ISLAM AND THE WEST POST 9/11

This book offers a chance for ... groups in Islam that have contributed to events pre and post Septe... clearer insights into Muslim/Christian relations today. Many books have focused on the events of September 11th but have been primarily journalistic. This book draws together both Muslim and non-Muslim scholars who have been studying Christian/Muslim relations for many years. They assess the impact of 9/11 on Islamophobia and antipathy towards Muslims. Providing insights into various multi-cultural communities whose relations with Islam have been affected, the authors look particularly at regions where there are large minority Muslim communities (US and UK) and large minority non-Muslim communities (Indonesia and Nigeria).

Assessing a number of issues impacting upon the teaching of Islam, this book allows readers to assess the consequences of the event and develop a more critical understanding of its implications.

Islam and the West Post 9/11

Edited by

RON GEAVES
THEODORE GABRIEL
YVONNE HADDAD
JANE IDLEMAN SMITH

ASHGATE

Published by
Ashgate Publishing Limited
Gower House
Croft Road
Aldershot
Hants GU11 3HR
England

Ashgate Publishing Company
Suite 420
101 Cherry Street
Burlington, VT 05401-4405
USA

Ashgate website: http://www.ashgate.com

British Library Cataloguing in Publication Data
Islam and the West post 9/11
1.Islam and secularism 2.Islamic renewal 3.East and West 4.Islam – Public opinion 5.Islamic fundamentalism 6.September 11 Terrorist Attacks, 2001 – Religious aspects – Islam 7.Islam and world politics
I.Geaves, Ron
297.2'7

Library of Congress Cataloging-in-Publication Data
Islam and the West Post 9/11 / edited by Ron Geaves ... [et al.].
p. cm.
Includes index.
ISBN 0-7546-5002-2 (hardcover : alk. paper) – ISBN 0-7546-5005-7 (pbk. : alk. paper) 1. East and West. 2. Islam–20th century. 3. September 11 Terrorist attacks, 2001–Influence. 4. Muslims–United States. 5. Muslims–Great Britain. I. Geaves, Ron.

CB251.I85 2005
305.6'97'090511–dc22

2004007849

ISBN 0 7546 5002 2 (Hbk)
ISBN 0 7546 5005 7 (Pbk)

Printed and bound in Great Britain by TJ International Ltd, Padstow, Cornwall

Contents

List of Contributors *vii*
Foreword *xi*

1 Introduction 1
Ron Geaves and Theodore Gabriel

PART I: THEORETICAL ISSUES

2 Is Islam against the West? 13
Theodore Gabriel

3 Self-critical Children of Abraham? Roots of Violence and Extremism in Judaism, Christianity and Islam 27
John J. Shepherd

4 The Finality of the Qur'an and the Contemporary Politics of Nations 51
Kenneth Cragg

5 Who Defines Moderate Islam 'post'-September 11? 62
Ron Geaves

PART II: THE CASE STUDIES

6 The Evolution of American Muslim Responses to 9/11 77
Marcia Hermansen

7 The Shaping of a Moderate North American Islam: Between 'Mufti' Bush and 'Ayatollah' Ashcroft 97
Yvonne Haddad

8 The Impact of 9/11 on British Muslim Identity 115
Dilwar Hussein

9 Endemically European or a European Epidemic? Islamophobia in a post 9/11 Europe 130
Christopher Allen

10 *Sharí'ah* Sanctions and State Enforcement: A Nigerian Islamic Debate and an Intellectual Critique 146
Lamin Sanneh

11 Perspectives on Radical Islamic Education in Contemporary Indonesia: Major Themes and Characteristics of Abu Bakar Ba'asyir's Teachings 166
Muhammad Sirozi

12 Israel as a focus for the Anger of Muslims Against the West 194
Colin Chapman

13 Conclusion 210
Jane Idleman Smith

Index 220

Contributors

Christopher Allen is a doctoral student at the University of Birmingham researching for his thesis entitled 'Deconstructing Islamophobia: a case study of Representations of Muslims in the British Press in the Aftermath of September 11'. He is the author, with J. Nielsen of *Summary Report on Islamophobia in the EU after 11 September 2001* (Vienna: European Monitoring Center for Racism and Xenophobia, 2002) and 'Reel Bad Arabs: How Hollywood Vilifies a People by Jack G. Shaheen', *The Muslim World Book Review*, Vol. 22, no. 4 (Leicester: The Islamic Foundation and the Institute of Islamic Thought, 2002).

Colin Chapman is Lecturer in Islamic Studies at the Near East School of Theology, Beirut, Lebanon. He was formerly Principal of Crowther Hall, Selly Oak Colleges, Birmingham and has taught also at Trinity College, Bristol. He is the author of: *Christianity on Trial*, Lion Publishing (1973); *Whose Promised Land*?, Lion Publishing (1983); *Shadows of the Supernatural: Popular Religion in the West*, Lion (1990); *Cross and Crescent: Responding to the Challenge of Islam*, IVP (1995); *Islam and the West: conflict, co-existence or conversion?*, Paternoster (1998).

The Rt. Revd. Kenneth Cragg, currently Honorary Assistant Bishop of Oxford since 1982 graduated D.Phil. from the University of Oxford. He was Asst. Anglican Bishop of Jerusalem from 1970-1984, and has also held the positions of Fellow in Jesus College, University of Oxford and Gonville and Caius College, University of Cambridge and Reader in Religious Studies at the University of Sussex. Kenneth Cragg was editor of the *Muslim World Quarterly* from 1952 to 1960. He is the author of numerous works on Islam, including *The Call of the Minaret* (3rd Edn, 1999); *Jesus and the Muslim* (2nd Edn, 1999); *Readings in the Qur'an* (2nd Edn, 1999); *Islam among the Spires* (2000), and *Muhammad in the Qur'an* (2002).

Theodore Gabriel was born in Kerala State, India, and graduated from the Madras Christian College. He did his postgraduate studies in Sociology and Anthropology at Shivaji University, Maharashtra, and later on did research in Anthropology and Religious Studies at the University of Aberdeen, Scotland, graduating M.Litt. in 1982 and Ph.D. in 1986. He has carried out research on Muslims in Kerala, the Lakshadweep Islands, Libya and Malaysia. He is the author of *Lakshadweep, History, Religion and Society* (Books and Books, 1986); *Hindu-Muslim Relations in North Malabar, 1498-1947* (E Mellen, 1996); *Christian-Muslim Relations, a Case Study of Sarawak, East Malaysia* (Avebury, 1996); and *Hindu and Muslim Inter-religious Relations in Malaysia* (E Mellen, 2000). He is also the editor of *Islam in the Contemporary World* (Vikas, 2000).

Ron Geaves is Professor of Religious Studies at University College Chester, England. He was formerly head of religious studies at University College Chichester and prior to that lectured at the University of Wolverhampton. He has been researching the Muslim community in Britain for the last twelve years and is primarily concerned with adaptation of Islam to non-Muslim European nations. He is the author of *Sectarian Influences within Islam in Britain* (1995) and *Sufis of Britain* (2001) in addition to numerous journal articles, contributions to edited books and conference papers on Muslim interaction with the West through migration processes. He has undertaken research in Pakistan, India, and Turkey and visited a number of Muslim nations including Afghanistan and Iran.

Yvonne Haddad is Professor of the History of Islam and Christian-Muslim Relations at Georgetown University's Centre for Muslim-Christian Understanding. She is the editor of *Muslims and the West*, *Muslims of America* and co-editor with John Esposito, of *Muslims on the Americanization Path?* She is the author of *Islam, Gender and Social Change*.

Marcia Hermansen is Professor of Theology at Loyola University, Chicago where she teaches courses in Islamic Studies and World Religions. She received her Ph.D. from the University of Chicago in Arabic and Islamic Studies. In the course of her research and language training she lived for extended periods in Egypt, Jordan, India, Iran and Pakistan and she conducts research in Arabic, Persian and Urdu as well as the major European languages. Her book, *The Conclusive Argument from God*, a study and translation (from Arabic) of Shah Wali Allah of Delhi's *Hujjat Allah al-Baligha* was published in 1996. Marcia Hermansen has also contributed numerous academic articles in the fields of Islamic Thought, Sufism, Islam and Muslims in South Asia, Muslims in America, and Women in Islam.

Dilwar Hussein graduated from King's College, University of London, in 1993. He is a Research Fellow at the Islamic Foundation focusing on Muslims in Europe/Britain and Muslim identity. He is on the editorial boards of the journals *The Muslim World Book Review* and *Encounters: Journal of Inter-Cultural Perspectives*. In addition to numerous book reviews, his publications include: 'The Holy Grail of Muslims in Western Europe: Recognition, Representation and Relationship with the State' in *Islam in the Public Sphere*, by J. Esposito and F. Burgat (eds.) (London: C. Hurst & Co., 2002). He has also written on *Muslims in Britain* (London: Foreign and Commonwealth Office, 2002), and on *British Muslim Identity* as well as *Muslims' Engagement in Politics*, Leicester: Islamic Foundation, 2003). His latest work is *British Muslims: Loyalty and Belonging* (Leicester: Islamic Foundation, 2004).

Lamin Sanneh is the D. Willis James Professor of Missions and World Christianity and Professor of History at Yale Divinity School. Born in Gambia, Sanneh is descended from the Nyanchos, an ancient African royal line. As such, his earliest education, in the Gambia, was with fellow chiefs' sons. Following graduation from the University of Birmingham with an MA, and University of London with a Ph.D. in Islamic History, he taught at the University of Ghana and at the University of Aberdeen, in Scotland. He served for eight years as Assistant and Associate Professor of the History of Religion at Harvard University, before moving to Yale University in 1989. He is the author of a dozen books including: *Translating the Message: The Missionary Impact on Culture* (1989); *The Crown and the Turban: Muslims and West African Pluralism* (1997); *Piety and Power: Muslims and Christians in West Africa* (1996); *Faith and Power: Christianity and Islam in 'Secular' Britain* (1998); *Abolitionists Abroad: American Blacks and the Making of Modern West Africa* (2000).

Muhammad Sirozi was awarded his Ph.D. by the Department of Educational Policy, Monash University in Melbourne, Australia, in 1998. He is currently Director of Graduate Studies at Palembang State Institute of Islamic Studies, Indonesia, and Fulbright Visiting Scholar, Center for International Studies, Ohio University, USA. He is researching the intellectual roots of Islamic radicalism in contemporary Indonesia.

John J. Shepherd was Principal Lecturer in Religious Studies and Social Ethics at St. Martin's College, Lancaster, from 1980 to 1997 and now works part-time in the same capacity. He graduated in Modern languages from the University of Leeds and holds a Diploma in Religious Knowledge from the University of Cambridge. He did his doctoral studies in Religious Studies at the University of Lancaster. He is the author of *Experience, Inference and God* (Macmillan, Barnes and Noble, 1975), and co-editor of *Contemporary Religions, a World Guide* (Longman, 1992) and *Longman Guide to Living Religions* (Longman, 1994) of which he was in charge of the Islam section. His translation from the German of Charlotte von Krischbaum's *The Woman Question* was published by Eerdmans in 1996. He has contributed several articles in academic journals on ethics in Islam and other world religions. He is the founding archivist of the recently established Ninian Smart Archive at Lancaster University

Jane Idleman Smith is Professor of Islamic Studies and Co-Director of the Duncan Black Macdonald Center for Christian-Muslim Relations, Hartford Seminary, in Hartford, Connecticut. She obtained her Ph.D from Harvard University in 1970, where she was employed from 1973-1980 as Assistant and then Associate Director of the Center for the Study of World Religions; Associate Professor in History of Religions, Harvard Divinity School, 1977-1998 and Associate Dean for Academic Affairs, Harvard Divinity School, 1980-1986. From 1987-1995 she was Vice President and Dean of Academic Affairs and Professor of History of Religion at Iliff School of Theology in Denver, Colorado. She is the author of numerous publications including *Muslim Minorities in the West: Visible and Invisible*, co-edited with Yvonne Yazbeck Haddad, (Walnut Creek: AltaMira Press, 2002); *Islam in America* (New York: Columbia University Press, 1999); *Muslim Communities in America*, edited with Yvonne Yazbeck Haddad (Albany:

State University of New York Press, 1994); *Mission to America: Five Islamic Sectarian Movements in the United States*, with Yvonne Yazbeck Haddad (Gainesville: The University Presses of Florida, 1993); *The Islamic Understanding of Death and Resurrection*, with Yvonne Yazbeck Haddad (Albany: State University of New York Press, 1981); *Women in Contemporary Muslim Society*, editor (Lewistown, Pennsylvania: Bucknell University Press, 1980). In addition she was co-chair, 'Consultation on Religious Freedom', sponsored by The World Council of Churches unit on Christian-Muslim Relations, Hartford Seminary, October 14–18, 1999; Islam Editor, *Encyclopedia of Women and World Religions*, Macmillan, 1995-1999 and recipient of US Speaker and Specialist Grant for the international seminar on 'Western Perceptions of Muslims: Muslim Perspectives on the West', USIS Islamabad, Georgetown Center for Muslim-Christian Understanding, and the Islamic Research Institute of the International Islamic University, October 4–6, 1997.

Foreword

The book is divided into two parts: the first part consists of a group of seven theoretical contributions that assess the relationship between Islam and the West and the second part provides a number of case studies.

The first part begins with Theodore Gabriel's assessment of the reasons why certain sectors of the Muslim world perceive the West as being anti-Islam, analysing a number of political, theological and value issues that have framed Muslim/Christian relations and also relations with the secular worldview of the West.

In Chapters 3 and 4, the authors address the radical changes that need to take place in interpreting tradition and scripture in order to promote world harmony. John Shepherd explores the possibility of a global ethic that would require the monotheistic religions to self-critically examine parts of their scriptural heritage that appear to endorse intolerance and violence. Kenneth Cragg utilises his deep knowledge of the Qur'an to present a cogent argument that Muslims need to engage with the wider world communities, in terms of morality, ethics and dialogue by drawing upon the Makkan revelation rather than the later Medinan episodes.

In Chapter 5, Ron Geaves assesses the reactions of the US and British governments after September 11th, 2001 (hereafter also referred to as 9/11) and argues that their political strategy of distinguishing terrorists from moderate Muslims is fraught with a number of risks that do not conform to contemporary reality, or to a real understanding of the nature of the Muslim world in the twenty-first century. He argues that the confrontation between the secular liberal worldview and the revival of absolutist religious worldviews results in a number of paradoxes, which can result in an 'iron fist' being displayed within 'the glove' of the liberal viewpoint of what constitutes right.

The second part of the book provides a number of case studies from different parts of the world which have been either affected by the events of 9/11, especially where Muslim minorities are concerned, or, alternatively, where Muslims are struggling for their voice to be heard by the international community. In Chapter 6, Marcia Hermansen explores the impact of 9/11 on American Muslims and their efforts to redefine Muslim identity in an American context. In Chapter 7, Yvonne Haddad looks at the impact of US policies since 9/11 on American Muslims caught between the efforts by the government to establish relations with a 'moderate' Muslim community, and the loss of individual freedoms and demonisation of the Muslim community.

Chapters 8 and 9 look at the impact of 9/11 on the British Muslim community. Dilwar Hussein explores the aftermath of 9/11 in the context of Muslim identity and the impact on the settlement and integration process, and assesses the risk of polarisation and radicalisation of opinion. Christopher Allen continues the theme by exploring the relationship between the events of 9/11 and increasing Islamophobia.

In Chapters 10 and 11, Lamin Sanneh and Muhammad Sirozi provide in-depth analyses of Nigeria and Indonesia; both nations struggling to deal with multi-faith issues within the context of Muslim majorities, and to develop relevant policies. Both authors focus on the consequences of movements to create Islamic states based on a strict implementation of *Sharí'ah* in each nation. In Chapter 12, Colin Chapman examines the struggle of the Palestinians to create a viable state for themselves and argues that Zionism has provided an insuperable problem with regard to Muslim relations with the West. In Chapter 13, Jane Idleman Smith concludes by summarising the main themes of the book and comments on Muslim relations with the West.

Chapter 1

Introduction

Ron Geaves and Theodore Gabriel

In calling this collection of essays 'Islam and the West' we are aware that we use the term 'West' not so much as a geographical location, but as a symbol for a way of life which certain segments of the Muslim populations of the world find threatening or at odds with their understanding of a comprehensive way of life given to them not by human progress or action but rather by an eternal and irrevocable revelation of the divine. The label, 'West', then, brings to mind a set of cultures that have established over the last two hundred years a series of more or less liberal and democratic regimes based on 'sovereignty of the people' rather than the truths of their own religious revelations and have, to the Muslim eye, replaced God's right to control all aspects of human individual and collective life, with the suspension of 'sacred' life to the private realm, preferring to trust in other agencies for the activities of public existence.

This way of life, known as 'secular', combined with a vigorous and aggressive free market capitalism has been extremely successful in the last decades of the twentieth century, and through a series of technological and communication breakthroughs has been able to penetrate most parts of the world, a process commonly known as globalization. However, not everyone has been happy with the results or able to participate in its benefits equally. The rich and the powerful have become more so, and the world's poor populations have proliferated. The divide between the world's rich nations and poor nations has increased.

One of the consequences of this process of globalization and promotion of a 'secular' free market – often oblivious to any moral codes or ethics arising from the world's religious traditions – has been the resurgence of a number of religious alternatives, often involving fundamentalist or foundationalist truth-claims based on the inviolability of various revelations.

Nowhere has this been more dramatic than amongst Muslims, although it should be noted that Islamic revivalism, commonly labelled 'fundamentalism' by the media needs to be explained within the context of that religion, rather than by attempts to find a common cause for religious revival in the second half of the twentieth century, even though, as the Appleby Project discovered, there are a number of common features. Muslims have historically responded to political or social crisis or invasion by non-Muslim forces, through religious revival. This reaction is built into the doctrine of 'Manifest Success', a theological position advocated in the Qur'an which links external success with the notion of being God's people.

Early Muslim success, linked to the dramatic expansion of the Arab tribes out of Arabia and into large swathes of territory belonging to the Byzantine Empire and all of the remainder of the Persian Empire, confirmed this special relationship with God. Later conquests and trading brought Islam to North Africa, India, South-East Asia, parts of China and into European territory in Spain and the Balkans. Muslims, like Christians in various parts of their history, could be reasonably confident that manifest success indicated that God was 'on their side' and the world would in due time embrace the 'true path'.

However, major setbacks such as the Mongol invasion in 1258, but much more crucially, the expansion of Europe and encroachment onto Muslim territory in the eighteenth and nineteenth centuries, were to seriously challenge the Muslim religious psyche. The European expansion was particularly threatening in that it introduced not only colonial domination that demonstrated the weakness of Muslim culture in the face of new technologies, scientific discovery and new methods of secular education, but faced Muslims with the possibility of a resurgence by Christianity deemed to be the previous and superseded revelation of God. The response to political failure and cultural decline in a 'Manifest Success' theology can only be religious revival. To a mentality, confident throughout history, that they would inherit the earth as God's last people, the only reason for failure had to be a lack of faith and commitment to God's revelation. Thus, one response was to return to the ways of God as written in the Qur'an and the Sunna of the Prophet. Another response, less theological, was to learn from the successes of the Europeans and establish their education, legal and political systems; a pragmatic solution that could lead to Islam becoming a private religion but losing its prominence in public institutions, as had happened to Christianity in the West. These two responses, as will be seen, provided the possibility of a serious clash of opinion, dividing the Muslim world into those who sought solutions through seeking rapprochements with Western political and cultural institutions, creatively borrowing in order to progress their own societies and those who saw this as a continuation of the failure to live by the tenets of Islam and thus doomed to failure in regard to any renaissance of Muslim life.

What is of no doubt, is that cultural interchange between Muslims and the Christian world, both in Europe and in the Byzantine East, had been going on for centuries, each creatively borrowing from the other, with the directional movement of knowledge depending on who was politically dominant. Thus in the Mediaeval period, western Europe was the recipient of Arab discoveries in science and mathematics and their philosophical developments achieved through a synthesis of Muslim and neo-Platonic ideas. The colonial period saw the movement reverse, and as pointed out by Lamin Sanneh, the Muslim encounter with European colonialism was more or less amicable leading to the 'genuine partnerships' and remarkable syntheses of western and Islamic legal codes.

However, resistance there was, and ironically for those who maintained that a return to God's way was necessary for Muslim renaissance, it was the estern-educated elites who led the way towards the end of colonial rule and the emergence of Muslim nation states, once again borrowing from European legal codes, political systems and either capitalist- or socialist-influenced economic systems. Yet, even in spite of the discovery of oil wealth in the Arab heartlands, there were those who saw the continuing lack of power and influence, which remained outside the Muslim world in North America, western Europe and the Soviet Union, the internal divisions between Muslim nations, the continuing poverty and lack of education and, above all, the internal corruption of Muslim regimes, as an indication that only a religious renaissance would resolve the problems. The rhetoric of an Islamic state, where Muslims governed themselves based on a full implementation of Islamic law, and removed governments that were influenced by western systems of governance and economic structures, began to find a ready audience, especially amongst those who were educated to university standard in law, engineering, accountancy and other professions, forming a new urban middle-class, increasingly disenfranchised by older elites that refused to share the rewards of wealth and status. Dissatisfied with western ideologies, both capitalism and socialism, which had to all intents and purposes failed both the common people and newly educated professionals, they turned to Islam as a political ideology as espoused by twentieth-century ideologues such as Maulana Mawdudi, Sayyid Qutb and Hasan al-Banna.

Thus, a number of movements were created throughout the Muslim world intent on creating revolutions by either militant or peaceful means that would lead to the creation of Islamic states, or even the ideal of one Muslim *khalifat*, arguing that even the ideal of nationalism was contrary to the Muslim concept of *ummah*, a transnational community of allegiance to God and His final revelation. The enemy was not so much the West, but those within the community of Muslims who were seen to have adopted western ways and departed from the comprehensive way of life revealed by God, known as Islam. However, increasingly, the struggle to determine how the Muslim nations should be governed and what part religion should take in the processes of governance has begun to implicate the western world, especially the USA.

The old colonial role of the West is not regarded as ended in many parts of the Muslim world, rather many consider that American dominance now manifests itself through forms of neo-colonialism and corporate capitalism. In addition, many of the movements founded to establish various forms of Islamic government regard the West as not only an enemy of Islam because of secular 'godlessness' but also for supporting the very regimes that they wish to remove. However, colonialism has brought with it other complications. Not only did the nineteenth century see the largest population movement of Europeans into other parts of the world, the collapse of the colonial enterprises has seen the corresponding movements of Muslim migrants into the homeland of the old adversaries. Thus, very few western nations do not have significant Muslim populations and very few Muslim nations are not wrestling with how to integrate western influence on lifestyles and culture into the Muslim paradigm. It is no longer a truism to state 'East is East and West is West'. Today, more Muslims live as minorities in non-Muslim countries than in the Arab heartlands.

To further complicate the contemporary scene, the Cold War had to some extent kept the Muslim world, especially its allegiance to Islam, under the sightlines of the main protagonists. Muslim nations were essentially seen as pawns in the game of gathering allegiances and gaining influence in various spheres of the globe. In the face of US support for Israel, a number of Middle-Eastern nations wooed the Soviet Union. In South Asia, the opposite was true. In the face of India's close relationship with the Soviet Union, the US wooed Pakistan. For a while, Afghanistan successfully played one off against the other for aid and development. However, the sudden collapse of the Soviet empire was to radically transform world politics and the perceptions of the world towards US dominance.

The invasion of Afghanistan by the Soviet Union had provided a catalyst for thousands of Muslim volunteers to converge on the north-west frontier of Pakistan where they were mobilised into the various factions of radical Islamic organisations engaged in *jihad* against the Russian military. The USA saw the opportunity to exploit the situation and embarrass their main foe. Military training, weapons and money were provided to the *mujahiddin*. So successful were the guerrilla strategies against the Russians, involving heavy casualities, that they had to pull out, leaving Afghanistan in the hands of tribal warlords and various *mujahiddin* groups. Several significant consequences were to come in the aftermath of the Russian defeat that transformed international relations, and especially the dynamics of the historical heritage of Islam and the West.

The collapse of the Soviet empire was not without impact on Muslim populations. New Muslim states were carved out in central Asia, needing to determine how to govern themselves. Chechnya became a battleground between Russia, determined to retain control of its strategic geographical position, and Chechnyan nationalists, equally bent on independence. The Balkans were plunged into chaos as aggressive nationalism, especially on the part of Serbia, resurrected the practice of ethnic cleansing, particularly aimed towards Bosnian Muslims, a remnant in Europe of the old Ottoman empire. The Palestinians opened a new *intifada,* marked by 'suicide bomber' attacks on both Israeli military and citizens as the prospect of a genuinely independent state diminished under the reality of Israeli settlements in the West Bank. At the same time, Saddam Hussein's Iraq chose to invade Kuwait, resulting in the first Gulf War and the presence of US troops stationed in Saudi Arabia. Other ongoing local Muslim issues continued to remain intractable, for example, Algeria and Kashmir.

With varying degrees of accuracy as to the religious factors in the conflicts, Muslims around the world saw the struggles as evidence of a conspiracy against Islam itself. The collapse of the Soviet Union had removed a traditional ally in a number of political issues and the US had now achieved a hegemonic dominance in world affairs. Its unreserved support of Israel, combined with its political support of a number of Muslim regimes regarded as corrupt, and its deep suspicion of the Islamic government in Iran, was all exacerbated by the presence of US troops so close to the two holy cities of Medina and Makkah. To millions of Muslims around the world it seemed as if the USA government had replaced its traditional enmity against communism with Islam. At the extreme end of this perspective, conspiracy theories abounded, resurrecting a new version of a Zionist plot to dominate world affairs. Anti-Israeli feeling amongst Muslims began to generate new versions of anti-Semitism, in which the Protocols of Zion, long condemned as forgeries after their use as anti-Jewish propaganda by the Nazi regime in Germany, again gained credibility in some Muslim circles.

However, it was developments in Afghanistan which were to prove, with hindsight, the most dangerous to western interests, and which would plunge relations between the West and Muslims into a critical stage. As mentioned, the Russian invasion had brought Muslim volunteers from all around the world to join the *mujahiddin*, armed by the US and battle-hardened in the vicious firefights with the Russian military, they came into contact with radical Muslim organisations in the north-west tribal areas of Pakistan, and often fought alongside *jihad* groups organised by various Islamic factions. Notable amongst these *mujahiddin* was the legendary Osama bin Laden, famous for his exploits against the Russians; a millionaire Saudi Arabian of Yemeni background, and the recipient of considerable US support. Although the story remains to be documented, Osama bin Laden was able to provide the resources, charisma and ideology for a more integrated international resistance against the perceived enemies of Islam. Linked by their experiences in Afghanistan, the *mujahiddin* volunteers dispersed, returning to support radical Muslim struggles in various parts of the world to overthrow corrupt regimes, or to fight in Bosnia, Chechnya, Algeria and Kashmir. Others remained in Afghanistan, intent on shaping an Islamic state in that nation. Somewhere in the midst of this activity, Osama bin Laden made the necessary contacts to found his al-Qa'eda organisation, more an umbrella movement able to link with various local *jihad* movements around the Muslim world than an international movement.

The power vacuum in Afghanistan was resolved by the victory of the Taliban over most other factions. They were a new radical movement created in the Afghan refugee camps in Pakistan where a passionate youth eager to reclaim their land came into contact with the teachings of revivalist Islam in the Deobandi-influenced rural *madrasas* of the North-West Provinces. The Taliban-dominated Afghanistan and the North-West Provinces provided the geographical space for *jihad* groups to live and train; al-Qa'eda gave the international dimension. However, few could have forecast the events of 9/11 even though there had been an earlier attack on the World Trade Center, or its dramatic impact on international relations.

However, the attacks on the USA were a logical continuation of the decision of Muslim revivalist movements pledged to *jihad* to include the West, especially the USA, in their struggle to impose their own vision of Islam on the Muslim world. The response of the US government to declare war on terrorism, although politically expedient has so far done very little to resolve the situation. The linking of the term 'terrorist' to *jihad* movements that may in some cases have justice on their side, provides the opportunity for any government, however corrupt or oppressive to brand its opponents prepared for armed insurrection as terrorists, and claim they are assisting in the US self-proclaimed war against such atrocities. On the other hand, such a policy fails to take into account the strength of popular Muslim support for such causes, particularly in Palestine, thus blurring the borders between 'terrorist' and 'moderate' Muslims, that the governments of the USA and Britain would like to keep clearly demarcated in the interests of their respective foreign policies.

Since the tragic events of 9/11, the situation in the world has done little to appease Muslim fears that they are the new enemy of the West. Afghanistan has been invaded and a new government installed in Kabul with little control over the rest of the country. The Taliban, under their leader Mullah Omar, are resurgent and able to flourish in the North-West Provinces of Pakistan, now under the control of an elected revivalist Muslim government. Osama bin Laden has attained a legendary status in the Muslim world, especially amongst disaffected youth. Conspiracy theories of denial of his involvement in 9/11 abound in the Muslim world, preferring to believe in Jewish/Christian conspiracies against Islam than admit that a pious man of the desert could have performed the atrocity. The Palestinian problem is at its most intractable as the hardline government of Ariel Sharon prepares to isolate the Arab population by building a wall between Israel and Palestinian territory. Iraq has been invaded by the military forces of the USA and Britain, Saddam Hussein removed from power, but Muslim opinion inflamed against what is perceived as renewed colonisation. Clumsy attempts to justify the war with overblown claims of 'weapons of mass destruction' and dubious links between Saddam Hussein and al-Qa'eda have only helped confirm Muslim suspicions. In addition, many regard the excursion into Iraq, the military presence in Afghanistan, the US build-up of military bases and commercial presence in Muslim Central Asia, and the Russian insistence on maintaining Chechnya as having more to do with petroleum geopolitics than efforts to support democracy.

Although al-Qa'eda and its allies in the Muslim world have failed to repeat the atrocity of 9/11 on either US or European soil, several bombs have exploded in Indonesia, Saudi Arabia, Turkey and other parts of the Muslim world, demonstrating how difficult it is to prevent such acts. The choice of locations for attacks since 9/11 would suggest that the targets have been chosen in places where the West and Islam most interact with each other, either in multi-cultural Muslim societies striving to maintain a delicate balance between Islamic values, democracy and pluralism or where western influence is strong, for example Saudi Arabia, which also follows tightrope diplomacy between its strong relations with the West and the Saudi regime's traditional links with Wahhabi strands of Islam.

Thus it would seem that it is either Muslim minorities in the West or Muslims living in societies which are trying to balance the demands of multi-faith or multi-cultural societies that have borne the brunt of the post 9/11 world. Muslim minorities in western democracies and larger and older minorities such as those in India have found themselves under suspicion and easily made the targets of either racism or the resurgence of ancient hostilities that brand them as 'other'. Muslim societies such as those in South-East Asia or Turkey, considered moderate by the West have become the target of the *jihad* movements, who regard them as almost apostate or at least, as hypocrites, failing to live by the tenets of Islam in public as well as private lives.

The contributors to this book have long experience of the relations between Islam and the West either as Muslim/Christian relation scholars, or as Muslims living in the West. It is on the areas mentioned above that we have chosen to focus rather than the Arab heartlands, with the exception of Palestine, so crucial to the resolution of the atmosphere of suspicion towards the West. It is in these places where the relations with the West have been most affected and where they are at their most creative. The collection is divided into parts: the first dealing with theoretical issues and the second containing a number of case studies specific to various regions around the world.

The traumatic events of 9/11 shocked the world and especially the United States, which had rarely suffered aggression from external enemies within its frontiers since its inception in 1776, in spite of its participation in two world wars and numerous other undeclared wars. The notable exception is the attack on Pearl Harbour which in itself becomes a mythic memory of heinous crimes against the nation. The leaders and people of the United States had never expected the homeland of the nation to be so vulnerable as to suffer acts of violence on some of its most prestigious sites. The destruction of two institutions symbolic of its economic and military might, the World Trade Center and the Pentagon, was so significant. The USA had long been the target of Muslim *mujahiddin* of various kinds, vexed by, to them, unwarranted interference in Muslim affairs, in Iran, in Lebanon, in Iraq, in Saudi Arabia and most culpably in Palestine. But these were acts of desperation, ill-organised and not of long-term consequence – the hijacking of a plane or a ship or the bombing of an embassy. But the present attack was symptomatic of a more clever, well-organised well-planned and more ruthless effort. Al-Qa'eda, masterminded by Osama bin Laden seemed quite different from earlier militant organisations. Indications of its potency had been forthcoming in the intrepid, well-planned and well-executed bombing of the USS Cole in October 2000. To get near a US warship, with all its sophisticated surveillance and protective equipment, let alone to bomb it, was no mean achievement, and testified to the calibre of the people who planned and carried out this act.

The response from the USA was automatic, led as it was by a conservative Republican 'Warrior President', though his critics have since challenged the warrior credentials. There was no move to consider international law, to give the Taliban any avenue of retreating with some honour and dignity, no intention or sign of giving a measured and reflective response to the threat of al-Qa'eda, nor any introspection as to the reasons behind why these attacks occurred. The bombing of Afghanistan was almost a gut response, a shooting from the hip, to the killing of so many Americans. The Taliban asked for evidence of Osama bin Laden's complicity in the attacks but this request was dismissed outright. They were given an ultimatum 'give up Osama or else'. As things stand neither of the objectives of capturing Bin Laden or eradicating the al-Qa'eda was realised. But the lot of the Afghans were no doubt considerably improved; the ousting of the Taliban with their draconian and anachronistic implementation of the *Shari'ah* was highly beneficial for civil liberties and particularly for the women of Afghanistan. World opinion was not hostile to the removal of the Taliban. Stories of the indignities suffered by women and the destruction of the Bamiyan Buddhas had totally alienated world opinion from the Taliban.

But then came the move to oust Saddam Hussein. The attack on Iraq was regarded by many as totally unjustified by the circumstances, and Saddam Hussein's links with terrorism quite nebulous to say the least. Saddam Hussein was being very well contained by sanctions and the patrolling of the Shi'a and Kurd areas by USA and British warplanes. Ideologically Saddam Hussein was not an Islamic extremist; the only possible allegations were his military ambitions and his oppression of the people of Iraq. The former has turned out to be a chimera, and the hasty removal of the weapons inspectors from the scene seems to indicate that the 'Weapons of Mass Destruction' rationale for the invasion was only a smoke screen for some other agenda. Regarding human rights, North Korea, China and Myanmar have even worse records without attracting such a response from the US or the United Kingdom. It would seem to an impartial observer that the invasion of Iraq and to a lesser extent the invasion of Afghanistan were partly motivated by the fact that these were comparatively soft targets; states without a credible air force, or a navy or a viable defence technology and having only rag tag armies. There was very little real opposition to the invasions. The attack on Iraq has aroused deep suspicion in Muslim minds all over the world, even among the most moderate and liberal groups, that the agenda was about gaining a stronghold in the heart of the Middle East and about petroleum geopolitics. Many are prone to allege an anti-Islamic agenda as well in the actions of the USA and the UK in recent times. Yvonne Haddad in a well-informed article tells of the lot of many Muslims in the USA, with the present curtailment of civil rights and rule of law. Haddad's article is a real eye opener to the lot of Muslims in the USA. Many would be shocked that this is happening in the USA, which has traditionally been the champion of human rights and civil liberties in the world as symbolised by the Statue of Liberty in New York. Civil rights are also slowly being eroded in the UK also, with new measures on the part of the Blair administration such as holding suspects indefinitely without trial and even moves to lower the threshold of evidence for convictions. These measures are being hotly opposed not only by civil rights pressure groups but also by eminent jurists and the bar. It now seems that the US administration is embarking on a dangerous and highly dubious course as far as civil rights are concerned. These measures seem to be intended mostly against Muslim immigrants, especially those of Arab origin and have raised the sceptre of another front in racial and religious discrimination in the USA.

Marcia Hermansen in a perceptive article has given a well-studied and graphic account of the response of the Muslim community in the USA to the happenings since the 9/11 attack. The response is certainly not homogeneous and many Muslims were genuinely horrified by the attacks. The more liberal among them have condemned the attacks outright and have called for the vision of a more enlightened, liberal and tolerant interpretation of Islamic teachings. The fact is that the attacks and the consequent happenings such as the invasion of Afghanistan and Iraq have polarised not only the Muslims and Christians of America, but also many factions with differing perspectives on Islam within the Muslim community of the USA.

The USA does not seem to have probed deeply or even reflected much on the reasons for the attack. Both Theodore Gabriel and Colin Chapman argue that the Palestinian issue is a major factor in Muslim hostility to the West. It is difficult to concur with Samuel Huntingdon's thesis of the clash of civilisations as clarifying the present situation. The clash of the West with other civilisations is nothing new – the whole colonial enterprise was fraught with such clashes of civilisations. Islamic fundamentalism in India or Indonesia or the Sudan is to some extent the product of the clash of the western values brought by the coloniser against indigenous mores. The stricter variety of Islam is to a great extent a consequence of the defensive response of Muslims in these areas to the imposition of western civilisation in the previously conquered areas. The other factor is of course the transmission of Wahhabism from Saudi Arabia. The fact that the Wahhabis control the holiest shrines of Islam, where there is a continual turnover of pilgrims from all over the world, and to where the *ulama* will turn for instruction, is no doubt the other factor in the rise of Islamic fundamentalism in many parts of the world. But of late, Muslim angst has been fuelled by Israeli high-handedness in the West Bank and other areas of Palestinian authority. The devastation of Palestinian abodes, the killing of innocent Palestinian bystanders during Israeli assassination attempts of militant leaders, the unnecessary shooting of children and most recently the building of a wall in Palestinian territory; such actions have dismayed and angered millions of Muslims all over the world. The ghettoisation of Palestinians in the less fertile areas of the land, their miserable economic status aggravated by Israeli isolationism, and the inhuman way protestors have been dealt with, echoes the policies of the Afrikaner white supremacist government in South Africa. The Israeli actions have only augmented support among Palestinians for Islamic hardliners there. The USA has not wholeheartedly advised and prevented Israel from carrying out its hardline policy. Israeli intransigence and chicanery in implementing international agreements, and the peace process in general, have not been justly and firmly dealt with by the US administration. Most of the Israeli atrocities are being carried out with US weapons and it seems to many Muslims with US tacit approval. Ron Geaves in his essay has pointed out the inability of the USA and its allies to distinguish between real terrorists and those who are fighting against oppression. The wholesale branding of all Muslims, engaged in defending their rights, as terrorists is not at all a solution for ending the violence or the threat that the USA and its allies face. The imbalance of US policy in Israel, the presence of US troops in the holy land of Arabia, and the support by the USA of undemocratic and allegedly corrupt governments have made the USA culpable in Muslim eyes.

Al Qa'eda is not as marginal in Muslim society as is made out by the West and many analysts. Because of continuing injustices perpetrated against Palestinians and the seemingly colonialist ambitions of the US and Britain these activists have more support among the Muslim masses than is publicly evident. Dilwar Hussein has drawn attention in his essay to how young Muslims have become radicalised by the increasing discrimination and loss of civil liberties that Muslims have to undergo in Britain post-9/11. Many Muslims, he states, view the so-called war on terror as a war on Islam.

Islamic fundamentalism and extremism is nevertheless a problem that the Islamic *ummah* has to tackle. Violence is never a solution to the world's problems. It can be argued that suicide bombing is the only way that militarily weak groups can defend themselves against oppression. However non-violence can also be a potent solution as manifested very clearly in Gandhi's Indian Independence movement. *Satyagraha*, the opposition to oppression by determined non-violent demonstrations and civil disobedience movements, was very effective against colonial British power. Is this not a *modus operandus* that the Palestinians can try out against Israel? As Lamin Sanneh points out in his eminently perceptive essay: should one's credibility totally depend on a calculus of the balance of terror? For too long the world has depended on mutually assured destruction as a deterrent to war. The military and economic pre-eminence of the US means that such a deterrent is no longer viable.

Kenneth Cragg in his erudite essay on the Qur'an points out that the Muslims encountered the brutality of the Quraysh oligarchy of Mecca with such a non-violent front while steadfastly remaining loyal to the commands of God. Cragg exhorts Muslims to turn to this Meccan paradigm rather than the Medinan policy of opposing violence with violence. John Shepherd in his essay rightly points out the ambiguity of scriptures – passages advocating violence and even genocide are intermixed with those exhorting pacifism. This is as true of Islam as of the Christian, Judaic and even Hindu texts. The aphorism *ahimsa paramo dharma* (non-violence is the highest duty) is a part of Hindu scriptures as much as Sri Krishna exhorting Arjuna to stand up and kill his enemies on the battlefields of Kurukshetra in the *Bhagavad Gita*. Shepherd points out rightly that the roots of religious extremism lie within the religions themselves. No amount of polemical sanitisation can invalidate this fact.

On the other hand, it seems that the literal interpretation of the Qur'an and the Ahadith without taking into account the historical and sociological context of the teaching, can be dangerous. Muhammed Sirozi in his illuminating essay on Abu Bakr Ba'asyir, the fundamentalist leader of Indonesia, points out that Ba'asyir's teachings are based on a narrow and literalist interpretation of the Islamic texts. Fundamentalists are moreover often highly selective in their reference to such texts, and as John Shepherd has pointed out, the scriptures can be used to argue one way or the other if the linguistic, cultural and contextual aspects are ignored.

The events of 9/11 are a watershed in Islam's relations with the West. Apparently, the polarisation of Muslims and the West has deepened. The Muslim diaspora in the West is in a very problematic situation. But the happenings can also be turned to the advantage of peace if both protagonists in this affair take time to sit back and reflect on what caused this confrontation and the traumatic consequences. The West has to reflect and probe into the causes of Muslim angst and rectify its policies to ensure justice for all. Muslims have to seek a new hermeneutic of their texts and the religion itself to revamp their relations with other faiths and other cultures, abandoning rigid and ossified perspectives and genuinely seeking avenues of peace and the well-being of the *ummah* as well as the whole world. Acting peremptorily without such reflection and restraint, and relying totally on a belief in the infallibility of political power, wealth and force, will not get the world out of this impasse. The contributors to this volume have a wealth of suggestions to give for amelioration of the present dangerous situation.

PART I
Theoretical Issues

Chapter 2

Is Islam against the West?

Theodore Gabriel

The perception has been gaining ground for some time now that Islam is against the western world and this has intensified since the incidents of 9/11. This is probably mainly a view from the western side but there might be a feeling in the Muslim *ummah* also that since western intervention in the Gulf in 1990, the recent confrontation in Afghanistan, and the present Iraqi crisis, that subsequent to the mitigation of tensions between the East and the West or between the Soviet and the western blocks, the main antagonisms in the world are indeed between the Muslim world and the West, and that the countries of the West view the Muslim world as hostile to them. Are these perceptions credible and valid?

We first have to define what is meant by the question 'Is Islam against the West?' By Islam we can mean both the religion itself or the practitioners of the Muslim faith. Andre Nusse points out that the same word 'Islam' is used to denote such different things as religious cult, society or the culture and symbols associated with Islam.[1] Thus we have to examine whether there is in Muslim faith and all its appurtenances thereof such as the Qur'an or the Hadith or its doctrines, laws and teachings elements intrinsically opposed to the West. On the other hand if by 'Islam' we mean the Islamic faith community we have to discern whether in their ideology or in its practical outworking there is evidence for hostility to the West as an entity, as opposed to particular western nations, on the part of the 1.2 billion Muslims in the world.

We also have to bear in mind that the Muslim *ummah* is by no means a monolith; there is considerable diversity in the Muslim world not only ethnically but also in approaches to other faiths, to religious conversion, to politics, war and a host of other aspects. There are three issues to be examined in this question 'Is Islam against the West'? One strand is in the religious domain and is mainly the issue of Christian–Muslim relations, since the West is often identified as the seat of the Christian faith, though with the decline of Christianity in the West this is becoming a more or less a fallacious premise, but paradoxically still one held by many non-western nations. Western nations are quite aware, with the possible exception of the USA, that with increasing secularism, apathy and even hostility to religion in the West the term 'Christian' may no longer be a proper epithet for the West. The second strand is ideological and cultural, and involves disparities in what may be called values and ways of life. Lastly and most importantly are the purely political issues.

1. Christian–Muslim hostility goes a long way back to medieval times and involves polemics between the two religions mainly fed by misconceptions and even deliberate distortions, and also physical confrontation, such as the Crusades, the Reconquista of Spain and more recently European colonial domination of Islamic regions, during which, events such as the Mappila Rebellion of 1920 in India, the rebellion led by the self-styled Mahdi in the Sudan, and the Padre Wars in Indonesia, brought Muslim communities into direct conflict with European colonial powers. John of Damascus seemed to consider Islam as a Christian heresy, stating that Muhammad established Islam as a result of having conversed with an Arian monk.[2] The significant point, however, is that John considered Islam as being sufficiently close to Christianity as to be considered a Christian heresy rather than a different religion altogether. Hitti points out that this was the most persistent and widely held image of Islam in medieval Christendom.[3]

But the two religions are not intrinsically opposed to each other, nor is there an innate hostility between the two. The Qur'an confirms this in Sura 5:85

> Strongest among men in enmity
> To the believers will thou
> Find the Jews and pagans;
> And nearest among them in love
> To the believers wilt thou
> Find those who say
> 'We are Christians'.

The Qur'an clarifies this and sets out that the reason for this fraternal feeling is the Christians' humility and lack of arrogance, perhaps in comparison to the Jews who reviled Mohammed's prophethood and the Qur'an at Medina. It is also to be remembered that the Prophet advised his followers who were not under clan protection to take refugee from persecution by the Quraysh with the Christian king of Abyssinia, the Negus.

The Hadith also often bears testimony to the strong influence of Christian scriptures, as in the one where Muhammad states that a person should forgive a servant 70 times.[4] Moreover, Christianity has much common theological ground with Islam. The figure of Jesus, central to the former and an exalted figure in the latter, is foremost in this commonality notwithstanding ontological and functional differences. The divinity and sonship of Jesus is a problem, but in a recent article David Thomas informs us some Muslim scholars such as Ahmad ibn Hait (d. 230AH) indeed admitted that Jesus was God's adopted son and though created was a second creator in addition to God.[5] This is not a typical response to Christian belief of Jesus as the Son of God, but tends to indicate that all Muslim opinions on this issue are not as negative as usually perceived. The Qur'an itself speaks of Jesus as a 'word' from God and a 'spirit' sent by him, and seems to be employing the very terminology used in the Gospel of St John. The figures of Abraham and the prophets, and ideas of afterlife, heaven and hell, resurrection and judgement by God, are again common ground between Islam and Christianity.

I would think that in modern times as well, Christianity, as a religion per se, is not seen to be an enemy by the Muslim *ummah* certainly at the level of informed Muslim leadership. In India where I come from I often found that Muslims emphasised that Islam and Christianity are revelations from the same source, 'The Well-guarded Tablet' in heaven, and referred to the two religions as the second and the third Veda, the first Veda presumably being Judaism. In India also there is much empathy between the two communities probably arising from the fact that both are religious minorities under threat from increasing Hindu fundamentalism, and keen to defend their religious and social institutions and rights against governmental interference prompted by demands of the Hindutva organisations. Christian–Muslim confrontation has never been a problem in independent India. Then, as I mentioned earlier, there is the question of whether Christianity is represented nowadays by the West. The centre of Christianity has shifted away radically from the western world to Africa, Asia and Latin America. It might no longer be legitimate to consider the western world as Christian.

2. There is no doubt that there are contrasts in the Muslim and the western way of life. Individual freedom and autonomy are highly respected and even cherished in western societies. Muslims emphasise community, fraternity and solidarity rather than individuality. To them matters such as the family, the authority of elders and respect for them, are highly important. There is a notion of the *ummah* that exists at various levels: the village, the town, the nation and the world. In all these concentric levels the group is more important than the individual. This probably has roots in the original forging of the community by the prophet. Arabia was a fragmented and disharmonious society in the days of what is known as the *jahiliyya*. Society was divided into clans and tribes and order was maintained only by the threat of violence between these social units. The vendetta was the tool by which law and order was kept. The Muslim *ummah* was on the other hand a united and even classless society in comparison in those primal days of Islam. As Ali Shariati puts it society moved from the *shirk* of classes and hierarchies, slaves and the free, women and men, to the *tawhid* of egalitarianism.[6] Thus individual and factional interests gave way to the interests of the community as a whole. This is another intrinsic contrast between western and Islamic societies, and also a source of tension between first and second generation Muslims in the western world.

To Muslims there is no activity outside the scope of religious law. The *shari'ah* is all-encompassing. The *shari'ah,* though its final form involves the deliberations of the *ulama*, analogical reasoning (*qiyas*), and even personal interpretation *(ijtihad*), and legal opinion (*fatwa*) of individual *muftis*, is mainly based on channels of revelation, firstly the Qur'an and secondly the Hadith. The community functions as a unit within the framework of the *shari'ah.* As John Shepherd states, in the West, 'law, but not morality, is codified and promulgated by the State, and its infringements, but not purely moral infringements incur statutory punishments…'.[7] This is not to say that western law disregards moral considerations. But in modern western societies many matters that are considered as more liable to moral scrutiny and judgement rather than legal investigation and action are still within the ambit of law in Islamic societies. This is because in the

West many matters that may not be detrimental to society as a whole are considered to be in the private domain and left to individual moral sensibilities. Moreover, the principles of natural justice rather than revelation form the foundation of legal systems in the western world and are subject to change as human value judgements and sensitivities change in course of time. What has been forbidden in the past may become legitimate in modern times. Many Muslims cannot brook such changes: tradition of the elders, the *sunnah*, is very important to them and the ease with which the western world has abandoned some of the older mores is not palatable to them. The abandonment of religion as the foundation of society, and the separation of religion and the State are according to them the roots of evil in western society, consequently creating loose moral values, drug addiction and increased crime, for example. Their apprehension is, however, that owing to colonial contacts, the media, and increased facility of global travel, their traditions and values might be infected by western individualism and liberalism and thus jeopardised. Western culture is therefore commonly seen to be a threat to the Islamic way of life and a force that erodes the religious and social norms of Islam.

Globalisation of trade and the burgeoning popularity of the media such as in satellite television and, more importantly, the internet are sources seen by many Muslim traditionalists as eroding the very fabric of Muslim society. In a recent revealing article Mark Levine points out that the consensus among Third World countries is that globalisation indicates a continuation of centuries-long western domination and hegemony. There is a feeling that America is using globalisation as a tool that can overthrow existing political, economic and cultural norms, realising its imperialist aims without causing the classic revolutionary reaction to it as evinced in the period of western imperialism.[8] Muslims are now exposed to western values and liberal perspectives much more than in any other age. Some states, Iran for instance, have totally banned the beaming and receiving of television programmes from the West. These programmes such as soap serials are very attractive to the younger generation and present a highly rosy picture of western culture and life, and it is certain that such programmes are clandestinely viewed by Muslim youth. It is next to impossible to control internet sources. Muslim nations often lack the sophisticated technology to monitor the use of the Internet by their citizens. Of course it is also possible to propagate Islamic ideals on the Internet and there are a plethora of such sources. But the very availability of hedonistic material on the TV and the Internet is a source of strong temptation to view such programmes, and forms a very potent ideological influence on Muslim youth. Many Muslim religious leaders resent this intrusion into their world, reacting against this perceived ideological and cultural colonialism, of a population already prepared for such influences by their experience of earlier political colonialism. Khomeini, for instance, believed that the Shah's westernisation of society was an 'imperialist and Zionist' plot for controlling Iran. To such a view, the westernisation of Iran was looked upon by the Shah as an instrument to weaken the hold of the clergy and consequently of Islam on Iran.[9] Syed Hossein Nasr in a perceptive article opines that lacking sufficient knowledge of, or confidence in, their own intellectual tradition, many modern Muslims have become like a *tabula rasa*, ready to receive impressions from the West.[10] It is to be remembered, however, that the lack of depth of knowledge in their own religious heritage can also be a factor in their ability to be influenced by Islamic politico-religious movements. We also have to take into account the fact that the Muslim diaspora in the West, when they visit their lands of origin, might also unwittingly disseminate elements of western culture into such societies. On the other hand, the Muslims in the West might introduce elements of Muslim culture into their host nations.[11] It cannot be forgotten that many Europeans are greatly attracted to Islam and have embraced the faith and some of the cultural appurtenances such as dress and food.

But does such ideological opposition lead to violent conflict as happened on 9/11? Such cultural and ideological infiltration of western values and ways of life is also alleged by other faiths, notably by the Hindutva parties of India. The Sangh Parivar, as they are called, is particularly opposed to globalisation of trade and mass media intrusion into Indian society. Establishments such as McDonald's have been picketed by activists of the VHP (Vishwa Hindu Parishad), and a World beauty contest disrupted by members of the RSS (Rashtriya Swayamsevak Sangh) in Bangalore. But no one contends that Hinduism or India is hostile to the West on these accounts. The hostility is at a local level where the two cultures meet and not on a global level. We can therefore say that there are misgivings regarding the general cultural trends in the West and its mostly non-deliberate intrusion into the Islamic world motivated by the financial ambitions of media moguls, international corporations, western media, and foreign policy of western nations, especially the USA, but to characterise these as antagonism to the people of the West may be too hasty a conclusion.

In classical jurisprudence, there are two aspects of Islamic belief that are relevant to the question of cultural interaction. One is the notion of *Dar al-Islam* and the other the idea of what is known as *jihad*. It is beyond the scope of this chapter to look into these concepts in detail. However, some brief comments on these concepts are made as follows: *Dar al-Islam* from the Arabic *darun* (house) can be translated as the Abode of Islam; this is a term that in the traditional context was applied to places where Muslims were in the majority. *Dar al-Harb* (abode of war) is where Muslims were in a minority and had to engage in *jihad* (struggle) for freedom to practice their faith and ways of life. But most western nations will be considered by Muslims as *Dar al-Sulh* (Abode of Peace) where Muslims are in a minority but have religious and cultural freedom. However, it is difficult to say that western nations are an ideal of *Dar al-Sulh* since Muslims living there are often faced with problems in observing their traditions, such as in the matter of apparel, food, burial of the dead and education of children. But these problems are not serious enough to warrant the term *Dar al-Harb* to be applied to them. On the other hand, there are Islamic movements that do not consider most Muslim nations to be *Dar al-Islam*. Sayyid Qutb, for instance considered Muslim nations with man-made constitutions as *Jahiliyya*.[12] Therefore, with the exception of these movements, this cannot be broadly speaking a context for the origins of hostility particularly to the West on the part of committed but reasonable and moderate Muslims who are the majority in the *ummah*. However, they might also acknowledge to varying degrees the critique of the Islamic movements that many of the Muslim states are un-Islamic or even anti-Islamic in their unquestioning and unchallenged submission to western ideals and norms of government and social order.[13]

The word *jihad* literally means striving or struggle and is often mistakenly translated as 'holy war'. For instance, on one occasion a man asked the Prophet 'Should I join the *jihad*?' He asked, 'Do you have parents?' The man said, 'Yes!' The Prophet said, 'Then strive by serving them!'[14] The Arabic for the term 'holy war' is actually *harbun muquaddasatu.* In the Islamic sense all religious *jihad* is defensive and is for protecting the cause of Allah (*Jihad fi sabil Allah*). In other words, it is waged against oppression of the faith and the faith community. When persecution ceased, and everyone was at liberty to profess the religion of his choice *jihad* has to cease (Qur'an 55:5-6). However, such *jihad* need not be in the form of an armed struggle. The following verse in the Qur'an suggests that peaceful methods may be employed to counter oppression:

> Lo! As for those whom the angels take [in death] while they wronged themselves, [the angels] will ask: 'In what you were engaged?' They will way: 'We were oppressed in the land.' [The angels] will say: 'Was not Allah's earth spacious that you could have migrated therein?' (Qur'an 4:97).

The Prophet's immigration to Medina when persecution in Makka became intense, provides Muslims with an example of non-violent *jihad* or *Hijrah* as a form of *jihad.*

3. Since the emancipation of Islamic countries from western domination in the twentieth century, the political relations between the two have been one of mutual interdependence in the majority of cases. Western nations have provided technical and scientific expertise to Islamic nations and some of the latter have supplied an important commodity, namely oil, to the West. Many Muslim nations are or have been in the past dependent on the West for developing their natural resources and marketing them and also for establishing modern infrastructure in these nations and training their youth in modern science and technology. Nations such as Saudi Arabia, and the UAE do have friendly links with the West mainly on these accounts, in spite of sharp ideological differences. We thus cannot disregard the element of symbiosis in the relations of Islam with the West. Moreover, Andre Nusse points out that western ideas such as liberty, fraternity and equality are accepted as Islamic ideals.[15] Some Muslims would even feel that Muslim civilisation has been the basis of western civilisation and the latter is simply an extension of the former.

However, I feel that the most significant factor in the interaction between Islam and the West are political issues that centre on the Palestinian question. The Palestinian problem seems to have been the *zeitgeist* in the attitudes of the Arab world and perhaps the entire Muslim *ummah* to the western world. But the Palestinian issue is not the only factor that has vitiated relations between Islam and the non-Muslim world. We find that the Kashmir issue is a political question that has been for a long time a bone of contention between Muslims and Hindu India. It is admitted that the operations of al-Qa'eda and other militant organisations have been directed not only against the West but also against perceived Hindu oppression of Muslims in Kashmir. Islamic militants have also fought against Eastern European nations such as Russia and Serbia. These instances invalidate the thesis of a general and innate opposition by Islamic faith communities to the West on political grounds. It would rather seem that opposition exists wherever and from whomsoever oppression of Muslim people is perceived. The thesis of Islam being intrinsically opposed to the West only disguises the problem of oppression of Muslim peoples and injustices against such populations, and distracts world bodies from seeking solutions for the legitimate grievances of such populations. The sanctions and subsequently unjustified war and conquest of Iraq, the high-handedness of Indian paramilitaries against the people of Kashmir, Russian excesses against Chechnya, and Israeli atrocities against Palestinians are legitimate causes from which attention can be diverted by characterising people seeking justice as terrorists, and these incidents as symptoms of a general Islamic antipathy to the West or to non-Muslim faiths.

We have to examine closely whether the Palestinian controversy involves anti-Semitic or anti-West attitudes. The patriarch Abraham is a highly regarded and important figure in all the three faiths of Judaism, Islam and Christianity. Muslims claim that in Medina, the first Islamic state, Jews and Christians had equal status with the Muslims. They had a fair measure of religious freedom. The Prophet regarded them as Muslims in the sense of those submitting to the one true God. He followed many of their rituals, observed their festivals and even wore similar apparel. Muslims, like Jews, prayed towards Jerusalem.[16] But Muhammad's overtures were rejected by the Jews who made fun of him and called him an impostor.[17] They said that Muhammad did not fulfil the criteria of prophethood as evinced in their own scriptures. More serious was their non-cooperation at a time of battle with the Quraysh, when the fledgling Muslim community was threatened by numerically vastly superior forces. Muhammad had to banish some Jewish tribes from Medina. After the battle of Ahzab, males of one tribe, the Banu Qurayza, who actively colluded with the Quraysh and spied for them, were executed and their women and children sold into slavery. But the decision to implement such draconian punishment did not come from Muhammed or the Mujahirrun (immigrants) but from one of the Ansar, the original inhabitants of Medina, Syed ibn Muadh, from the Aws tribe, a tribe who were actually allies of the Jews.[18]

Such examples not withstanding, we see that there was no history of a deeply ingrained anti-Semitism in Islam as in the case of medieval Europe or Nazi Germany. Jews were accepted as Muslims in the sense of being strong monotheists who submitted to the one true God. They were given religious freedom and equal rights with Muslims and Christians in the constitution of Medina. In Spain, Muslims and Jews lived happily together during the long period of Islamic rule. During the Crusades both communities were equally victimised by overzealous Christian warriors.

All individuals or communities who criticise Israel cannot be designated as anti-Semitic. There are many who in other ways are totally unbiased and free from any racist tendencies but criticise the Israeli occupation of Palestine. It will be unjust and inaccurate to class them as anti-Semitic. This is the case with most Palestinians, though as the atrocities, the violence and the hostility escalates, this might turn into anti-Semitism. Moreover, a person can be anti-Zionist without being anti-Semitic. Zionism began as more of a political than religious ideology and like any other political creed will invite criticism, without the critique and the critic being characterised as racist. One can be anti-communist without being anti-Chinese, for instance and anti-capitalist without being anti-American. On the other hand, many who support Zionism are anti-Semitic. There are many fundamentalist evangelical Christians who support Zionism as a necessary pre-condition for the coming of Jesus Christ.

Nusse opines that the origins of modern day anti-Semitism in the Arab world can be traced to European anti-Semitism and the term 'Jewish Nazism' relates to the expulsion of the Muslims from their homelands which is depicted as a kind of holocaust.[19] However, there is a significant difference. Anti-Semitism in the Arab world is not racist as it was in Europe but is related to the conquest of land, and is to be used as a weapon in the struggle against Zionism, not against Jews per se. However, there are signs of anti-Semitism in the revival of the Protocols of Zion as a genuine document and the idea of worldwide conspiracy of domination by Jews, which were once a part of Christian and Nazi anti-Semitism, are now prevalent in the Muslim world. This is no doubt a reaction to the mounting oppression of Palestinians by Israel, and more of a recent than well-established phenomenon.

For the Jews the idea of a promised land has been a powerful motivating force. They are, like the Muslims, a people called from nomadism to enlandisement by God. Kenneth Cragg states, 'righteousness has to be "earthed", not disparate, visionary and immaterial; cultivation and tenancy spells a very physical reverence in which Yahweh is adored'.[20] But they never did drive out completely the indigenous people from the territories they occupied. Joshua 15:63 states, for instance, that the Jebusites were never expelled. And there have always been warnings from God that they were not to expel certain people from the lands that God had allotted to them. [21]

Theodore Herzl, a Hungarian Jew (1860-1904) was the architect of the movement known as Zionism. He proposed a solution to the Jewish problem, to their sufferings and persecution in Europe. Herzl wrote:

> The Jewish question exists wherever Jews live in perceptible numbers. Where it does not exist, it is carried by Jews in the course of their migrations ... This is the case in every country, and will remain so, even in those highly civilized – for instance France – until the Jewish question finds a solution on a political basis. The unfortunate Jews are now carrying the seeds of anti-Semitism into England; they have already introduced it into America... We are one people-our enemies have made us one in our respite, as repeatedly happens in history. Distress binds us together, and, thus united, we suddenly discover our strength. Yes, we are strong enough to form a State, and, indeed a model State. We possess all human and material resources necessary for the purpose...[22]

In short he proposed the formation of a Jewish state as the way to resolve the problems Jews faced in Europe.

Herzl's ideology seems to have been supported by Lord Balfour, British Foreign Secretary, who in 1917 declared the intention of creating a Jewish state in their ancient homeland 'without prejudice to the civil and religious rights of the existing non-Jewish population of Palestine'. However, the wishes of the Palestinians were not at all considered in arriving at this decision. In a secret memorandum submitted to the British cabinet he said Britain was committed to Zionism. And Zionism, 'be it right or wrong, good or bad is rooted in age-long traditions, in present needs and in future hope, of far profounder import than the desires and prejudices of the 700,000 Arabs who now inhabit that ancient land'.[23] The Jewish state would have had much more legitimacy if the Palestinians and neighbouring Arab countries were consulted before implementing the decision to settle Jews into Palestinian territories. But Britain was a great colonial power then, the empire on which the sun never set, and was in no mood to consult its subject peoples on matters of importance. [24] The initial moves in what is termed Zionism were European in origin, not American, and it is strange that nowadays in spite of our Prime Minister's determined effort, the USA and not Britain or Europe is regarded as the villain in the entire issue. The settlement of Jews in Palestine was unfortunately decided upon without consulting the Palestinian residents or neighbouring Arab states of the region. The Arabs regarded the *aliyas* as an unwelcome intrusion. Like the proverbial camel the Jews soon pushed out the indigenous occupants, and thus the Palestinian problem, which has global repercussions, came into being.

The idea of a 'promised land' is both anachronistic and disruptive to peace. But this is advanced by many orthodox Jews and inhabitants of the illegal Jewish settlements in Palestinian land as supporting their occupation. The idea of a people chosen by God is also a concept that prompts separatism and racism. In Old Testament times these ideas had a certain relevance in calling a nomadic people to enlandisement and to providing an example of a people totally committed to God and living a disciplined life in conformity with sacred law. The God of the Biblical scriptures is not an unjust God who displays favouritism, but a God who has called every one to worship him and live a life in conformity with moral ideals–the Israelites may have been a channel through which these revelations were communicated to a world that was steeped in sinful acts and bizarre religious practices such as sacrificing their own children to appease gods, just as Muhammad and the first Muslims were the channel through which God exhorted the Arabs and even the world into submission to his will and to abandon a licentious and profligate life.

The USA was never a colonial power, and had sympathies for India and other subjugated nations emerging from colonialism. But America has made itself unpopular in the entire Arab world with its unstinting support of Israel in the UN Security Council and by supplying arms and financial assistance. In a recent speech Mr. Afif Safieh, the Palestinian Ambassador to the United Kingdom has pointed out that since the negotiating partners in the peace process are so unequal, Israel is able to dictate conditions rather than agree to negotiate a solution.[25]

Without outside mediation and intervention the peace process has become a process without peace and an end in itself, whereas a solution is urgently needed to end the tragic scale of suffering in the region. Israel has the advantages of an unwritten alliance with the only remaining superpower and has all the advantages of such an alliance but none of the restraints of being the junior partner. Israel has never taken a conciliatory stance and in recent times seems bent upon achieving a military rather than a political solution to the problem. Its policies and actions provide fuel for Islamic militants. Moreover the USA is perceived in the Muslim world as unnecessarily meddling in Middle Eastern affairs. The European colonial powers, perhaps with the exception of France, have stayed clear of domestic politics in their former colonial possessions. The USA, moreover, seems to seek a military solution to political problems and does not seem to tackle the root causes of Muslim *angst*. It is to be noted that there is a wide disparity in the relations between the US and the Arab administrations, as contrasted with considerable elements of the Muslim masses and their attitudes towards the USA. It would thus be truer and more accurate to state that the Muslim *ummah* is against the USA on account of its arbitrary support of Israel and seeking to intervene in Middle Eastern affairs, so far from their homeland, rather than against the West. The invasion of Iraq is also looked upon as motivated by economic and political self-interest rather than concern for Iraqis or other averred altruistic motives. The apparent agenda of reshaping the Middle East and gaining control of natural resources and exerting US hegemony is a strong motivation for a vicious armed struggle against the USA and Britain.

This was brought home to me very clearly when with a group of British academics I visited Libya in 1986. US war planes bombed Tripoli when we were there and soon food supplies in Tripoli dwindled. We faced the prospect of being marooned in Tripoli facing starvation. My western colleagues were very apprehensive and huddled together in a room afraid to go out. But many of the local people and Palestinians resident there came to us and pacified us promising us that we were safe, and that they would bring us required supplies if food ran out in the hotel where we were accommodated. It was brought home to me very strongly that their attitude was anything but hostile to westerners in spite of the bombing and the death of the Libyan leader's child.

It is also significant that pre- and post-9/11 there have been very little threats or violence against any European nation, even against Britain, which is seen as the staunchest ally of the USA among the European nations. Moreover, there are other Muslim populations in confrontation with what are perceived as oppressive regimes. In Kashmir the target of Muslims is Indian occupancy, in Chechnya the Russians, in the Philippines the Filipino administration. The attempt to give a racial or geographical interpretation to the happenings seems to lack validity. Some quarters have voiced the opinion that it is the affluence of the USA, and presumably the whole western world, that has provoked Islamic militancy. That is to say that it is a question of jealousy. But we cannot forget that there are some Muslim nations that are as affluent as the US or Europe. Such jealousies do not seem to operate in their own context, at least not to the extent of launching an attack. Moreover some of the leaders of Islamic *jihadis* are themselves very wealthy figures. So it does not seem principally to be an economic motivation, cultural and ideological contrasts do play a part, though probably a minor part, in Islamic attitudes to the West. Poverty and oppression in parts of the Islamic world do have a role in fostering fundamentalism, extremism and fanaticism. Also there has been in the past, and even today, a feeling that the West has tried to exploit natural resources in the Islamic world for its own benefit. It was one of the allegations against the Shah's regime in Iran that it allowed such exploitation. In Libya I saw graphic posters depicting the contrast in the flow of natural wealth pre- and post-Fatah revolution. In the pre-Fatah days oil wealth is seen as benefiting only the West and the Sultan, and after the revolution as going towards development of Libya. However, in recent times most Arab nations would see the West as a partner in utilising natural resources rather than as an exploiter.

Now we must examine closely whether the violence associated with the 9/11 incident in New York, and other events usually termed terrorism, is representative of the Muslim community or originating from the Islamic faith itself. Al-Qa'eda, the Taliban and such militant outfits in the Islamic world are mainly groups who subscribe to an ideology known as Wahhabism or Salafism. The Taliban, for example, are Afghanis schooled in an Indian variant of Wahhabi ideology. The Hamas is an offshoot of the Muslim brotherhood whose ideology is also akin to Salafism. Salafism or Wahhabism has its intellectual roots in the Hambali Madhab of Islam, and of the thoughts of Ibn Taymiyya, a fourteenth century Syrian Hambali theologian. Essentially the Wahhabis go back to the Qur'an and the Hadith and permit the use of *ijtihad* (personal interpretation). They reject transmitted knowledge and the authority of the canon, and the roots of the law such as *qiyas* and *ijma*. They have reopened the gates of unconditional *ijtihad*, with the consequent dangers of erroneous interpretation of scripture. They disregard classical *tafsir* – even that of the renowned at-Tabari – on the grounds that it contains Biblical references. There is here the danger of reducing what is believed to be God's knowledge to one's own knowledge by saying that only one interpretation of it is the right one. We can see that the evangelicals in Christianity have very similar notions, and in this respect the Wahhabis may be called the fundamentalist evangelicals of the Islamic faith. My Wahhabi friends in Lakshadweep used to call other Muslims *Khurafis* indicating that they consider only themselves as true Muslims. They also do not observe the pre-requisites for framing new *fatwa*s, such as knowing the Qur'an by memory, close knowledge of Hadith and *fiqh*, and the rules of interpretation.

Wahhabi ideology has spread far and wide, with the backing of petro-dollars from their headquarters, Saudi Arabia, and has a strong presence now in every Islamic nation. When I was in Malaysia I noted that it has made considerable inroads into traditional Malay Islam, a relaxed and tolerant form of the faith, incorporating much from the Hindu-Buddhist-animist culture of the Malays. This is true especially of urban educated sections such as university students. The Wahhabis aim to purge all syncretistic influences from Malay Islam and transform it into a pure Arab and Wahhabi form.

The Wahhabis also form alliances with local Islamic groups and form legal political parties wherever feasible. Expatriate Muslims from Saudi Arabia, who have gone there either to work or to study Arabic extend Salafi influence considerably to many Islamic nations. In the Lakshadweep Islands where I taught for twenty years the ideology is disseminated by Arabic teachers in the state high schools; these teachers are either trained in Saudi Arabia or have been students in Wahhabi-oriented *madrasas* in Kerala State, notably the Farook College in Feroke. However, they are a minority in the islands and not well favoured by the Lakshadweep islanders, there being a strong element of Sufism in their religious praxis. But in many other Islamic societies their influence is growing. Having presented their ideology as a panacea for all the evils blighting the lives of Muslims in the world, they have a strong appeal to the Islamic youth.

I am not embarking on a wholesale indictment of Wahhabi ideology. I suppose it is as legitimate an ideology to have as any other religious ideology, though different from traditional Islam. After all, their aim was to revert back to the ideals presented by the early days of Islam when it was led by the Prophet. But their attempts to reform Islam seem naive and simplistic in the sense that they discount the historical evolution of Islam which has been enriched by centuries of contact with other cultures and civilisations, and by the deliberations of knowledgeable minds who sought to contextualise and adapt their faith to the different locales and cultures that Islam found itself in. Theirs is a particular interpretation of the scripture and the Islamic faith which looks upon all these developments as *bida* (innovation). The problem also is that since Wahhabism does not rest on well-founded and stable methodological principles it is liable to misuse by extremist groups.

Wahhabism is not by itself a violent ideology. But there are subsets who Vincenzo Oliveti terms the Salafi Takhfiris,[26] probably because they consider other Muslims as heretics. In their hands the Wahhabi ideology has exploded into an ultra-violent form and has led to the slaughter of innocent civilians, women and children, expressly forbidden in the Qur'anic principles governing *jihad*. The Qur'an, as I mentioned earlier, makes clear that *jihad* is only envisaged as defensive warfare, and has to be engaged within strict limits: that is, no wholesale slaughter of innocent civilians and destruction of property. The Qur'an states:

> To those against whom war is made, permission is given
> (to defend themselves), because they are wronged – and
> verily, Allah is Most Powerful to give them victory –
> (they are) those who have been expelled from their homes
> in defiance of right – (for no cause) except that they say,
> 'Our Lord is Allah'... (Qur'an 22:39-40)

> Fight in the cause of Allah against those who fight against
> you, but do not transgress limits. Lo! Allah loves not
> aggressors. ... and fight them until persecution is no more,
> and religion is for Allah. But if they desist, then let there
> be no hostility except against transgressors (Qur'an 2:190, 193).

The Prophet's own laws of *jihad* communicated by Abu Bakr are as follows:

> Do not betray: do not carry grudges; do not deceive; do not mutilate; do not kill children; do not kill the elderly; do not kill women. Do not destroy beehives or burn them; do not cut down fruit bearing trees; do not slaughter sheep, cattle or camels, except for food.[27]

Suicide is a sin in Islam. The belief is that the human life span is determined by Allah and to take one's own life and hasten one's own death is interfering with Allah's will, and closes the door to divine mercy.[28] But the Salafi Takhfiris abide by a *fatwa* that anyone who commits suicide while killing their enemies or dies while withholding information from them when captured, is a martyr and is directly eligible to Paradise.[29] This provides a strong motivation for the type of self-immolation witnessed in acts such as that of 9/11. Such people who gain considerable media attention are erroneously taken to be representative of the Muslim *ummah* by the media and political analysts and thus give Islam an undeservedly negative image. It is true that the Salafi Takhfiris seem to have a very hostile attitude to the West, but it is evidently fallacious to postulate this for the Muslim *ummah* in general.

In conclusion, I feel it will be too simplistic to see the happenings of 9/11 and later, as Islam against the West or as a war between religions, civilisations or races. The danger inherent in such views is that it tends to obscure genuine grievances on the part of Islamic communities who are dealt with unjustly by non-Muslim forces, for instance Israel in Palestine or indirectly by the USA in Palestine and in Iraq. It is also necessary to make a fine distinction between those who fight injustice on the part of vastly superior forces through guerrilla warfare and those who indulge in acts of violence to cause terror in civilian populations.

Notes

[1] Nusse, Andre, *Muslim Palestine, The Ideology of Hamas*, London, Routledge-Curzon, 1998.
[2] See Sahas, Daniel J., *John of Damascus on Islam: the Heresy of the Ishmaelites*, Leiden: E.J. Brill, 1972, p. 68.
[3] Hitti, Philip, K., *Islam and the West*, Princeton: D. Van Nostrand Co., 1962, p. 50.
[4] The similarity to Matthew 18: 21-22 is striking.
[5] See Thomas, David, 'The Question better not asked', in Gabriel, T. (Ed.), *Islam in the Contemporary World*, New Delhi: Vikas, 2000, pp. 20-41, p. 25
[6] See Enayat Hamid, *Modern Islamic Political Thought*, London, The Macmillan Press, 1982, p. 156.
[7] Shepherd, John, 'Islamic Ethics and the Ethics of Liberalism the Logic of a Creative Synthesis', in Gabriel, T., (Ed.), *Islam in the Contemporary World,* New Delhi:Vikas, 2000, pp. 1-20, p. 3.
[8] Levine, Mark, 'Muslim Responses to Globalisation', in *ISIM Newsletter*, no. 10, July 2002, p. 1.
[9] Irfani Suroosh, *Revolutionary Iran*, London: Zed Books, 1983, p. 79.
[10] Nasr, S.H, 'The Western World and its Challenges to Islam', in Ahmad, Khurshid, *Islam its meaning and Message*, London: Islamic Council of Europe, 1975, p. 225.

[11] On the other hand, they may be practising their religion more conservatively than their counterparts in Muslim countries, a consequence of the apprehension of being in a minority situation and in reaction insulating themselves from extraneous influences in religious practice.
[12] Nusse, op. cit., p. 76.
[13] In opposition to classical jurisprudence, Qutb and Mawdudi, along with a number of revivalist movements of the twentieth century consider the contemporary world, including Muslim states, to be *Dar al-Harb*. Thus there is a struggle *(jihad)* to bring all the world from a state of *kufr* to Islam, rallying around the implementation of *shari'ah* in both personal and public life.
[14] From Saleh al-Bukhari.
[15] Nuse, op.cit., p. 106.
[16] See Rodinson, Maxim, *Mohammed*, Penguin Books, 1973, pp. 160-161.
[17] Geiger, Abraham, *Judaism and Islam*, Ktav publishing house, 1970, p.12.
[18] See Rodinson, op. cit., p. 212.
[19] Nusse, op. cit., pp. 33-34.
[20] Cragg, Kenneth, *Palestine the Prize and Price of Zion*, London: Cassell, 1997, p. 21.
[21] See Deuteronomy 2: 5, 9, 19.
[22] Quoted in Chapman, Colin, *Whose Promised Land?*, Tring: Lion Publishing, 1986, p. 40.
[23] Ibid., p. 58.
[24] For instance, Gandhi or the Indian National Congress were aggrieved that the British had dragged India into the Second World War without consulting the Indians.
[25] See *Oxford Centre for Islamic Studies News Letter*, Autumn 2001, p. 3.
[26] Oliveti, Vincenzo, *Terror's source*, Amadeus Books, 2002, p. 72.
[27] Robinson, Neal, *The Sayings of Muhammad*, London: Duckworth, 1991, p. 32.
[28] Qur'an 3:45. See also the discussion on euthanasia, in Ibn Ally, 'Islam', *Ethical Traditions in Six Religions*, Morgan, Peggy (Ed.), Edinburgh: Edinburgh Univ. Press, 1996, p. 247.
[29] Such notions also exist among the Hamas, the Al Aqsa Martyr's Brigade and other Palestinian groups but the Salafis are the ones who most strongly adhere to this ambiguous principle.

Chapter 3

Self-critical Children of Abraham? Roots of Violence and Extremism in Judaism, Christianity and Islam

John J. Shepherd

They made war on Midian, as Yahweh had ordered Moses, and put every male to death.... Moses was enraged... . He said 'Why have you spared the life of all the women...? Kill all the male children and kill all the women who have ever slept with a man; but spare the lives of the young girls who have never slept with a man, and keep them for yourselves.' (Numbers 31:7, 14-18)

The seventh day must be a holy day for you, a day of complete rest, in honour of Yahweh. Anyone who does any work on that day will be put to death. (Exodus 35: 2-3)

You [Jews] are from your father, the devil... . There is no truth in him at all. (John 8: 44)

And the people [Jews], every one of them, shouted back, 'Let his blood be on us and on our children. (Matthew 27:25)

Idolatry is worse than carnage. (Qur'an 2:191)

Fight against such of those to whom the Scriptures were given as believe neither in Allah nor the Last Day, who do not forbid what Allah and His apostle have forbidden, and do not embrace the true faith, until they pay tribute out of hand and are utterly subdued. (Qur'an 9: 30)

Believers do not generally take their religion seriously in its entirety–a fact at times much deplored by those in religious authority, but more to be welcomed by the world at large. For religious commitment can conduce rather readily, and apparently logically and as a matter of principle, to religious extremism. The above quotations are redolent of religious intolerance in general, and holy war, genocide and anti-Semitism in particular.[1] Or consider the rather different case of Origen, so in thrall to scripture as to be prepared to harm himself, not others, by castrating himself in response to Matthew 19:12 – 'There are eunuchs who have made themselves so for the sake of the kingdom of Heaven. Let anyone accept this who can'. Two contrasting (though not necessarily mutually exclusive) types of response to such phenomena are available. Stated crudely: blame Origen, or blame

Christianity. Anti-religious sceptics apart, there is a strong tendency to plump for the first of these two strategies. Portray Origen and his ilk as 'extremists' and one can then exculpate the religion: extremists do not represent the 'true' religion; they are guilty of deficient understanding and distorted faith.

The attractions of this strategy are considerable. It comforts non-extremist insiders, and it enables sympathetic outsiders to be constructively tolerant. This may be of great importance politically and socially. Hence, for example, the well-publicised meeting at No. 10 Downing Street between British Muslim leaders and the British Prime Minister in the wake of 9/11. Again, President Bush's 'war' is on 'terrorism', not on 'Islam'. Nevertheless, despite its merits, this strategy also suffers from three potential disadvantages. First, within a given religion arguments about what is to count as the 'true' religion can be messy and inconclusive. Second, adherents of any given religion are notoriously better at exonerating their own religion in this way than they are at exonerating other people's religions, so that partisan idealisation/vilification takes place. Third, and especially, it lets religions – one's own or someone else's – off the hook too easily. For typically, the roots of religious extremism do actually lie in religion. Social and political circumstances may condition or even determine the extent to which the roots bear fruit. Yet responsibility for the roots lies in the religion itself.

There is, admittedly, a difficulty at this point, not logically, but psychologically and morally. In the wake of 9/11, for example, one does not want to risk encouraging Islamophobia by 'attacking' Islam. In the wake of the Holocaust one does not want to risk encouraging anti-Semitism by 'attacking' Judaism. On the other hand, the academic study of religion has its own set of responsibilities, and teaching, or more generally communicating, sanitised versions of religion is not part of its proper purpose. In any case, and additionally, shielding religions from pertinent critical questioning is not conducive to their long-term health. Ideally, admittedly, such critical questioning needs to be conducted not simply by outsiders but also by insiders. Criticism needs to include self-criticism, as an exercise in healthy open-mindedness. Yet if criticisms are valid, their provenance – from among fellow-believers, or from among outsiders – is in fact irrelevant. Many of the criticisms to be considered here are also, we shall see, examples of internal criticism. It is my contention, though, that a move to a greater degree of self-criticism would be a constructive, though not uncostly, response to the atrocities of 9/11, especially if it could be seen as appropriate, not just for Muslims, but for all the children of Abraham.

One conclusion that reflection on 'Muslim extremism', 'Jewish extremism', 'Christian extremism' points to is that members of faith communities today have a problem. On the one hand, they live their religious commitment in a society and in a world that is increasingly self-consciously pluralistic, and open at many levels to recognising and developing a trans-religious and indeed global ethic of humanitarian concern, human rights, and mutual religious tolerance. On the other hand, their own religious tradition originated in quite different circumstances, where mutual religious intolerance was deemed a duty, and was absorbed as part of that tradition – or, indeed, in good measure inspired it and helped constitute its very identity.

Thus the Jewish tradition celebrates, as in good measure foundational, what is euphemistically termed the 'entry into the promised land' – an event that in practical terms is described as a bloody conquest with periodic divinely sanctioned massacres and would-be genocide, inaugurating a history of intolerance and persecution of idolaters and deviants. The Christian tradition has absorbed this inheritance into its bloodstream, so that Christian groups have been able, at diverse times and in sundry places, to see themselves as a new chosen people entering a new promised land in equally ruthless fashion – a ruthlessness extendable to a cruel anti-Semitism fuelled by their own New Testament as opposed to the inherited Old. The New Testament, indeed, contains passages that would, one imagines, be actionable under British laws against incitement to racial hatred were they to be published fresh today. In the Muslim tradition, of course, hatred of idolatry lies at its very root, and the career of Muhammad, as described in Muslim sources, contains scenes of bloodshed and murder which are shocking to modern humanitarian sensibilities, as are related teachings in the Qur'an. Fragments of support for these thumbnail summaries are to be found in the scriptural quotations that preface this essay. Let me now explore them more fully in a way that highlights their far from purely academic significance.

On 25 February 1994 a Jewish zealot, Baruch Goldstein, walked into the Ibrahim Mosque portion of the Tomb of the Patriarchs in Hebron and cold-bloodedly massacred twenty-nine Muslims, some children, at their morning prayers, and wounded many more before being beaten to death himself by other potential victims. The atrocity evoked virtually universal revulsion – and yet: 'within two days of the massacre the walls of religious neighbourhoods of west Jerusalem (and to a lesser extent of many other religious neighbourhoods) were covered by posters extolling Goldstein's virtues and complaining that he did not manage to kill more Arabs'; at his funeral a rabbi eulogised him as a 'holy martyr ... from now on our intercessor in heaven', adding, 'he heard the cry of the land of Israel, which is being stolen from us day after day by the Muslims ... The Jews will inherit the land not by any peace agreement but only by shedding blood'; and after the funeral the army provided a guard of honour at his tomb, which subsequently became a centre of pilgrimage: 'Thousands of Jews from all Israeli cities, and even more from the United States and France, have come to light candles and pray for the intercession of "holy saint and martyr", now in a special section of paradise close to God and able to obtain for them various benefits, such as cures for diseases from which they suffer, or to grant them male offspring.'[2]

Goldstein's supporters may be extremists, but their extremism is neither unprincipled nor illogical. For the settler movements of which he was part are based on the clear Biblical thesis of the Promised Land; and even if their relentless discrimination against Palestinian occupants (and owners) of the land spills over into murder, Biblical precedent is again at hand by way of justification. The Hebron massacre occurred on Purim, a festival celebrating deliverance of the Jewish communities of the Persian Empire from planned genocidal attacks as recounted in the Book of Esther. The counterpart to their deliverance, though, was their proceeding to large-scale killing 'to avenge themselves on their enemies'

(Esther 8:13). 'They slaughtered seventy-five thousand of their opponents' (Esther 9:16). The way was open for Goldstein's action to be hailed as 'a Purim miracle', and for it to engender wishes for further massacres.[3]

More generally, in settler circles, the Palestinians are liable to be identified with the Amalekites – referring to whom Samuel, relaying 'the words of Yahweh', tells Saul: 'Now, go and crush Amalek; put him under the curse of destruction [the ban] with all that he possesses. Do not spare him, but kill man and woman, babe and suckling, ox and sheep, camel and donkey' (1 Samuel 15:1, 3). Inspired by such a verse, a former Campus Rabbi of the religious Bar-Ilan University in Israel published an article for students on 'The Commandment of Genocide in the Torah', writing for example that 'the day is not far when we shall all be called to this holy war, this commandment of the annihilation of Amalek'. The message is passed on through the religious schools: 'These boys are taught that the Arab is Amalek.... "It says in the Torah that you have to destroy all the remnants of Amalek," said [thirteen-year-old] Oren.'[4]

The settlers, of course, are a supreme obstacle to the peace process. At first against Israel's government policy, but subsequently, often with its acquiescence or indeed active support (not least by Ariel Sharon, known in Israel as 'the godfather of the settlements'), the settlers have sought, successfully, to create a situation on the ground that militates against the establishment of a viable Palestinian state in the occupied West Bank. For, as of 2002, Amnesty International, quoting the Israeli human rights organisation B'Tselem, reveals that 'the settlements control 41.9 per cent of the land area of the West Bank, although their built-up areas cover only 1.7 per cent'.[5] Their very existence vitiates any peace process, while at the same time being nurtured by central tenets of scripture.

Not all would be as extreme as those who relish the prospect of eliminating 'the Amalekites', but the idea of expulsion or 'transfer' of the Palestinians as a means of redeeming the lands of 'Judaea and Samaria' commands strong support. Its roots lie in part in that crucially, indeed cruelly, flawed early Zionist slogan of 'a land without a people for a people without a land'. Yet it lies too, critically, in Torah and Talmud. As Rabbi Yisrael Ariel of the Gush Emunim settler movement puts it, the traditional commandment of 'inheritance and residence' means quite simply 'conquering and settling the land'. 'The Torah repeats the commandment "You shall dispossess all the inhabitants of the land" tens of times'. Quoting an eminent Talmudic scholar he goes on: 'The substance of this commandment is to expel the inhabitants of the land whoever they may be'.[6]

A step in the opposite direction, accommodating Palestinian claims to rightful residence, is from this perspective sheer religious betrayal. In signing the Oslo Agreement in Washington in September 1993, Prime Minister Yitzhak Rabin unwittingly signed his own death warrant. For it provoked significant numbers of rabbis to resurrect two long-forgotten Jewish laws, the 'law of the pursuer' (*din rodef*) and 'the law of the informer' (*din moser*), according to which a Jew should be killed or at least severely wounded if that person endangers the life or property of a fellow Jew, or delivers them to non-Jewish authority. Devised, it should be said, for entirely different circumstances, they are nevertheless there as part of the tradition, and 'before long Orthodox rabbis in Israel and the United States were consulting one another, orally and in writing, about whether Rabin fell into the category of a *rodef* or a *moser*. In the United States hundreds of Orthodox rabbis signed a statement declaring that he did', by virtue of having abandoned rule over parts of the Land to the Palestinian Authority. 'By so branding Rabin, they [and others in Israel like them] effectively declared open season on his life. Any Jew who was faithful to the *halacha* [Jewish religious law] was entitled, if not actually obliged, to kill him'.[7] To a 'fanatic of the holy trinity: the people of Israel, the Torah of Israel, and the Land of Israel', this was enough, and the polite, devout Yigal Amir, highly skilled in Talmudic argument, duly shot and killed a Rabin whom he regarded as an arch religious traitor to the world of the Jews.[8]

The Biblical record is not, admittedly, either precise or necessarily consistent about the precise identity and borders of this Promised Land. Yet that the West Bank is a better candidate for inclusion than much of the area originally allocated to Israel by the United Nations (e.g. the strip along the Mediterranean including Tel Aviv and Jaffa) is hardly open to dispute, given the accounts of the states of historic Judaea and Samaria as recorded in the Hebrew Bible.[9] For such as Amir, though, even Israel's de facto borders today fall very far short of what is required. For does not the Torah record God's promise to Abraham: 'To your descendants I give this land, from the river of Egypt to the great river, the river Euphrates' (Genesis 15:17), a promise subsequently repeated to Moses (Exodus 23:31, cf. e.g. Deuteronomy 11:24). Hence, to the alarm of all other nations in the Middle East, a religiously motivated Greater Israel movement can claim Biblical sanction for aspirations to territorial expansionism.

The settler movements, then, although 'extreme' from the combined perspectives of mainstream Judaism and international diplomacy, nevertheless have extremely deep roots in the authoritative Biblical account of a divinely ordained right to the Land, and of a divinely sanctioned ruthlessness in its retrieval and retention. Their stance is not irrefutable. There are anti-Zionist Jews who tie the redemption of the Promised Land to the prior coming of the Messiah, and regard the present State of Israel as an irrelevance (or worse, as do members of the Neturei Karta group, for example). So Jewish extremism of the kind instanced above is not mandatory. Nevertheless, it has considerable plausibility. Once grant the key premises – Promised Land, Chosen People, Torah as direct divine revelation – and the extremist conclusions can without undue difficulty seem seductively logical. They are, indeed, far from obviously illogical. A further example of an extremist deduction from these premises is that of anti-Gentile racism. Once again the case of Baruch Goldstein is instructive. A trained paramedic, and member of the army medical corps, he refused on religious grounds to treat wounded or sick Arabs. Moves to have him court-martialled foundered, so powerful has the influence of the ultra-religious in Israel apparently become.[10]

The ultimate root of this attitude is the fact that the theology of a Chosen People, reinforced by traditional rules against intermarriage with Gentiles, created an acute us-them condition, in which, indeed, according to the Biblical accounts, ruthless ethnic cleansing was engaged in by God as well as his chosen people (Exodus 23:23, Deuteronomy 7:1-6). In connection with the later Exilic period Karen Armstrong notes 'a new hatred of the *goyim*', while Lemche contrasts the relative benignity of Deutero-Isaiah with 'the racist bias of the historical writers'.[11] This deep-rooted intolerance could only be reinforced by the hatred and persecution of Jews by Gentiles, especially Christian Gentiles, down the ages. Be that as it may, in Jewish religious law the distinction between Jew and Gentile can be crucial. According to the highly revered Maimonides, murder of a Jew by a Jew is a capital offence, but a Jew murdering a Gentile is not. (So Goldstein was not, one could argue – not 'really' – a 'murderer', and accordingly the ultra-religious refused to label him one.)[12]

The same Maimonides – for many Jews perhaps the greatest of the traditional authorities – commenting on the Talmudic saying 'Gentiles are neither to be lifted [out of a well] nor hauled down [into it]' – writes: 'As for Gentiles with whom we are not at war...their death must not be caused, but it is forbidden to save them if they are at the point of death; if, for example, one of them is seen falling into the sea, he should not be rescued, for it is written: "neither shalt thou stand against the blood of thy fellow [nor will you put your neighbour's life in jeopardy] – but [a Gentile] is not thy fellow'.[13] If this is the peacetime prescription, one can imagine the inferences to be drawn regarding Gentiles in time of war, and drawn they were, and are.[14]

Maimonides was also a doctor – indeed, he became personal physician to Saladin's vizier, who was in practice virtually the ruler of Egypt. Nevertheless, following through on his judgment that a Gentile is not one's neighbour, he wrote: 'and from this learn ye, that it is forbidden to heal a Gentile even for payment...'.[15] Goldstein was a great admirer of Maimonides, and his refusal to treat Arabs emerges as having the sanction of revered tradition. He is not alone. 'On July 7, 1983, in broad daylight, Arab terrorists repeatedly stabbed Aharon Gross, a Jewish Seminary student in Hebron, dumping his mutilated body in a bloody heap just outside the Casbah. Miriam Levinger, a registered nurse, was summoned to help the dying victim. But thinking he was an Arab, she walked away, leaving the young Jew to die.'[16]

The conflict-laden context of contemporary Israel is fertile ground for the further reaches of negative religio-ethnic exclusivism. The tradition's 'the best of Gentiles – kill him; the best of snakes – dash out its brains' has a modern counterpart in the Gush Emunim leader Rabbi Levinger's comment on Goldstein's victims: 'I am sorry not only about dead Arabs but also about dead flies'.[17] The dehumanisation can extend even further. The tradition's 'it is permissible to try out a drug on a heathen, if this serves a purpose' finds a modern counterpart in the proposal of another Gush Emunim rabbi, Rabbi Dov Lior, that captured Arab terrorists be used 'as guinea pigs for medical experiments'.[18] Thus the inhumanity of Nazi Dr Mengele is now to be exercised by the co-religionists of his victims. Against this there was indeed an outcry, but it should not be overlooked that as a proposal the rabbi's view was not without religious precedent. [19]

An even starker, tragically ironic, comparison with Nazism is Jewish extremist concern with racial purity. Again, the ultimate roots are Biblical. The injunctions against intermarriage with Gentiles in the books of Ezra and Nehemiah mean that the Jews are to keep themselves 'pure' and 'uncontaminated', and while this is intended primarily religiously, as the descendants of Abraham, an ethnic component is also implied. Indeed, the notion of an affinity between Ezra and Nehemiah's prescriptions and Nazi racial purity ideology was given oblique support from the famous German Biblical scholar Gerhard Kittel in 1943: 'The radical eradication of connubium [marriage] between Jews and non-Jews carried out by National Socialism is not, as almost all the world outside Germany claims, an unprecedented act of cruelty against the Jews ... but in reality a healthy compulsion for Jews who assimilate to return to their own foundations and their laws'. Ezra and Nehemiah could hardly have disagreed. Thus 'anti-Semitism has a grotesque mirror image in the Old Testament itself'.[20]

Construing this religio-ethnic anti-assimilationism in terms of 'blood' is but a short step. Commenting on the shooting to death of a thirteen-year-old Arab girl in July 1989 by his own yeshiva (seminary) students rampaging through Nablus, Rabbi Yitzhak Ginzburg, addressing an Israeli court, was adamant: 'It should be recognized that Jewish blood and a *goy*'s [Gentile's] blood are not the same'.[21] Unsurprisingly, and entirely logically, ultra-orthodox rabbis therefore resist the idea of Jews receiving blood transfusions from Gentiles. It might cause them to behave in ways contrary to the Torah.[22] Analogously, Rabbi Kook, the Elder, a revered and highly influential figure amongst the ultra-religious in Israel, said: 'The difference between a Jewish soul and souls of non-Jews – all of them in all different levels – is greater and deeper than the difference between a human soul and the souls of cattle'.[23]

Yet another Jewish extremist concern with deep Biblical roots is the question of Jerusalem. The Temple Mount, sacred to Jews as the site of the First and Second Temples, is sacred to Muslims as the site of Muhammad's ascent to heaven during his Night Journey, and is dominated by the Dome of the Rock and the al-Aqsa Mosque. In 1984, a meticulously planned plot was uncovered to destroy the Dome with explosives – an event that would have convulsed the Muslim world and led to incalculable consequences. To the plotters, it would have cleared the way for the building of the Third Temple - and the arrival of the Messiah.[24]

The grounds for believing this are very far from being clear injunctions such as those considered above. Thus, for example, to at least one of the plotters the Dome was the 'abomination' of the Book of Daniel (see Daniel 11:31, 12:11) – an identification that is historically worthless and theologically speculative.[25] Yet if scripture does not, in this respect, furnish clear prescriptions, it potentially does something equally dangerous. For by bestowing authority on eschatological visions and apocalyptic prophecies in a book like Daniel, it issues an open invitation to later generations to 'read the signs of the times' – an invitation whose acceptance may herald slaughter as well as personal catastrophe.[26]

Among those apparently accepting the invitation was Jesus, who, at least as described in the earliest gospel, Mark, also referred mysteriously to Daniel's 'abomination' (Mark 13:14, cf. Matthew 24:15). The New Testament contains, as well as the 'little apocalypses' of which these verses are part (see also Luke 21), much fuel for eschatological speculation, not least in its final book, the Book of Revelation, and it is in its Christian forms as much as (perhaps more than) any other that eschatological speculation has reaped a bloody harvest.[27] Its contribution to the Middle East maelstrom could yet be in character. For an alliance has sprung up between Messianic Jews and Messianic Christians (the latter largely American conservative evangelicals) to promote a rebuilt Temple as preparation for the coming of the Messiah. They disagree, of course, as to this Messiah's identity (as also regarding their respective fates upon his arrival), but combine pragmatically in anticipation – at the expense, if things were to go according to plan, of all respect for Muslims and their own distinctive spiritual sensibilities.

For Jews of this outlook, Messianic fervour received a massive boost with the Six-Day War of 1967 which restored to Jewish control so much of 'the Land'. This was surely a sign of imminent salvation. For their Christian counterparts, the creation of the State of Israel, and the return of the Jews to the Promised Land, is a sure sign of the coming of the End. Yet, especially for believers in the 'dispensational pre-millennialism' of John Darby, Christ's second coming will be preceded by the Antichrist desecrating the Temple with Daniel's 'abomination' – an undertaking beyond even his powers in the absence of the said edifice. So its rebuilding is essential. [28]

The forms of cooperation are various, ranging from fundraising to the quest for 'Red Angus cattle suitable for Old Testament Biblical sacrifices' ('genetically red … also excellent beef quality'). The importance of these particular sacrifices derives from Numbers 19, according to which the ashes of an unblemished red heifer are required in order to cleanse any person tainted by contact with death. Today, in view of the centuries-old interruption of Temple sacrifices, all are thus tainted, and therefore, according to Israel's leading rabbis, barred from entering the Temple Mount (a real problem, as it happens, for those plotting to blow up the Dome of the Rock – they claimed exceptional circumstances). Accordingly, an unblemished red heifer needs to be reared and sacrificed as a necessary condition of the beginning of the rebuilding of the Temple. Enter American born-again cattlemen quoting Genesis 12:2-3 ('I shall bless those who bless you, and shall curse those who curse you') – a standard evangelical justification for Christian support of infidel Israel.[29]

The fundraising mentioned above may be part of a programme whereby churches in America sponsor particular settlements in the West Bank – sponsor, in other words, possibly the prime obstacle to long-term peace between the Israelis and the Palestinians. They do so, though, in the conviction (well-grounded if one accepts the full authority of scripture) that, in line with Biblical teaching, it is simply the case that the land ('the Land') belongs to the Jews. And so leading American evangelical Jerry Falwell, commenting on the strong alliance between evangelical Christians in America and Messianic Jews in Israel, can claim, memorably, that 'America's Bible Belt is Israel's safety belt'. [30]

The relationship between the two contrasting groups (Messianic Jews and Christians) is warm, but in it, as Gershom Gorenberg puts it tellingly, 'lies the mutually exploitative core of the ties between Christian believers in the End and Israeli rightists: The Jews accept political, financial, and moral support. Often they believe they are bringing the redemption, and disregard or downplay what their allies hope to see happen to Jews. The Christian millennialists believe the Jews have no idea of the catastrophic consequences of their actions [they will be victims of Armageddon] – and encourage them to move forward. And perhaps it wouldn't matter, except that well-intentioned people warming themselves with the idea that Jews building the Temple will lead to the world's final salvation sometimes lend their hands to extremists who act, not in the realm of myth, but in a real country where real conflicts claim real lives'.[31]

There is, admittedly, a certain irony in Christians, whose theology virtually hinges on denying that the Jews are any longer the Chosen People, mobilising to support their continued claim to the Promised Land. The irony is all the sharper, perhaps, considering that Christians have so often seen themselves as the new Chosen People – with rights to a new Promised Land. If examples of this are 'historical', then they are not necessarily 'purely' so. Historical examples continue to have contemporary resonances. Distressingly, they all too often also bear the marks of intolerance and violence associated with their prototype.

Perhaps the most notorious and uncontroversial recent example to note is that of apartheid South Africa. To the Afrikaners, the Great Trek of 1836-1838 is their very own Exodus, commemorated in style on their very own 'Day of the Covenant', 16 December 1938. This new name for an established annual celebration symbolised, in effect, a shift from thinking of themselves as 'being like' the children of Israel to thinking of themselves as 'being' a new Chosen People. Like the children of Israel, this new *volk* had a Promised Land that needed to be 'redeemed' against the wishes of its inhabitants, a task for which it needed to keep itself 'pure' – racially pure. Laws against intermarriage follow logically. Indeed, according to one acute analyst, 'one can accurately predict most Afrikaner legal, political, and cultural developments in the first two-thirds of the twentieth century by reading carefully the books of the Pentateuch'.[32]

The 1938 Day of the Covenant in South Africa had had an important antecedent three hundred years earlier when the General Assembly of the Church of Scotland in 1638 proposed a National Covenant, followed in 1643 by the Solemn League and Covenant. These Scottish Presbyterian developments of Calvinist theology, though politically powerful for a season, hardly outlived the seventeenth century – except in Ireland, amongst the Ulster-Scots. There the Calvinist emphasis on 'the elect' fused with inspiration drawn from the Hebrew scriptures to engender a sense among the Scottish settlers in northern Ireland that they too were a chosen people sent to redeem the land from idolaters. This mind-set proved extremely durable, and in 1912 Ulster Protestants, faced with the prospect of minority existence under Catholic rule should the British government succeed with its third Home Rule bill, as seemed likely, overwhelmingly endorsed 'Ulster's Solemn League and Covenant', pledging themselves 'to stand by one another … in using all means which may be found necessary to defeat the present conspiracy to set up a Home Rule Parliament in Ireland'.[33]

The threat of religiously rooted civil insurrection in Ulster – along with all manner of other complicating factors which cannot be pursued here – led to the Partition Act of 1920, and the emergence of a Northern Ireland committed to religious segregation. Once again a 'people' was to be kept 'pure' by systematic policing of boundaries – including, yet again, the upholding of a taboo against intermarriage, in the service of a religio-ethnic racism, in a way that would have been all too clearly understood by Ezra and Nehemiah. The basic injustice, in the form of systematic discrimination, that flowed from this mind-set led, 'inexorably' one might think, to the Troubles, a situation still far from completely resolved as the twentieth century gave way to the twenty-first. Neither in South Africa nor in Ulster could these discriminatory covenantal polities be sustained indefinitely in a world increasingly sensitised to the values of human rights – and in which, relatedly, more liberal Christian theologies have extended their sway. Yet the sense of being 'chosen' has continued to be powerfully represented in another offshoot of seventeenth-century British covenantal theology, the USA.

In Britain itself, indeed, a theology of the 'chosen people' left an indelible mark, despite the decline of covenantism as such. Already John Foxe, author of *The Book of Martyrs* (the only book to rival the Bible itself in popularity), had seen Henry VIII and Elizabeth I as 'appointed by God to lead the English people out of the land of bondage (foreign papal control) into freedom' – the clear implication being that those thus led were chosen successors of the children of Israel.[34] Later, for the composer Handel, the theme of Britain as a new Israel was celebrated in a series of great oratorios based on the Hebrew scriptures – *Judas Maccabaeus* being composed explicitly to highlight parallels with the Duke of Cumberland's victory (against 'idolaters' – the Jacobites) at Culloden. The ultimate outcome of 'chosenness' would be the British Empire itself, whose enemies could be variously described as Canaanites, Moabites, Amalekites, Philistines, and so on, in a Hebrew scripture/Old Testament-inspired negative litany. [35]

Meanwhile, though, another offshoot of Puritan theology had taken root in America, regarded from Pilgrim Fathers times as the new Promised Land for a new Chosen People – with a new set of Canaanites in the familiar role of divinely destined victim. 'Many Puritan preachers were fond of referring to Native Americans as Amalekites and Canaanites – in other words, people who, if they would not be converted, were worthy of annihilation. By examining such instances in theological and political writings, in sermons, and elsewhere, we can understand how America's self-image as a "chosen people" has provided the rhetoric to mystify domination'. [36]

America, indeed, retains to this day a powerful sense of 'manifest destiny' and sacralised identity. As one journalist was to testify in the wake of 9/11, 'one of the strongest lessons of my Massachusetts childhood was the purposefulness of the United States. All human history seemed to have been leading to the creation of God's Own Country'.[37] America's 'manifest destiny' is part of divine Providence, and 'God bless America', absorbed in the context of this whole typology, is widely taken, not least, but not only, in the American Bible belt, to imply favoured son status. In a striking observation regarding this deep-rooted religio-nationalism Clifford Longley adds: 'as for questioning whether the treatment of the American flag as sacred amounted to idolatry, Americans would regard it as sacrilege even to mention the possibility (which perhaps proves the point)'.[38]

In respect of the above examples, Christianity has built on the election theology constitutive of Judaism. In terms of intolerance, though, it has added its own distinctive voice in the form of anti-Semitism. This is now well-trodden territory, and I can be brief. Two of the key texts here were cited at the outset, but other unpleasant passages occur (see, for example, Matthew 23:33-35), and the vilification of 'the Jews' in the Gospel of John and the Book of Acts provides blanket cover for anti-Semitic prejudice. The Fourth Gospel is for Christians a much loved text, while yet also being, on reflection, 'a notorious contribution to the heart and sinews of Christian anti-Semitism'. [39] Of course, 'anti-Judaism is the left hand of Christology', as Rosemary Ruether has put it. For 'no one can come to the Father except through me' (John 14:6), and 'only in him (Christ) is there salvation' (Acts 4:12) – so 'the Jews' are damned. [40] Yet anti-Judaism is one thing, anti-Jewish rhetoric is another. The problem is that in the New Testament expressions of the former are too often clad in virulent examples of the latter.

Admittedly, the early Christians were not unusual in this respect. 'A reading of the Hebrew Bible in conjunction with the Talmud will reveal a world of rhetorical abuse unlike anything else in world literature ... People are never accused of making mistakes or of failing to live up to an ideal, they are accused of adultery and murder, of worshipping false gods and lying, of cannibalism and robbery (e.g. Mic: 3:1-3; Isa: 59:1-8; 65:1-7; Ezek: 22:23-31)'.[41] Yet while this illuminates the situation, it does not relieve its gravity, and Robert Carroll's conclusion is judicious when he writes: 'I find the anti-Jewish rhetoric of the New Testament's discourses on the Jews vicious beyond toleration. I know many good Christian scholars have found it possible to exonerate the New Testament writings from all blame in this matter of Christian anti-Semitism. I do not find it as easy to separate biblical rhetoric from the consequences of people taking such rhetoric seriously'. [42]

Among the people taking it seriously were some of the most eminent figures in church history, from Origen and Ambrose to Luther, and 'in spite of official church pronouncements to the contrary, about one-third of the clergy still blame "the Jews" for crucifying Christ'. It was only in 1946 that the Jesuits revoked a rule laid down in 1592 forbidding admission to the order of 'men of Jewish origin, calculating ancestry to the fifth generation'.[43] Such is the power of New Testament propaganda – for that, to speak plainly, is what much Christian scriptural anti-Judaism is.

The third of our religions, Islam, has not, historically, been anti-Semitic, and neither has it propounded a self-preferring Bible-based covenantal theology of the kind found in both Judaism and Christianity. Yet a legacy of aggressive intolerance is one that it shares with its sibling religions. This is apparent both in the Qur'an as interpreted in mainstream Islamic tradition, and also in the early Islamic conquests (and subsequently).

Taking the second point first, recent Muslim apologists have often strongly resisted the view, advanced by various non-Muslim authors, that Islam was spread by the sword, arguing that this is at best a misapprehension and at worst outright prejudice. Yet, that Muslim armies swept out of Arabia in a series of astonishing conquests is not in dispute. What the apologists are referring to, I take it, is that the Jewish and Christian populations thus conquered were not faced with forced conversion. Thus a distinction is drawn between Arab expansionism and the promotion of Islam, and we read, for example, (in a non-apologetic study,) that although there were exceptions, 'protection and tolerance for religious practice and places of worship is a condition that occurs in the reports for all regions, including Persia'.[44]

Equally clearly, though, those defeated by the Arab armies were faced, if not by forced religious conversion, then with forced submission in the name of religion, in accordance with the Qur'anic verse 9:29, quoted at the outset of this paper. As the Muslim general Khalid wrote to an Egyptian governor:

> Become a Muslim and thou art safe. Otherwise, take a *dhimmi*'s covenant and pay *jizya* [accept protected status as a subject person and pay a poll tax]. If you refuse these terms, you will have none but yourself to blame for what happens. For I am come against you with a people that loves death as you love life.

Again, to followers of a rival prophet to Muhammad, Musailama, captured in battle, Khalid put the question 'O Banu Hanifa, what say you?' 'They answered, "You have a prophet, and we have a prophet". He put them to the sword.'

Meanwhile, Muhammad's immediate successor as Muslim leader, the caliph Abu Bakr, wrote to Arab tribes who felt released from treaty obligations with Muhammad following his death:

> We will treat as an unbeliever whoever rejects Allah and Muhammad, and we will make holy war upon him. I have sent So-and-so with an army and have given his orders to fight no one and kill no one, until he calls the people to prayer. Whoever obeys will not be troubled. But whoever refuses will be treated as an enemy. For such there is only the sword and fire and indiscriminate slaughter.[45]

The judgment is inescapable that, taking the full range of evidence into consideration, and making every allowance for the particularities of local circumstance (e.g. personal feuds, antagonisms or rivalries), the early Islamic conquests constituted, if not 'war conducted with the aim of spreading the true faith', then at the very least 'war conducted with the aim of spreading...the rule of the state that ensured the dominance of that faith'.[46] The distinction between Arab expansionism and the promotion of Islam is not finally sustainable. We may look forward from this conclusion, and we may look back. Looking forward, we are not surprised to find the Muslim jurists developing what was to become the classical Muslim doctrine of *jihad* understood as holy war, dividing the world into two antagonistic spheres, *dar al-Islam*, the realm of Islam, and *dar al-harb*, the realm of war, with the obligation of the former to seek to extend its sway militarily ('by the sword') at the expense of the latter. Quoting the Qur'an in support of this dichotomy becomes both axiomatic and, given the Qur'anic verses quoted, plausible.[47]

Looking backward, we are not surprised to find Qur'anic passages which underpin this religious war ethos, and to find accounts of Muhammad as religio-militaristic exemplar. After all, Abu Bakr and his immediate companions and successors knew Muhammad better than anyone else, and clearly saw themselves as continuing the instantiation of his ideals in the wars they prosecuted.

The Qur'an is admittedly not unambiguous about religiously inspired warfare. Certainly there are verses which support modern Muslim apologists' claims that in Islam *jihad* is a purely defensive concept.[48] Yet the view upheld as authoritative within Islam was that less aggressive verses like 2:190, 'Fight for the sake of Allah those that fight against you, but do not attack them first. Allah does not love the aggressors', was to be regarded as trumped by the 'sword verse', 9:5 'Slay the idolaters wherever you find them. Arrest them, besiege them, and lie in ambush everywhere for them. If they repent and take to prayer and pay the alms-tax, let them go their way.' Numerous other verses extol the duty to fight for the religion of Allah, and 'as for those who are slain in the cause of Allah...He will admit them to the Paradise he has made known to them' (47:5). Note, too, that the 'idolaters' in 9:5 are required to pay the alms-tax, not the poll-tax mentioned in Khalid's ultimatum to the Egyptian governor. The latter applied to *dhimmis*, protected peoples like Jews and Christians, whom the Qur'an calls 'People of the Book'. The former, *zakat*, was, as it still is, an obligation for Muslims. Thus for 'idolaters', as opposed to 'People of the Book', the choice prescribed by 9:5 is Islam or death.[49]

This religious intolerance is to be found not only in the Qur'an but also in the career of Muhammad himself, who is described in Muslim sources as capable indeed of considerable ruthlessness. He was persuaded, much against his inclination, according to Muslim sources, to spare one Jewish clan in Medina, the Banu Qaynuqa, and exile them rather than have them put to death. Another Jewish clan, however, the Banu Qurayza, were less fortunate. The circumstances are much debated, but not the outcome. It is chilling to read how, as described in the Muslim sources, between six and eight hundred Jewish men were forced, with Muhammad's approval, to dig mass graves before being executed into them. Their wives and children were taken by the Muslims as slaves.[50]

Arguably these killings were, in their immediate context, political rather than religious. The men were killed for being ready to betray Muhammad to his Makkan enemies, not because they rejected his claims to prophecy. Nevertheless, Muhammad is portrayed as being ready to advance his cause ruthlessly if necessary. According to Ibn Ishaq, Muhammad, upset by a poetess (a mother of five children) who had criticised him, asked who would rid him of her. He then thanked the man who, in response, duly murdered her in her sleep with the words 'You have helped God and His apostle, O Umayr', and refused all punishment for him. Another poet critical of Muhammad – a centenarian – was also (again according to the Muslim sources) similarly dispatched at Muhammad's behest.[51]

The campaigns completed or inaugurated immediately prior to Muhammad's death indicate that aggressive holy war was entirely legitimate according to his worldview. Muhammad's career and the doctrines of Islam revolutionized both the ideological bases and the political structures of Arabian society, giving rise for the first time to a state capable of organising and executing an expansionist movement.

> The Islamic conquest of the Near East cannot be viewed ... as something separate from the career of Muhammad the Apostle or from the conquest of Arabia during the *ridda* wars [conducted by Abu Bakr immediately following his death]. It must be seen as an organic outgrowth of Muhammad's teachings and their impact on Arabian society, of Muhammad's political consolidation, pursued by traditional and novel means, and especially of his efforts to bring nomadic groups firmly under state control.[52]

In view of these examples, and this exemplar, the emergence of modern Muslim holy warriors is far from unintelligible, even if some of their actions are theologically questionable and indeed Islamically indefensible. Their ethos is authentic even if its application is flawed.

Thus, for example, to read the remarkable document labelled by its translator 'the creed of Sadat's assassins', and emanating from the extremist Islamist group that killed the Egyptian President, is to find oneself in a thought-world imbued with the imperative to religiously sanctioned violence found in the Qur'an, and backed by the *Sunnah* (accounts of words and actions attributed to Muhammad). The author, indeed, is extremely well versed in both, and marshals his evidence to good effect in support of 'the neglected duty', that is, *jihad* in the sense of holy war or indeed holy revolution. As the translator correctly comments, 'No one reading the text ... can fail to be impressed by its coherence and the force of its logic'. It is very far from being the ranting of an ill-informed rabble-rouser.[53]

Not that the argument is irrefutable, and indeed a detailed and authoritative refutation was to emerge from the al-Azhar University in Cairo: this is not the place to enter into the details of argument and counterargument. The point, rather, is that the argument is far from absurd, drawing extensively, not on quirks and exceptions and what one might call the lunatic fringe of Islam, but on teachings and precedents central to the tradition (including the precedent set by yet another assassination instigated by Muhammad).[54]

This is much less the case with that other notorious feature of contemporary extremist Islam, the 'suicide bomber'. In Israel the strategy was partly a response to Goldstein's massacre of non-combatants in Hebron, though it had already been applied in Lebanon. There, it was partly a product of Lebanon's distinctively Shi'ite Islam, where the theme of martyrdom features more prominently anyway. Yet, even in Lebanon it was controversial, for in Islam, while martyrdom is lauded, suicide is forbidden. Thus the practice of 'self-chosen martyrdom' (a perhaps not inaccurate euphemism) presents a genuine moral dilemma, and is far from uniformly condoned, let alone receiving unconditional theological approval: in Lebanon the spiritual leader of Hizbollah, Sayyid Muhammad Husayn Fadlallah, came under persistent pressure to issue a *fatwa* sanctioning suicide bombings, but consistently refused to do so.[55]

The dilemma becomes all the more acute if, instead of selecting political and military targets, as happened in Beirut in 1983 with the attacks on the American Embassy and the barracks of the American marines, purely civilian targets are intended, as is the case in Israel, and was even more notoriously the case in the attacks of 9/11. Muslim critics of these outrages point vigorously to the traditional ban, in Islam, on targeting women and children in warfare. On the other hand, anyone in self-critical mode will observe that in 'total war' the distinction between combatant and non-combatant does begin to be eroded – think of the relentless Allied bombing of German cities in WW2, which made the original 'atrocity', the bombing of Coventry, seem in comparison, relatively speaking, a minor skirmish. In respect of Israel it is not only (many) Muslims who take the view that in this conflict at least there are no innocent parties - many Israelis regard 'innocent' Arabs as enemies as well, and so terror becomes a currency to be exchanged. This does not mean that it is justified – Muslim critics are surely right. On the other hand, in a religion with such a strong tradition of jihad as 'holy war', and with scriptural sanction for martyrdom in the path of God, one cannot wonder at its becoming a seductive option from the perspective of well-grounded despair. The threshold of religiously justified violence has already been set too low.

As illustrated by this last example, my argument has not been that in each of the three religions examined that the extremists, considered dispassionately, carry the day, logically and theologically. It has been, rather, that in each of these offspring of Abraham there is ample material for extremists to draw on, and since this material is either central to their respective theologies, or prominent in their respective authoritative scriptures and traditions, these theologies, and these scriptures and traditions, are as deserving of criticism as the extremists they nurture. Let us be fair to the fanatics. They too, in a sense, are victims of the religions they seek to serve.

My further point is that purely internal debates, about what counts as 'true' Judaism, 'true' Christianity, 'true' Islam, are not in themselves an adequate response to the problem that principled extremism poses. The arguments can be too finely balanced. Are the Gush Emunim settlers in the West Bank really betraying the theology of the Chosen People? Is it clearly and unambiguously the case that anti-Semitism rests on a purely idiosyncratic reading of the New Testament? Is it conclusively proven that Islamic terrorists (or 'terrorists', in view of the indiscriminate propagandistic use of the term) can draw no authentic sustenance from traditional sources on *jihad* and/or the example of the Prophet? I think not.

What is needed, therefore, is a shift in the centre of gravity of debate. If the Gush Emunim settlement policy is to be rejected, this is not, ultimately, because it is theologically questionable, but because the dispossession of a people is morally (and legally and politically) indefensible. If anti-Semitism is to be rejected, this is not, ultimately, because it is incompatible with a more nuanced reading of the Gospels, but because it is incompatible with any basic morality drawing on elementary conceptions of shared humanity. If Muslim terrorism is to be condemned, this is not, ultimately, because Muhammad is misunderstood, but because it violates the tenets of basic human rights.

In sum, West Bank Jewish settlements, Christian anti-Semitism, and Muslim terrorism (taking, for the moment, these three examples as representative) are not morally wrong because theologically questionable – they are theologically questionable because morally wrong.

There are, in short, moral criteria of religious truth, and religions need to be held accountable in these terms. This conclusion is not predicated on a rejection of religion. It is predicated on commitment to a basic humanism. This commitment is one which insiders and outsiders alike may share. Generally, indeed, they do – which is why the views examined here are accurately described as 'extreme'.

By the same token, of course, 'extremists' will resist the claim that their religiously rooted extremism may properly be trumped by moral values held as being epistemologically independent of religion. 'The Bible is the sole standard of right for the church', declared the Dutch Reformed Church in South Africa in 1986; 'It is forbidden to think about any thought that may cause a Jew to doubt one principle of the Jewish religion', wrote Maimonides, several centuries earlier; 'it is not for true believers – men or women – to take their choice in their affairs if Allah and his apostle decree otherwise', says the Qur'an.[56] This resistance needs to be engaged with. It is to engaging with it that the centre of debate needs to shift, for the issue of moral criteria of religious truth is critical to the ever more urgent task of rendering religions safe for human consumption.

The application of such criteria is open to all, insiders and outsiders alike, for they are, putatively, universal. If, though, their validity is accepted, it imposes on the several children of Abraham in particular the obligation to be vigilantly self-critical. That there are those active in accepting this challenge is apparent from many of the authors quoted here. Nevertheless, the task is a daunting one. For the process of critical questioning can quickly turn into a process of religious unravelling. Can scripture be regarded as sacred, if they generate the dispossession of a people, religiously rooted anti-Semitism, and acts of terrorism? Should they, indeed, be regarded as 'scriptures'?[57]

It may be, therefore, that the long-run implication of my analysis is that in becoming self-critical religions need to become self-transcending. That is to say, instead of being Jewish, Christian, Muslim, people will need to become post-Jewish, post-Christian, post-Muslim – not in the sense of having rejected their faith (though that has to be envisaged as a possibility), but in the sense of having transmuted it. They continue to draw spiritual nourishment from belonging to it, without feeling the need or the duty to be committed to its wholehearted practice and preservation. Liberal Christianity has already moved far in this direction, with contemporary Quakers perhaps representing its best practical exemplification. The 'open Judaism' advocated by Dan Cohn-Sherbok is also very much in this mould. On the other hand, a self-critical approach does not have to go to this length in order to yield positive results, and less drastic initial findings may indeed be more politic in the short term.[58]

In the end, education is perhaps the key. The 'extremist' views considered here are nourished above all in the Orthodox and ultra-Orthodox yeshivas of Judaism, in the Bible institutes of American conservative evangelicals, in the conservative and ultra-conservative *madrasas* that multiplied, for example, in Pakistan and from which were to emerge the Taliban.[59] Common to these is not, or not necessarily, an entirely unquestioning approach to their respective religions; it is, though, an approach that is at best selective in its questioning, and one where to each question there is presumed to be a safe, orthodox answer. Thus there can be no real rocking of the boat, given the absence of that open-mindedness that is its necessary precondition. Yet if the preceding analysis is basically sound, each of these boats is in very urgent need of some very vigorous rocking.

The alternative is to acquiesce, even from within the precincts of the academic study of religion, in further generations of believers becoming captive to their Book, and in so doing, risking becoming victims of what, from a modern humanitarian perspective, must be deemed immoral aspects of its teachings. Equally, even when its teachings are innocent, they may become victims of its status. A young son in rural north-west Pakistan felt obliged to murder his widowed mother at the behest of religious elders, for the sin of persisting in leaving the house to try to eke out a living in the market. All concerned apparently believed that this action was morally right because the Qur'an commanded it – which, of course, it does not.[60] Yet when the Qur'an's iconic status can be invoked in this bogus way, how much easier is it for extremists to tap into it when they can quote chapter and verse. Either way, the Book is then in practical terms being treated virtually as a new idol. The enemy evicted by the front door has effected re-entry in disguise through the back.

Most Jews, Christians and Muslims, certainly in this country but also elsewhere, simply want to get on with their lives and not have anything to do with extremist versions of their faith. They find it possible to do so by drawing on the tolerant, moderate aspects of their tradition, while ignoring, or indeed lacking adequate knowledge or awareness of, the other, intolerant aspects. The latter, though, are there and they are producing cruel effects, as they gradually become highlighted afresh – not, or certainly not necessarily, by wicked deviants, but by people of integrity who can legitimately command respect, and, hence, a following. 'What puzzles me', writes Mark Juergensmeyer, 'is not why bad things are done by bad people, but rather why bad things are done by people who otherwise appear to be good ..., by pious people dedicated to a moral vision of the world'.[61] The reason, of course, is that the religions that engender the piety simultaneously inspire the immorality.

Important work can indeed be done by tolerant insiders concerned to advocate what they claim to be the 'true' faith while striving vigorously to remain within an exclusively religious or theological traditional framework. On the other hand, their arguments can appear strained – as in various prominent attempts to claim a natural harmony between 'Islam' and 'human rights'.[62] Equally strained is the global ethic thesis advocated by Hans Küng and others, according to which all religions accept ('really'), as an 'irrevocable directive', a 'commitment to a culture of non-violence and respect for life'.[63] The evidence adduced here militates decisively against this view.

Rather, there is a nettle here that remains ungrasped: the religions of the children of Abraham (and no doubt others) are inherently ambiguous at best, if not indeed inherently flawed, in respect of issues of intolerance, discrimination, violence, and hatred. Grasping the nettle requires elevating allegiance to the values of mutual tolerance and respect for basic human rights above all else, thereby in effect sanctioning them as moral criteria of religious truth, and thus as universal human values to which religions are required to submit, and by which they are under an obligation to be judged. This, arguably, is the true Copernican revolution required of religions – to place themselves in the service of a basic humane morality, rather than regarding basic morality as orbiting around (one of) them.

The step needed is possible logically (indeed logically it is compelling); it is not impossible psychologically; it is not, everywhere, possible politically. All the greater, therefore, is the responsibility for promoting open-minded critical engagement with the issues where it can be done: they are not going to go away.

Notes

[1]The quotations are taken from *The New Jerusalem Bible*, and *The Koran*, trans. by N.J. Dawood, fourth revised edition (Harmondsworth: Penguin Books, 1974). Translations of the Qur'an sometimes differ from each other quite significantly, but the substance of the verses quoted here is the same in other translations such as those by Arthur J. Arberry, *The Koran Interpreted* (London: Oxford University Press, 1964), Mohammed Marmaduke Pikthall, *The Meaning of the Glorious Koran* (New York and London: Mentor Religious Classic, no date), and Abdullah Yusuf Ali, *The Holy Qur'an* (Ware: Wordsworth Classics, 2000) [first published 1934].

[2] Israel Shahak and Norton Mezvinsky, *Jewish Fundamentalism in Israel* (London and Sterling, Virginia: Pluto Press, 1999): 100, 102, 111. See also e.g. Dilip Hiro, *Sharing the Promised Land: An Interwoven Tale of Israelis and Palestinians* (London: Hodder and Stoughton, 1996): 312-318; Gershom Gorenberg, *The End of Days: Fundamentalism and the Struggle for the Temple Mount* (New York and London: The Free Press, 2000): 203-208.

[3] Shahak and Mezvinsky, op. cit. 108; see also pp. 104, 109.

[4] Nur Masalha, *A Land without a People: Israel, Transfer and the Palestinians 1949-96* (London: Faber and Faber, 1997): 208; David K. Shipler, *Arab and Jew: Wounded Spirits in a Promised Land* (New York: Penguin Books, revised edition 2002): 117 see also ibid., p. 135, 'as the eleven- and twelve-year-old boys in Kiryat Arba explained, they are learning in their yeshivas that the Arab is Amalek, the enemy tribe that God instructed the Jews to fight eternally and destroy'. That the indigenous population was always set to cause a problem was recognised early on in parts of the Zionist movement, see also David J. Goldberg, *To the Promised Land: A History of Zionist Thought* (Harmondsworth: Penguin Books, 1996), chapter 11. Their stake in their future was chillingly dismissed by Lord Balfour: 'In Palestine we do not propose even to go through the form of consulting the wishes of the present inhabitants of the country.... Zionism, *be it right or wrong, good or bad*, is rooted in age-long traditions, in present needs, in future hopes, of far profounder import than the desires and prejudices of the 700,000 Arabs who now inhabit that ancient land'[italics added], as quoted in Karen Armstrong, *Holy War: The Crusades and Their Impact on Today's World*, 2nd edition (New York: Anchor Books, 2001): 520-521.

[5] *Amnesty International News Review* (July/August, 2002): 9. See also B'Tselem, *Land Grab: Israel's Settlement Policy in the West Bank*, which can be accessed on www.btselem.org.

[6] As quoted (translated from the original Hebrew) in Nur Masalha, ibid., p. 206. On the relevant teachings of the Torah, see also the classic study by Gerhard von Rad, *Holy War in Ancient Israel*, ed. and trans. Marva J. Dawn (Grand Rapids, Michigan: William B. Eerdmans, 1991, 3rd ed.) [first published 1958]. A more recent and more nuanced study is Susan Niditch, *War in the Hebrew Bible: A Study in the Ethics of Violence* (New York and Oxford: Oxford University Press, 1993). Less detailed and specialised are: Gerd Lüdemann, *The Unholy in Holy Scripture: The Dark Side of the Bible* (London: SCM Press, 1997),

chapter 2; Michael Prior, CM, *The Bible and Colonialism: A Moral Critique* (Sheffield: Sheffield Academic Press, 1997), chapter 1; Peter Partner, *God of Battles: Holy Wars of Christianity and Islam* (London: HarperCollins, 1997), chapters 1-2; Jack Nelson-Pallmeyer, *Is Religion Killing Us? Violence in the Bible and the Qu'ran* (Harrisburg, PA: Trinity Press International, 2003), passim.

[7] Michael Karpin and Ina Friedman, *Murder in the Name of God: The Plot to Kill Yitzhak Rabin* (New York: Henry Holt and Company, 1998; London: Granta Books, 1999): 107-108.

[8] The description of Amir by a friend is quoted in Karpin and Friedman, ibid., p. 10. For a historical survey of Jewish attitudes to 'the Land', see also Dan Cohn-Sherbok, *Israel: The History of an Idea* (London: SPCK, 1992).

[9] The issue of the reliability of the Biblical account is, admittedly, another matter. The respected Danish scholar Lemche, for example, concludes that 'the land of Canaan', according to 'the source material from the 1st millennium BCE – outside the Hebrew Bible ... was mainly to be identified with the central areas of the Phoenicians in Lebanon, and perhaps also included the neighbouring areas to the south on the coastal plain of Acre, and perhaps even the Valley of Jezreel', Niels Peter Lemche, *The Canaanites and Their Land: The Tradition of the Canaanites* (Sheffield: Sheffield Academic Press, 1991): 61. The historical issues receive further examination in other writings of Lemche's, and see also too Keith W. Whitelam, *The Invention of Ancient Israel: The Silencing of Palestinian History* (London and New York: Routledge, 1996). The controversy generated by such conclusions testifies to their current political relevance. For an interpretive discussion, see also Michael Prior, op. cit., chapters 6-7.

[10] See also Shahak and Mezvinsky, op. cit., pp. 96-98. Jewish theologian Marc Ellis writes starkly that 'Baruch Goldstein and Yigal Amir are not foreign to Judaism but rather have become an integral part of it. Do they speak a language that other Jews are unable to understand? Do they emerge from a religious and political culture distant and isolated from the Jewish people and its history?' Marc H. Ellis, *Unholy Alliance: Religion and Atrocity in Our Time* (London: SCM Press; Minneapolis: Augsburg Fortress Publishers, 1997): 191.

[11] Karen Armstrong, op cit., p. 14; Lemche, op. cit., p. 165.

[12] 'If an Israelite kills a resident alien, he does not suffer capital punishment at the hands of the court .... Needless to say, one is not put to death if he kills a heathen.' Maimonides, *Mishneh Torah*, Book 11, Treatise 5 'Murder and the Preservation of Life', chapter 2, paragraph 11. The quotation is from the translation by Hyman Klein, *The Code of Maimonides*, Book 11, *The Book of Torts* (New Haven and London: Yale University Press, 1954): 201. On not labelling Goldstein a 'murderer', see also Shahak and Mezvinsky, op. cit., pp. 99-100.

[13] Maimonides, *Mishneh Torah*, Book 11, Treatise 5, chapter 4, paragraph 11, quoted from Klein (trans.), op. cit., p. 208. See also Israel Shahak, *Jewish History – Jewish Religion* (London: Pluto Books, 2002): 75-76 on the significance of the Jew-Gentile distinction. See also too Shahak and Mezvinsky, op. cit., p. 43, where they quote a certain Rabbi Yitzhak Ginsburgh: 'If a Jew needs a liver, can he take the liver of an innocent non-Jew to save him? The Torah would probably permit that. Jewish life has an infinite value. There is something more holy and unique about Jewish life than about non-Jewish life'. Shahak and Mezvinsky continue: 'It is noteworthy that Rabbi Ginsburgh is one of the authors of a book lauding Baruch Goldstein, the Patriarchs' cave murderer. In that book Ginsburgh contributed a chapter in which he wrote that a Jew's killing non-Jews does not constitute murder according to the Jewish religion and that killing of innocent Arabs for reasons of revenge is a Jewish virtue. No influential Israeli rabbi has publicly opposed Ginsburgh's statements; most Israeli politicians have remained silent; some Israeli politicians have openly supported him'.

[14] See also Shahak, op. cit., pp. 77-79.

[15] Maimonides, *Mishneh Torah*, 'Idolatry' 10, 1-2, as quoted in Shahak, op. cit., p. 80 (see also Shahak and Mezvinsky, op. cit., p. 100). Maimonides continues, 'but if you fear him [the Gentile] or his hostility, cure him for payment, though you are forbidden to do so without payment'(ibid.).

[16] Robert I. Friedman. *Zealots for Zion: Inside Israel's West Bank Settlement Movement* (New Brunswick and New Jersey: Rutgers University Press, 1992): 29. Shahak, op. cit. p. 78 (see also ibid., p. 113, note 6); Shahak and Mezvinsky, op. cit., p. 100. See also the discussion of the wider spectrum of views in the Talmud and elsewhere in the entry, 'Gentile', in the *Encyclopedia Judaica*, vol. 7 (Jerusalem: Keter, 1971): 411-413.

[17] See also the discussion of the wider spectrum of views in the Talmud and elsewhere in the entry, 'Gentile', in the *Encyclopedia Judaica*, vol. 7 (Jerusalem: Keter, 1971): 411-413.

[18] Joseph Karo, *Beyt Josef*, section 'Yoreh De'ah' 158, as quoted in Shahak, op. cit., p. 81, with the comment that Karo [1488-1575] is quoting Maimonides [1135-1204]; Gorenberg, op. cit., p. 164, see also Shahak and Mezvinsky, op. cit., p. 103.

[19] The whole context in which people like Maimonides and Karo worked was, of course, very different from that of modern Zionist extremists. At least some of the Talmudic legal discrimination against Gentiles arose from Christian Gentile discrimination against Jews. 'Thus, the Talmud rules that the commandment to restore lost property to its owner (Deut. 22:1-3) does not apply when the gentile is the owner (BK 113b). This is because gentiles do not act reciprocally in such cases', *Encyclopedia Judaica*, vol. 7, p. 412. Moreover, from the fact that the Talmud prescribes various kinds and degrees of discrimination, it does not, of course, follow that most Jews have observed them most of the time – see also ibid., 'Gentile', passim. See also Jacob Neusner, Tamara Sonn and Jonathan E. Brockopp, *Judaism and Islam in Practice: A Sourcebook* (London and New York: Routledge, 2000): 190-209, 'How the Outsider is Treated in the Law of Judaism'.

[20] Gerhard Kittel, 'Das Konnubium mit Nicht-Juden im antiken Judentum', *FJF*, 2,2, p. 59, as quoted in Lüdemann, op. cit., p. 75. Additional comment by Lüdemann, ibid., p. 74.

[21] As quoted in Friedman, op. cit., p. xxvii. Ginsburgh continued (ibid.), 'Any trial that assumes that Jews and *goyim* are equal is a travesty of justice'.

[22] See also Shahak and Mezvinsky, op. cit., p. 41.

[23] Ibid., p. ix.

[24] On the Temple Mount plot see e.g. Roger Friedland and Richard Hecht, *To Rule Jerusalem* (New York: Cambridge University Press, 1996): 233-237; Gorenberg, op. cit., pp. 128-137; Dilip Hiro, *Sharing the Promised Land: An Interwoven Tale of Israelis and Palestinians* (London: Hodder and Stoughton, 1996): 35-43; David S. New, *Holy War: The Rise of Militant Christian, Jewish and Islamic Fundamentalism* (Jefferson, North Carolina, and London: McFarland & Company, 2002), chapter 19. New notes that since the Six Day War of 1967 there have been 'more than two dozen separate violent attempts to take Temple Mount' (ibid., p. 154).

[25] See also Gorenberg, op. cit., p. 132.

[26] See also New, op. cit., passim, and p. 187: 'Temple Mount is the focal point of "the colliding eschatologies of monotheism"' – quoting Jeffrey Goldberg, 'Israel's Y2K Problem', *The New York Times Magazine* (Oct. 3, 1999): 40. The significance of Islamic eschatology and apocalyptic, both historically and today, is much neglected. See also David Cook, 'Muslim Fears of the Year 2000', *Middle East Quarterly*, vol. 5 (1998): 51-62, and his major historical study, *Studies in Muslim Apocalyptic* (Princeton, New Jersey: The Darwin Press, 2002). Relevant aspects of Cook's work feature briefly in Gorenberg, op. cit., pp. 43-45, 72, 186-191.

[27] See also ibid., pp. 1-2, and (p. 42) 'if we're wondering why so many Christians obsess about last things, we have Jesus to blame' – a quotation from the editor of the journal

Christian Century; see also more generally Norman Cohn, *The Pursuit of the Millennium* (London: Secker and Warburg, 1957).

[28]On Darby's dispensational pre-millennialism and fundamentalist Christian attitudes towards the State of Israel see also e.g. Karen Armstrong, *The Battle for God: Fundamentalism in Judaism, Christianity and Islam* (London: HarperCollins, 2000): 135-140, 214-218; New, op. cit., chapter 3.

[29] See also Gorenberg, op. cit., chapter 1, 'Cattlemen of the Apocalypse'. The quotation is from p. 22. See also New, op. cit., chapter 17.

[30] Falwell's comment occurred in a television interview featured in the programme 'Dangerous Liaison: Israel and the USA', Channel 4, 2002. On the alliance between American evangelical Christians and messianic Jews in Israel generally see also Gorenberg, op. cit., pp. 164-167; Friedman, op. cit., p. 144; New, op. cit., chapters 1-17.

[31] Gorenberg, op. cit., pp. 172-173; see also Friedman, op. cit., pp. 142ff.

[32] Donald Harman Akenson, *God's Peoples: Covenant and Land in South Africa, Israel, and Ulster* (Ithaca and London: Cornell University Press, 1992):73, and see also ibid., p. 70. Chapters 3, 7, and 10 focus on the key ramifications of these ideas in the South African context. See also too Michael Prior, op. cit., chapter 3.

[33] As quoted in Akenson, op. cit., p. 187.

[34] Foxe as quoted in Clifford Longley, *Chosen People: the Big Idea that Shaped England and America* (London: Hodder & Stoughton, 2002): 125. See also ibid., p. 213. That this 'big idea' shaped more than England and America (and South Africa) is demonstrated in Anthony D. Smith, *Chosen Peoples* (London: Oxford University Press, 2003).

[35] On Handel see also Longley, op. cit., p. 39.

[36] Robert Allen Warrior, 'A Native American Perspective: Canaanites, Cowboys, and Indians', in R.S. Sugirtharajah (ed.), *Voices from the Margin: Interpreting the Bible in the Third World* (Maryknoll, NY: Orbis Books, 1991): 293. Aspects of American incorporation of Puritan theology are explored too in Michael Walzer, *Exodus and Revolution* (New York: Basic Books, 1985).

[37] As quoted in Longley, op. cit., p. 4.

[38] Ibid., p. 70. This, of course, illuminates George Bush's religious rhetoric in the wake of 9/11 and in the run-up to the invasion of Iraq – a rhetoric that jars on the much more secular sensibilities prevalent in Britain. On the Bible and colonialism in Latin America as opposed to North America see also Michael Prior, op. cit., chapter 2.

[39] Robert P. Carroll, *Wolf in the Sheepfold: The Bible as Problematic for Theology*, 2nd edition (London: SCM Press, 1997): 95. See also Marc H. Ellis, op. cit., p. 88 - Is it possible that within the concentric tradition of reading is a barbarism which erupted into Auschwitz and that barbarism is located within the tradition rather than outside of it?' 'The Bible doesn't teach you tolerance; that I want you to know ... Biblical people are extremists', as quoted in Shipler, op. cit., p. 122. 'My fundamental claim is that religiously justified violence is first and foremost a problem of "sacred" texts and not a problem of misinterpretation of the texts', Nelson-Pallmeyer, op. cit., p. xiv.

[40] Rosemary Ruether, *Faith and Fratricide: The Theological Roots of Antisemitism* (New York: Seabury Press, 1974; London: Search Press, 1975): 8.

[41] Carroll, op. cit., p. 104 (see also Lüdemann, op. cit., p. 116).

[42] Carroll, op. cit., p. xiv.

[43] On Origen, see also Lüdemann, op. cit., pp. 98-99. On Ambrose, see also Clark M. Williamson and Ronald J. Allen, *Interpreting Difficult Texts: Anti-Judaism and Christian Preaching* (London: SCM Press, and Philadelphia, PA: Trinity Press International, 1989): 15-16. See also too e.g. Dan Cohn-Sherbok, *The Crucified Jew: Twenty Centuries of Christian Anti-Semitism* (London: HarperCollins, 1992), chapter 3, 'The Church Fathers and

Jewish Hatred' and Ruether, op. cit., chapter 3, 'The Negation of the Jews in the Church Fathers'. On Luther, see also Williamson and Allen, op. cit., pp. 19-21, and Lüdemann, op. cit., pp. 125-126. See also too Gorenberg, op. cit., p. 226, 'in the 1930s ... the Nazis massively reprinted Luther's treatise'. On the clergy 'still' (but admittedly in 1971, and attitudes are changing) blaming 'the Jews' see also Williamson and Allen, op. cit., p. 8.

44 D.R. Hill, *The Termination of Hostilities in the Early Arab Conquests A.D. 634-656* (London: Luzac & Company, 1971): 175-176.

45 Tabari, *Annales* (Leiden) ed. de Goeje, I.4, p. 2022, as quoted in Adolph L. Wismar, *A Study in Tolerance as Practiced by Muhammad and his Immediate Successors* (Columbia: Columbia University Press, 1927, reprinted New York: AMS Press, 1966): 75; Tabari, op. cit., pp. 1939-1940 as quoted in Wismar, op. cit., p. 67; Tabari, op. cit., pp. 1883-1884, as quoted in Wismar, op. cit., p. 66. For an example of benign Muslim apologetics in this regard see also e.g. 'Abd-al-Rahman 'Azzam, *The Eternal Message of Muhammad* (London: Quartet Books, 1979) [first published in Arabic in 1946], chapter 18.

46 Fred M. Donner, 'The Sources of Islamic Conceptions of War', in John Kelsay and James Turner Johnson (eds), *Just War and Jihad: Historical and Theoretical Perspectives on War and Peace in Western and Islamic Traditions* (Westport, Conn.: Greenwood Press, 1991): 49.

47 The literature on *jihad* is extensive. See also e.g., in addition to Kelsay and Johnson, op. cit.: James Turner Johnson and John Kelsay (eds), *Cross, Crescent, and Sword: The Justification and Limitation of War in Western and Islamic Tradition* (Westport, Conn.: Greenwood Press, 1990); Majid Khadduri, *War and Peace in the Law of Islam* (Baltimore: The Johns Hopkins Press, 1955); Shaybani, Muhammad al-, *The Islamic Law of Nations: Shaybani's Siyar*, trans. and intr. by Majid Khadduri (Baltimore: The Johns Hopkins Press, 1966); Rudolph Peters, *Jihad in Classical and Modern Islam: A Reader* (Princeton, NJ: Markus Wiener, 1996); Reuven Firestone, *Jihad: The Origin of Holy War in Islam* (New York: Oxford University Press, 1999); and at a more popular level, Peter Partner, *God of Battles* (see note 6 above). For a succinct summary of the relevant Qur'anic verses see also Faruq Sherif, *A Guide to the Contents of the Qur'an* (London: Ithaca Press, 1985): 113-116.

48 On *jihad* as defensive, see also e.g. Ann Elizabeth Mayer, 'War and Peace in the Islamic Tradition and International Law', in Kelsay and Johnson (eds), *Just War and Jihad*, pp. 202-205; Peters, op. cit., chapter 7; Brigadier S .K. Malik, *The Quranic Concept of War* [Foreword by General M. Zia ul-Haq] (Lahore: Wajidalis, 1979); 'Abd-al-Rahman 'Azzam, op. cit., chapter 14.

49 On *jihad* as aggressive, see also e.g. Faruq Sherif, op. cit., pp. 92-93, 113-115; Firestone, op. cit., passim; Rudolph Peters, *Islam and Colonialism: The Doctrine of Jihad in Modern History* (The Hague: Mouton, 1979), chapter 2 (see also ibid., pp. 112-115). South African Muslim theologian Farid Esack refers dismissively to the way in which, post-9/11, 'jihad was critiqued and repackaged as entirely non-threatening' – Farid Esack, 'In Search of Progressive Islam Beyond 9/11', in Omid Safa (ed.), *Progressive Muslims: On Justice, Gender and Pluralism* (Oxford: Oneworld, 2003): 83.

50 On the Banu Qaynuqa see also e.g. A. Guillaume (ed.), *The Life of Muhammad: A Translation of Ibn Ishaq's Sirat Rasul Allah* (Lahore: Oxford University Press, 1967): 363-364; Maxime Rodinson, *Mohammed* (Harmondsworth: Pelican Books, 1973): 172-173. On the Banu Qurayza see also e.g. Ibn Ishaq, trans. Guillaume, op. cit., pp. 461ff.; Rodinson, op. cit., pp. 211-214; W. Montgomery Watt, *Muhammad: Prophet and Statesman* (Oxford: Clarendon Press, 1961, repr. 1978): 171-175; Martin Lings, *Muhammad: his life based on the earliest sources* (London: The Islamic Texts Society & George Allen & Unwin, 1983), chapter LXI. According to Ibn Ishaq, indeed (one of the earliest sources), 'Then the apostle went out to the market of Medina (which is still its market today) and dug trenches in it. Then he sent for them and struck off their heads in those trenches as they were brought out

to him in batches ... There were 600 or 700 in all, though some put the figure as high as 800 or 900 ... This went on until the apostle made an end of them' (op. cit., p. 464).

[51] Ibn Ishaq, trans. Guillaume, ibid., pp. 675-676. See also Rodinson, op. cit., pp. 171-172 (and see also ibid., pp. 167-168). It is a measure of the lack of self-critical discipline so often to be found that a currently widely respected Muslim scholar can summarise the poet's murder (he does not mention the poetess's) as 'an over-zealous Muslim infuriated by his verses set out to silence the poet' – whereas according to Ibn Ishaq he was responding to Muhammad's 'Who will deal with this rascal for me? [op. cit. p. 675]'. See also Akbar S. Ahmed, *Discovering Islam* (London and New York: Routledge & Kegan Paul, 1988): 23. (Ahmed adds for good measure, in respect both of the murder and of the case of the Banu Qurayza, 'harshness and violence were simply not part of the Prophet's nature. Yet on religious matters he was firm and unequivocal', ibid.)

[52] Fred McGraw Donner, *The Early Islamic Conquests* (Princeton, NJ: Princeton University Press, 1981): 8, 90.

[53] Jansen, op. cit. p. xvii.

[54] For the translation of the original 'neglected duty' text see also ibid., pp. 159-234. Discussion of the precedent set by 'the night expedition to murder Ka'b ibn al-Ashraf' is to be found on pp. 211-214. See also Ibn Ishaq trans.Guillaume, op. cit., pp. 364-369; Rodinson, op. cit., p. 176 (and see also too p. 189). For a summary of the argument of 'the neglected duty' text see also Jansen, op. cit., pp. 5-31. For the response from al-Azhar, see also ibid., chapter 2.

[55] Martin Kramer, 'The Moral Logic of Hizballah', in Walter Reich (ed.), *Origins of Terrorism: Psychologies, Ideologies, Theologies, States of Mind* (Washington, DC: Woodrow Wilson International Center for Scholars, 1900): 141-149. The whole issue is aired, highly polemically from an Israeli Jewish perspective, but nevertheless informatively, in Raphael Israeli, *Islamikaze: Manifestations of Islamic Martyrology* (London and Portland, Oregon: Frank Cass, 2003). See also more generally John L. Esposito, *Unholy War: Terror in the Name of Islam* (New York: Oxford University Press, 2002): 99-100; John L. Esposito, *What Everyone Needs to Know About Islam* (New York: Oxford University Press, 2002): 124-127; Mark Juergensmeyer, *Terror in the Mind of God: The Global Rise of Religious Violence*, updated edition with a new preface (Berkeley and Los Angeles, CA: University of California Press, 2001): 58, 73, 77, 175; Jansen, op. cit., pp. 217-218. Suicide is also forbidden in Judaism – but then there is the example set by Samson's 'self-chosen martyrdom' as he pulls down the temple, killing large numbers of Philistine men and women (Judges 16:23-31). In a frightening modern comparison, Israel's nuclear weapons programme and policies have been labelled 'the Samson complex', and 'the Samson option', see also New, op. cit., pp. 172ff., and Seymour M. Hersh, *The Samson Option: Israel, America and the Bomb* (New York: Random House, and London: Faber and Faber, 1991).

[56] Akenson, op. cit., p. 307; Shahak and Mezvinsky, op. cit., p. 122; Qur'an 33:36. For a perceptive analysis of the mind-set behind such remarks, see also Charles Kimball, *When Religion Becomes Evil* (San Francisco: Harper, 2002).

[57] Michael Prior's judgment (as a Roman Catholic) that 'a faith nourished on the Bible as understood by the prevailing biblical scholarship conflicts with universally agreed perspectives on human dignity and rights' (op. cit., p. 259) is one example of the kind of prioritising of moral criteria that I am advocating. From a contemporary revisionist Shiite thinker comes the related view that 'being humane is the condition of the truth of religion', Mahmoud Sadri and Ahmad Sadri (eds), *Reason, Freedom, and Democracy in Islam: Essential Writings of Abdolkarim Soroush* (New York: Oxford University Press, 2000): 129.

[58] On 'open Judaism' see also Dan Cohn-Sherbok, *The Future of Judaism* (Edinburgh: T & T Clark, 1994), chapter 7. Chief Rabbi Jonathan Sacks stirred up serious controversy with his 'dignity of difference' thesis, despite its blandness compared with the scale of the

problem as outlined here; yet even small steps in the right direction are welcome and may indeed be important. See also Jonathan Sacks, *The Dignity of Difference: How to Avoid the Clash of Civilizations*, revised edition (London and New York: Continuum, 2003).

[59] On the ultra-Orthodox yeshivas, see also Shahak and Mezvinsky, op. cit., chapter 2; on the Bible institutes, see also New, op. cit., chapter 3; on the madrasas, see also Ibrahim M. Abu-Rabi', 'A Post-9/11 Critical Assessment of Modern Islamic History', in Ian Markham and Ibrahim M. Abu-Rabi' (eds), *9/11: Religious Perspectives on the Causes and Consequences* (Oxford: Oneworld, 2002): 28-37. The deeper issues raised by current madrasa-style education are explored in Fazlur Rahman, *Islam and Modernity: Transformation of an Intellectual Tradition* (Chicago and London: University of Chicago Press, 1982).

[60] 'Correspondent – License to Kill', BBC2 (25.3.00).

[61] Juergensmeyer, op. cit., p. 7.

[62] An impressive example of working very firmly within the tradition, in this case to review the ethical foundations of the Islamic legal system, and radically reappraise the status and position of women, is Khaled Abou El Fadl, *Speaking in God's Name: Islamic Law, Authority and Women* (Oxford: Oneworld, 2001). See also too the collection *Progressive Muslims* (see note 49 above), to which El Fadl also contributed. Less convincing as a purely internal defence is Abdullahi Ahmed an-Naim, *Toward an Islamic Reformation: Civil Liberties, Human Rights, and International Law* (Syracuse, NY: Syracuse University Press, 1990). His admirable conclusions are predicated on the thesis that for Muslims only the so-called Meccan suras of the Qur'an are authoritative, not the (troublesome) Medinan suras. This radical break with tradition is surely, certainly from an outsider's perspective, a step in the direction of an 'open Islam' (see note 56 above), where this kind of 'hermeneutic of wishful thinking' (Ebrahim Moosa, 'The debts and burdens of critical Islam', in *Progressive Muslims*, p. 125) is no longer necessary. More generally, on the topic of human rights, see also Ann Elizabeth Mayer, *Islam and Human Rights: Tradition and Politics*, 3rd edition (Boulder, CO and Oxford: Westview Press, 1999).

[63] Hans Küng and Karl-Josef Kuschel (eds), *A Global Ethic: The Declaration of the Parliament of the World's Religions (London:SCM Press, 1993):24.*

Chapter 4

The Finality of the Qur'an and the Contemporary Politics of Nations

Kenneth Cragg

The study of power and authority . . . draws us, like it or not, to . . . what is harshest, ugliest and most dangerous in human conduct . . . of all spheres of human public activity, that which entails social control is the one most likely to be touched with pathology.[1]

The first part of this dictum on the problematics of political power would certainly find echoes in Islam. The second would be an apt observation on the violence of 9/11. Ever since the crucial *Hijrah* of the Prophet and the early converts to Islam from Mecca to Medina, Muslim religion has been committed to, and reliant on, a religious marriage with political power. The logic of that watershed in Muhammad's *Sirah*, from which, significantly, the Muslim Hijri calendar begins, could well be caught in an adaptation of Matthew 6.33: 'Seek ye first the political kingdom and all else shall be added to you,'[2] except that 'first' – in the same *Sirah* there had been the thirteen exclusively 'religious' years in Mecca. They were years in which the Prophet was told many times: 'Your sole responsibility is the *balagh*, the message you utter.'[3] During that defining period of the 'essential Islam of the word' he had neither sought nor enjoyed the luxury of power. On the contrary, he had been physically vulnerable and in heavy soul-distress from the bitter scorn and hostility of his Meccan populace, to whom he seemed an upstart and a renegade, a menace to the pagan status quo. 'In truth you are vexing your very soul in grief over the way they are,' we read in Surah 18.6. It will always be a question for the Islamic mind whether that Meccan situation requires to be held finally determinative of Islam, as having not merely chronological but essential priority over all else.

A conviction in the affirmative is the purpose of these paragraphs, reinforced by the nature of the current world of nations as in a fifteenth Muslim (a twenty-first) century we find them to be. The post-Meccan power-quest and power-structure are firmly embedded in the text of the Qur'an, as is the age-long resultant politicisation of Islam. Therefore, to suggest that the Meccan precedent might now be paramount involves the traditional Muslim doctrine of the Qur'an's finality as 'a mercy to all worlds,' both across time as well as place. If its finality is dynamic, its religious theme of human tenancy of the earth under God must duly belong with how that tenancy obtains in a technological world of nation-states urgent for global community across both hemispheres. That vocation cannot now know itself divinely summoned in terms congenial to the tribalism of the Hijaz as the seventh century knew it. Moreover, a static finality is a contradiction in terms. Is it not arguable that the Meccan call of the Prophet to embrace Islam translates more aptly in the present global context into an open human co-existence in which its Muslim political expression in both majority or minority areas, functions as befits an authentic religion responding to the contemporary world? Given the long tradition in which a Medinan Islam saw itself summoned to perpetual, political establishment, that must be a bold and taxing suggestion. Yet, in all realism, there is no denying the essential priority of the Meccan story and any sane individual refusing the urgency of inter-religious compatibility – not doctrinally which will always be impossible – but in the physical equations of political power as committed to the modern nation-state. Insofar as 9/11 placarded one shape of the Muslim mind the question looms as large as that day's drama.

The case is not for a de-politicised Islam in any absolute way but for a perception – by any and every religion – of power as a tributary to moral ends not unilaterally identified and/or imposed by Islam or any other creed in exclusive terms. Before arguing the contemporary urgency of this plea, and the reasons that make it radical, it will be well to review the Qur'an's sense of its own textuality.

It is clear that it 'gathered' into a whole via sequences. Its *tanzil*, or 'sending down,' transpired *'ala mukthin,*' 'at intervals,' (17.106) though the despisers, tauntingly, wanted it 'all at once' (25.32), *jumlatan wahidatan.* That periodicity was important on several counts. It bore witness to Muhammad's tenacity while pleading with Qurayshi obduracy. For all exegetes to come, it furnished what are called *asbab al-nuzul*, 'occasions of revelation,' in relation to which passages are to be understood. The place and time to which a deliverance belonged must be clue to the sense it carried. The entire Qur'an, through its twenty-three years, impinges precisely on the same time-measure of Muhammad's textual recipience of *wahy.* Its time-and-place incidence, both textual and biographical, is paramount to its very being as scripture.

The question, therefore, has to follow; how does the role in the text of those two score and three years translate into the fifteenth of the centuries imposing on its relevance? Given unfailing divine sovereignty how would the divine option for that where and when relate to our here and now, where alone in this generation the claim of the scripture cannot be 'dated' – as all texts are – in more than a calendar sense, if they are to guide all ongoing centuries. To discern their guidance must be the task of those to whom the Qur'an appeals for *tadabbur*, or responsible reflection, (Surahs 4.82 and 47.24) by people who do not have 'locks on their hearts.' Out-of-dateness would be impossible in an abiding revelation. Only reverent reading from then to now, from there to here, as the business of fidelity, can ensure the continuity of its authority.

A retrospective inclusiveness of the Qur'an has long been central to Islamic doctrine. 'The Seal of prophethood' is held to embrace and confirm all previous prophethood, all of whom in their sundry dates and places had 'the same message.'[4] If past ages could be contained in the text with comprehensive truth, how would future ages be incorporated? The text would have to be capable of a perceived relevance ascertained only by a wise readership alert to different time settings. To what 'occasions' in the current scene can the Qur'an be seen to be speaking and who is to say? How might 9/11 be one of them? Nothing in the Qur'an coincides date-wise with any times after 632 C.E. Being rightly read, all of it must synchronise with every turning century and with this one intensely.

Idolatry, for example, is not now what it then was – a harsh plural worship based on tribal loyalties, with natural forces still outside rational control and so needing to be venerated or placated. Contemporary idolatries, are in Qur'anic phrase – *min duni-Llahi*,[5] in the far more subtle terms of techniques, sciences, enterprises and structures made into false absolutes of human pride and self-sufficiency. There is no less need, no less relevance, for the Qur'anic summons that 'only God is God.' It is only that it has now to address a sophisticated and subtle pseudo-worship – 'idols' in the market-place and corridors of power not dethroned by the likes of Abraham's axe and which even Muhammad's preaching in its Meccan terms might no more effectively dissuade.[6] Yet that preaching, in its great positive of divine unity and human vocation into creaturehood, held everything needing to be said to both Muhammad's audience and the contemporary population of the world.

There will be ample indications later of a never obsolescent Qur'an vis-à-vis our contemporary world. The need is that its significance be brought to bear, not only on current secularity but even against aspects of some Muslims' rendering of Islam which an up-to-date reading would have to disown. What is not in mind is the notion some twentieth century Muslims have proposed which reads the Qur'an as having somehow anticipated modern inventions or attainments, like the Suez Canal, or photography, X-ray, such as Kamil Husain condemned in his *Al-Mutanawwic*, as quite distorting the evident spiritual intention of the scripture.[7]

Nor is the plea here about scriptures of any faith somehow expressing themes beyond their own cognition or conscious intention. Some Biblical studies, Jewish and Christian, have inclined to that concept, of sacred text having a sort of 'after-life' as divinely intended for them so that they are no longer bound by the first and immediate sense of the words. To think the text had meanings hidden from themselves had much to do with the religious need for 'development' of doctrine – as with John Henry Newman, in wanting to think itself always latent in the 'intention' of the hallowed sources even if long unconsciously undetected there.[8] Such situations are part of the perennial problem of how a time-set Scripture avails as 'revelation' beyond the culture or the *zeitgeist* of its prime matrix and its accomplished shape.

Rather, the purpose here in mind is the more concrete duty to apply the Scripture – in its there and then immediacy – to a lively register here and now of the precedent its salient themes might yield for the guidance of a manifestly changed human landscape. Ideally, such duty and register should be the task and privilege of a communal mind rather than the ingenuities of esoteric learning or of exegetical subtlety. If the Qur'an is 'about man and his behaviour, not God, whose existence is strictly functional,'[9] then obedience to 'His Word' is most right when it is most operative in the social order. Nowhere is the well-being of the social order more at stake than in the political structure. There, too, both the peace and the wealth of nations are forever in primary – and forever vulnerable – trust. If 'sovereignty is God's' (Surahs 2.107, 3.26, 3.189, 5.17, 5.40, 5.120, 9.116, 24.42, 35.13, 39.6, 43.85, 45.27, 48.14, 57.2), in which He has no partner (25.2), then the political order in the human scene is at once the crucial factor in any right theology. But, since that sovereignty presides via creation and creaturehood and the reach of 'sent prophethood' over all mankind, the political realm in its human custody must recognise in such delegacy from God a responsibility that is no less inclusive, no less comprehensive, in its workings.

What, then, of the nation-state? Or what, also, of a single Muslim *Ummah* with which, in the name of one religion, some Muslim minds reject the nation-state?[10] Answer here must come inside the wider formulation that will best embrace it, namely that the logic of contemporary globalism – for deeply religious reasons – requires the conscious relinquishing of unilateral religious annexation of the political order, by exclusive privilege in power possession. This need in no way entail any abeyance of faith's relevance or religion's task, and no surrender to outright 'secularisation,' but only a more duly religious vision and practice of what is due from faith to society. The pure gain will be deliverance from that menace of the pathological which always looms when faiths bind themselves into the corruptible instincts of power. The benefit will be a spiritual reckoning with the agnosticisms present in religious diversity[11] and in the irreligious world that would be otherwise ignored by a power quite excluding them from its counsels.

To see the religion/power equation this way will at once seem totally un-Islamic whether in theory or practice, and against all the logic of a defining *Hijrah* and long instinctive practice. Why it might not be so has first to make the case from where humankind now is and join it to the finality the Qur'an claims. The task is akin to the earlier instance concerning idolatry. The sovereignty that – in seventh century Arabia – demanded the end of superstitious plural worships, and currently would dethrone all false modern absolutes, must be similarly dissociated from unilateral power–faith equations too unkindly in the global human scene.

Globalisation of what was once only locally 'a common good' is now mandatory but evident enough. The inter-penetration and inter-dependence of human societies are manifest on every count of sanity and compassion and, indeed, brutal fact. For every psychic and cultural reason, intense 'separateness' abides, but this only makes the terrestrial logic of things the more exacting. To all the human anxieties here religious faiths owe more than a perpetuation of their ancient divisiveness. For too long they have corroborated the enmities of human tribes and the theisms have done so in the name of the Lordship they claimed was One. Must they continue to sanction alienations in the very trust of their universal reach?

Contemporary history is confusedly questing for some degree of inter-responsibility, whether through the United Nations, or global response to climate issues, illiteracy, population pressures and multiple migration, through governmental or non-governmental agencies or a concert of both. 'The wealth of nations' is more than a euphemism. It is a vision that remains distant, as is an ending of poverty. Indeed, 'nations' per se are both the irrepressible reality and the perennial issue, with all the sanctions of ethnicity, language, culture, tradition and locale. If Islam is to be worthy of the name, its instinctive divide of the world into *Dar al-Islam* and *Dar al-Harb* is the more menacing precisely in being the more obsolete. All religions, indeed, will be steadily the less warrantably religious in remaining self-sufficient and self-satisfied in their nexus with the global scene.[12]

To sense that this is so, has to follow from the measure there is currently, in the West if less so in Asia, of how 'insane' and 'criminal' religions can be, not least when in single league with political power that arises from secular humanism. A growing dismay or despair is liable to cry: 'a plague on all their houses!' Society is perceived to be better without these fanatics, and their fanaticisms are endemic. They refuse to be rescued from themselves, being captive to their own perversity. They are better totally excluded from the realm of politics, to which – on this view – they have only a threatening bigotry to bring. One need not be a Nietzsche to feel impelled to warn one's fellows that to breathe clean air one must keep away from churches; or a James Joyce to say: 'We have had too much of God in Ireland.'[13]

Such verdicts must be heeded, for they may well intend a truer humanity providing a better present than religion has so far succeeded in achieving. There can be moral discernment in 'the will to disbelieve'.[14] Faiths that do not register the indictments they receive are liable to forfeit their integrity. Events, dramatic or mundane, which reveal their image, betray religions to themselves. Nor will they deal with the case against them that demands an entire secularisation if they refuse the disclaiming pleas of a moral secularity.

In any Islamic attentiveness to these aspects of globalism, far away in this point of time as it may be, there might be a beginning in the age-long concept of *Dhimmi* status for tolerated minorities. A far happier policy than elimination or persecution, it was a sort of 'let them be ...' stance, allowing personal status laws of marriage and kinship, ritual practice and child faith-nurture – all to the good. In practice there was inferiorisation and social disadvantage, with dire consequences to the vital statistics of the subject faiths. Why not now a religious polity that 'let the other be . . .' not merely in *Dhimmi* shape but in full participatory potential in the body social? What is now called 'civil (or 'civic') society' means precisely this. 'Letting be' of all and sundry in a common citizenship so that none are penalised or effectively disenfranchised, while the State holds the ring neutral – consistent with law and order – for all components irrespective of their numerical size. In such a shape, any one religion might still have a hegemony for long historical and cultural reasons, provided that in dominating, it did not domineer. Societies do not forthwith forego identity because they undergo internal migration. To absorb migrants lays a necessary vocation on all religions involved – that of a tolerance both given and accepted honestly.

But surely the idea behind the *Dhimmi* system rules out this argument altogether, based as it was on the principle that only Islamic rule could properly ensure and safeguard Islamic faith. The *ahl al-Dhimmah* were human evidence of that dictum. The creation of Pakistan was a resounding historic witness to its validity.[15] If power is inescapable, as the crucial factor in human affairs, then all the more reason why it should be exclusively wielded by the right religion. *Dhimmi* status was only the corollary of the fact in enthroning the valid while confining the invalid one to the politically harmless as 'merely religious,' thus sharply witnessing to something Islam could never be. The point was underlined both ways.

Yet 'merely religious' was all Islam was in the Meccan years. To be sure, the Quraysh did not grant it *dhimmi* status. On the contrary, they hounded and oppressed it as darkly incompatible with their vested interests in pagan pilgrimage and trade. It was the pain of that hostility, its implicit veto on the faith, that argued what the *Hijrah* achieved, namely power to prevail. So then, it was the faith that sought the power, not the power that gave birth to the faith. In that situation, there is no doubt whose was, and is, the primacy. In a civil society the Medinan theme of exclusive power would be ended but the Meccan reality would abide, freed to be and proclaim itself but in the different idiom of a contemporary citizenry.

Is there anything wrong for Muslims in a perceptive return to Mecca, whither all Hajjis go, whither all mosques direct their careful *qiblahs*? Writing on *The Hijrah: Story and Significance*, a recent author remarks: 'In Medina to be a Muslim was to ride the winning horse ... It was easy to become a Muslim in Medina,' because 'failure to declare oneself so was to remain in the fringe of society.' Significantly, he goes on:

> In Makka there was no ground for hypocrisy . . . the phenomenon only emerged when the victory of Islam was clear . . . Perhaps (Meccan innocence of power) was because Islam needed a period of time in which to establish itself peacefully and on the merit of its own intrinsic spiritual and moral strength without the further support of military force.[16]

Could the case for a civil society, now, be more tellingly stated? If 'intrinsic worth' suffices what need of further concert for truth?

The writer is close to the strange evolution of the Qur'anic term *fitnah.* Basically 'what tests faith's mettle.' In Mecca it was the tribulation of a persecuted belief-system; in between it was the human yearning to escape the dangers of armed combat, a yearning which the Qur'an reproved; at length in Medina it became the trouble the establishment had from internal sedition or *nifaq.*[17] Must it not be that Islam was truer – as a religion – when it was tested by verbal contradiction in Mecca than when it was sanctioned in Medina against wily sedition?

The issue here is closely related to that *ikraha* which, according to Surah 2.256, ought never to belong with religion. Usually rendered 'compulsion,' the root word means whatever 'makes hateful or odious,' the quality religion ought never to have, by which its behaviour towards others belies its truth-professing. Such outlawing – in the Qur'an's own text - of *ikraha* is more readily ensured when the power-dimension is absent from faith-witness.

It is noteworthy, in respect of what can or should obtain between those two, that the Qur'an itself is strangely silent on many matters attaching to things political. The Caliphate, for example, though assumed through thirteen centuries, finds neither mention nor definition in the Qur'an, where – with the solitary exception of

David the king – the only *Khulafa* (pl.) are ordinary human mortals, peasants, traders, craftsmen, set over the earth as tenant-custodians, rendering thanks and glory to their divine Lord. There was, of course, the symbol of post-Hijrah Medina and the rulership of Muhammad and the urgent necessity of perpetuation of that authority (prophethood apart) after the shattering community trauma of his death.

Yet it would seem that nowhere was there explicit directive for the *Hijrah* in the Qur'an – only the pressing logic of Mecca's obdurate refusal to be persuaded by *balagh* (message). Islam may be 'not like any other religion in that it lays down clear and unambiguous claim to government,'[18] but was emigration to that end ever explicitly laid down? It is true that when fighting was underway the Qur'an has commands about not shrinking and directives about prayer under combat or the disposal of 'spoils.' Given that context, the repeated order: 'Obey God and obey the *Rasul*' is apposite enough, underwriting both the campaign and the faith-meaning. Does it mandate the *Hijrah* itself, sustained as it would come to be by many other directives as to alms and disciplines? In Surah 9.107 it is clear that there was a 'mosque of dissension,' with 'Muslims' at sharp odds with the 'loyalists,' even after Mecca had capitulated. It would be left to 'sources of law' outside the Qur'an to build up the corpus of law that decisively affirms and establishes political Islam.[19]

Muslim legists who have recognised the significance here for current issues have, of course, to concede the basic symbol that Medina carries and how there is no eliding it either from the Qur'an or the *Shari'ah*. In whatever guise – Caliphate, Sultan, Mamluk, Emir, King, Republic – *Dawlah* is seen as wedded to *Din* and *Din* to *Dawlah*. Islam was destined to govern and governing to be the destiny of Islam.

Yet the Islamicity in that partnership in no way duly follows. On the contrary, it has frequently proved a contentious or, further, a subversive issue. The Islamic adequacy of the rule or the State can be called into question and allegiance withheld. Such dispute, politically, about 'Islamic quality' becomes intrinsically a religious theme. The very centrality of the political returns us to the doctrinal. We, or rather, the Muslim society, are back in *Din*, made the more crucial by the very majesty of politics. Clearly every society (*polis*) needs enforceable law for its very order (police) but the efficacy of that power element turns on the law-abidingness that the law deserves and receives. This, in turn, hinges on religious minding of the law's worth and dignity.[20]

The will to 'submission' to any Islamic political order has always been in question throughout Muslim history. The Caliph Umar's title of *Amir al-Mu'minin* was used in deliberate distinction from *Amir al-Muslimin*, since the latter, as only outward 'conformists,' lacked true belief.[21] Promptly the Khawarij withheld obedience from the Ummayyads as being 'unworthy' Muslims not warranting the fealty of 'true' Muslims. The Shi'ah developed their doctrine of *taqiyyah*, reserving a hidden purpose of dissent until a time when it might become open revolt, meanwhile never consenting 'in the heart.' Last century the Islamicity of Pakistani statehood has always been in question by elements ready to disallow its successive actual – and changing – expressions. General Zia al-Haqq differed sharply from *Al-Qa'id al 'Azam*, M.A. Jinnah, the founder of the nation.

Pacific minds, like the *Murji'un*, throughout history realised that the 'right' equation between the religious ideal and the political actuality was ever elusive and that sanity had to 'leave the issue of legitimacy' in suspense ('*irja*') and hope and, meanwhile, get along with the viable. Thus the primacy of *Din* as the monitor has to concede the ever unsatisfactory necessity of *Dawlah*, however awkward the partnership.

Inevitably the same quandary attaches to the concept of *jihad*, the aegis of force in the ensuring of Islam by the *mujahid*'s measure of its quality. The tragedy of 9/11 is that of an extreme reading of *jihad* as demanding a suicidal and implacable hostility to perceived *kufr*, Satanism or anti-Muslim villainy as only fit to be destroyed. The tragedy is only deepened by the sense that Islam and internationalism could never feasibly align that way – a way which could only propose some bitter, perpetual anarchy.

It is also clear that there is no panacea that the political order can offer. The political, at best, can only yield a modicum of justice, compassion, liberty and well being. Its being always imperfect is no argument against commitment to it but only a realisation that the ideology from which it draws its warrant and its inspiration sets it again squarely within the responsibility of the religious faith.

This surely means the relevance, at least in contemporary history, of the converse between religions and their theologies, seeing that the global issues are more than any one religion either can, or does, monitor in isolation. The glass of events in which 'they all see darkly' is more than ever common to each.

Seeing that political power is always approximate in what it can deliver for religious ideology, as it is unlikely that both sets of truth claims will be identical on every issue and, being approximate, is also always at risk of disagreement it follows that religious faith should be distinguishable from the organs of power exercise. This was the great strength of the Hebrew prophets like Isaiah and Jeremiah. They could accuse the corridors of power because they were not of them. 'Obey God and obey the Prophet' would be a dangerous formula if 'the prophet' were also the state. Only in being outside the political can the religious be its honest mentor. Religions are well able to develop pathological excesses. The temptation is only the greater if they wield political power. Thus the quest for 'civil society' is a quest for the health of the religious mind not to say also its perspicacity. Allied to this is the large question as to the role of private conscience in the attainment of public good and so, also, of how conscience operates inside the dogmas of religious law and system.[22]

If, in sum, we are asking whether Islam can ever rethink its religio-politico reality, as both credal faith and legal structure, to be compatible with the 'civil society' concept and ready to be in co-existence with its other global shapes, there is one final fact to consider: maybe as much as a quarter of all Muslims are now precisely in that situation in a dispersion outside Muslim statehoods and orthodox versions of Muslim *Ummah*. Migrants are thus 'Makkan Muslims' in most cases, but usually minus the persecution. In most foreseeable circumstances they are adjusting to being 'just a religion,' where religion and politics are separated in secular societies. This position has arisen by their own *Hijrah* as economic migrants or in other cases where they exist as minorities in non-Muslim societies; for example, the frontier shaping of a Pakistan that excluded them.[23] This fact of present history has profound significance for the inner development of Islam and one that could have wide implications for the Islam of continuing *Dar al-Islam* or of nations, as in Africa, of duo-religious character.

Certainly, one reaction of diaspora Muslims is to conspire towards the Islamicisation of their new and chosen homelands and to contrive, at whatever cost, their transit to Islam. Thus the writer earlier quoted on *Hijrah*:

> To be accepted as a full Muslim in a non-Muslim society is a false hope. It is important that all such hopes … of being accepted with honour and justice and equality should be shed and exposed as mere fantasies. Non-Muslim societies will never accept nor enable a truly conscious Muslim, who is aware of his full identity as Muslim, to realise the ideals of Islam.[24]

This counsel of confrontation comes from an institution enjoying full facilities near Leicester for Muslim self-expression and fulfilment. Its logic, of course, turns on who is 'a full Muslim' and 'truly conscious.' Happily, there are contrasted verdicts about how to live both in full Islamicity and genuine compatibility with non-Muslim regimes. Thus Sayyid Ahmad Khan in British India, Maulana Azad in post-independence India, affirmed fully Islamic fidelity. Similar co-existence in full authenticity is advocated throughout the western dispersion of Muslims.

These are however beset by the contrary attitude of those whose presence is inherently subversive, and who pervert the hospitality they enjoy. The resulting suspicion, kindled and harboured, leaves the situation open to social deterioration and reciprocal bad faith. The lot of minorities has always been exacting and the genuine reception it most needs turns, in part, on their own resilience. There are many dimensions of the Qur'an and Islam that point to hope rather than despair in this context. Some we have earlier explored. 9/11 underscored how critical is the 'Islam and the West' formula so frequently made. When merged into that of *Din wa Dawlah*, the realm of religion and the realm of politics, the passions and the confusions multiply. The hope of a 'civil' concept of nationhoods, cognisant of the mutuality of one global humankind, must surely be the moral summons to religions, unhardening their dogmas and making gentle their hearts.

It is important to remember that the 'civil society' ideal means no necessary marginalisation of religion, so that faith retreats into a private option which it could never rightly be. That the State holds a neutral ring for all *might* mean that religions per se are forfeiting their truth claims. Duly understood, they are being invited to hold and to present these the more patiently and the more perceptively by virtue of their enjoying no advantage but their quality of mind and soul. Does not the Qur'an tell all Muslims '*Alaikum anfusukum*', 'your souls are in your souls' trust.'?[25]

Notes

[1] David Vital: *A People Apart: The Jews in Europe, 1789-1939*, Oxford, 1999, p. vi.
[2] An adaptation made by the Convention People's Party in Ghana en route to gaining independence. See Kwama Nkrumah: *My Autobiography*, London, 1957, p. ix.
[3] Surahs 5.99, 13.40, 24.53, 29.18, 36.17 and 42.48.
[4] For thinking, as opposed to dogmatic minds, there has always been a problem about this backward reaching 'identity' of all prophetic word and theme. The greatest Hebraic prophethood, for example, was never in a Qur'anic situation speaking to a Meccan sort of *Jahiliyyah* of untutored paganism. It called to a Yahwist or Elohist people long nurtured in a theism, but one to which they were disloyal. Even when plural worships beguiled them, Hosea's grief's about the Ba'alim by which Israel was deceived were sharply contrasted with Muhammad's pre-*Hijrah* anguish over a people still perversely darkened. When Isa, (Jesus) is included in the 'sameness' of all the prophets the alleged inclusion becomes still more in question. The *sitz-im-leben* of them all differs so direly that identity of message is too bland a claim. Even so, if they all arrived where they are finally and identically 'sealed' in unison, the ongoing relevance beyond the 'sealings' (with which we are concerned) becomes, all the more, a crucial exegesis.
[5] Perhaps best translated: ' . . . to the exclusion of God' it is – highly frequently – the Qur'an's indictment of pagan living.
[6] On the exploits of the Qur'anic Ibrahim as an iconoclast, see Surahs 6.74-82, 21.51-73 and 26.69-104.
[7] The title in English meaning: 'Miscellanies,' Vol. 1, Cairo, 1957. See discussion in my: *The Pen and the Faith*, London, 1985, pp. 126-44. His point is that, as divine revelation, the Qur'an is both beyond, and indifferent to, such supposed embellishments of its authority.
[8] The theme of doctrinal 'development' was critically important to his mind. It enabled him to sustain what was essentially 'ecclesiastical' as being also 'scriptural,' in that it was there implicit in the text, ready for when a right-minded Church made it explicit. The stance was both a tribute to the text and a subduing of it.
[9] Fazlur Rahman: *Major Themes of the Qur'an*, Minneapolis, 1980, pp. 3 and 1.
[10] For many in Islam the nation-state, even a Muslim one, offends against the essential unity of Islam, for which they reserve the Quranic word *Ummah* (though others use it to refer to any separate Muslim nation). See, for example, the thought of Sayyid Qutb. See loc.cit. note 7, pp. 53-71 and bibliography, p. 174.
[11] Religious faith owes agnostics and sceptics an attentive ear. Their reasons for 'belief withheld' may well deserve to come within the ken of dogma. In the immediate context of Qurayshi paganism, the Qur'an had strong impulse to be confrontational (cf. Surah 109). The temper of the world is different now. Being simplistic – either way in faith or unfaith – is not to have the measure of human perplexity.
[12] The familiar divide between Islam and non-Islam no longer rides with the wide dispersion of Muslims in the world of non-Islamic regimes. (See below). In any event, its legitimacy, only and always, stood in the political dimension alone. For much that is doctrinal and spiritual belongs also elsewhere, while *Dar al-Islam* is well populated with *non-Dhimmi* non-Muslims who interact with its ethos.
[13] One might compare how W.B. Yeats saw his native land:

'Great hatred, little room,
Maimed us at the start.
I carry from my mother's womb
A fanatic heart.'

Of much more than Ireland is this true.

[14] Indeed, both belief and unbelief are much more a matter of will than of logic. A strenuous allegiance can be highly inconvenient for the selfish soul no less than for the lazy mind. Iris Murdoch insisted that she had 'opted' for an agnosticism about 'the traditional God,' which she would not think to prove.

[15] See the illuminating discussion, near the time, of its creation in Wilfred Cantwell Smith, *Islam in Modern History,* Princeton, 1957, pp. 206-255.

[16]Zakaria Bashier: *Hijrah: Story and Significance*, Leicester, 1983, pp. 71 and 101.

[17] Ibid. p.101. The writer notes that in Mecca there was no hypocrisy.

[18] Ibid. p.103.

[19] Namely tradition, analogy and consensus of the community. When in 1924 the new regime in Turkey abolished the historic Caliphate, an Egyptian scholar, Ali Abd al-Raziq wrote his *Islam wa Usul al-Hukm* ('Islam and the Sources of Jurisprudence,') demonstrating that the Caliphate had never been essential to Islam. More recently see the writings of the jurist, Muhammad Sa'id al-Ashmawi, especially *Al-Islam al-Siyasi*, ('Political Islam'), Cairo, 1987.

[20] The linkage is clear in the very derivation of the words. A mundane example from the realm of traffic would be the 'Highway Code' which requires what also serves the common 'good' of safe mobility. That, however, has a certain sanction from the fact that there is a risk in flouting it. Society at large is not so minded to be 'law-assenting'.

[21] Believers were thus distinguishable from the 'Muslims' who had merely 'submitted' to power without sincerely consenting to faith. There is precisely the same situation in Surah 49.14.

[22] How conscience might, or might not, duly belong with faith in revealed scriptures was explored in my: *The Weight in the Word: Prophethood, Biblical and Qur'anic,* Brighton, Sussex Academic Press, 1999, pp. 88-101

[23] Though, to be sure, minority status carries odds against one's identity, as in India where the very precedent of Pakistan – creation suggested to Hindus that their majority people should be a Hindustan with only Hindus as genuine 'Indians'. Happily, for a time Nehru style 'secularism' held that at bay but perhaps not forever. Even 'secularism' can aid Islam.

[24]Zakaria, *Op.cit.*, p. 104

[25] Surah 5.105. A final responsibility for 'you being the you that you are'?

Chapter 5

Who Defines Moderate Islam 'post'- September 11?

Ron Geaves

The tragic events of 9/11 and the resulting conflict with the al-Qa'eda and the Taliban have created a new politically motivated discourse in which the British and the US governments have attempted to differentiate between 'terrorists' and the majority of Muslims in the world who are increasingly defined as 'moderate'. This is not only an overwhelmingly simplistic analysis of the religious and political realities of the Muslim world, it raises a number of methodological questions concerning how religious commitment is regarded in pluralistic, secular and liberal Western democracies.

The branding of those individuals and movements that transform the rhetoric of *jihad* into actual violent acts against Western institutions as 'terrorists', functions as an attempt to pursue a political strategy of retaliation without appearing to alienate an increasingly uneasy Muslim world. It is also tempting to brand 'terrorists' as evil or psychopathic individuals without attempting to understand that there are underlying rational as well as emotive explanations of their behaviour arising from a deep sense of injustice originating in perceived prejudices and imbalances in US foreign policy towards the Muslim world. These injustices include the unbalanced US policy in Israel, the presence of US troops in Saudi Arabia and the support of various regimes in the Muslim world considered to be corrupt or opposed to Islam. To this list, can be added the second war in Iraq leading to invasion and apparent colonisation, and the unresolved situation in Afghanistan. Although there are millions of Muslims who were shocked at the events of 9/11, many of those share the belief in a conspiracy against the Muslim world which has intensified since the collapse of the Soviet empire led to the demise of communism as the traditional opponent of US-led Western capitalism.

Manifest Success

The prevailing mood of political and social pessimism among many Muslim populations is in stark contrast with the Islamic theology of 'Manifest Success' and the firm and widespread conviction that Islam is the final option offered to humanity by a just and merciful creator. The theology of 'Manifest Success' dates back to the origins of Islam and the changing relationship of the small Muslim community to the Arab world around them as events unfolded in Makkah and Medinah. Originally, Muhammad and his small band of followers were mocked and reviled in Makkah and increasingly faced persecution from the indignant merchant hierarchy of the city. The Qur'an's revelations during this period encouraged steadfastness and exhorted Muslims to remember that all the prophets of God had faced such trials from temporal authorities. The persecution was therefore perceived as proof of Muhammad's prophetic mission.

However, this was to change in Medinah, after the Muslims' overwhelming victory over the superior forces of the Makkan merchants at the battle of Badr. The Medinan situation and the significant victories achieved, culminating in the surrender of Makkah and the defeat of the goddess worshipping tribes of Ta'if, transformed the Prophet's reputation from an eccentric but tiresome minority voice to that of a successful warrior and leader of thousands. The Muslim problem became one of how to deal with the numbers of tribes and individuals who formed allegiances with them and embraced Islam to be a part of the success story and seek the protection of the powerful. It is at this stage of development that the Qur'an's revelations become more concerned with the issue of hypocrisy.

As the Muslim success story continued after the death of Muhammad with the conquest of the Persian and Byzantine territories, the issue of 'Manifest Success' and the problem of hypocrisy became central to both Muslim rulers and the pious. The theological idea that material success demonstrates God's favour is also common in the Jewish sacred writings and results from a combination of the linking of God to a particular people and their fortunes and the idea of a divinity who works through providence. There is one drawback with such a theological position and the emerging Muslim community had already felt its sting at the battle of Uhud shortly after Badr. At Uhud, the Muslims suffered a setback and narrowly avoided disaster. The question then became, how do God's chosen people assess material failure. The only acknowledgeable reason for such desertion by God has to be a failure on the part of his chosen community to follow his will in the proper manner. Thus a pattern was established throughout the history of the Sunni Muslim world that material failure is met by religious revival. Increasingly, hypocrisy is associated with nominal allegiance to the faith, and although many would have been content to associate the spread of empire with Manifest Success, any set back was likely to be regarded by the pious as the empire having neglected true Islam in favour of the 'hypocrites'.

Until the invasion of the Mongols, Sunni Muslims had been unused to serious failure as the Muslim faith spread to Europe, India and beyond, rapidly overtaking Christendom as the foremost civilisation of the world. The main bone of contention for Muslim theologians and the pious was the issue of 'hypocrites' or those who joined the ranks of victors for reasons other than purely religious ones. For many pious Muslims this included their own rulers, and although the opinion prevailed that judgement should be left to God, there were those who pursued either the alternative routes of rejection, renunciation of power and focus on personal piety, or the route of armed struggle against nominal allegiance to the religion and corrupt regimes that did not observe the law of God. Both alternatives stressed that they were returning to the original faith of the Prophet and his companions. The latter groups introduced a strong political dimension to their struggles, perceiving themselves able to destroy an aberrant form of the faith that had co-operated with pre-existent forms of *jahiliyah* (ungodliness) and corrupted the purity of Islam. This, they claimed had been achieved by mixing Islam with forms of government, religious and cultural customs belonging to former civilisations which had either departed from God's revelation or had never received it in the first place. Their solution was to divide the world into *dar al-Islam* (the world of Islam) and *dar al-Harb* (the world of war). The innovation of such groups was that *dar al-Harb* could also include corrupt regimes and nominal allegiance to Islam inside Muslim territory and *jihad* could be declared against the 'hypocrites'.

The eighteenth and nineteenth centuries brought the greatest threat to the Muslim world in its history with the rise of European power and several colonial empires that not only challenged Muslim hegemony but also gained control of considerable territory. It is not surprising that the modern period has seen the rise of a number of movements which believe the solution to the problem is a return to the revelation and the prophetic example and declarations of *jihad* against the modern 'hypocrites' of the Muslim world who are blamed for the loss of 'Manifest Success'. In doing so such movements, although taking on twentieth century political forms, followed a line of resistance that dated back to the early history of the faith, having its roots in the relationship between the faithful, their deity and historical events during the time of Muhammad.

Reform and revival

For the last two centuries, there have been those who have responded to change in the world's balance of power by asserting religious renewal based upon reform and revival as the solution to Muslim decline. Prominent amongst these groups were the nineteenth century Wahhabi movement which originated in Saudi Arabia and spread to most parts of the Muslim world, generating new variations in the Salafi movements of the twentieth and twenty-first centuries. Although the Wahhabis were essentially religious rather than political in their motivations and focused their attention on perceived corruptions and innovations to a 'pure' Islam believed to have been practised by the Prophet and the early Muslim community in Medina, they created a conflict which continues to the present day over who has ownership of an authentic Islam. As documented by Esposito, the twentieth century inheritors of the Wahhabi critique of traditional Islamic belief and practice added an anti-western and anti-Zionist rhetoric. They asserted the idea of a Judeo-Christian conspiracy to their already strong conviction that *jihad* is permissible against Muslim individuals and governments who do not fully implement Islamic law and live according to the Qur'an and Sunnah of the Prophet.[1] Such movements strived by all means available to establish Islamic states where their vision of an Islam based upon seventh century fundamentals could be implemented.

Categories of Muslims

Thus most Muslim countries have struggled, not only with deep-rooted economic and social problems in the latter part of the twentieth century, but with religious and ideological positions that have deeply divided their communities. These divisions fall into approximately four categories:

1. The various nineteenth and twentieth century revivalist movements committed to *islah* (reform) and *tajdid* (renewal) in which renewal involves a return to a perceived golden age of ideal practice and correct belief under the leadership of the Prophet and the first four caliphs. These movements are themselves divided on both means and objectives. Some wish to achieve a series of Islamic states to replace the existing Muslim nations who are believed to be seriously and fundamentally flawed by their compromise with western systems of law and government; others wish to replace the nation states with a single Muslim geographical region ruled over by a restored caliph. Some believe that these respective aims can be achieved by education and by functioning within the existent political structures; others are fully committed to violent *jihad* against prevailing authorities and western powers if they should contribute towards maintaining these power structures.
2. The Sufi orders (*tariqas*) organised around the authority of living or deceased *shaykhs,* and traditional Muslims who maintain allegiance to one of the four schools of law, but also love and respect the lineages of pious and saintly men and women who form the heart of Sufism within Islam. Such Muslims will accept the idea of the Prophet as intercessor, may visit the tombs of holy men, and honour the authority of tradition and local custom which is not in contradiction to Islamic law.
3. Islamic modernists who are not antagonistic to the western world and believe that its political systems, scientific and technological advances and educational methods should be utilised to rejuvenate Muslim society. They maintain that these aspects of Western civilisation are in accord with the spirit of Islam.
4. Large numbers of Muslims who are not particularly devout although they maintain a nominal allegiance to the religion of Islam, but who possess a stronger sense of belonging to Muslim culture as manifested in a particular locality.

The revivalist movements are just as likely to declare *jihad* against the other three as they are with western civilisation, and the Sufis are not necessarily moderate in their expression of religious sentiment or hostility to perceived godlessness in western secular societies. As with the revivalist movements, they are likely to be hostile to the modernists and perceive the fourth category as fallen Muslims to be reclaimed for the faith.

Problems arise when the governments of Britain and the United States attempt to define 'moderate' from among these categories. Muslims themselves are likely to have a different understanding of 'moderate' from that of outsiders. The Muslim world's experience of two hundred years of European/Christian domination followed by globalisation processes in which US-led capitalism is perceived as a form of economic colonialism, has led to a lack of Muslim self-confidence. This is demonstrated by seeking western good opinion, on the one hand, while perceiving the West as culturally arrogant and indifferent to the fate of Muslim populations, on the other. The Muslim discovery of the West has revealed antipathy to Islam and educated Muslims are increasingly aware of orientalism. Since the publication of Edward Said's seminal work, orientalism can be described as the corporate institution for dealing with the Muslim world – making statements about it, authorising views of it, describing it, settling it and ruling over it, either by force, economic power relations or intellectual ownership.[2] Sardar has described orientalism as an 'intellectual and cultural tool' seen to be a 'deliberate and calculated exercise' which gives weight and credence to the views of non-Muslims and making Muslims a partial witness to their own history, religion and culture.[3] Once we begin to think of orientalism as a kind of western projection to assert cultural and intellectual superiority over the Muslim world in which the West defines the Muslim reality and relays it back as the ideal model of Muslim perception of themselves, then we can begin to understand the problematic nature of powerful western leaders defining for Muslims who is a 'terrorist' and who is 'moderate'.

In addition to the problem of orientalism, discerning whom to deal with in the Muslim world is complex for western leaders attempting to determine who is 'moderate'. Although western leaders may be naturally inclined to negotiate with Muslims who fall into categories three and four, this is not as straightforward as it might appear. Muslim modernists have never made much headway among their own people. Although they can be defended on the grounds of loyalty to Islam, demonstrating how it can be liberal, rational and progressive, they are also open to the criticism of being too defensive and apologetic when under fire from western civilisation – they can be accused of selling out to the West; at the worst they can be criticised as a Muslim form of 'Uncle Tom'.

Muslims believe Islam to be a religion which incorporates the final revelation of Allah to an errant humanity. Even those who do not live devout Muslim lifestyles, obedient to the Qur'an and Sunnah of the Prophet, are likely to see this as their own weakness rather than the fault of the revelation. The doctrine of 'Manifest Success' underpins Muslim psychological understanding of their community. Failure in the world is the sign of Allah's displeasure with his final people and success is warmly welcomed as a sign of Allah's favour. Western domination of the world undermines Muslim belief in themselves as the final community of Allah and can lead to religious revival and the hope of seeing a reversal in fortunes. Those who maintain their religion or successfully stand up to the West, are perceived to be worthy of respect amongst Muslims even when they take to extreme manifestations of resistance or uphold questionable political regimes. Orthodox or traditional Muslims who maintain their faith as central to their lives will never accept nominal Muslims as 'moderate', rather they will perceive them as 'failed' or disobedient to the revelation of Allah and in need of transformation or 'reversion' to the faith.

The traditional Muslims of category 2, spiritually led by the Sufi *tariqas*, represent the most interesting case to be defined as 'moderate'. On the one hand, the western world, particularly orientalist scholars, has long been fascinated by the mysticism of the Sufis. This is especially true in the United States where figures such as Rumi are household names. Sufism is perceived as quietist, pietist and non-political. On the other hand, Sufi *tariqas* may well be tempted to claim the title of 'moderate' and the opportunities of leadership in Muslim communities that this might afford. For many years now Sufis have been on the receiving end of a vociferous critique from the revivalist movements. This has manifested in several forms, from accusations of corrupting Islam by introducing non-Muslim innovations to declarations that they are outside the fold of Islam. Such critique has even resulted in civil war in some Muslim nations as the revivalists claim the right to declare a *jihad* of orthodoxy against tradition. In recent years, there have been signs of various spiritual leaders amongst the *tariqas* beginning to fight back by utilising the methods of dissemination of publicity and forms of organisation so successfully used against them by the revivalist movements. Astute leaders may see the West's new found hostility towards the revivalist cause discrediting it in the Muslim world and providing a new opportunity for the *tariqas* and their supporters to claim that they are the authentic Islam which has always been the 'moderate' form of the religion, albeit with strong commitment to practice of both the esoteric and exoteric realms of the religion. This provides the opportunity to distinguish between a faith-based revival of the religion and a political Islam as the basis of Islamicisation.

However, the West should be cautious of alliances with the Sufi movements. Carl Ernst (1997) has pointed out that although both the officials of previous colonial governments and modern Muslim secular leaders have recognised the importance of courting prominent *pirs* and *shaykhs* and acknowledging their authority, this was often undertaken because government structures were aware of the possibility of the *tariqas* becoming competing political forces.[4] Turkey under Ataturk suppressed the Sufi orders, whilst in Egypt there exists a bureau which lists and supervises over eighty 'official' Sufi *tariqas*. However, the government of India has long recognised the opportunity of utilising the loyalty of the traditional Muslim masses for the Sufis and condemning extreme forms of militant Islam by praising Sufism as the tolerant form of Islam, in contrast to what is described as rigid religious bigotry.[5] It would be tempting for the governments of Britain and the USA to follow the same road. Britain's Muslim community is predominantly Sufi-orientated and in the USA there are certainly Sufi leaders who would welcome government support and encouragement in the face of Wahhabi/Salafi tendencies in the North American Muslim community. However, it should be remembered that historically the Sufi orders have been centres of resistance to colonial rule in Sudan, Algeria and the Caucasus. In the Soviet Union they maintained the resistance of Islam against the anti-religious attitudes and policies of the Communist regimes, and perhaps, more importantly in terms of perceptions of Sufis, they formed the backbone of the Chechnya resistance to Russian occupation and dominance. Ernst notes that in the nineteenth century, Sufi leaders were perceived by colonial regimes as similar to depictions of contemporary fundamentalist movements, that is crazed, fanatical figures who were able to inspire their followers with an ' irrational and blind devotion that made them capable of anything'.[6]

Religious pluralism and liberal democracy

George Lindbeck (1984) cites the experiment carried out by Bruner and Postman in which a red six of spades and black four of hearts were introduced into a sequence of otherwise normal playing cards. All the subjects perceived the cards incorrectly, but as the exposure time was increased, they became confused.[7] Using this example, one can say that the events of 9/11 introduced in a traumatic manner religious cards that were analogous to the black four of hearts or the red six of spades. A reality, similar to a card that doesn't look right, which seemed impossible, had been introduced and consequently concepts or theories had to be created that allow for this anomaly.

Utilising Lindbeck's categories of the experiential/expressive and the cultural/linguistic, the British government's approach to moderation seems to imply a type of experiential/expressive model in which different religions are diverse expressions of the same common core experience. However, in this case the core is transferred from that of a universal deity experienced internally as a common mystical experience usually posited by essentialists, to that of 'moderation' that fits into the liberal/secular worldview of religion. However, Lindbeck suggests a cultural/linguistic alternative in which religions are perceived as 'comprehensive interpretive systems, usually embodied in myths and narratives and heavily ritualised, which structure human experience and understanding of self and the world'.[8] He goes on to state that 'becoming religious involves being skilled in the language, the symbol system of a given religion, which is a kind of cultural linguistic framework or medium that shapes the entirety of life and thought'.[9] In this model there can be no common core, as the experiences that a religious form creates in the adherent are as diverse as the interpretive schemes they embody.[10] Simply put, different believers have different experiences and different religions, and the varied strands within them create radically diverse 'depth experiences' of what it means to be human.[11] Lindbeck's argument proposes that there is no common framework and that different religious traditions may have disputing notions of reality, truth and 'categorial adequacy'.[12] The black four of hearts and the red six of spades belonged to another sequence, and had rudely entered the interpretive framework of secular/liberal ideology.

Lindberg goes on to say that this does not prohibit dialogue between faiths; on the contrary, our world necessitates such communication, but the cultural/linguistic model avoids the error of assuming that our deepest experiences and commitments are not necessarily the same. Dialogue has to go beyond selecting groups that appear to share the same core values. The US and British government's branding of certain forms of Islam as 'terrorist' and 'evil' is an attempt to destroy the out-of-sequence cards so that dialogue takes place only amongst those recognised as part of the sequence. As Lindberg correctly points out, this theory of dialogue runs the risk of disguising the multiplicity of problems and motives.[13]

Implicit to the British government's claim to be the ally of 'moderate' Islam is a brand of 'religious pluralism' which allows into the pack certain forms of religion that conform to a particular world view. Comparisons are made between religions by invoking a 'correspondence theory' of truth in which the superior religion is the one least free of error as determined from the standpoint of a particular religious viewpoint. Thus the pack can be ordered without the unwelcome intrusion of cards from another sequence. Surin (1989) has pointed out that Lindberg's ideas have at least furnished us with 'the rudiments of a theory which eschews the correctly fashionable ideology of 'religious pluralism'.[14]

Gavin D'Costa (2000) goes even further than the notion of a 'correctly fashionable ideology' and argues that there is a 'god of modernity' hidden within correct notions of religious pluralism.[15] He points out that figures from various religious traditions such John Hick, Radhakrishnan and the Dalai Lama are welcomed in the West as they posit forms of religion that are acceptable to the liberal/secular worldview. D'Costa states that the inevitable conclusion of such pluralism is the formation of another party which invites disputants to actually leave their parties and join the pluralist one.[16] He argues that inter-religious harmony will thus have been attained but that no religion would be left except liberal modernity espousing a unitarian, deistic, or agnostic deity.[17]

Following this logic, the liberal/secular worldview is not as pluralist as it appears. It is indeed another form of absolutism in which such pluralists usually differentiate between corrupt or pathological forms of religion and major world religions as long as an essential core is defined that fits the liberal/secular worldview's own grand narrative. Muslims looking on might well be convinced that the secular/liberal worldview contains an iron hand inside a soft glove as they watch the bombs drop on Afghanistan and Iraq and the conditions of the prisoners held in the camps on Cuba, and see that being a moderate Muslim is simply defined as sharing the world view of the powerful.

Although both the US and British governments have attempted to downplay the idea of a 'clash of civilizations',[18] preferring to make the distinction between pathological terrorists and a moderate majority in the Muslim world who are deemed to agree with the worldview of western liberalism, from the perspective of millions of Muslims this dichotomy is too simplistic. Above all the divine attributes, the Qur'an emphasises justice, and it is here in this world that Allah's final people of revelation struggle for social justice, even if its perfect and ultimate resolution is in the next. Since the early days of persecution by the wealthy of Makkah, Muslims have perceived their religion as a voice for the poor and oppressed. Seen from the perspective of social justice, it is not a dichotomy of views, but a pyramid in which a broad base yearns for fair treatment and justice from the hands of the powerful and an apex is prepared to struggle for such justice through armed conflict.

Madeleine Bunting, *The Guardian's* religion correspondent has noted that 'liberals are guilty of an often polite but pervasive distaste for Islam (reminiscent of English anti-Semitism) in which Muslims find credence for a clash of civilisation theories'.[19] I cannot agree that this has parallels with English anti-Semitism, as there is a lack of a religious dimension and rather a more overt racism based on ethnic identity in this case. Although ethnicity may be a problem in racist attacks on Muslim minorities, the liberal critique of Islam is proffered up by those who generally abhor racism and is part of the secular world's deep suspicion of serious religious commitment, especially where it is combined with the 'fundamentalist' thrust to bring religion back to the public as well as the private sphere.

The perceived suspicion of religion by secular liberals helps to define and fuel a confident Muslim identity both in Muslim majority nations and where Muslims live as a minority in western nations. Both the liberal school of thought and devout Muslims have believed in a linear progress, the former through the means of technological, educational and economic advances and the latter through the unfolding final victory of God. Both have believed in social justice and the advancement of conditions for the world's downtrodden but the reality must be faced by the school of liberal thought which believes in social progress, that the market economy has failed to deliver either social or political equality across the globe, and it is this very imbalance that has contributed to the increase of radical religious solutions, violence and instability.

Madeleine Bunting argues that for this reason the world is experiencing a powerful but grotesque re-emergence of religion in a modern distorted form,[20] but in the case of Islam, the modern versions of violent dissent against perceived injustices, and the failure of the Muslim world to embrace the religion in the form that the Prophet was supposed to have exemplified and his companions imitated, has existed since the very beginning of the faith. Contemporary manifestations may throw up very modern dilemmas where Abu Hamza, a vociferous critic of the West and open supporter of Osama Bin Laden, is defended by the Islamic Human Rights Commission for his right to express his views and be permitted to use the Finsbury Park mosque from which he has been denied entry. The Chair of the Commission, although disagreeing with Abu Hamza's stance, supports his right to freedom of speech and perceives double standards at work when rabbis in Britain are allowed to make statements in support of Israel without criticism.[21]

Modernity and religion

These apparent contradictions are part and parcel of what Peter Cox defines as 'the problem of forging emancipatory discourses in the post-colonial and post-modern context'.[22] Modernity sees itself as such an emancipatory discourse but not all Muslims would agree. Modernism has borrowed from old religious providence models of human evolution to posit the ideal of progress in which the process of emancipation within liberal secular societies has been viewed in terms of entry into the value world of modernity itself. In this model of social evolution, pre-modern conditions that include allegiance to God-centred worldviews are seen as binding or even enslaving the human being. A reductionist discourse from the social sciences is drawn upon to establish religious worldviews as existing in a

Durkheimian sense to maintain and control social systems in some form of absolutist and homogenous hegemony which conflicts with relativism and liberal pluralism.

Much of twentieth and twenty-first century Islamic revival has to be seen as a response to colonial and post-colonial discourse and conditions. Rist (1997) has argued that one of the justifications for colonialism was the objective of taming and educating the savage into the 'civilised' culture of the coloniser;[23] in return the colonised nation was offered the reward of entry into democratic citizenship given by birthright to Western liberal societies.[24] Many Muslims have felt that emancipation from the colonial project involved the loss of the world of enchantment as embodied in societies whose allegiance was to the supranatural. Tradition too came to be regarded as anachronistic. Cox argues that the appeal of nationalism 'arises in a void left by the banishment of enchantment from emancipation'. By the same token, fundamentalism or radical religious/political solutions occur to reclaim God's world from both nationalism and secular discourse.

If there is an element of post-colonial discourse and an innate sense of the superiority of the modernist project in the western powers dealing with the Muslim world then the challenge for those who call upon moderate Muslims to reject violent forms of emancipatory discourse is to provide an entry into the globalised market that restores economic parity and to look at political solutions which undermine the balance of power that remains with the former colonial powers. Muslims need to feel that they are not being invited to participate, either as members of the world's nation states or as minorities within secular liberal democracies, merely as poor relations who are only accepted if they surrender their worldview or risk being regarded as an embarrassment who serve to remind the 'emancipated' of once 'how they used to be' before enlightenment and progress were achieved.[25]

These debates over freedom of speech, the freedom of the individual and the law of God first emerged seriously amongst Muslim minorities at the time of the publication of *The Satanic Verses* by Salman Rushdie. At this time, young Muslims in Britain found a political expression that was independent of the mosque but asserted a voice of dissent that borrowed its worldview from the Qur'an and the Prophet of Islam rather than western secular liberal values. In doing so, some of them discovered that there were voices in the Muslim world that shouted more vociferously, sometimes with the rifle and the bomb, but the message was the same. The world's injustices cannot be put right until Muslims themselves live according to the laws of God, and western attempts at social justice through democracy are doomed to failure since they do not constitute part of a revelation that insists upon God's sovereignty.

The voices of militant Islam are as much a radical cry against perceived political and social injustices as they are religious movements. The attempt by politicians such as the US Secretary of State to link all such movements to al-Qa'eda is naïve as it neglects the historical and contemporary reality of Muslim militancy. The struggle is not going to be between western democracies led by the USA and Britain against a single pathological movement. Since the second half of the twentieth century such movements have manifested throughout the Muslim world attempting to reform or overturn their own governments through the revival of Islam. As stated by Jason Burke, all were committed to a holy struggle, by both peaceful and sometimes violent means, to transform their societies through the implementation of Islam modelled on the life of Muhammad and the Qur'anic revelation.[26] Gradually their attitudes towards the West have shifted towards perceiving the USA as leading a Crusader-Zionist alliance against Islam. Britain and the USA are not fighting a single enemy but are struggling against a political religion whose goals strike a chord with millions of Muslims, especially those alienated by social injustice and poverty or who are on the receiving end of the policies of harsh and corrupt regimes seen to be supported by western powers. The Qur'an's dichotomy of evil versus good goes right back to a titanic struggle between God himself and Shaitan (Satan), the *djinn* who would not submit to divine authority. This struggle between good and evil will only end just prior to the time of final judgement when the world will embrace Islam and the *Shaitan* will be defeated. Western governments would be advised to tread with care in trying to resolve problems with the Muslim world. Alongside any attempts to defeat Islamic radicalism must be major concessions that help to remove perceptions of social injustice. Failure to do this will surely create a new generation of radical Muslim dissent convinced that 'Manifest Success' can only be achieved by religious revival manifested in the realm of ideology. Increasingly, 'moderate Islam' may stand in danger of being perceived as no Islam at all.

On the other hand, Peter Cox argues that many contemporary emancipation projects recognise that 'the re-enchantment and re-spiritualisation of the world, both of human and non-human nature' needs to be re-created; 'not as an irrelevancy to the emancipatory project, but as part of very process of re-establishing liberty'.[27] Muslims who participated in February 2003 at the largest peace demonstration ever held in Britain in opposition to war with Iraq found themselves in strange company but the result may be a realisation that there are others who want to re-sacralise the world without recourse to radical fundamentalisms. However, the voice of 'moderation' may still be radically opposed to the absolutism inherent in the liberal philosophy and politics of the powerful. The old divisions of *Dar al-Harb* and *Dar al-Islam* may need to be reinterpreted or radically revisited in order for Muslims to fully participate in twenty-first century emancipatory discourses and struggles, especially when so many millions of Muslims now live in Western pluralist societies.

Jeremy Henzell-Thomas writes that 'a closed, exclusive, puritanical, hostile, and inward-looking version of Islam, which regards all non-Muslims as enemies and infidels and refuses to engage with the rest of humankind, corresponds with no period of greatness in Islam and will bring none'.[28] However, as a Muslim convert, Henzell-Thomas pleads for Muslims to commit themselves to the project of establishing a just and fair 'new world order' through full engagement. Yet he argues that engagement with a pluralist worldview must be more than tolerance consisting of 'a passive form of hostility' or 'a shaky truth'. He borrows from the work of Diane Eck who warns of the dangers of confusing relativism with pluralism and asserts that the challenge for pluralist societies is 'to create the space and the means for the encounter of commitments, not to neutralise all commitment', for 'unless all of us can encounter one another's conceptual, cultural, religious and spiritual expressions and understand them through dialogue, both critically and self-critically, we cannot begin to live with maturity and integrity in the world-house'.[29]

Conclusion

The situation in the 'world-house' is too critical for powerful western politicians to be using rhetoric to convince us of the integrity of their foreign policies post-9/11. The populace is becoming aware of the difference between linguistic manipulation for self-serving motivations and genuine discussion and dialogue. Although there are serious voices both within and without Islam who consider that religious discourse has lagged behind secular humanistic discourse on major issues such as human rights, political participation, environmental issues, women's rights and social justice, these are too important to be hijacked as part of a political dichotomy between secular 'relativists' and religious 'absolutists' crudely occupying the oppositional camps of the colonists and colonised in this post-colonial world.

Muslims need to feel confident that they can engage with the above issues without surrendering their own worldview that embraces the absolute and the immutable truths provided by revelation and joining an emancipatory discourse that does not view them as equal partners or even worse, demands that they join the voices of powerful elites and surrender their own enchanted world in order to be accepted as participants in dialogue in regard to humanistic discourse.

Whilst many Muslims feel that they are unequal participants of a world order that maintains the 'hegemony of Eurocentric culture' in which economic, social, political and ideological inequalities are not addressed, they will continue to remain disaffected and alienated. Islamicisation throughout the Muslim world and among Muslim minorities need not be a call to political radicalism and *jihad*, but rather an affirmation of faith, but as one British Muslim representative of the Islamic Foundation stated to me, as long as Western governments engage in wars with Muslim nations or fail to consider solutions for injustices against Muslim people, as a moderate Muslim with deep loyalties to Britain, he observes increasing numbers of Muslim youth enter the camp of the extremists and he has no argument but silence to use against them.

Notes

[1] Esposito, John (1988) *Islam-The Straight Path*. Oxford: Oxford University Press, pp.126-127 and pp.170-172.

[2] Said, Edward (1978) *Orientalism*. Harmondsworth: Penguin

[3] Sardar, Ziauddin (1990) *Distorted Imagination: Lessons from the Rushdie Affair*. London: Grey Seal, p.3.

[4] Ernst, Carl (1997) *The Shambhala Guide to Sufism.* Boston: Shambhala Publications, pp. 208-209.
[5] Ibid., pp.209-210.
[6] Ibid., p.209.
[7] Lindbeck, George (1984) *The Nature of Doctrine: Religion and Theology in a Post-Liberal Age.* London: SPCK, p.9.
[8] Ibid., p.32.
[9] Ibid., p.34.
[10] Ibid., p.40.
[11] Ibid., p.41.
[12] Ibid., p.49.
[13] Ibid., p.54.
[14] Surin, Kenneth, (1989) *The Turnings of Darkness and Light.* Cambridge University Press, p.179.
[15] D'Costa, Gavin (2000) *The Meeting of Religions and the Trinity.* Edinburgh: T & T Clark.
[16] Ibid., p.20.
[17] Ibid., p21.
[18] Huntingdon, Samuel (1996) *The Clash of Civilizations and the Remaking of the World Order.* New York: Simon & Schuster.
[19] Bunting, Madeleine (20 January 2003) 'The Fight for Tolerance', *The Guardian,* p.17.
[20] Ibid.
[21] Dodd, Vikram (18 January 2003) 'Controversial cleric vows to defy mosque ban', *The Guardian.* p.4.
[22] Cox, Peter (2002) 'Re-enchanting Emancipation'. An unpublished paper given to the Social Studies Research Seminar, Chester College, p.1.
[23] Rist, Gilbert (1997) *The History of Development: From Western Origins to Global Faith.* London: Zed Books.
[24] Mies, Maria (1996) 'The French Revolution cannot take place for women' in Sheth, D.L. and Nandy, A. (eds) *The Multiverse of Democracy: Essays in Honour of Rajni Kothari*: New Delhi: Sage, pp.168-182.
[25] Eder, Klaus (1993) *The New Politics of Class: Social Movements and Cultural Dynamics in Advanced Societies.* London: Sage, ch.7.
[26] Burke, Jason (9 February 2003) 'First Casualties in the Propaganda Firefight', *The Guardian,* p.17.
[27] Cox, Peter, op.cit. p.7.
[28] Henzell-Thomas, Jeremy (2002) *The Challenge of Pluralism and the Middle Way of Islam,* Occasional Paper Series, The Association of Muslim Social Scientists, p.18.
[29] Eck, Diane (1993) *Encountering God.* Boston: Beacon Press, pp.195-196.

PART II
The Case Studies

Chapter 6

The Evolution of American Muslim Responses to 9/11

Marcia Hermansen

The lives of American Muslims will never be the same after the events of 9/11. The dramatic and tragic events sent a shock wave through diverse communities of Muslims living in the United States. Elements of individual and communal identity were destabilised and accented in the wake of the terrorist attacks including racial categories, concepts of citizenship, and ideologies about Islam. In particular, American Muslims, whether immigrants, Euro-American or African-American converts, were shocked and surprised to find cultural tensions that they may have already experienced in the Muslim community embodied and exaggerated in reaction to the events.

In the aftermath, suddenly those American Muslims who were perceived to be articulate or to have some expertise in religious knowledge were constantly called upon to 'be present' at interfaith vigils, prayer services and so on – in order to demonstrate their sympathy and inclusion in the American fabric. As time went on these individuals were further enjoined to speak, explain, comment, and analyse. The government and the media coalesced in seeking out Muslim representatives, and this was the rub. Who speaks for Islam? One British scholar described this quest for Muslim spokespersons as the search for 'a new stereotype, an acceptable Other, a liberal Muslim that can be manipulated and domesticated'.[1] In America the issue was often one of image and representation. Requirements of being visibly Muslim and of signalling both American and Muslim identity simultaneously came down to the level of TV hosts seeking out soccer moms in *hijabs*, brown folk who spoke good English, and so on. This by the way, often excluded American converts who were either too black, too white, or too liberal to fit the image requirements.

Among advice offered to American Muslims, the American scholar of Islam, John Esposito, suggested they had to put forth more women and young people speaking accent-free American English in order to articulate their community's message. 'Unless you tap the next generation, you are not going to make it through the next few months', he said, suggesting that by using representatives who speak English as Americans do, Muslims would avoid appearing as though they were a predominantly foreign group.[2]

Since this chapter is about the ongoing evolution of American Muslim responses to 9/11, it is necessarily a commentary upon commentaries. I will try to provide some sense of order to this material by isolating certain prominent themes as an aid to better understanding the voices that are speaking and why they are being called to speak regarding these issues. I will consider these responses of American Muslims chronologically as well as with regard to the speakers and their perspectives.

9/11 was such a major event for Americans that public culture as a whole shifted. Some of the impact on American Muslims, in particular academics, intellectuals, and activists, was part and parcel of this broader social and historical watershed.[3] For example, the focus on public intellectuals, the polarisation of the ideological left and right, and the exacerbated tensions across racial and ethnic lines all affected Muslims at the same time as they were impacting broader public culture in the USA.

The initial arena of response was overwhelmingly in the media. For days, everyone was glued to the television. An analyst of British media commented that in the UK there was a shift over time in media representation and commentary about 9/11. This developed from an initial concern with maintaining order and being sensitive and civil, to analysing the threat within, and ultimately to cracking down on extremists through surveillance of immigrants.[4] In the United States one may trace a similar trajectory, with a heightened intensity due to the facts that the attacks occurred on American soil.

The first memories of American Muslim responses for me are personal and anecdotal, followed by television and print commentaries, then later op-ed Internet articles. As I prepared this chapter about two and a half years after the event, the most recent development is the growing number of books and articles by American Muslims who continue to discuss issues impacting them in the shadow of the attacks, thereby providing us a sense of a continuing process of reflection and analysis. In the chapter I will present some major themes of the responses in this same chronological order.

Personal

Many American Muslims probably remember the initial first shock of the attacks followed by dread and fear of backlash. Some American Muslims of Indian background, whom I know, expected communal riots to break out where their homes and businesses would be burned in retaliation. While too many isolated incidents of violence occurred, I think most Americans demonstrated civility and restraint. As a white American Muslim, the most disturbing reaction for me was that of individual immigrant Muslims I knew who expressed a sense of happiness and smug vindication about the attacks. Other American convert Muslims and some of my fellow academics who teach Islamic Studies at university level experienced this and it festered like an ugly secret. No one would talk about it to the media or outsiders because of the fear that it could cause further backlash against the vast majority of Muslim Americans who were innocent of such thoughts and appalled by the violence.[5]

The next several months passed in a horrible nightmare, filled with apprehension, confusion, and a sense of disassociation. The brief hope that somehow we (the USA) would transcend the impulse to revenge, or 'bomb them with butter' – as an e-mail that made the rounds at that time, proposed[6] – was shattered, initially by the bombing campaign on Afghanistan, and later by the invasion of Iraq.

Initial Themes: Language, Terminology and the Rise of the Muslim Public Intellectual

Language

Among the themes that I find significant among early responses to the terrorist attacks is a heightened sensitivity to language and terminology, evident in discussions regarding the origin, true meaning, misuse, and manipulation of terms, especially those with religious resonance. A notable example was a flurry of concern over President Bush's ill-conceived employment of the terms 'crusade' and 'infinite justice' in his early speeches. The prominent American Muslim teacher Hamza Yusuf Hanson, in a CBC radio interview on September 23, 2001 talked about his September 20 private meeting with President Bush and five other religious leaders. He told the President that 'Infinite Justice' was a poor choice of name for the American military operation against terrorism, and that 'crusade' would evoke similarly negative reactions among Muslims. The President told him that 'the Pentagon doesn't have theologians and they're the ones that name these things', and he said the name would be changed.[7]

A case of contested definition of terms arose from the assertion by some Muslim respondents and their sympathisers that 'Islam means peace'. This, of course, is too simplistic; while the Arabic root (s-l-m) does convey a concept of peace or acceptance, it is *salam*, not Islam, that literally means 'peace'. The 'correctors' in the media and elsewhere objected to what seemed to be a disingenuous blurring of terms on the part of Muslims. Another turn of phrase that became commonplace was 'hijacking Islam' coupled with the formulation that Islam must be recovered or 'taken back'. Karen Armstrong, a well-known writer on religion, invoked 'the true, peaceful face of Islam' and advised that 'the vast majority of Muslims, who are horrified by the atrocity of Sept. 11, must reclaim their faith from those who have so violently hijacked it'.[8] *The Economist* headlined a piece 'The need to speak up,' calling for moderate Muslims in the West to deplore and repudiate people 'explaining and even trying to justify the [Sept. 11] crimes'.[9] In 2002, Michael Wolfe, an American Muslim discussed later in this paper, edited a collection entitled, *Taking Back Islam: American Muslims Reclaim their Faith.*[10]

In fact, both Muslim and non-Muslim commentators sometimes hesitated or stumbled on words or ideas that had now taken on other connotations. A long exchange over the word '*jihad*' occurred, with its already inflammatory connotation of 'holy war' often coming to the fore. For example, a devout Muslim

American student, Zayed Yasin, who was selected as Harvard valedictorian in spring 2002 entitled his speech, 'My American *jihad*', playing on the religious meaning of '*jihad*' as struggle in the name of God. 'First, I wanted to talk about the unity between Islamic and American values,' Yasin said. 'I also wanted to try to reclaim the word 'jihad' from the way it's been misused and abused.'[11] This title, in turn, was considered inflammatory by those who could only respond to the militant associations with the term '*jihad*'.

In another instance of the delicate balance between explaining and justifying while grasping for meanings behind explicit words, is illustrated by my experience at an interfaith meeting. I, along with other Muslims, was addressing a predominantly Christian audience. One woman in the audience kept asking another of the Muslim panellists how she felt about the attacks. The Muslim presenter kept recounting examples of the failures of American foreign policy. Finally, sensing the increasing agitation of the questioner I intervened and said the attacks were a terrible and evil thing. This was what the woman really needed to hear, and it seemed difficult for some Muslims to get the point and directly address the real question on people's minds. Explanations for the attacks could not be heard until a speaker's own position on the events was clarified.

An odd confusion that is still present is an American Muslim response that tries to find the 'silver-lining' in the events of 9/11, in terms of 'Oh, now Americans are interested in Islam' or 'reading the Qur'an'. Such an attitude bespeaks an insularity and misreading of the current climate that is truly disturbing and does not augur well for the future of such Muslims in America.

The Rise of the Muslim Public Intellectual

Islam, despite its associations with other crises and conflicts of national and international scope, had never been of such interest to the American public. All of the major television networks mounted specials on the Islamic religion[12] usually at the expense of reviewing the more relevant recent political history of Muslim societies and American engagement with them. Established intellectuals as well as new voices, both Muslim and non-Muslim, appeared in the public arena in the aftermath of the attacks, along with the familiar experts on terrorism. One prominent commentator was the novelist Salman Rushdie situating himself as a New Yorker, who contributed an essay entitled, 'Yes, this is about Islam.'[13]

> The restoration of religion to the sphere of the personal, its depoliticization,is the nettle that all Muslim societies must grasp in order to become modern ... If terrorism is to be defeated, the world of Islam must take on board the secularist-humanist principles on which the modern is based, and without which Muslim countries' freedom will remain a distant dream.

One thread of such interventions was that Muslims must liberalize and modernize. Another was 'What went wrong?' the title of a book by the noted historian, Bernard Lewis, considered by American Muslims to be not only an academic critic of Islam, but a voice ideologically inimical to Muslims and particularly identified with support for Israel. In fact, the elephant in the room, or perhaps one should imagine many elephants in various corners of the American psyche – that made its presence felt in many interventions was the spectre of the Israeli-Palestinian conflict. 'Yes, this is about Palestine' (liberals and Muslim sympathizers) vs. 'No, this is not about Palestine' by anti-Muslim, neo conservative, and pro-Zionist commentators. It couldn't be about Palestine, for them, because that would mean that something should be done to equitably resolve a dispute that might threaten American interests and lives. As intellectuals of various backgrounds took up positions on the left/right continuum, conservatives often used the attacks to define a new sort of 'patriotism' that would caricature liberals or immigrants as being at best soft on terrorist threats and at worst a threat to national interests.

Due to the intensity of the issues involved, various strands of the identities and positions of public intellectuals were engaged at numerous levels. One example that comes to mind is a review by the late Palestinian-American literary critic, Edward Said, that addressed the two books, Bernard Lewis', *What went wrong?* and Karen Armstrong's, *Islam: A Short History*. In the review Edward Said criticized Karen Armstrong for orientalizing her subject,[14] stating that she, like Bernard Lewis, 'frequently suggests great distance and dehumanization rather than closeness to the experience of Islam in all its tremendous variety.' The point that I wish to make here is that as a progressive Said was troubled by shared aspects in the views of each of these disparate authors, despite the fact that their political positions and receptions in the Muslim community are diametrically opposed. Some of the newer 'Muslim' public intellectual voices that were heard will be treated in the next section.

Second Phase: Progressive Islam, 'Good' Muslim/ 'Bad' Muslim

Progressive Islam: Mandela, Martin Luther, or the Mahdi - who are Muslims waiting for?

The creation of a 'progressive' Muslim theology seemed to be a desideratum within at least some segments of the media that searched out Muslim spokespersons who might simultaneously convey authentic Muslim identity and liberalism. An initial concern was defining the elements of this 'progressive Islam'. The liberal and non-sectarian religion website, *Beliefnet*, presented the following checklist:

Six Tenets of Reformist/Progressive Islam

- Gender equality
- Mosque and State separation
- Non-literal Qur'anic interpretation
- Interfaith dialogue
- Embracing modernity
- Emphasis on the arts[15]

Several of these 'progressive' themes were addressed in commentary after the attacks. For example, a national public radio program featured music and poetry from the Muslim world to counter, or at least to complicate, the prevailing emphasis on harsh political commentary on Muslims and Islam. Even the austere discourse of Muslim student associations was moderated on some campuses by Muslim students who heeded the call to mount poetry readings rather than the usual sermons and convert testimonial panels. Gender equality was a theme that also began to receive a broader hearing in the community. A number of reports by Muslim women about how poorly they were treated at mosques circulated within Muslim discussion groups and in Muslim publications. The 'visibility' of Muslim women who retained their headscarves despite the risk of being insulted or even assaulted, created a permanent shift in the perceptions of Muslim males as protectors. For example, Muslim male students on campuses offered to walk 'sisters' home from late night studies, but it was clear that many times females faced the new challenges alone, and therefore garnered a new independence and respect.

In terms of interfaith, an astounding and unexpected grassroots outpouring of sympathy and support for Muslim organisations and mosques, coupled with an overwhelming response by local churches and in some cases, synagogues, offering support and scheduling inter-faith programs, left many Muslim conservatives non-plussed. Some spoke of a change of heart at recognising the essential "goodness" of non-Muslim neighbours. As time passes, however, this interest in Muslims has waned, and the flurry of interfaith events, vigils, and Muslim guest speakers has settled down.

Attempts to create liberal or progressive Muslim institutions have not yet born fruit although a conference was held in 2003 in Washington, and the first Saturday of every month is being designated as a 'meet-up day' for aspiring progressives to sign up on line and organise at the grass roots level in various cities.[16] An example of academic work by American Muslim scholars responding to 9/11 is the volume of papers edited by Omid Safi, entitled *Progressive Muslims: On Justice, Gender and Pluralism* that offers theological, legal, and cultural positions on such topics largely from a liberal academic viewpoint.[17] The aftermath of 9/11 has inspired a burgeoning internal Muslim critique of established cultural and religious attitudes and practices. These range from the academic progressive Muslims of the Safi collection, to a more populist genre of what it's like to be Muslim in America (Michael Wolfe and Gul Hasan), to a 'why I don't like Islam anymore' (Ibn Warraq and Irshad Manji).[18]

Along with the quest for a liberal or progressive Islamic theology, and its spokespersons, calls for a reform movement headed by someone with moral authority and political weight in the Muslim world, a Muslim Mandela, if you will, went unanswered. For Muslim liberals, invoking universal norms of human rights and gender justice seemed more urgent in the wake of further egregious examples of misguided literalism as in the case of the Saudi school girls who were burned to death because conservative police would not let them run from their school without head coverings.

Explicit parallels to the Protestant reformation within contemporary Islam, in terms of a democratisation of authority and expansion of literacy were often taken up in academic or popular discourse, for example, in Dale Eickleman's article, 'Who Speaks for Islam: Inside the Islamic Reformation'.[19] Eickleman contends that broader social changes such as mass literacy, greater personal autonomy, and new media globalisation will contribute to a 'democratisation' of religious authority in an expanded public sphere. In other contexts specific Muslim intellectuals such as Iran's Abdol Karim Soroosh or Europe's Tariq Ramadan were designated as 'Muslim Martin Luthers'. At times this image was paired with the notion of a 'crisis of authority' in Islam. Some non-Muslim commentators suggested that a Pope might be the answer, rather than a Luther, or at least a 'Muslim Vatican II'. On the other hand, conservative Muslims deplored the attention being paid to the new liberal voices, in one case terming them the 'neo-mods' of the community who have caved in to secularist pressures.[20]

I propose the final term 'mahdi' not only for the sake of alliteration but also as a reminder that millenarianism is the tendency of some of the more radical Islamic groups. Those who clamour for the restoration of the Caliphate such as the members of Hizb al-Tahrir might also see the solution to the problems of Muslims in reinstating a Caliph's papal-type authority.

Good Muslim /Bad Muslim[21]

The assertion that one could be American and Muslim at the same time took on a stronger urgency as the definition of a 'loyal' American in the larger culture now entailed a new sense of solidarity that seemed to exclude foreigners. The media quest to surface 'the good Muslims' or 'the moderate Muslims' brought to a fore an interesting assortment of American Muslim commentators, often, but not always, liberal.

The 'Good' Muslims

Karen Leonard, in her essay on American Muslims after 9/11, comments on the fact that many of the new, moderate, American Muslim voices were those of persons who were not part of the formal networks of Islamic organisations.[22] Most of these latter organisations and the mosques affiliated with them were influenced by political Islam and conservative identity politics. The 'moderate' voices, on the other hand, tended to come from academia or from the convert community. I will briefly discuss several 'good' Muslim voices given media prominence after 9/11: Muqtedar Khan, Khaled Abou El-Fadl, Shaykh Hisham Kabbani, Hamza Yusuf Hanson, and Michael Wolfe.

M.A. Muqtedar Khan, a young Indian-origin Ph.D. in Political Science from Georgetown, had been known for his enthusiastic 'modern' view. While still a student he had developed a reputation as 'the Cyberspace Mufti'. A self-described 'more liberal voice', he gave advice that was no doubt controversial among more traditionally-trained *fiqh* specialists.[23] After 9/11 Khan wrote a forceful essay and posted it on his website; 'A Memo to American Muslims' was immediately circulated by email, quoted in newspaper editorials, and reprinted in many venues:[24]

> Muslims love to live in the U.S. but also love to hate it ... As an Indian Muslim I know for sure that nowhere on earth, including India, will I get the same sense of dignity and respect that I have received in the US ... If ... Sept. 11 had happened in India, the biggest democracy, thousands of Muslims would have been slaughtered in riots on mere suspicion and there would be another slaughter after confirmation. But in the U.S., bigotry and xenophobia has been kept in check by media and leaders ... It is time that we acknowledge that the freedoms we enjoy in the U.S. are more desirable to us than superficial solidarity with the Muslim world. If you disagree then prove it by packing your bags and going to whichever Muslim country you identify with ... It is our responsibility to prevent people from abusing Islam. It is our job to ensure that Islam is not misrepresented.

Khan's voice was clearly breaking from the immigrant Muslim consensus in the USA with its prevalent exhortations for solidarity with the world's oppressed Muslims being a major theme of popular discourse in sermons, meetings, and conversations. The Muslim voice raised with the call, America, love it or leave it, was something new and signalled a growing rift over where ultimate loyalties lay. In 2002 he published a book, *American Muslims: Bridging Faith and Freedom,*[25] discussing social and political developments in the American Muslim community and its response to the attacks on America.

Khaled Abou El Fadl, who holds a Chair in Islamic Law at the University of California, Los Angeles, had been a featured columnist for *The Minaret,* a magazine issued from the relatively liberal Islamic Center of Southern California in Los Angeles.[26] El Fadl was known for his independent views, particularly about women in Islam.[27] Coincidentally, he had published a piece entitled 'Terrorism is at Odds With Islamic Tradition' in the *Los Angeles Times* on August 22, 2001.[28] After 9/11, he became a prominent Muslim voice, appearing on CNN, and writing powerful indictments of Muslim leadership.[29] Trained in both Islamic and American law (at Cairo's Al-Azhar, the University of Pennsylvania, Yale, and Princeton), Abou El Fadl analysed the current situation as arising from the 'crumbling of the Islamic civilization [that] has removed the established institutions to seriously challenge the extremists'. Characterising extremist theology as 'a combustible brew of puritanism, ethical and moral irresponsibility and rampant apologetics' in a series of articles and books he demonstrates the intellectual stranglehold of authoritarianism in Muslim legal and theological reasoning and attitudes.[30] Long a critic of the science-trained new spokesmen for American Muslims,[31] known by some as the 'professional' Muslims, Abou El Fadl was admiringly profiled in January, 2002, in the *Los Angeles Times.*[32]

Abou El Fadl emerged as a media personality after 9/11 and also received death threats due to his outspoken liberalism and critique of the terrorists and extremist legal positions. He offers some of the more sophisticated legal and philosophical analysis of the position in which Muslim moderates find themselves.

One theme of his analysis is the critique of authoritarian and rigid interpretations of Islamic law. His calls for a new interpretation consonant with universal philosophical ideals of goodness and beauty, while resonant with an American audience or liberal Muslims, have been criticised by others as compromising Islamic authenticity and jettisoning the classical process of legal reasoning so as to conform to the dominant liberal (white) cultural norms.[33] Shaykh Muhammad Hisham Kabbani is son-in-law and American representative (*khalifa*) of Shaykh Nazim, a Cypriot Naqshbandi Sufi with a worldwide following. Originally from Lebanon, Kabbani arrived in the United States in 1991 and rapidly tried to establish a position on the American Muslim scene. When his overtures were rebuffed by the conservative, and anti-Sufi Muslim organisations, Kabbani turned his attention to winning friends in the American political establishment in Washington.

Aspects of Shaykh Nazim's and Shaykh Hisham's[34] teachings include a millenarianism, apparently handed down from his teacher, Abdullah Daghestani. Earlier lectures of Shaykh Nazim often referred to the anticipation of the coming of the Mahdi.[35] The approach of the Y2K period had the Shaykh encouraging his followers to adopt survivalist measures in the face of anticipated disruptions of basic services in urban areas.[36] Shaykh Kabbani has been very active in publishing, for example his hagiographic work on the Order[37] and a seven volume set compiling traditional Muslim arguments in support of Sufism.[38] His movement became heavily embroiled in debating certain elements of the American Muslim community, often termed Salafis[39] or Wahhabis, who are doctrinally conservative and explicitly anti-Sufi. After 9/11 the image of the Wahhabi as a 'bad' Muslim spread well beyond the narrow confines of Sufi vs. literalist interpretations, to a broader association of Wahhabism with violence and extremism, positioning Shaykh Hisham at least in some quarters, as a moderate voice of American Islam, despite the fact that his movement was considered marginal by the majority of American Muslims.

The climactic event in the polarisation of the Naqshbandi-Haqqanis and the conservative mainstream Islamic organisations had been a State Department briefing in 1999 at which Shaykh Hisham categorized the majority of American Islamic Centres as espousing extremist ideologies – 'the ideology of extremism has spread to eighty percent of the (American) Muslim population'.[40] This allegation in turn led to a condemnatory statement issued on the part of a number of mainstream Muslim organisations including Islamic Society of North America, Islamic Circle of North America, American Muslim Council, Muslim Students Association, and the Warith Deen Muhammad group.[41] In a subsequent interview, Shaykh Hisham attempted to explain his statements but still continued to offer specific criticism of a number of Muslim organisations for collecting funds in the name of charity and sending them to the Middle East for political ends.[42] This issue emerged in the public sphere after 9/11 with the arrests and freezing of assets of numerous America-based Islamic charities such as Benevolence International and Global Relief due to accusations that they had supported terrorist organisations.

The Naqshbandi-Haqqanis had over time consciously developed an identity of being the 'good Muslims' in America; moderate, democratic, willing to participate in interfaith dialogue, meeting with the Clintons and sponsoring 'unity conferences' for Muslim leaders from various groups. An editorial by Shaykh Hisham in the *Muslim Magazine*, an organ of this organisation, characterises their position in some of the following ways – 'we should take the middle course and avoid extremes', and, 'We remain committed to our top priority of maintaining tolerant, open lines of communication with all.'[43]

After 9/11, however, Shaykh Kabbani was 'back in the spotlight as never before', appearing on CNN, the 'Today' show, MSNBC, national public radio and more, as 'the Muslim who dared to blow the whistle on his brethren.'[44] Kabbani seems now to spend more time in Washington lobbying than with his Sufi disciples. In one post-9/11 interview Kabbani reiterated his opposition to Wahhabism as a politically subversive interpretation of Islam, and equated it with the communist threat, thereby positioning it as the ultimate 'Other'.

> And in that ideology (Wahhabism), of course, people are going to be violent. Until today no one tried to stop that kind of ideology. It's equal to communist ideology, which America always came out against and fought.[45]

While Sufis have traditionally perceived Wahhabis as natural doctrinal opponents, the broader and more politically charged spectre of a Wahhabi political agenda and specific Saudi influence was explored in the American media in the aftermath of the attacks, and Saudi Arabia itself was increasingly portrayed as a problematic ally.

Hamza Yusuf, a white American convert to Islam had become a sort of culture hero among Western Muslim youth before 9/11.Yusuf's reputation and following arose from his skill at 'being more Muslim than the immigrant Muslims'. This is epitomised by his mastery of Arabic, often wearing traditional garb, and denunciation of decadent Western mores in the light of both classical Islamic sources and the discourse of modern Western academic scholarship on religion and critical theory, combined illustrations from popular culture. Hamza Yusuf was one of the Muslim 'leaders' called to the White House after the attacks and his public denunciations of the extremism of the hijackers and repudiation of some of his former positions left some more radical of his admirers disillusioned, for example accusing him of turning to the White House rather than the 'black house' (the Ka'ba).

His words about hijacking Islam (above) were repeatedly quoted and paraphrased and his views were welcomed by the President, the media, and the American public. In an interview published 16 September, 2001, Hamza Yusuf called the World Trade Center attackers:[46]

> ... enemies of Islam ... mass murderers, pure and simple ... I think that the Muslims – and I really feel this strongly – have to reject the discourse of anger. Because there is a lot of anger in the Muslim ... world about the oppressive conditions that many Muslims find themselves in ... we have to move to a higher moral ground, recognizing that the desire to blame others leads to anger and eventually to wrath, neither of which

are rungs on a spiritual ladder to God. It's times like these that we really need to become introspective.

At the same time Hamza Yusuf offered some explanation of the context, saying that what Americans were now feeling 'has been business as usual for Lebanese people, Palestinian people, Bosnian people'. When the reporter immediately asked about Israeli people, his answer was sympathetic: 'Certainly the fear element is there for Israeli people ... there are still a lot of Jewish people alive who remember the fear and terror of what happened in Europe ...' Answering the reporter's questions about the meanings of *jihad*, martyrdom, and suicide in Islam, Yusuf ended by saying, 'If there are any martyrs in this affair it would certainly be those brave fire fighters and police that went in there to save human lives and in that process lost their own.' His words resonated widely with the American public.[47]

Hamza Yusuf's call for antagonistic Muslims living in the West to go back where they came from brought a critical response from some Muslims of immigrant background born in the West who found Yusuf's 'love it or leave it' position to be implicitly racist.[48] This illustrates the exacerbation of divisions of American Muslims along racial lines where white American Muslims became increasingly distanced from Arab and South Asian Muslims in America.

Michael Wolfe is an American writer and a Caucasian convert to Islam. He first achieved public profile with a televised documentary on the *Hajj*, aired on the widely watched NBC television series, *Nightline* in 1997. At the time of the terrorist attacks Wolfe was well into preparing a full-length documentary on the life of the Prophet Muhammad that was independently financed by a grass-roots fundraising effort among American Muslims. This was ultimately shown nationwide on public broadcasting (PBS) affiliates in December 2002. By then the script of the documentary had been revised to include significant footage of American Muslims who were living their lives with the Prophet Muhammad as their inspiration, including a New York City firefighter. This program was generally well-received by the American public, although some right wing commentators objected that it was apologetic regarding some aspects of Islamic history, and that it portrayed Muslims and their Prophet in too favourable a light.

This leads me to another theme, the strong right wing Christian condemnation of Islam as a terrorist faith and the Prophet as a poor moral example by the likes of prominent evangelical clergy with political connections to the White House such as Jerry Falwell and Franklin Graham. While most liberals and convert Muslim in America probably saw this as insignificant ranting, for many immigrant Muslims and Muslims overseas such comments were seen as disturbing emblems of a new Crusader mentality emerging in the USA.

But back to Michael Wolfe, he remains a Muslim op-ed commentator on *BeliefNet* and *the American Muslim*, albeit rarely in mainstream print media. His volume *Taking Back Islam*, an attempt to rally liberal Western Muslims and their supporters in order to present a humane and accessible face of the religion, was widely distributed.

The 'Bad' Muslims

The 'Bad' Muslims are obviously the terrorists, but beyond this the association was subsequently broadened to encompass extremist, Wahhabi and even fundamentalist and conservative Muslims. The concept of supporting terrorism quickly became conflated with critiquing American foreign policy. The latest to be tarred by this brush being liberal academics who teach in Middle East studies programs (most of who are not Muslim but became guilty by association).

The campaign to define Wahhabi influence in the United States gathered steam in the media with the ambiguity of Saudi foreign and domestic policy being exposed and criticised. The small numbers of actual Saudis living in the United States and the vagueness of trying to characterise particular teachings in mosques and Islamic schools as 'Wahhabi' made identifying the purveyors of these tendencies problematic. The condemnatory gaze thus broadened to include Muslim conservatives, including most of the major organisations, charities, the Council for American Islamic Relations, and many Islamic schools, mosques, Muslim Student associations and so on. Muslim charities were among the more suspect elements and the directors of some were arrested and their assets frozen due to the problematic nature of their support for organisations with multiple objectives.

A deeper theoretical issue and broader basis for distrust was the issue of whether fundamentalism, due to its binary construction of the world, truth, and the other, was a stepping stone on the path to undertaking violent behaviour.

Third Phase: race, identity and reflections

Race and Identity

Sherman Jackson, an African American scholar of Islamic law and professor at the University of Michigan stated at a seminar I attended in 2002 that 'After Sept. 11th the door to American whiteness was closed to immigrant Muslims'. He meant that for Muslim immigrants from the Middle East or South Asia who had previously thought that by falling into the Caucasian category they would be able eventually to 'pass, a new distrust of the foreign and explicitly the Muslim would permanently exclude them from the American national consensus'.

This is an important observation highlighting the destabilisation of racial categories that affected everyone in America in specific and unique ways. Commentators tried to define by comparison the new collectively stigmatised role for Muslims. Muslim Americans found support in the Japanese community that strongly identified with the theme of 'guilty by association' that had led to the internment and seizure of assets of many loyal Japanese Americans during World War Two. The theme of being 'the enemy or alien within' was later portrayed in Muslims being the new 'Irish'[49] (in Britain) or even being like the 'gays' of 1980s America. The second comparison was made by Michael Wolfe in an op-ed piece, 'The New Angels in America' written after viewing Tony Kushner's famous play about Aids in the 80s broadcast on national television. Wolfe proposed that 'like gays in the 1980s, Muslims today are stigmatised based on the lethal outcome of behaviours practised by a few'.[50] In another article, Wolfe explicitly positions himself as a white, college-educated 50-something male who perceives that the social privilege normally accorded those elements of his identity eroding after becoming Muslim.[51]

After 9/11, white American Muslims were often seen as collaborators by both Muslim immigrants and the American public at large. On the part of Muslim immigrants, they were seen as being not Muslim enough because they generally found the terrorist attacks abhorrent and were willing to support the American political positions so as to avoid identification with some aspects of Muslim internationalist causes. On the other hand, due to a series of well-publicised cases of American converts to Islam who became traitors – beginning with the American Taliban, John Walker Lindh, and continuing with military figures turning on their comrades or being willing to co-operate with the enemy in other ways – the identity of the convert Muslim, white or black, became more suspect.[52] The ambivalence of being a 'white' American Muslim is illustrated by the perception by themselves and others that white converts are 'pet' Muslims of the immigrant community, at times spoiled and tokenised and at others 'domesticated', to be shown off and paraded around, but not taken very seriously.[53]

Michael Wolfe's statement that, 'Many Muslims suspect that Islam's traditional lands have less to teach us than they think' is very American, and at the same time discloses the ambivalence of 'American privilege' as 'white privilege', of expecting to lead and surpass. The assertion of the ISNA vice-president, Ingrid Mattson, also a Caucasian, that 'American Muslims (now) have a special obligation', in my opinion does not imply privilege of any particular race but suggests an emerging and significant, nationally and internationally, American Muslim identity, and of course, this is among the more contentious and contested issues. Muqtader Khan, an American Muslim of Indian background, agrees that American Muslims have a special 'manifest destiny', presenting their role as being potentially '*mujaddids*' for the community.[54] While the *mujaddid* is traditionally conceived of as a reformer who will arise at the beginning of every century, Khan argues that:

> by interpreting reality through Islamic lenses and simultaneously reinterpreting the sacred texts with a steady eye on contemporary conditions, the *mujaddids* systematically reduce the distance between text and time, between reason and revelation, between conscience and consciousness, between the here and the hereafter, and between values and politics'.[55]

Oddly, the only three examples of *mujaddids* he names are Khomeini, Syed Maududi, and Hassan al-Bannah, hardly the anticipated role models for progressive American Muslims.

The identity of being an 'American Muslim' became contested after the attacks. For example, one magazine, 'The American Muslim'[56] offering commentary on 9/11 and other American Muslim related topics re-emerged as a presence on the Internet as a response to the vacuum of non-Salafi discourse in the institutions of the Muslim community. Its editorial board and policies reflect the perspectives of American convert, Sufi, and/or liberal Muslims. At the same time the Muslim Brotherhood (*Ikhwan al-Muslimin*), a worldwide Islamist group, through their organisation in the USA known as the 'Muslim American Society', issued a glossy, expensively-produced magazine bearing the same name. However, the similarity ends with the name. The Islamist magazine displayed a truly inappropriate cover after the attacks with horror movie style lettering reading 'Sept. 11th', the main theme of the articles being 'isn't it wonderful the Muslim women in America are still wearing their *hijabs*'.[57] In my opinion, the name 'American Muslim' in this second case is a complete misnomer.

The difference in perceptions between 'indigenous' and immigrant Muslims is epitomised in an intellectual exchange wherein Sherman Jackson, an African-American scholar of classical Islamic law, critiqued a paper of Abou El Fadl.[58] This discloses some important ideological divisions among American Muslims. Jackson finds the claim that Islamic legal pronouncements should be evaluated and accepted or rejected on the basis of universals such as justice or beauty (a term often invoked by Abou el-Fadl) to be problematic. Abu El Fadl, according to Jackson, asserts universal norms as superseding the particular and regional flexibility of classical Islamic legal procedures and reasoning. Basically, Jackson states that Abou Fadl offers an essentialistic and idealistic perspective, since it does not reflect 'concrete social, political, or interpersonal contexts and is not grounded in cultural, historical, or even ideological perspectives but instead is reflective of a transcendent, "natural" order whose validity is obvious to everyone, save the stupid, the primitive, or the morally depraved'.[59] For Jackson, positions such as Abou El Fadl's lend credence to the efforts of liberal Muslims who were already declaring that the sacred law of Islam is out of step with modern sensibilities and needs to be brought into conformity with 'universally recognised' rights and obligations.[60]

Jackson resists the move to reconcile Islam with the dominant culture and positions himself as rejecting attempts to instate what is in fact the norms of 'whiteness' as establishing what is normative for everyone, thereby ensuring the 'domestication' of Islam whereby it forfeits the ability to challenge the dominant culture. Liberal and upwardly mobile immigrant Muslims are, according to Jackson, 'American Muslim romantics'. Jackson characterises this romanticism as a sort of 'chic, designer fundamentalism' appealing to tradition to make it appear liberal, whereas most classical jurists did prohibit music, most of the arts, and even the artistic embellishment of mosques.[61] At the same time, Jackson contends that classical Islamic legal tradition can accommodate and authenticate multiple interpretations.

The post-9/11 shift that Jackson points to is that throughout the twentieth-century, the understanding of Islam in the West upheld Middle Eastern ways as normative for all Muslims and the right to define 'Islamic' remained almost their exclusive prerogative. For Jackson, 9/11 brought Muslim émigrés to the West into the act of becoming authoritative spokespersons for tradition.[62]

Jackson's voice, speaking both as an intellectual and an activist, has often been raised to critique the humiliation and marginalisation of African-American Muslims on their own turf, as it were, with the arrival of the immigrant 'professional' Muslims post-1970. These newcomers to the American scene arrogated to themselves the right to define what was Islamically normative. This can be illustrated by an anecdote recounted by Jackson of how visiting Arab Muslims wanted males in an African-American congregation to be informed that they didn't know how to urinate properly.

Jackson seems to resist the shock of 9/11 as empowering liberal immigrant Muslims to become authorities who reject classical tradition in the name of universal ideals. He states:

> If the basic aim of the romantics is to disassociate themselves from the views and actions of extremists in the Muslim world, this can be done by simply declaring that Muslims in the West reject and disagree with these views and actions. There is no need to make categorical statements about these actions from the perspective of Islamic law.[63]

I think this exchange is very powerful in epitomising the divergences of opinion that exist, not only at the level of philosophy, but in terms of shifting social/racial locations. Muqtader Khan, after 9/11, interviewed a number of African-American Muslim intellectuals and found that they resented the lack of attention given to their voices and issues on the part of both immigrant Muslims and the American media and government portrayal of Islam.[64]

In fact, African-American Muslims were relatively overlooked by the media post-9/11, although Siraj Wahaj, *imam* of the Tawqa mosque in Brooklyn, New York, spoke out strongly: 'I now feel responsible to preach, actually to go on a *jihad* against extremism ... and to urge other religious leaders to do the same.'[65] Like Hamza Yusuf, an immensely popular figure among young American Muslims, Siraj Wahaj was included in several American Muslim panels and meetings around the country.[66] African American Muslims often felt under-represented in the media[67] and particularly slighted by Oprah, the hostess of a popular talk-show who was herself African-American, but who had only Arab Muslim spokeswomen on her daytime TV show, that was presented in an attempt to assuage prejudice against Islam and American Muslims. In some cases, however, African-Americans have been recognised as potential mediators between American culture and authorities and the Muslim immigrant community,[68] and some have become more outspoken in exposing and criticising their marginalisation by both American Muslim organisations and the media's construction of who is an American Muslim.

Reflections

American Muslim responses to 9/11 are still in a process of development several years after the terrorist attacks. The divisions among American Muslims across racial and doctrinal lines are probably greater than they were before, and part of this comes from the challenge of whether to engage with the broader society or not. For example, in many cases I find conservative mosques and schools in America proceeding as if nothing had changed, in fact, some are more intransigent in their insularity than previously.

Individual Muslims who had already been more liberal or accommodating have probably shifted more so in that direction, and a greater public presence of alternative views, as exemplified by articles on the web site 'Muslim Wake Up' demonstrates the broader circulation of progressive ideas in the Muslim American community.[69]

However, the liberal and progressive Muslims have to date largely failed in mounting an effective institutional response. Although the spectre of outside scrutiny can sometimes be useful for liberal Muslims in demanding moderation in intra-Muslim discourse, for example, mosque sermons; I don't see much evidence of a genuine change of heart on the part of the conservatives who control the majority of Muslim institutions.

Among the circuit of speakers and teachers who appeal to young adult Muslims attending campus seminars, '*deen* intensives', and so on, I do see the emergence of a more liberal discourse with respect to ideas of gender equality and civic responsibility. In fact, civic responsibility has emerged as a bridge issue across conservative and liberal Muslims after 9/11. According to Karen Leonard, 'Muslim organisations have now rallied and declare themselves even more fervently to be American, democratic, and supportive of civil liberties.'[70] Upholding the American Constitution and civil rights are shared concerns of American and Muslim liberals, and Muslim conservatives who feel most under threat and scrutiny.

If real changes are to happen in the American Muslim community, I feel that they are most likely to emerge among the cohort that was of high school or college age at the time of the attacks. The intense challenge to identity that occurred has forced some substantial re-evaluations among younger American Muslims and has forged some new alliances so that one may observe, for example, increased inter racial co-operation, and greater acceptance of intercultural and even doctrinal diversity.

As a final comment I might note the local nature of American Muslim responses. Perusing the media, Muslim and mainstream, one is struck by how an established moderate Muslim culture surrounding a particular centre in Los Angeles affected the image of Islam in the media of that city. Another example would be how relationships of trust already built up among a number of religious congregations in Chicago through ongoing activities of the Parliament for the Worlds Religions, facilitated a speedy and effective interfaith response to 9/11 that included Muslims.

While Internet sites and television media may strive to inform about a topic such as Islam and even to an extent create by projection, a certain kind of Muslim intellectual, shape a particular discourse or even movement; it seems to be at the local, grassroots and embodied level that real change takes place and from which a genuine response emerges.

Notes

[1] Elizabeth Poole, *Reporting Islam: Media Representations of British Muslims* (New York: I. B. Tauris, 2002), 16.
[2] 'Muslims Urged to Work on Improving Image', *Los Angeles Times*, Oct. 7, 2001, B3.
[3] For a multi-disciplinary discussion of whether 9/11 was in fact a watershed see Mary Dudziak, *9/11 in History: A Watershed Moment* (Durham: Duke University Press, 2003).
[4] Elizabeth Poole, *Reporting Islam*, 13.
[5] I reflect on some of the issues raised by alienation among American Muslim youth after 9/11 in, 'Putting the Genie back in the bottle: Identity Islam and Muslim Youth Cultures in the United States' in Omid Safi, ed., *Progressive Muslims on Justice, Gender and Pluralism* (Oxford: Oneworld, 2003), 303-319.
[6] This widely-circulated e-mail was written by Kent Madin. It is still available on numerous web-sites.
[7] *Newsweek* 'The Muslim moderator', Vol. 120 No. 34. Yusuf had said that 'Infinite Justice is an attribute of God and Muslims would consider using that phrase as almost a proclamation that America considered itself God. Cited in Karen Leonard, 'American Muslims Before and After September 11, 2001' in *Economic and Political Weekly* (Mumbai), 37:24 (June 15, 2002), 2293-2302, p. 2295. In this essay I owe many references to Leonard's article and she has generously allowed me to quote copiously.
[8] *Time*, 158: 15 (Oct. 1, 2001). Armstrong's article 'Has Islam been Hijacked?' is included in the anthology *Taking Back Islam: American Muslims Reclaim their Faith*, ed. Michael Wolfe and the Producers of *beliefnet*. (Emmaeus, PA: Rodale, 2002), 11-14.
[9] *The Economist*, Oct. 13, 2001, 14.
[10] Michael Wolfe, *Taking Back Islam*.
[11] http://abcnews.go.com/sections/nightline/DailyNews/jihad_marash020605.html, ABC News, June 5, 2002.
[12] Caryn James, 'Islam and Its Adherents Ride the Publicity Wave' in *New York Times*, October 6, 2001.
http://www.nytimes.com/2001/10/06/arts/06OPRA.html?ex=1078376400&en=d0dba45da0bfd346&ei=5070 Viewed March 1, 2004.
[13] Salman Rushdie, 'Yes, this is about Islam', *New York Times*, Nov. 2, 2001.
[14] Edward Said, 'Impossible histories: why the many Islams cannot be simplified', *Harpers*, July, 2002.
[15] Deborah Caldwell, 'Something major is happening: Are we witnessing the beginnings of an Islamic Reformation?' http://www.beliefnet.com/story/92/story_9273.html. Viewed January 19, 2004.
[16] As of March 2004 one signs up at Muslim Wake Up http://muslimwakeup.com/index.php
[17] Omid Safi (ed), *Progressive Muslims*.
[18] Irshad Manji, *The Trouble with Islam* (Toronto: Random House, 2003) has sparked controversy, not only due to her identity as a lesbian Muslima, a media personality and her lack of academic background in the subjects she is supposedly critiquing, but also due to her promotion by American political conservatives.
[19] Dale Eickleman, 'Who Speaks for Islam: Inside the Islamic Reformation' in *An Islamic Reformation?*, Michaelle Browers and Charles Kurzman (eds.), Rowman & Littlefield, 2004, 18-26.
[20] Abid Ullah Jan, 'The Neo-Mods of Islam' on http://paknews.com/PrintPage.php?id=1&date1=2003-05-05&news2=articles1. Viewed Feb. 25, 2004. 'If neo-cons are problem (sic) for the Christian world, neo-mods, are the problem of Islam.'

[21] This was the title of an article by Mahmood Mamdan, 'Good Muslim, Bad Muslim: A Political Perspective on Culture and Terrorism', *American Anthropologist*, 104:3 (2002):766-776.
[22] Karen Leonard, 'American Muslims Before and After September 11, 2001', 2295.
[23] Emily Wax, 'The Mufti in the Chat Room: Islamic Legal Advisers Are Just a Click Away From Ancient Customs', *Washington Post*, July 31, 1999, C1.
[24] *Los Angeles Times*, Oct. 10, 2001, B12; the full text was printed in *The Minaret Pakistan Link* and many other publications.
[25] Muqtedar Khan, *American Muslims: Bridging Faith and Freedom* (Beltsville, MD: Amana Publications, 2002).
[26] The Islamic Center of Southern California, which publishes *The Minaret*, is one of the most successful inter-ethnic Islamic congregations in the USA and makes a self-conscious effort to formulate and represent an American Islam.
[27] These are laid out in his books: *Conference of the Books: The Search for Beauty in Islam* (New York: University of America Inc., 2001); *And God Knows the Soldiers: the Authoritative and Authoritarian in Islamic Discourse* (New York: University Press of America, 2001); *Speaking in God's Name: Islamic Law, Authority and Women* (Oxford: Oneworld Publications, 2001), *The Place of Tolerance in Islam* (Boston: Beacon Press, 2002.
[28] *Los Angeles Times*, August 22, 2001, B13.
[29] Khaled Abou El Fadl, 'Derangements', *The Minaret*, special edition, Oct. 2001, 11; 'When God Asks the Child', *The Minaret*, November/December 2001, 11.
[30] Teresa Watanabe, 'Extremists Put Own Twist on Faith', *Los Angeles Times*, Sept. 24, 2001, A13.
[31] See instances in Karen Leonard, 'American Muslim Politics: Discourses and Practices', *Ethnicities*, 3:2 (June 2003), 147-181, and Abou El Fadl's comments in his books, cited above.
[32] Teresa Watanabe, 'Battling Islamic Puritans' *Los Angeles Time*, January 2, 2002. Also at http://www.scholarofthehouse.com/batlosantimj.html a website devoted to El Fadl. Viewed March 1, 2004.
[33] Sherman Jackson, 'Islam(s) East and West: Pluralism between no-frills and designer fundamentalism', in Mary Dudziak (ed.), *September 11 in History: A Watershed Moment* (Durham: Duke University Press, 2003), 112-135.
[34] Shaykh Hisham Kabbani, *The Approach of Armageddon?: An Islamic Perspective* (Washington, DC : Islamic Supreme Council of America, 2003).
[35] In Islamic religious symbolism the Mahdi is a Messianic figure who will appear near the end of time to battle the forces of evil.
[36] Andrew W. Vidich, 'A Living Sufi Saint: Shaykh Muhammad Nazim Adil al-Haqqani and the Naqshbandi Method of Self-Transformation' Ph. D. Thesis, Berne University, 2000, 322.
[37] Shaykh Hisham Kabbani, *The Naqshbandi Sufi Way* (Chicago: Kazi Publications, 1995).
[38] Shaykh Hisham Kabbani, *The Encyclopedia of Islamic Doctrine* (Chicago: Kazi, 1998). Large portions of this and other texts are available at: http://www.naqshbandi.net/haqqani/toc.htm.
[39] 'Salafi' or 'following the way of the early pious Muslims' is an Arabic term now used to refer to Muslims who prefer literalist interpretations, although it has come to have political connotations of conservative activism as well.
[40] The full text of the briefing was on the Haqqani website as 'Islamic Extremism: A Viable Threat to U. S. National Security', transcript of Jan. 7, 1999. It has now been removed. The *Los Angeles Times* covered some of these tensions in Teresa Watanabe, 'Holy War of Words', April 15, 1999.

[41] Available on the Internet at http://www.musalman.com/islamnews/kabbani.html Viewed March 1, 2004.
[42] Muhammad Hisham Kabbani, 'The Muslim Experience in America is Unprecedented', *Middle East Quarterly*, June 2000, v. 7 i. 2:61-72.
[43] Shaykh Hisham Kabbani, editorial, *Muslim Magazine*, Vol. 3, 1-2, Spring 2000, 6.
[44] Karen Leonard in 'American Muslims Before and After September 11', 2296 citing Laurie Goodstein, 'Muslim Leader Who Was Once Labelled An Alarmist Is Suddenly a Sage', *New York Times*, Oct. 28, 2001.
[45] Michael Savage, 'A Man of Peace Unmasks False Prophets of Hate', April 5, 2002, NewsMax http://www.newsmax.com/archives/articles/2002/4/5/11503.shtml. Viewed Jan. 11, 2004.
[46] Richard Scheinin, 'Expert says Islam Prohibits Violence Against Innocents,' *San Jose Mercury News*, Sept. 16, 2001.
[47] Cited in Karen Leonard, 'American Muslims Before and After September 11, 2001', 2295.
[48] amshed Bokhari, 'The Great White Sheikh' at http://www.islamonline.net/English/views/2001/11article8.shtml. Viewed Jan. 11, 2004.
[49] Among them, Ghayasuddin Siddiqui, head of the Muslim Parliament, at a House of Commons hearing on Guantanamo Bay found on: http://www.theirishworld.com/homepage.asp?fname=2003-09-26\news\2.htm.Viewed March 1, 2004.
[50] Michael Wolfe, 'The New Angels in America', found on: http://about.beliefnet.com/story/137/story/13719_1.html. Viewed Feb. 21, 2004.
[51] Michael Wolfe, 'How does it Feel?' http://www.beliefnet.com/story/82/story_8281_1.html. Viewed March 1, 2004.
[52] Michael Wolfe, Ibid.
[53] Muqtader Khan in *American Muslims,* uses the expression 'trophy Muslims', 20.
[54] Ibid., 4-6.
[55] Ibid., 5.
[56] http://www.theamericanmuslim.org. A previous print version of the magazine, put together by the same editor, Sheila Musaji, had been suspended some years earlier.
[57] *The American Muslim*, Vol. 2 (5, December 2001).
[58] Mary Dudziak (ed.), *September 11 in History,*
[59] Sherman Jackson, 'Islam(s) East and West: Pluralism between no-frills and designer fundamentalism' in Mary Dudziak (ed.), *September 11 in History*, 112.
[60] Ibid., 112-3.
[61] Ibid., 113.
[62] Ibid., 117.
[63] Ibid., 130.
[64] For example, The US State department website currently has a photo album on line about Muslims in America, almost all of whom appear to be immigrants. http://usinfo.state.gov/products/pubs/muslimlife/htm. Posted February 20, 2004.
[65] Peter Ford, 'Listening for Islam's Silent Majority', *Christian Science Monitor*, Nov. 5, 2001.
[66] Imam Siraj Wahhaj was listed as a well-known social activist/leader on a Houston panel on 'Practicing True Islam', Oct. 20, 2001, along with several professors, editors, and directors of Muslim organisations. After 9/11 African-American Muslims reported increased scrutiny and suspicion of them, although less than of Arabs (Tania Fuentez, 'Black Muslims Complain of Increase in Discrimination', *Pakistan Link*, Oct. 26, 2001, PL5; John W.

Fountain, 'African-American Muslims: Sadness and Fear as They Feel Doubly Vulnerable', *New York Times*, Oct. 5, 2001.
[67] In January, 2002, African-American Muslim followers of Wallace Deen Muhammad still reported 'feeling snubbed by Muslim immigrants'. They referred back to the fall of 2000 when 'a coalition of American Muslims endorsed George W. Bush for president' and they were 'left out of the process'; they also felt 'relegated to the background' in meetings following Sept.11. Mary Rourke, 'One Faith, Two Minds', *Los Angeles Times*, Jan. 30, 2002, E1, 3. Muqtader Khan considers the mutual alienation of the immigrant and 'indigenous' American Muslim communities to be one of the major challenges facing Muslims in the USA, *American Muslims*, 18-26.
[68] Felicia R. Lee, 'An Islamic Scholar with the Dual Role of Activist', featuring Professor Aminah McCloud of Chicago, *New York Times*, January 17, 2004.
[69] Muslim Wake Up http://muslimwakeup.com/index.php
[70] Karen Leonard, 'American Muslim Politics', 166.

Chapter 7

The Shaping of a Moderate North American Islam: Between 'Mufti' Bush and 'Ayatollah' Ashcroft

Yvonne Haddad

The events of 9/11 have refocused the preference of American policy makers for 'moderate' Islam, one that has been promoted by certain sectors in the American establishment since the fall of the Soviet Empire and adopted by President Bush since 9/11.[1] The Bush administration has launched several initiatives to foster, nurture and empower 'moderate' Muslims, at the same time that the Justice Department under John Ashcroft has promoted legislation and measures that allow search, seizure, and incarceration of Muslims and Arabs without evidence or recourse to legal advice. This chapter will outline some of the policies and measures implemented since 9/11 by the Bush administration and assess their impact on the American Muslim community that feels abandoned by a president it supported and helped elect. It will also discuss the pressures from government and political lobbies that are attempting to create a 'moderate Islam'.

For over a century, Muslims have lived in the USA mostly on the margins of its political life. Several factors contributed to their marginality: their size, their ethnic diversity and their lack of experience in playing the democratic game. At the same time other factors and interests in American society contributed to their exclusion, including American traditional antipathy towards Arabs and Muslims at least as far back as the founding of the Republic,[2] and the contemporary political and religious domestic interests of both the pro-Israel lobby and the Christian Right, both of which managed to keep Arabs and Muslims out of the mainstream. Muslim reluctance to engage in American political activity was finally put aside during the 2000 presidential election when a coalition of Arab-American and Muslim-American political action groups endorsed the Bush-Cheney ticket and contributed financially to the Republican Party.[3] Many continue to believe that they provided the margin of difference that delivered the presidency since they reportedly cast over 50,000 votes for the Republican ticket. Muslim elation at their success slowly dissipated as they faced the reality of their impotence in reshaping policies defined and pursued by both Republican and Democratic administrations during the last three decades of the twentieth century according to American security and national interests.

Several events contemporaneous with the increased emigration of Muslims to the USA after 1995 have had a profound impact on Arab and Muslim involvement in the American political process: the 1967 Israeli pre-emptive strike against Egypt, Syria and Jordan, the Iranian Revolution, the Rushdie Affair and the Gulf War. The Israeli attack and the pro-Israel propaganda in the US that justified it brought into existence American-Arab organizations eager to improve the negative image of Arabs in America. These organizations identified as Arab and included both Christian and Muslim immigrants from Lebanon, Syria, Palestine, Egypt, etc.[4] The Gulf war energised a new generation of Muslim activists and hastened the appearance of American Muslim organizations seeking to achieve parallel goals under the umbrella of a Muslim identity. Basic to both Muslim and Arab organizations was a confidence in the guarantees of the American constitution to enable them to voice their views and to create advocacy groups that can inform, correct falsehoods, and seek recourse in the democratic system, in the process negotiating a place for Islam, Arabs, and Muslims in the American mosaic.[5]

Most of the Muslims who immigrated to the USA came after the repeal of the Asia exclusion Act in the 1960s. They entered an America that had passed the Civil Rights Act of 1964, the Voting Rights Act of 1965 and the Immigration Act of 1965. It was an America going through an identity crisis, one that was uncomfortable with its racist past, one that had begun to tolerate hyphenated identities. They found the accommodation made by earlier American Muslim citizens to be unacceptable. Casting around for a model of organization for the survival of their identity, they decided to emulate the Jewish community. They noted that although the Jewish community constituted less than 3% of the American population, this fact had not impeded its shaping policies and exercising equal power in a society that increasingly defined itself as Judeo-Christian. In the process, they sought equal representation hoping for a day when the USA would define itself as Christian-Jewish-Muslim. They emphasised difference and distinctiveness as the mark of being Muslim, perceived as a means of ensuring survival of the community and the perpetuation of its faith in the next generation. It became clear that if they would not define themselves, others would continue to define them.

Always latent in American society, prejudice towards citizens of Arab ancestry increased in the 1970s as they were targeted as security risks and held accountable for the acts of individuals overseas. In 1972 the Nixon administration formed a special committee to restrict Arab immigration to the USA, collect data on the immigrants in the US, and compile dossiers on Arab American leaders and organizations.[6] By the end of the 1970s, apprehension in the American Arab community intensified when they obtained information through the Freedom of Information Act that the American administration was considering preparing two military compounds in the South for the possible internment of Arabs and Iranians living in the USA.

Early Islamic activism in the West had been related more to circumstances in the countries left behind than to events in America. Some of the immigrants came because they feared persecution on account of their affiliation to Islamic movements. They found the USA hospitable to their goals and were afforded the opportunity to work for opposition groups seeking an Islamic alternative to governments overseas.[7] American interests overseas that promoted Islamisation facilitated their activities and encouraged their enthusiasm and eagerness to establish Islamic institutions and to foster Islamic states to act as a firewall against the spread of Communism.[8] In their annual conventions in the USA, prominent Muslims from overseas were repeatedly invited to address the Muslim community in the US.[9]

Muslim activists took advantage of the fact that the USA afforded more freedom to think, reflect, organise, publish and propagate in the USA than in the autocratic Muslim nations they left behind. Once they realised that they were in the West to stay, they started to build permanent institutions to ensure an Islamic future in the USA. They began to envision their role as participants in western societies, propagators of Islamic values that would help rescue the West from its social degeneration. As events unfolded during the 1980s and 1990s Muslim activism began to focus more specifically on the American context.

For the Muslim community in the USA, the Gulf War brought unexpected consequences. Muslims noted Arab and Muslim nations joined the coalition against Saddam Hussein, demonstrating their loyalty to the USA and putting to rest the Zionist argument that Israel is 'the only reliable American ally in the region'. They expected an easing of anti-Arab/anti-Muslim rhetoric in the USA. The election of Bill Clinton as president of the USA had a negative impact on policies they cherished and hoped to see implemented. Clinton was elected with the support of the pro-Israel Lobby eager to punish George Bush senior for threatening to cut off aid to Israel if it did not cease to construct the settlements on the West Bank of the Jordan. At the insistence of Senator Joseph Lieberman, Democrat of Connecticut, Clinton brought 27 activists from the Israeli Lobby to formulate and implement his policy vis-à-vis the Middle East. This precipitated a definite shift in American policy vis-à-vis Islamic nations, dubbed by some as the 'Bibi-sation' of American foreign policy, in reference to Bibi Netenyahu's urging Americans to identify Arabs and Muslims as terrorists.[10]

During Clinton's second term, several Muslim states were identified as 'rogue states'. Even Pakistan, which had been a consistent and reliable ally since the 1950s, was being shunted aside in favour of India. All of these events helped foster the growing perception that Islam is the new American enemy, a green menace that has replaced the red menace of the Soviet Union. American Muslims have become increasingly aware that their marginalised reality has empowered ideologues who waste no opportunity to paint Muslims as terrorists and a threat to the USA. Islamophobes such as Steven Emerson, Daniel Pipes and Bernard Lewis became the goad that spurred Muslims to respond and challenge the veracity of their charges.[11]

At the same time, the Clinton administration, using the politics of symbolic access and inclusion, initiated overtures to the Muslim community that appeared aimed at making Muslims feel included in the political process. In 1993, the Department of Defence commissioned the first Muslim chaplain in the armed forces. This was followed by the appointment of chaplains in all branches of the armed services as well as by the construction of an Islamic prayer hall on a military base in Norfolk, VA. The Department of Defence recognised the Graduate School of Islamic Social Sciences as the endorsing agent for the suitability of such chaplains. The administration also appointed the first Muslim ambassador, the first Muslim federal judge, the first Muslim Deputy Secretary of Agriculture, and a Muslim member in the Congressional Commission on International Religious Freedom.

The Clinton Administration made other symbolic gestures, such as hosting the first Ramadan *iftar* (breaking the fast) dinners in 1992. Succeeding *iftars* were hosted by the Department of Defence (in 1997) and the Department of State (in 1999 and 2000), and by Hillary Clinton at the White House in 1996, 1997, 1998 and 1999). In 2000 it was hosted by Bill Clinton since Hillary was running for the Senate from New York and feared Jewish backlash. Robert Seiple, Ambassador-at-Large for Religious Freedom, held regular Roundtable meetings with leaders of Muslim organizations starting in February 15, 1999 to discuss issues of mutual concern. Even the Postal Service issued a special commemorative *Eid* stamp on November 13, 2000.

While some in the Muslim community celebrated inclusion and symbolic access, others were apprehensive about policies simultaneously adopted in the 1990s by various agencies of the federal government that targeted Muslims in the USA, in the process restricting their human and civil rights. These laws were particularly harsh in relation to Arabs and Palestinians. For example, in the aftermath of the Oklahoma City bombing in 1995 the media coverage precipitated a backlash against innocent Arab Americans which led to scores of injuries, incidents of harassment and physical abuse, and attacks on mosques and Islamic institutions. Jingoistic journalists such as Steve Emerson and Connie Chung insisted that the Oklahoma City bombing was the work of Middle Eastern terrorists and had the markings of their *modus operandi*. President Clinton appeared on television and warned Americans not to blame or target the Muslim community. The Congress passed HR 1710, the Anti-Terrorism and Affective Death Penalty Act of 1995 after the Oklahoma City bombing and signed into law by President Bill Clinton on April 24, 1996. The bill gave the right to the American government to try and incarcerate Arab-Americans without evidence. It also sanctioned, among other security measures, airport profiling of potential terrorists. The profile was not of a Timothy McVeigh, the perpetrator of the Oklahoma City bombing, but of an Arab or a Muslim. A further denial of First Amendment rights to non-citizens was sanctioned by a Supreme Court decision in 1999 in the LA Eight case against Palestinian Christians and Muslims. Clinton also signed Executive Order No. 12947 on January 23, 1995, which banned contributions to Palestinian charitable institutions by American citizens, depriving orphans, widows and the needy of American financial assistance. It also allowed for seizing the assets of any American citizen who donated funds to NGOs and civic organizations on the State Department's list of terrorist organizations, including those that support Palestinian relief agencies such as schools, hospitals, orphanages, libraries, women's organizations and community centres, in the process curtailing Arab civil liberties and human rights.

President Bush and American Muslims

With the election of the Bush-Cheney ticket, the leadership of the American Muslim community expected better relations with the White House. However, from the start, Muslims noted the absence of even symbolic Muslim participation during the inauguration ceremonies while other religious communities were represented by their leaders. Some in the Muslim political leadership insisted on seeing this as an oversight rather than a snub. When the administration was notified of this absence, an attempt was made to rectify the situation. A Muslim from Michigan was included at President Bush's announcement of his faith-based voluntary work initiative which he hoped would be undertaken by churches, synagogues and mosques. This belated gesture of including Muslims was openly condemned by the reverend Jerry Falwell, leading some Muslims to expect a Presidential condemnation of 'hate speech'. None was issued. Other Muslims doubted the President's ability to do so, given his dependence on the Christian Right. 'The administration was only keen in seeking token participation of Muslims without involving them in the decision-making process,' one Muslim editorial read.

Another public slight to the Muslim community early in the Bush Administration came when the White House announced that it intended to celebrate *Eid-ul Adha* to which Muslims were invited; the event was first postponed and finally cancelled. When leaders of Muslim organizations asked to meet with the President, their request was ignored. A Muslim journalist wrote in response that the Bush Administration may honour Muslims not as representative of Muslims but as donors to the Republican Party. It may even recruit Muslims to issue statements supporting President Bush, and even recruit Muslims to join the US propaganda machinery in different parts of the Muslim world. However, it is not serious in appointing Muslims representing the community in positions of significance.[12] It was not until November 19, 2002 that President Bush invited Muslims to an *Iftar* dinner at the White House. While some of the Muslim religious leaders were not invited, ambassadors from Muslim nations were heavily represented and the event was a grand affair since the dinner was served in the State Dining Room. On November 29, 2002, Secretary of State Colin Powell hosted the American Muslim leaders at the State Department.

Muslims suspect that the reason President Bush cancelled the first *Iftar* was his concern about potential criticism for socializing with Muslims. Such criticism would come from the pro-Israel Lobby which insists on depicting the Muslims as terrorists or as supporting terrorism, or from the Christian Right who see Muslims as outside the pale of a Christian or a 'Judaeo-Christian' state. Seeking to clear the air, the leadership of mainline Muslim organizations asked for a meeting with the White House. While they were about to meet, a security agent came in and escorted out one of the participants, Abdullah al-Arian, claiming that he was a security risk. This happened despite the fact that all the participants had been vetted and approved by security agents prior to the meeting and the fact that al-Arian was working on the Hill in the office of Congressman Bonier. Muslim leaders in attendance were offended and walked out of the meeting. Eventually, the White House arranged a meeting on September 11 to try to patch things up.

By the early part of 2001, some in the Muslim community were beginning to doubt that President Bush was going to act on what they saw as his pre-election promises. While leaders of the Arab and Muslim organizations recognised the constraints under which the Bush Administration was operating, they were disappointed by the slow process of alleviating the harassment of Arabs and Muslims. On May 23, 2001, The American-Arab Anti-Discrimination Committee published an advisory, reporting an increased frequency during the previous month of passenger profiling of Arab and Muslim Americans at airports. Most disappointing to the group was the fact that the organization had been working with the Department of Transportation and the Federal Aviation Administration since the profiling was instituted in 1996 in the hope of expediting the amelioration of these hardships. The Arab and Muslim community had endorsed George Bush for president precisely because he had voiced concern during the presidential debates about the profiling of Arabs. At the end of August 2001, Muslims were coming to believe that they had achieved numerical parity with the Jewish community in the USA. At the same time, they were increasingly becoming aware that they still lacked clout and influence. The leadership of both the Arab and Islamic organizations appeared to be more realistic and began to advise patience. They warned that politics is the art of the possible. Professor Agha Saeed, who was instrumental in creating the coalition that made the Muslim voters important players in the last presidential election, outlined the challenges that Muslims faced and advised that they continued to attempt political engagement in the USA by exercising their rights as citizens. He noted that Muslims need 'to acquire a better knowledge about the USA, its political institutions and its governance and the means by which consensus is gained'; that they should continue to fight all efforts that seek to demonise Muslims and exclude them from participation in the political process; that they should learn how to gain 'real access to the political process since symbolic access has not been effective'; and that they need to 'earn the right to co-author America's vision of itself and its future'.[13] Such calls for political participation have proved effective for many immigrant Muslims. A survey of Muslim leadership of mosques issued on April 26, 2001 shows dramatic support (over 70%) for the proposition that Muslims should be involved in American institutions and should participate in the political process.[14]

Thus while the leadership of Muslim organizations continued to be hopeful that Arabs and Muslims can no longer be taken for granted in future elections since their vote can make the difference in critical states, many in their constituency increasingly felt jilted by the Bush-Cheney administration that had courted them during the campaign. An editorial in a national Muslim publication out of California that played a major role in building a coalition to support the Bush-Cheney ticket read: 'Mr. Bush is no different than other politicians who make promises only to break them, and who will say anything to achieve power in order to serve the agenda of their special interest groups'.[15]

A few voices in the American Muslim community were increasingly asking: 'What has the Muslim community gained from the Bush-Cheney team?

Broken promises and more broken promises'.[16] While some hesitated to pass judgment on the policies of the new administration regarding issues of deep concern to Muslims as well as on its reluctance to implement meaningful Muslim participation in the political process, others were wondering whether they had been hoodwinked into endorsing Bush for president. The question then was whether the Bush administration had decided that even the politics of symbolic access practiced by the Clinton administration were unpalatable to its supporters in the Christian Right and the watchdog groups of the pro-Israel Lobby, which it needs to placate if it harbours any hopes for a second term.

President Bush and American Muslims after 9/11

This policy of ignoring the Muslims changed after the catastrophic attack of 9/11 that shattered America's sense of security and self sufficiency. President Bush visited the Islamic Centre in Washington, DC in an effort to calm public anger and retribution against Muslims. To the consternation of many of his supporters, he declared Islam a 'religion of peace'. The government now sought engagement with the Muslim community for a price. Not only did it demand their repeated denunciation of revolutionary groups overseas, it asked for what was perceived by Muslims as a rejection of some of the basic tenets of their faith, namely a restructuring of their Islamic organizations and a recasting of their faith as 'moderate Islam'.

On September 14, 2001, three days after the catastrophic attack on the World Trade Center and the Pentagon, the people of the USA were brought together by President Bush through television in a National Day of Mourning held at the National Cathedral. The event was attended by four former presidents (George H.W. Bush, William Clinton, Jimmy Carter and Gerald Ford) as well as members of the cabinet and Congress and ambassadors of foreign nations. The service was led by religious functionaries of various faith communities. For the Muslims living in fear of backlash from an angry American population, it was a special moment of inclusion. Muzzammil Siddiqui, president of the Islamic Society of North America participated. He prayed:

> We turn to you, our Lord, at this time of pain and grief in our nation ...We see the evil of destruction and the suffering of the many of our people before our eyes. With broken hands and humbled hearts, and with tears in our eyes, we turn to You, our Lord, to give us comfort ... Help us in our distress, keep us together as people of diverse faiths, colours and races, keep our country strong for the sake of good and righteousness, and protect us from all evil. Amen.[17]

Some in the Muslim community were relieved and hailed the inclusion of Muslims by the Bush administration. Others questioned Siddiqi's participation since he stood under a huge suspended cross in the nave of the Cathedral. Still others saw that he was being used by the Bush administration as a cover in the attempt to project a pluralistic picture to Muslims overseas, at the same time that it initiated a dragnet targeting Muslims and their institutions in an effort to ferret out possible collaborators with the hijackers.

President Bush set the tone of a nation grieving, and at the same time, one that is determined to combat terrorism and protect itself from further attacks. Bush affirmed: 'Our responsibility to history is already clear: to answer these attacks and rid the world of evil ... This nation is peaceful, but fierce when stirred to anger. This conflict was begun on the timing and terms of others. It will end in a way, and in an hour of our choosing'.[18]

The quest for national security in the aftermath of 9/11 and the desire of the administration not to be caught napping again has led to new legislation that makes it necessary to initiate new research into the integration and assimilation of Muslims and Islam into the American fabric. To date, scholars have been comparing the immigration and integration of Arabs and Muslims in the USA and their incorporation into the American religious mainstream to that of other ostracised religious groups deemed undesirable by the founding fathers of the republic, such as Mormons, Catholics, and Jews. It is increasingly clear that in the aftermath of 9/11, it may be more productive to compare the treatment of Arabs and Muslims and their assimilation into American society with that of the experience of the Germans during World War I, the Japanese during World War II and the Communists during the Cold War. The measures adopted by the Bush administration are reminiscent of those taken during critical moments in American history that made it necessary to suspend American legal protection and constitutional guarantees for all citizens and to scrutinise persons identified as a potential threat to the nation.

The attacks of 9/11 appear to have resolved the internal debates among policy makers in the USA that were initiated after the collapse of the Soviet Union, as a growing number of political and religious officials cast around for a new enemy. Some of them had found it convenient to designate 'fundamentalist Islam' as the imminent threat, 'the other' that needs to be eliminated. Israeli leaders for several decades had been identifying Islam as 'the enemy'. The attacks of 9/11 revealed a growing consensus among many of the Beltway pundits in Washington DC as well as the press. Israel and America were depicted as co-victims of Islamic hatred of Judaism and Christianity. The right wing Christian community had already shifted its interpretation of the signs of the end of times after the Israeli victory of 1967. Included among the signs was now a major battle between Muslims and Jews restored to Israel, a cataclysmic event that will herald the imminent return of the Messiah. Millenarian Christians welcomed the intensification of conflict between the two faiths since it would mean the final redemption of the Jews and urged Israel to hold firm. Their preachers, casting away all pretence at political correctness, engaged in demonizing Islam and its Prophet with gusto reminiscent of the discourse that launched the Crusades and justified European colonization of Muslim nations.

The events of 9/11 brought further restrictions on the Arab/Muslim community. The Bush Administration initiated and the Congress passed HR3162, commonly known as USA PATRIOT (Providing Appropriate Tools Required to Intercept and Obstruct Terrorism) Act of October 24, 2001. It basically lifted all legal protection of liberty for Muslims and Arabs in the USA. It sanctioned the monitoring of bank transactions, telephone conversations, email messages, books purchased or borrowed from libraries, credit card purchases, etc., without notification, of any and all individuals, organizations and institutions deemed suspicious. It has been assessed as violating the Constitution by the American Bar Association, the American Librarians Association and the American Civil Liberties Union. Former Congresswoman Mary Rose Oakar, President of the American-Arab Anti-Discrimination Committee, argued that it was 'completely incompatible with basic civil liberties, most notably freedom from unreasonable search and seizure by the government guaranteed by the Fourth Amendment to the Constitution'.[19] Arabs and Muslims have noted that while the Anti-Terrorism Act had sanctioned the incarceration of Arabs and Muslims with secret evidence, the Patriot Act as implemented by Attorney General John Ashcroft has sanctioned their incarceration with no evidence. Two hundred and forty-seven cities and towns, including a New York Borough a few blocks from Ground Zero, have gone on record rejecting the legislation and its extensive powers to monitor, deport, freeze assets and incarcerate, as violating the Constitution. When several Arab and Muslim organizations and civil rights groups sued the American government, insisting that the PATRIOT Act is un-American, given the need for security the Supreme Court upheld the government action.

The security measures adopted by the Bush Administration are perceived both overseas and among many in the Muslim community in North America not as anti-terrorism but as anti-Muslim. It appears that these measures reveal a fundamental challenge to the Muslim definition of the role of women in society that many Muslims deem as prescribed by God in the Qur'an. The Department of State has established bureaus specifically charged with the task of empowering and liberating the women of Islam. It has implemented this charge in a variety of programs such as funding women's organizations in various Muslim countries, training women from the Middle East and North Africa to participate in the political process, and bringing delegations of women from overseas to learn about women's activities in the USA and about American democracy, pluralism, and tolerance. One delegation of high powered Arab women included the mayor of a North African city, the vice mayor of a Palestinian town, and a banker from the Gulf. Some in the group expressed indignation at the presumption that they needed empowerment. Their message was that the American government should change its policies to promote economic development in the area, rather than create a gender divide. They identified American partiality towards Israel and its failure to condemn Israeli violence as one of the core reasons for Arab anger at the US. Some even questioned whether the goal of the US government is not in essence to liberate women from Islam and its values.

Another measure adopted by the American administration that has been interpreted as a part of a war on Islam is the monitoring by CIA agents at American embassies overseas of Islamic textbooks for anti-western, anti-American or anti-Israeli content. This monitoring has enraged some Muslims who have accused President Bush of becoming a 'Mufti', the arbiter of what true Islam is. At a Christian–Muslim dialogue meeting in Cairo sponsored by the Middle East

Christian Council, one of the participants, responsible for the educational programs of the Organization of the Islamic Conference in Sub-Saharan Africa, expressed great concern about the CIA project. I do not mind if they question my students, my teachers or my principals about what they believe', he said. 'But they cannot tell me what Islam is'. He expressed willingness to discuss revisions in the curriculum if and when the USA government begins to censor Jewish educational institutions in Brooklyn that teach hatred of gentiles and produce gun-toting settlers for the West Bank as well as Christian institutions such as that in Virginia run by Pat Robertson that teach hatred of Islam and Muslims. While some have dismissed reports about American censorship of school texts as fanciful since they are persuaded that the USA believes in freedom of religion and speech and would not resort to such action, there is evidence that such a project is underway. A college professor from Abu Dhabi who was a member of a committee to remove objectionable material from textbooks reported that she was very surprised to find a copy of her report at the American Embassy.[20]

Muslims overseas have not hesitated to express their anger at the Bush administration. Wajih Abu Zikri, writing in *al-Akhbar*, published in Cairo, reported that President Bush sent personal messages to Islamic scholars, including Shaykh Yusuf al-Qaradawi, asking them to 'delete those verses and sayings that Bush sees "inappropriate" from the Qur'an'. He went on:

> President Bush pushed far his crusade, thinking that Islamic education must stop. The Islamic religion should be abolished from all school curricula. The Islamic religion schools should even vanish from the world, and the verses of the holy Koran, that he believe incite the defence of Muslim dignity and respond tit for tat to aggression should be struck out. Bush wants to teach our children to turn the other cheek, and the back to be kicked at will.[21]

Muslims have been deeply disturbed at the decision of the Bush administration to monitor NGOs, civic, charitable and religious organizations, both overseas and in the USA. The government has also published a list of suspect organizations whose assets have been frozen. In effect, the American government is perceived by Muslims to have assumed a veto power over *zakat* (tithe), one of the basic tenets of the Islamic faith by monitoring charities and organizations that support orphans and widows in an effort to curb the transfer of funds to terrorist organizations. Leaders of Islamic organizations have met with the administration asking for clarification as to what and who is considered by the American government as a legitimate recipient of such charities.

Another action by the Bush administration that has eroded Muslim confidence that the declared war is really on terrorism and not Islam itself is the raiding by several federal agencies of the homes and offices of the national Muslim leadership in Northern Virginia. Muslims see this as a demonstration by the US government that it is now looking for a new Islamic leadership. The raids came as a major surprise to many Muslims who had previously criticised this leadership precisely because it was cooperating with the American Government.

Such action raised serious questions about what kind of Islam America will now tolerate.

A few individuals have stepped up and volunteered to 'lead the Muslims into moderation'. Several have been supported and funded by various agencies of the USA government. Their mission is to provide new reflections and interpretations of Islam. They have opened offices and are in the process of leading others into 'right thinking'. To date, they appear to have few followers since they are perceived as agents of the effort to undermine Islam. An important collection of essays *Progressive Muslims: On Justice, Gender and Pluralism*[22] has recently been published by several Muslim academics.

American policy makers tend to see the world in polarities, a fact that is evident in war rhetoric and policies engaged in by the American administration. The War on Terrorism bifurcated the world into good and evil, civilised and uncivilised, democratic versus despotic, of free versus held hostage, at the same time insisting on policies that were the antithesis of the American ideals of democracy, tolerance and civilization that the American elite were claiming to be the target of the terrorists. In the process a search for an evil to be vanquished that had been in process for two decades appears to have become a dividing line. Islam replaced communism as the enemy of freedom, Godliness, civilization and all that is good. The USA, while claiming that its goal is the creation of democratic governments in all Muslim nations, is demanding that these same governments demonstrate their Islamic moderation by prosecuting, if not persecuting, suspected terrorists. As Aihwa Ong observed:

> By sharply drawing a line between moderate Muslim leaders and radical Muslim rebels, the US-orchestrated war on terror has increased the power of authoritarian Asian regimes. It has allowed them to brand a spectrum of local opposition or separatist groups as terrorist or al-Qa'eda-linked. The terrorist discourse is used as a resource against political opponents, to disguise military actions against insurgents at home, and to link sectarian violence at home and terrorism on the global stage."[23]

The Bush administration has made it clear that it expects moderate governments to implement other measures to assure American interests. These include curbing free speech, called 'inflammatory' if it is directed against American or Israeli policies. [24] Various administration officials have weighed in on how to promote moderate Islam. Paul Wolfowitz, US Deputy Secretary of Defence said in 2002 at the Brookings Institutions Forum, that:

> In winning this larger struggle, it would be a mistake to think that we could be the ones to lead the way. But, we must do what we can to encourage the moderate Muslim voices. This is a debate about Muslim values that must take place among Muslims. But, it makes a difference when we recognise and encourage those who are defending universal values. And, when we give them moral support against the opposition they encounter, we are indeed helping to strengthen the foundations of peace.[25]

The two strongest lobbies in Washington, the Christian Right and the Zionists, have had a field day since 9/11. The demonstrated ability of the Muslim community to organise, register voters and get them out to vote for a particular candidate concerned supporters of Israel. 'I worry very much from the Jewish point of view that the presence and increased stature, and affluence, and enfranchisement of American Muslims ... will present true dangers to American Jews'.[26] Pro-Israel journalists such as Martin Peretz referred to Muslims in the USA as a 'fifth column'.[27]

Pro-Israel lobbies have worried and stalked Arab and Muslim activists and organizations for several decades. After 9/11, they swung into action and shared their files with reporters and the media in order to facilitate the investigation of Arab and Muslim individuals and organizations. Solomon Moore reported in the *Los Angeles Times* on November 3, 2002, that such organizations, as 'the Anti-Defamation League, The Jewish Defence League, the Middle East Forum think tank have provided news organizations with reams of official documentation on Muslim leaders in recent weeks'.[28] Pro-Israeli lobbies were instrumental in derailing the nomination of Salam al-Marayati, founder and director of Muslim Public Affairs Council, to the National Commission on Terrorism. His views were exposed by the 'Zionist Organizations of America in coalition with the Conference of Presidents of Major American Jewish Organizations, AIPAC, The American Jewish Congress, The American Jewish Committee, and the Anti-Defamation League'.[29] They also protested the nomination of his wife Laila al-Marayati to the USA Commission on International Religious Freedom.

A detailed litmus test of moderate Islam was provided by Daniel Pipes, the Presidential appointee to the US Institute of Peace. He is perceived by Muslims as the pro-Israel provocateur who has initiated a relentless campaign against 'militant/extremist/terrorist Islamists', in the process calling for what could be considered a new Inquisition reminiscent of what obtained in Spain during the fifteenth century. His views on what constitutes 'moderate Islam' are noted for their inconsistencies. Many dismiss him as a 'designated demoniser', since he set up Campus Watch asking students to report on faculty members who expressed ideas that disagreed with his orthodoxy. The President of the USA appointed him to the Institute despite vigorous opposition from the Muslim community as well as some Christian and Jewish leaders who saw him as a divider of the nation when what was needed was a healer, and despite opposition to his nomination by scholars and intellectuals as well as senators Ted Kennedy, Christopher Dodd, Tom Harkins and Jim Jefferds, members of the senate committee that was approving his appointment. Whether Bush's insistence on appointing him during the Congressional recess was based on a shared view of 'Islamists' or due to the pressure of the pro-Israel lobby is hard to tell.

In an editorial in the *Jewish World Review*, Pipes sets out to distinguish between 'real and phony moderation', which he asserts cannot be divined by 'amateurs like US government officials'. He goes on to affirm that:

> The best way to discern moderation is by delving into the record, public and private, Internet and print, domestic and foreign, of an individual or institution. Such research is most productive with intellectuals, activists, and imams, all of whom have a paper trail. With others, who lack a public record, it is necessary to ask questions. These need to be specific, as vague inquiries ('Is Islam a religion of peace?' 'Do you condemn terrorism?') have little value, depending as they do on definitions (of peace, terrorism).[30]

For Pipes, there is a need to question Muslims regarding their views on a variety of issues including their attitude towards violence, whether they condone or condemn resistance fighters who 'give up their lives to kill enemy civilians'. They need to condemn by name a list of organizations that he provides. He also challenges the Muslim view of modernity, expecting them to renounce specific teachings of the Qur'an regarding women and the right to resist occupation by foreign troops who expel Muslims based on religious discrimination, in the process denying their right to choose and identify their own religion and culture: 'Should Muslim women have equal rights with men (for example, in inheritance shares or court testimony)? Is *jihad*, meaning a form of warfare, acceptable in today's world? Do you accept the validity of other religions? Do Muslims have anything to learn from the West?'[31]

Under the rubric of secularism, Pipes asserts that to be considered moderate, Muslims have to renounce certain teachings of their faith. What is peculiar is that the questions he posits regarding Islamic laws have parallels in Israel, a state he generally defends as modern, democratic and secular:

> Should non-Muslims enjoy completely equal civil rights with Muslims? May Muslims convert to other religions? May Muslim women marry non-Muslim men? Do you accept the laws of a majority non-Muslim government and unreservedly pledge allegiance to that government? Should the state impose religious observance, such as banning food service during Ramadan? When Islamic customs conflict with secular laws (e.g., covering the face for drivers' license pictures), which should give way?[32]

Pipes is also eager to question Muslims about their understanding of pluralism, whether they consider Sufis and Shi'ites as fully legitimate Muslims (hence admitting to his targeting of Sunni Muslims.) 'Do you see Muslims who disagree with you as having fallen into unbelief? Is *takfir* (condemning fellow Muslims one has disagreements with as unbelievers) an acceptable practice?' Furthermore, he provides a category for 'self-criticism' in which he implies that anyone who does not question his/her faith is not moderate. 'Do you accept the legitimacy of scholarly inquiry into the origins of Islam? Who was responsible for the 9/11 suicide hijackings?' [33]

As for defence against militant Islam, Pipes wants to interrogate Muslims on whether they accept being singled out for suspicion, profiling, incarceration or expulsion. 'Do you accept enhanced security measures to fight militant Islam, even if this means extra scrutiny of yourself (for example, at airline security)?' He further demands that they acquiesce to measures that impede their right to religious freedom based on accusations without evidence. 'Do you agree that institutions accused of funding terrorism should be shut down, or do you see this as a symptom of bias?' Finally, he demands that they renounce any missionary activity in the West. 'Do you accept that Western countries are majority-Christian and secular or do you seek to transform them into majority-Muslim countries ruled by Islamic law?' That he demands an Inquisition is in the text of his opinion piece, 'It is ideal if these questions are posed publicly – in the media or in front of an audience – thereby reducing the scope for dissimulation'.[34]

To prove that he is not against Islam itself but against extremists, Pipes has provided several other articles that define:

> moderate 'Anti-Islamist Muslims' – who wish to live modern lives, unencumbered by *burqas, fatwas* and violent visions of *jihad* – [they] are on the defensive and atomised. However, eloquent, their individual voices cannot compete with the roar of militant Islam's determination, money (much of it from overseas) and violence. As a result, militant Islam, with its West-phobia and goal of world hegemony, dominates Islam in the West and appears to many to be the only kind of Islam.

Anti-Islamist Muslims that Pipes approves of include 'freethinkers or atheists. Some are conservative, others liberal'. Among those on his favoured list are Abdelwahab Meddeb of the Sorbonne 'who wrote the evocatively titled Malady of Islam, in which he compares militant Islam to Nazism', Ibn Warraq, a self described convert from Islam who attempts 'to embolden Muslims to question their faith', and Ayaan Hirst Ali of Holland who has called Islam a 'backward' religion.[35] Others include Irshad Manji, author of *The Trouble with Islam: A Wakeup Call for Honesty and Chang*,[36] as well as a slew of journalists and authors including Saadallah Ghaussy, Hausain Haqqani, Salim Mansur, Khaleel Mohammad, Tashbih Sayyid, Stephen Schwarts, Khalid Duran and Tahir Aslam Gora.[37] Also on the list of 'moderate Muslims' is Shaykh Mohammad Hisham Kabbani who in a January 1999 address at the Department of State warned against the imminent danger to America from Islamic extremists armed with 20 nuclear bombs. He also warned that 80% of mosques in the US have been taken over by extremists who have an unhealthy focus on the struggle of the Palestinian people.[38] Pipes has also published a list of approved Islamic organisations.[39]

Aware of the reaction of Muslims worldwide to its policies and attempting to deal with the majority, the USA Government has decided that it has failed in public diplomacy, and not policy. In an effort to enhance its image overseas, the Department of State has supervised the production of several videos that attempted to demonstrate American pluralism, tolerance and inclusion of Muslims. The videos featured Muslim Americans touting the freedom they enjoy in the USA and the fact that their fellow workers appreciate their contributions.[40] Unfortunately they were aired around the same time the Justice Department was implementing a program that required Muslim males living in the USA to register. The press was televising worldwide the arrest of nearly 14,000 males who came to register and were now to be deported, as well as the thousands who trekked north and sought asylum in Canada.[41]

It is clear that the attacks of 9/11 have had a major impact on the presidency of George Bush who has declared that it has 'changed America forever'. The question continues to be whether this change is to be marked simply by increased vigilance and security measures by Ashcroft's Department of Justice, or if it serves as an historical demarcation leading to a permanent shift in American foreign policy. Muslims wonder if it has led to what amounts to a declaration of unrelenting war on the Islamist interpretation of Islam, or whether that war is aiming at undermining mainstream Islam. A visiting scholar at the Carnegie Endowment for International Peace, Husain Haqqani, himself a self-proclaimed moderate, recently urged the USA and other Western powers to revise their definition of what constitutes extremists and moderates in the Muslim world. Rather than considering moderates only as those who 'toe the line', he said, moderate Muslims should be defined as those who want to engage as equals with others in the contemporary world and believe that violence, force and coercion are not appropriate ways in which to respond. Moderate Muslims, he said, are those who 'need to be embraced and strengthened'.[42]

The Muslim world wonders what President Bush meant when he declared 'The battle is now joined on many fronts. We will not waver; we will not tire; we will not falter; and we will not fail. Peace and freedom will prevail'.[43] Will this peace include a resolution of the Arab and Israeli conflict such that Palestinians can live in dignity without fear of Israeli repression? Or is President Bush marching to the drum of Pope Urban who declared a Crusade over a millennium ago, or of Napoleon who invaded Egypt proclaiming that he had come to restore Islam to its genuine teachings? Only George Bush knows.

Notes

[1] Some of the information in this chapter is extracted from *The Charles Edmondson Historical Lectures* delivered at Baylor University, to be published as Yvonne Yazbeck Haddad, *Not Quite American? The Shaping of Arab and Muslim Identity in the United States*, Waco, Texas: Baylor University Press, 2004. I would like to thank Baylor University Press for the permission to republish some sections. Special thanks go to my research assistants Nicholas Reith and Ahmed Humayun for their help in locating and compiling information for this chapter.

[2] See for example: Timothy Worthington Marr, *Imagining Orientalism in America from the Puritans to Melville*, Ph.D. diss. New Haven: Yale University, 1997; Marwan M. Obeidat, *The Muslim East in American Literature: The Formation of an Image*, Ph.D. diss, Indiana University, 1985.

[3] The American Muslim Political Coordinating Council (AMPCC) was formed as an umbrella organization representing the American Muslim Alliance, The American Muslim Council, The Council on American-Islamic relations and The American Public Affairs Council.

[4] These organizations include the following: (1) The America-Arab University Graduates (AAUG) which was founded in 1967 by professionals, university professors, lawyers, doctors, and many veterans of the Organization of Arab Students (OAS). (2) The National Association of Arab Americans (NAAA), was organised in 1972 and modelled after the pro-

Israeli lobby, the American Israel Public Affairs Committee. Its leadership seeks to meet with members of congress and educate Arab Americans on the political process. (3) The Arab-American Anti-Discrimination Committee (ADC) was founded in 1980 by former Senator from South Dakota, James Aburezk, and modelled after ADL to fight racism and prejudice and discrimination against Arabs. It is currently the largest grassroots organization with chapters throughout the USA. (4) Arab American Institute (AAI) was established in 1984 when Jim Zoghby split from Aburezk. It encourages participation in the political system and seeks to get Arab Americans to run for office. It established Democratic and Republican clubs and was active in Jesse Jackson run for office in 1988.

[5] They include the following: (1) The American Muslim Alliance (AMA) focuses on voter registration, political education and leadership training and seeks Muslim participation as voters and elected officials nationwide in both parties. (2) The American Muslim Council (AMC) was established in 1990 with a focus on increasing Muslim participation in the political process. It gained legitimacy by arranging for Muslim religious leaders to open the House of Representatives with a Muslim invocation, hosted hospitality suites at the Democratic and Republican party conventions in 1992 and 1996 and worked for a more balanced Freedom from Religious Persecution Act and for the repeal of secret evidence. (3) American Muslims for Global Peace and Justice (Global Peace) established in 1998 is focused on creating networks working for human dignity, freedom, peace and justice. (4) American Muslims for Jerusalem (AMJ) incorporated in 1999 works for presenting accurate information about Muslim concerns about Jerusalem. (5) The Council on American Islamic Relations (CAIR) was established in 1994 to promote a positive image about Islam and Muslims and seeks to empower Muslims in America through political and social activism. (6) Muslim American Society (MAS) was founded in 1992 by the Ministry of Warith Deen Muhammad, an African American Sunni convert group, to promote a better society. It has a political arm, Muslims for Better Government, involved in voter registration and political education. (7) The Islamic Institute was founded in 1998 to create a better understanding between the Muslim community and the political leadership. (8) Muslim Public Affairs Council (MPAC) is involved in political activism.

[6] Ayad al-Qazzaz, 'The Arab Lobby: Toward and Arab-American Political Identity', *al-Jadid*, 14, January 1997, p. 10.

[7] Omar Afzal, 'Learn not Copy: Movements Facing Challenges of the West', The Message, March 1996, p. 23.

[8] Afzal, 'Learn not Copy', p. 23.

[9] Afzal, p. 23.

[10] His publications include: with Biyamin Netanyahu, editor, *Jerusalem Conference on International Terrorism. International Terrorism Challenge and Response: Proceedings of the Jerusalem Conference on International Terrorism.* New Brunswick: Transaction Books, 1981; *Terrorism: How the West Can Win.* New York: Farrar, Straus, Giroux, 1986; *Fighting Terrorism: How Democracies Can Defeat Domestic and International Terrorism.* New York: Farrar, Straus and Giroux, 1995.

[11] Among the most vociferous is Steven Emerson who produced the controversial documentary *Jihad in America* aired on PBS in which he claimed that Muslims use mosques for terrorist training. He also appeared before the House International Committee where he asserted that Radical Islamic networks now constitute the primary domestic – as well as international – national security threat facing the FBI and other law enforcement agencies. Steven Emerson, *Testimony of Steven Emerson: Subcommittee of Africa House International Relations Committee*, US House of Representatives, April 6, 1995, p.4. He was one of the first journalists to ascribe the Oklahoma City bombing to Muslim terrorists as vindication of his analysis and assessment. He has also published an article and is in the process of writing

a book on the topic. Steven Emerson, 'The Other Fundamentalists', *The New Republic*, June 12, 1995, 21-30.
[12] 'Has the Bush Administration Benefited Muslim Americans?' *The Minaret*, 23, 5 (May 2001) 7.
[13] Agha Said, 'The American Muslim Paradox', in *Muslim Minorities in the West: Visible and Invisible*, Yvonne Yazbeck Haddad and Jane I. Smith' Lanham, MD: Altamira Press, 2002, 39-58.
[14] Ihsan Bagby, Paul M. Pearl and Bryan T. Froehle, *The Mosque in America: A National Portrait*, released by the Council on American-Islamic Relations, Washington, DC, April 26, 2001, 4.
[15]'Has the Bush Administration Benefited Muslim Americans?' *The Minaret*, 23, 5 (May 2001) 10.
[16] 'Has the Bush Administration Benefited Muslim Americans?' *The Minaret*, 23, 5 (May 2001) 7.
[17] Ayesha Ahmad and Neveen A. Salem, 'Faiths Come Together at national Cathedral on National Day of Mourning', *Islam On Line* accessed 1/31/2004.
[18] 'President's Remarks at National Day of Prayer'.
http://www.whitehouse.gov/news/releases/2001/09/2001.
[19] Other Arab American and Islamic organizations that joined ADC in the brief include: Muslim Community Association of Ann Arbor, Arab Community Centre for Economic and Social Services, Bridge Refugee and Sponsorship Services, Council on American and Islamic Relations, Islamic Center of Portland and Masjid as-Sabir of Portland, OR.
[20] Interview with Fatima Al-Saawegh.
[21] Wajih Abu Zikri, A New American Religion for Muslims," *al-Akhbar*, December 26, 2001. FIBIS-NES-2001-1226.
[22] Omid Safi, ed., *Progressive Muslims: On Justice, Gender and Pluralism*, Oxford: Oneworld Publications, 2003.
[23] Aihwa Ong, 'A Multitude of Spaces: Radical versus Moderate Islam', paper presented at the AAA annual meeting in New Orleans, November 21, 2 9 September 2003. 002, p. 4. 13
[24] Farish A. Noor, 'The Other Malaysia: Panopticon Revisited', November 6, 2002, Malayskini.org.
[25] Paul Wolfowitz, 'Remarks at A Brookings Institution Issues Forum, September 5, 2002. http://servizi./Radicalparty.org/documents/index.php?fune+detail&par=130.
[26] Daniel Pipes as quoted in Dave Eberhart, 'Muslim Moderate Kabbani Firm on Terrorist Nuclear Threat', Newsmax.com, November 19, 2001. See also Robert I. Friedman, 'The Wobbly Israel Lobby; For the Once Potent AIPAC, It's Been a Very Bad Year', *Washington Post*, November 1, 1992.
[27] Martin Peretz, 'When America-Haters Become Americans', *The New Republic*, October 15, 2001.
[28] As reported in the *Los Angeles Times* by Solomon Moore, November 3, 2002.
[29] News Release, January 23, 2002.
[30] Pipes, Daniel. 'Identifying Muslim Moderates'. *Jewish World Review*, 25 November 2003 / 30 Mar-Cheshvan, 5764.
http://www.jewishworldreview.com/1103/pipes_2003_11_25.php3
[31] The organizations to be condemned include: Abu Sayyaf, Al-Gama'a al-Islamiyya, Groupe islamique armée, Hamas, Harakat ul-Mujahidin, Hizbullah, Islamic Jihad, Jaish-e-Mohammed, Lashkar-e-Tayyiba, and Al-Qaeda.
http://www.jewishworldreview.com/1103/pipes_2003_11_25.php3
[32] http://www.jewishworldreview.com/1103/pipes_2003_11_25.php3
[33] Ibid.

[34] Pipes, Daniel. 'Identifying Muslim Moderates'. Jewish World Review, 25 November 2003 / 30 Mar-Cheshvan, 5764.
http://www.jewishworldreview.com/1103/pipes_2003_11_25.php3

[35] Daniel Pipes, '[Moderate] Voices of Islam', New York Post, 23 September 2003. http://www.danielpipes.org/article/1225. *The Trouble with Islam: A Wake-Up Call for Honesty and Change.*

[36] Irshad Manji, *The Trouble with Islam: A Wake-Up Call for Honesty and Change*, Toronto: Random House Canada, 2003.

[37] http://www.Jewishworldview.com/1103/pipes

[38] Dave Eberhart, 'Muslim Moderate Kabbani Firm on Terrorist Nuclear Threat', Newsmax.com, November 19, 2001.

[39] These include: The Islamic Supreme Council of America, the Council for Democracy and Tolerance, American Islamic Congress, Society for Humanity and Islam in America, Ataturk Society and the Assembly of Turkish American Associations. http://www. Jewishworldview.com/1103/pipes

[40] Jane Perlez, 'Muslim-as-Apple-Pie Videos are Greeted with Skepticism', *New York Times*, October 30, 2002.

[41] See for example, Mae E. Cheng, 'Legal Catch-22 for Immigrants', *Newsday*, December 14, 2003.

[42] Dannheisser, Ralph. 'Islam Compatible With Democracy, Not Monolithic, Muslim Panelists Say'. US Embassy Malaysia,
http://usembassymalaysia.org.my/wf/wf0909_islam.html

[43] George Bush, 'Presidential Address to the nation', October 7, 2001, http://www.whitehouse.gov/news/releases/2001/10/2001.

Chapter 8

The Impact of 9/11 on British Muslim Identity

Dilwar Hussein

Background

I often begin presentations on 'Muslims in Britain' by saying that 'it is an "interesting" time to be a Muslim!' The visible presence of Muslims in Europe has been perceived, by many, to be a real challenge to the status quo of the culture and traditions of European states. World events, such as those of 9/11, have had such sweeping effects on Islam and Muslims across the world that only time will allow us to record. Is this a clash of civilisations? Maybe – maybe not. Only in the luxury of a retrospective analysis can such questions be truly answered, for today, we are still living through the moment. It hasn't just been 9/11 though – over the last four decades event after event has reminded the world of the presence of Muslims. The Saudi oil embargo in the 1970s, the Iranian Revolution in 1979, the Iran-Iraq war in the 1980s, the Satanic Verses affair in the late 1980s and early 1990s, the eruption of Bosnia in the 1990s, the Gulf Wars in the 1990s, 9/11 in 2001 and then the 'War on Terror' and conflicts in Afghanistan and Iraq.

In this Chapter I hope to give an overview of the presence of British Muslims then look at 9/11 and the impact that this has had on the British Muslim community so far. Before I continue I should mention that I will at times use the word 'community' as a sociological construct to refer to the Muslim presence in Britain, though the term has its limitations. First, some approaches in Europe are not comfortable with the term because of its connotation of group life and ghettoisation, for example in France the individual citizen is given a very prominent place in social space and the nature of the relationship between the individual and the state is seen to negate the sense 'community' as used in the UK. The second reason is that due to the very diverse nature of the British Muslim presence it is difficult to always talk of a single entity where so much difference exists in terms of first language, political allegiance, religious sub-denomination etc. It may therefore be more accurate to talk of 'communities' in plural. An example could be given of comparative differences between the Muslims of Gujarati/East African origin living in Leicester and the Muslims of Mirpuri/Pakistani origin in Bradford. There are significant differences of class, educational levels, employment skills base and household income, leading to very different dynamics of community formation and interaction with the life of these respective cities. What makes matters worse and better at the same time is the ambiguity surrounding, and number of different sociological definitions of, the term 'community'.

Muslim communities in Britain

The UK contains one of the most diverse Muslim communities in Europe. It may come as a surprise to some that Islam and the British Isles have had centuries of interaction. The mention, in Arabic, of the Muslim declaration of faith on coins minted by King Offa (d.796) is a cryptic example of this. One such coin along with the Ballycottin Cross (dated to the ninth century), containing an inscription of the '*basmala*', were, until recently, held in the British Library. Despite this early interaction it was in the eighteenth century that the first Muslims began to form communities in Britain. As the migrants were mainly sailors, most of these communities were formed in areas of the major port cities such as Liverpool, Newcastle and London. Two significant communities were formed in Woking and Liverpool with a number of converts playing an important role in the community. These communities were quite small and localised and it was much later, after the Second World War, that more significant numbers of Muslims migrated and settled. A key reason for migration was that the post-war economy in Britain needed labourers. Additionally, in the recently decolonised regions of the world, economic and educational conditions were not satisfactory. This led to a 'push-pull' effect which, over two decades, brought a significant number of Muslims to the UK, mainly from the rural areas of Pakistan and Bangladesh, invited to participate in migration as a result of their historic relationship with Britain through colonisation and now part of the new commonwealth. In addition to this South Asian presence, a number of Muslims came from different parts of the Arab world, mainly for educational purposes. Over the years, these communities have been joined by Muslims originating from Africa, Europe and far East-Asia, as well as converts from the UK, to form an ethnically diverse community. About half of the 1.6 million[1] British Muslims now present were born in the UK.

The UK does not have a system of 'recognition' of religion as found in some other EU states such as Germany or Belgium. Instead the relationship is a complex one governed by less formal arrangements and discrete references in the legal system that may be of relevance to the minority concerned. The Jews and Sikhs are viewed as ethnic groups and are therefore protected when it comes to discrimination. There are also some limited provisions for Jews to observe elements of Jewish law in personal matters. Citizenship has generally been easier to obtain in the UK as compared to some other countries in Europe and most people from the minorities residing in the UK today are British citizens.

With the arrival of migrants in the 1960s and 1970s a very pronounced debate started to take place as to the position and status of these migrants. The tone of the debate in the early stages was very similar to that in other parts of Europe. Should these minorities be sent back? Would they take away jobs from British people? Would they be an economic burden? Perhaps the most vociferous participants in the political debate were Enoch Powell of the Conservative Party and Roy Jenkins of the Labour Party. They stood poles apart. It was within this debate that the British notion of multiculturalism was crystallised: 'a flattening process of uniformity, but cultural diversity, coupled with equal opportunity in an atmosphere of mutual tolerance.'[2]

Though Muslim communities began to form in the UK from the early nineteenth century, the most significant institutions that remain in existence were initiated by migrants who settled around the time of, and after, the Second World War. The first major initiative to establish Muslim organisations in the post-war period was the formation of the Islamic Cultural Centre and the Mosque Trust in 1944 and the subsequent opening of the London Central Mosque at Regents Park in 1977.

Statistical data on Muslims in Britain

The 2001 census was the first one in recent times to include a question on religious affiliation.[3] This was a quite a controversial step and initially created a great deal of debate within the different religious communities of the UK and also among liberal circles. Eventually it seemed that the major faith communities endorsed it. The response to the question was surprisingly high considering that it was left as a voluntary one with just over 92 per cent of people answering the question. About 15.5% of the UK population stated that they had no religion. Some of the data on religious affiliation is still being cross-correlated with other factors such as economic deprivation, crime, housing and employment but the most basic datasets were released from February 2003 onwards.

Census 2001 figures for religious affiliation in UK[4]

Religious Affiliation	*Value*	*Percentage*
Christians	42,079,000	71.6
Muslims	1,591,000	2.7
Hindus	559,000	1.0
Sikhs	336,000	0.6
Jews	267,000	0.5
Buddhist	152,000	0.3
Other	179,000	0.3
No Religion	9,104 15.5	
Not Stated	4,289 7.3	

As the census data for 1991 was based on ethnic categories alone a real comparison cannot be made with the last census. However, analysts had relied on the groups with known significant Muslim populations to extrapolate a figure ranging from 1.3 to 1.6 million for 1991.

Regional distribution of Muslims in England

The largest Muslim communities have been formed around the old industrial cities and nearly half the Muslims are located within the greater London area. English cities with five largest Muslim populations were:

London	607,000
Birmingham	140,000
Gtr Manchester	125,000
Bradford	75,000
Kirklees	39,000

The breakdown in terms of local government administrative authorities shows that London contains the local authority with the highest Muslim percentage – Tower Hamlets – with 36.4%. Also of the top ten populated local authorities, four (Tower Hamlets, Newham, Waltham Forest and Hackney) are in London.

Local Authority	*Value*	*Percentage*	*Ranking*
Tower Hamlets	71,389	36.4	1
Newham	59,293	24.3	2
Blackburn with Darwen	26,674	19.4	3
Bradford	75,188	16.1	4
Waltham Forest	32,902	15.1	5
Luton	26,963	14.6	6
Birmingham	140,033	14.3	7
Hackney	27,908	13.8	8
Pendle	11,988	13.4	9
Slough	15,897	13.4	10

The table below shows the numbers of adherents of different faith groups in England and Wales broken down according to age profile.

Age	*Christian*	*Buddhist*	*Hindu*	*Jewish*	*Muslim*	*Sikh*
0 - 15	6,824,189	17,286	115,808	44,577	522,860	80,755
16 - 24	3,463,825	19,491	83,620	25,489	281,628	55,113
25 - 49	12,619,115	75,177	238,774	82,385	567,182	134,397
50 - 59	5,217,434	20,264	56,787	36,617	81,944	28,259
60 - 64	2,121,798	4,584	20,956	13,004	36,510	10,566
65 - 74	3,726,398	5,092	25,779	25,375	42,850	13,506
75 and over	3,365,727	2,559	10,697	32,480	13,652	6,762

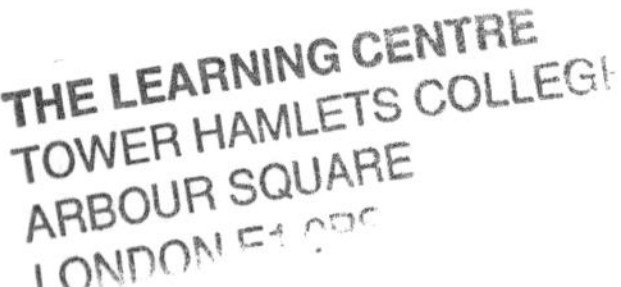

The table shows that age profiles vary considerably across the faith communities and that Muslim and Sikh communities have a very high proportion of young people. 33.8 % of Muslims and 24.5 % of Sikhs are aged 0–15, and 18.2 % of Muslims and 16.7 % of Sikhs are aged 16–24. The England and Wales average is 20.2% aged 0–15 and 10.9% aged 16–24. The table also shows that Christian and Jewish groups have an aging population; the average is 16% whereas there are 19% Christians and 22.3 % Jews above the age of 65. This is important to our discussion on identity as it reveals the large proportion of young Muslims – for whom identity is a highly topical issue.

Political life

British Muslims began joining the mainstream political parties in the 1960s and the first councillor, Bashir Maan, was elected in 1970. Until quite recently the affiliation was almost exclusively with the Labour Party. Currently there are over two hundred Councillors,[5] two Members of the House of Commons, four Members of the House of Lords and one Member of the European Parliament, that are of Muslim origin. It is difficult to estimate the number of Muslims that are members of the various parties.

Table: Number of Muslim Councillors according to Party in 2000[6]

Party	*Muslim Councillors*
Labour	166
Liberal Democrat	27
Conservative	20
Justice	6
Total	**219**

According to the Institute of Public Policy Research (IPPR) there is still a strong case of under representation of ethnic minority candidates (including Muslims) in political positions[7]. The report, which calls for urgent positive action, found that there are only twelve black and Asian MPs, a figure which should be around 47[8] in order to be more reflective of the demographic situation of the UK. 2.5% of the councillors are from ethnic minority backgrounds while there should be around 6% and there should be around six black and Asian members of the Greater London Assembly (GLA) whereas in reality there are only two.

Table: IPPR Estimate of ethnic minority under-representation in political positions[9]

	Current situation	*More reflective situation*
MPs	12	47
Councillors	2.5% (530)	6% (1,272)
Members of GLA	2	6

Muslims have traditionally been keen supporters of the Labour Party. However, in recent years there has been a gradual increase in support for the other two mainstream parties as well. This has probably been egged on by dissatisfaction with some of the Government's foreign policy choices and also domestic stances on matters such as the repeal of Clause 28 and the lowering of the age of consent for gay relationships. The reasons for supporting the Labour Party find their roots in the immigration stance that Labour took in the 1970s, along with of course the fact that being factory workers, first generation Muslims would have had strong links with the unions. The local elections of 2003 saw Labour losing a large number of seats. Though there are no studies yet to prove why, it is thought that anti-war sentiment played a large role in shifting votes from Labour to the Liberal Democrats. In Leicester for example, the previous four Muslim councillors (all Labour) lost their seats. At the same time there were four new councillors of Muslim background, but this time with affiliation to the Liberal Democrats. Patricia Hewitt, a Labour MP for Leicester commented that Muslims were registering their protest against the Labour party and acknowledged that she was not surprised by the lack of support for Labour in the Muslim community.[10] A number of groups including the Muslim Association of Britain (MAB) led vociferous campaigns asking Muslims not to vote for Labour out of protest for the Government's stance on the war in Iraq. Especially after the events of 9/11 there has been considerable scrutiny on the Muslim communities in the UK, especially in terms of loyalty, belonging and identity.

Identity – The definition of self[11]

Modern societies produce a heightened sense of the individual and the notion of self-identity thus becomes very important. The daily choices we make vis-à-vis clothing, food, newspapers, all speak volumes about who we are and send out images, conscious or sub-conscious, about the type of person we think we are. Choices of belief, personal philosophy, career, and relationships similarly give out such signals. Yet self-identity is not just a matter of one way traffic, for we constantly influence others and are influenced by external factors, be that the people around us, the pervading culture or the context in which we live. Because of the individualisation of society and the break from traditional modes of social roles, this notion of self-identity becomes more powerful. The individual has achieved a greater scope of choice to shape his/her self, to be an individual. As Giddens puts it:

> What to do? How to act? Who to be? These are focal questions for everyone living in circumstances of late modernity – and ones which, on some level or another, all of us answer, either discursively or through day-to-day social behaviour.[12]

Giddens also points out the connections between the most 'micro' and 'macro' levels that impinge on social identity and social change.[13] Sociology cannot make sense of each of these levels by looking at them in isolation. If, for example, one is to consider the changes in morality in Britain post World War Two – looking at relationships outside marriage, increases in crimes of a moral nature or the increase in sexual imagery in the public domain – such changes cannot be accounted for adequately by looking at the either the micro or micro levels. They were not led by social institutions or the state, yet neither did individuals spontaneously change their minds about moral behaviour. Most of such changes were influenced by a decline of religious authority and the rise of rationalism and materialism in British society. These changes were in turn affected by other social factors and influences. Changes in laws regarding family and gender roles would have come from the macro level, yet their demands would have stemmed from the micro level. The change within the micro level would have been caused by social movements at the macro level, which of course would have come from people's experiences and dissatisfaction at the micro level. Change is therefore a result of a very complex interaction of micro and macro forces. Agencies such as the media naturally play a significant role in the shaping of our images of self, others and the relationships between the self and the other. While news and documentaries may inform us or 'report' to us, such information is also re-appropriated by society and a closed cause and effect loop is set up. Hence information in the media does not merely reflect the world, but constantly shapes it as well.

The transient and multiple nature of identity

Foucault looks at identity as something that is not within a person, but something that is the result of people interacting. People do not possess a real identity; rather an identity is a temporary construction that is constantly shifting. Identity is thus relational. For Foucault the notion of self is related to power. Power, which may be defined as the ability to influence the environment, is an action which individuals engage in. Power is not possessed, it is exercised. And where there is power, there is bound to be resistance. Hence identities are not given, but are the products of ongoing processes, meaning that identities are constantly produced and transformed through social interaction.[14] Not only are identities transient but single individuals rarely occupy or appropriate single identities. An individual may be a father, husband, son, cousin, uncle, office worker, sportsman, etc. all at the same time, shifting effortlessly from one role to another or indeed juggling different roles at the same time while negotiating his way through life. Similarly when considering a religious and national group such as Muslims living in Britain, multiple layers of identity may come into play.

What do we mean by Muslim identity?

In previous writings I have proposed that the most important elements that impinge on the formation of a Muslim identity are threefold:

1. The concept of self
2. The concept of territory
3. The concept of community

1. Self

Muslim identity is forged by the complex interchange of numerous factors, perhaps the most influential among these being the concept of God and man's relationship with God. For a Muslim, God is One (*Tauhid*) and is the Creator, Sustainer and the final Judge of all affairs. He is the Lawgiver and the Sovereign, but above all He is Merciful and Forgiving. And while man is created as vicegerent of God (*Khalifah*), as His Trustee on earth, God is ever conscious that man is liable to weakness and forgetfulness. In fact the word for man (*insan*) means the 'one that forgets'. Man is therefore deputed, but encouraged to constantly bear his Lord in mind (*dhikr*) in order to be conscious of Him (*taqwa*) and accomplish His duty as *khalif* with justice and diligence. This strong relationship between man and God is designed to keep God at the hub of man's life such that the divine spirit touches all of man's actions whether this worldly or that worldly – in fact there is no such division, for God is the Guide in all affairs. In order to remind mankind, throughout the ages, God has chosen messengers and given them inspiration and revelation to bring people back on track. This role now rests with the believers who are encouraged to 'call unto good things', to 'promote what is right and discourage what is wrong'. This spiritual relationship (*rabbaniyah*) sets the scene for man's many and varied roles in life.

The Muslim is therefore a subject of God, in fact His deputy, who lives not for himself only but to bring goodness to humanity. The concepts of *tauhid* (God's unity and uniqueness), *istikhlaf* (viceregence), *dhikr* (remembrance), *taqwa* (God-consciousness) and *rabbaniyah* (relationship with God) form the core of a Muslim being and essence.

2. Territory

Traditional Muslim societies were not based on the nation state and Muslims lived in territories where it was not uncommon to see people of various ethnic and linguistic backgrounds sharing the same geographical space. To this day the debate goes on as to how legitimate nation states are within the Islamic framework.

Another fundamental idea in the conception of space is the role of religion in public life. Until secularism became firmly established in the post-Ottoman era, Muslim societies saw a greater fusion of religious, political, economic and social life, as Ernest Gellner comments: 'it has one important sociological consequence: the absence of accommodation with the temporal power. Being itself Caesar, it had no need to give unto Caesar'. [15]

This said, there was always recognition within Muslim societies of distinction between the public and private, and political and religious domains leading to a *de facto* division of powers. However, this was not as pronounced, particularly in the case of the latter, as in modern secular states. During early Islamic history, Muslim scholars derived specific geo-political terms to define the way in which the law should apply to Muslims living within and outside the Muslim territories. The region that was under Muslim rule was defined as *Dar al-Islam* (abode of Islam) and the 'other' regions were variously described as *Dar al-Harb* (abode of war), *Dar al-Kufr* (abode of unbelief), *Dar al-'Ahd* and *Dar al-Sulh* (abode of treaty), *Dar al-'Amn* (abode of security), etc. Many more definitions were coined, but by far the most popular to the scholars were the first two, leading to what Tariq Ramadan calls 'a binary vision of the world':[16] the world of Islam and the world of 'Others'. The implication this had on jurisprudence was serious. Though there were differences among the various schools, most of them disliked that a Muslim should live outside *Dar al-Islam*. Permission was granted for traders, students, preachers, etc., but these were generally seen as exceptions granted for a minimum time. Upon close scrutiny one can deduce that the vital criteria of *Dar al-Islam* were seen to be factors such as personal security, justice, freedom of worship and avoidance of corruption. One may, therefore, raise questions about the situation today, where in some cases Muslims have been forced to flee from Muslim countries and seek refuge in countries in the West because of political problems. It is bearing these factors in mind that some contemporary scholars are questioning the whole approach of this binary vision. Is it possible in this globalised world to have such a vision, especially when no such entity exists that the scholars can unanimously identify as *Dar al-Islam* against which a *Dar al-Harb* can be defined? Furthermore, it is pointed out that the terms are of juristic origin rather than having their basis in either the Qur'an or the *Sunnah*. The Qur'an reminds that: 'to God belongs the East and the West',[17] that regardless of political or moral expression in different countries the *whole* earth belongs to the Creator.

3. Community

The Qur'an relates the story of many messengers, saying that God sent the messengers 'to their brethren',[18] who were non-Muslims. The prophets addressed their community as 'my People!'[19] (*Qawmi*). Hence there is a fraternal relationship between the Muslim and his community, regardless of their belief. The Muslim is one of 'them', 'they' are part of the *Qawm*. The Qur'an further clarifies this:

> O mankind! Behold, we have created you from a male and female, and have made you nations and tribes, so that you might come to know one another. Verily the noblest of you in the sight of God is the one who is most conscious of him ...[20]

Thus, plurality of cultures and ethnic groups is acknowledged as a positive factor to enhance human life, rather than be a cause of prejudice. The notion of *ummah* which attempts to unify Muslims across the globe does not negate one's duties to those who are neighbours, fellow countrymen or part of one's *Qawm*. The idea of the concept of *ummah*, as theoretical as it may be, is to transcend the bonds of kinship, language, region and ethnicity. Such ties, identified as *asabiyah* by the fourteenth century Muslim historian and sociologist Ibn Khaldun (d. 1406), are frowned upon when taken as the normative in group cohesiveness. In expressing national or local ties, the question of physical manifestations of belonging is often a point of debate among Muslims. As a citizen, can a Muslim engage in acts of patriotism – perhaps the most visible of which are acts such as displaying the flag or reading, or standing for, the national anthem? According to Shaikh Faisal Mawlawi:

> Muslims living in non-Muslim countries are to respect the symbols of those countries such as the national anthem, national flag, etc. This is part of what citizenship dictates as per modern customs...Thus, standing up for the national anthem is not a form of prohibited loyalty. If a Muslim is to change a wrong action in a majority non-Muslim country, let him do that through *Da'wah*, wisdom and fair exhortation. At the same time, he should not obey any rules that involve disobedience to Allah.[21]

One other question that is often posed is 'which are you first: Muslim or British?' In light of the above discussion on justice, such a question is actually a non-issue. In fact, there are two distinct identities involved here: one is a religious and philosophical identity and the other is a national or territorial identity. Just as one could be Christian and British, or Humanist and British, so one can be Muslim and British, without the need for contradiction, tension or comparison between the two.

At the centre of debates such as Muslims expressing an identity that is British, or indeed engaging in the political process of a Western country (that may be at odds with some sections of the Muslim world) is the notion of loyalty (*wala'*). To whom is loyalty due? According to a *fatwa* of the European Council for Fatwa and Research *wala'* can be divided into two areas:

> 1. Loyalty in religious matters. It refers to creedal loyalty, which lies in believing in Allah and shunning other beliefs that run counter to the Oneness of Allah. This kind of *wala'* is due to Allah, His Messenger and the believers. Almighty Allah says: "Your friend can be only Allah; and His messenger and those who believe, who establish worship and pay the poor due, and bow down (in prayer)".[22]

> 2. Loyalty as regards worldly matters: This refers to transactions between people living in the same society or between different societies, regardless of the distance and the religion. It is permissible for Muslims to engage with non-Muslims in commercial transactions, peace treaties and covenants according to the rules and conditions prevalent in those countries. Books of Jurisprudence do contain many references about such kind of dealings.[23]

Loyalty is hence multi-faceted and operates at different levels. Each one of us regularly balances loyalties to ourselves, our families, our work commitments and careers, our friends, the community, the nation, etc. Often these loyalties can clash, but this is not a case just for Muslims, but for all people. A person with a passion for the environment, for example, may have personal views about how to live and consume that do not agree with the views of the majority, or at least with some state policies. Living in any society involves a constant negotiation of our different values and ideas, allegiances and loyalties. The very framework of most modern constitutions, as well as international treaties on Human Rights are designed to facilitate this by giving room for freedom of individual thought and belief.

The impact of 9/11

Only time will tell how serious and consequential an occasion 9/11 will be in the vast expanse of human history. Will it stand out as a moment such as Martin Luther's Protest against the Catholic Church, the Industrial Revolution or the collapse of Communism? Yet, even if it does not reach such magnitudes of change, there is no doubt that the events of 9/11 have had some significant effects, especially on the Muslim world. As for those Muslims living in Britain the effects may not be as pronounced as Muslims in the US, or Afghanistan, but they are important nonetheless.

We saw, while looking at the notion of identity, that it is relational, it operates not in isolation but in a context and 9/11 has radically influenced the context for British Muslims. British Muslims have been detained in Guantanamo Bay, British Muslims have been arrested on suspicion of terrorism, mosques and homes have been raided, and some have pointed to London as a 'hub of Islamic terrorism' (sic). With all this a spotlight has been placed over the British Muslim community that has brought with it a number of important consequences. In some ways perhaps 9/11 has merely acted as a catalyst of history, speeding up a process of change that was bound to happen, for its consequences are not entirely positive or negative. Indeed it is difficult to judge the effects in many cases.

The Muslim Council of Britain (MCB) issued a press statement condemning the attacks on 9/11 three hours after the incident and then held a press conference two days later gathering a large number of Muslim leaders to a similar statement. Countless other Muslims institutions through websites, emails, press statements, talks, study circles, leaflets etc. all condemned the attacks. Despite this, hate mail, offensive phone calls, arson attacks on mosques and attacks on individuals, thought to be Muslim, began to occur at an alarming rate. It was the

Runnymede Trust that popularised the term 'Islamophobia' with the launch of their report in 1997, *Islamophobia: A Challenge for us all.* The issue was also highlighted by the University of Derby's *Project on Religious Discrimination* in 2000, commissioned by the Home Office. It was also raised by the Parekh Report on *The Future of Multi-Ethnic Britain* in October 2000. After 9/11 a paper launched by the Psychology Department of Leicester University in 2002 concluded that there have been increased experiences of discrimination against the British Muslim community after 9/11. On a European level The European Union Monitoring Centre (EUMC) on racism and xenophobia identified in a report[24] that there has been a significant rise in physical and verbal attacks on Muslims, as well as a heightened climate of discrimination, after 9/11.

The climate now allowed for a revitalisation of the Far Right in British Politics and the British National Party launched a new 'Campaign to Keep Britain Free of Islam'. One of its leaflets downloadable from the BNP website stated that Islam stood for Intolerance, Slaughter, Looting, Arson and Molestation of women. There was even an attempt to recruit Sikhs and Hindus into the campaign to isolate and target Muslims as a common enemy. The BNP distributed thousands of tapes, CDs and leaflets and in subsequent local government elections has gone on to win more support than they ever had before. Furthermore, in the name of responding to the rise of the Right the Government has taken up harsher stances on issues such as immigration and asylum, so as not to lose the 'Middle-England' vote.

All of this has somewhat polarised views at different levels. There has been very negative media coverage[25] of Muslims and Islam while at the same time, an openness from some sections of the media that would have been unimaginable prior to 9/11, such as the *Daily Telegraph* special supplement on Islam[26] and a number of other opinion pieces, articles and programmes. At the level of politics, while the general climate crept towards a constriction of civil liberties and new counter terrorism laws were rushed in through Parliament, new opportunities were also created for dialogue with Government and a number of meetings were held with the Prime Minister and other senior Ministers. At the level of the general public, while there was a well documented rise in Islamophobia, new opportunities for dialogue were also created between faith and cultural institutions, individuals and communities. Initiatives such as open days run by Muslim institutions or the annual Islam Awareness Week spearheaded by the Islamic Society of Britain (ISB) have taken on a renewed importance and have attracted widespread support from non-Muslims. Partnerships between Muslims and non-Muslims have also been strengthened through campaigns such as the 'Stop the War' actions and now the greater involvement of Muslims, through many of those left-wing affiliations, in the anti-Globalisation movement. Within the Muslim community, polarisation of views has also occurred with some becoming further radicalised. François Burgat's notion of 'bilateral radicalisation' probably holds true in this case as well, that in the process of observing the reactions to 9/11, the attacks on Afghanistan and Iraq, while feeling that there is a double standard at play when dealing with the Muslim world, it is especially young Muslims who feel more isolated and alienated. They become further distanced by observing that fellow Muslims want to deal with the establishment that has betrayed them, and thus they turn to radical alternatives outside the 'system' of both the State and the traditional structures of the Muslim community. It is difficult to state what proportion of Muslims would take this option but a MORI Poll, carried out on behalf of a British-Asian newspaper, *Eastern Eye*, in November 2001 showed that there were only minor differences between Muslims and other Asian religious groups in expressions of loyalty. The question asked was: 'How loyal, if at all, would you say you are to Britain?'

	All %	*Hindu %*	*Muslim %*	*Sikh %*
Very loyal	49	62	42	55
Fairly loyal	41	30	45	40
Not very loyal	5	4	6	4
Not at all loyal	1	0	2	0
Don't know	4	3	5	1
Not stated	*	1	0	0

To coincide with the 1st annual memorial of 9/11, the MCB (Muslim Council of Britain) launched a book, *The Quest for Sanity: Reflections on September 11 and the Aftermath*. The book contains a series of (mainly) short articles looking at the effects of 9/11 globally and locally and mentions a pilot youth survey conducted by the MCB in December 2001 to ascertain the reaction of young British Muslims to 9/11.[27]

One of the significant effects of 9/11 was to break the taboo of Muslims speaking out against the extremists within. Prior to 9/11 most Muslims were very wary of 'washing their dirty linen in public', a phenomenon present within many communities especially where there is a perceived sense of struggle against the outside world (often in terms of racism, disadvantage, discrimination, etc). One would expect that subsequent to an incident such as 9/11 the Muslim community would close ranks to defend itself against the 'outside'. However, people felt that it was this very attitude that had led to the growth of a small but significant number of extremists, and for the first time major institutions and community leaders across the West began to pinpoint and talk of individuals who would bring disrepute to Islam, some even calling for radical preachers to be expelled. Tariq Ramadan in Switzerland wrote of the need to criticise Muslim extremism, Yusuf Islam famously stated that 'they have hijacked my religion',[28] the Islamic Society of Britain categorically denounced suicide bombings and declared them to be 'a major sin'[29] and Hamza Yusuf, in the US, declared that if there were any martyrs on 9/11 it would have been the people who risked their lives while trying to save the victims of the attack.[30] The ensuing months and years have resulted in a heartfelt search for how to deal with extremism within the Muslim community with a frankness and honesty that was clearly not there before.[31] How to deal with the anger, frustration, hatred and radicalisation (of young men in particular) and stop the extremist tendencies attracting any more support? How have we allowed Islam, a beautiful spiritual force, to be interpreted in such a way as to lend support to such ugly and evil acts?

Certainly the climate hasn't helped. The War on Terror is read by many as 'War on Islam' or 'Crusade'. The attack on Afghanistan and Iraq, the hyper-power with which the US seems to dominate world events and the almost equivalent hyper-power of the media to arbitrarily declare truth and falsehood – such that Baudrillard commented cynically in the 1990s that the Gulf War did not happen. Such developments have created a deeply politicised context in which 'Islam' has been assumed as the nexus. Thus perhaps the most widespread impact on British Muslims is that events such as 9/11 (and the *Satanic Verses* affair, the Gulf War and the Ethnic Cleansing in Bosnia previously) emphasise the 'Islamic' component of an individual's identity over the 'ethnic' or 'national' component. Sophie Gilliat-Ray suggests that:

> Nationalist ties appear to be a secondary means of identity for many young British Muslims. Given the racism so deeply embedded in parts of British Society, feelings of 'belonging' to this country may be insecure, while at the same time they do not feel that an identity based upon being of Pakistani origin offers a viable identity in this country. Religion provides a way out of this identificational *impasse*, and presents a secure foundation for identity based upon time-honoured religious myths and rituals.[32]

A context such as 9/11 thus gives primacy to an Islamic identity with a secondary ethnic affiliation as opposed to a cluster of ethnic or national identities that are somehow loosely connected via the thread of a vaguely religious Islamic identity. Identity thus becomes more politicised and as that identity is often forged in oppositional terms, it also becomes more defiant.

Notes

[1] This figure is from the 2001 Census. Some have argued that accounting for growth and the fact that the question was a voluntary one, the actual figure in 2003 is closer to 1.8 million. See the works of Muhammad Anwar based at Warwick University.

[2] Roy Jenkins, *Essays and Speeches*. 1967. Quoted in Phillip Lewis, *Islamic Britain: Religion, Politics and Identity among British Muslims*, London: I.B. Tauris. 1994. p. 3.

[3] A similar question did exist prior to this one but was removed in the 1800s.

[4] All the census data mentioned is crown copyright and can be found on www.statistics.gov.uk.

[5] Based on figures for 2000.

[6] 'Muslim Councillors in the UK: May 2000', compiled by *The Muslim News*, 2001.

[7] Rushanara Ali and Colme O'Cinneide, *Our House? Race and Representation in British Politics*, London: IPPR, April 2002.

[8] According to Muhammad Anwar this figure should include about 20 MPs of Muslim origin, see: Anwar, Muhammad, 'British Muslims: Socio Economic Position', in Mohammad Seddon et al., *British Muslims: Loyalty and Belonging*. The Islamic Foundation and COF, Leicester, 2003, p. 65.

[9] Rushanara Ali and Colme O'Cinneide, *op cit.*

[10] Peter Hetherington, 'Lib Dem surge changes the landscape', *The Guardian*, Friday May 2, 2003.

[11] For a fuller discussion on British Muslim Identity see also: Dilwar Hussain, 'British Muslim Identity' in Dilwar Hussain et al. (eds.) *British Muslims Between Assimilation and Segregation*, Leicester: Islamic Foundation. 2004.
[12] Anthony Giddens, *Modernity and Self-Identity,* Stanford University Press. 1991. p.70.
[13] David Gauntlett, *Media, Gender and Identity: An Introduction*, Routledge, London and New York. 2002.
[14] Vered Kahani-Hopkins and Nick Hopkins, 'Representing British Muslims: the Strategic Dimension to Identity Construction', *Ethnic and Racial Studies,* Vol. 25. No. 2, March 2002, pp. 288-309.
[15] Ernest Gellner, 'A Pendulum Swing Theory of Islam', in Robertson, Roland, (ed.) *Sociology of Religion*, Penguin, 1976. pp. 127-138.
[16] Tariq Ramadan, *To Be a European Muslim.* Leicester: Islamic Foundation. 1999.
[17] Qur'an, 2: 115.
[18] See Qur'an, 7: 65, 7: 73, 7: 85, 11: 50, 11: 61, 11: 84.
[19] Ibid.
[20] Qur'an, 49:13.
[21] http://www.islamonline.net/fatwa/english/FatwaDisplay.asp?hFatwaID=79294 (Date of Fatwa: October 2002).
[22] Qur'an, 5: 55.
[23] http://www.islamonline.net/fatwa/english/FatwaDisplay.asp?hFatwaID=78491 (Date of Fatwa: August 2002).
[24] Jorgen Nielsen and Christopher Allen, *Anti-Islamic reactions within the European Union after the recent acts of terror against the USA*, European Monitoring Centre on Racism and Xenophobia, October 2001.
[25] See: Elizabeth Poole, *Reporting Islam*, London: IB Tauris. 2002.
[26] November 2001.
[27] See: *The Quest for Sanity: Reflections on September 11 and the Aftermath*, Middlesex: The Muslim Council of Britain. 2002.
[28] *The Independent*, October 2001.
[29] Leaflet: Terrorism and Islam: Exploding the Myths, see www.isb.org.uk.
[30] *San Jose Mercury News*, September 16, 2001.
[31] See for example: M. Hashim Kamali, 'Fanaticism and its Manifestation in Muslim Societies' in Aftab Ahmad Malik (ed.), The *Empire and the Crescent: Global Implications for a New American Century*, Bristol, UK: Amal Press. 2003. pp.175-207.
[32] Gilliat, Sophie, 'Back to Basics: The Place of Islam in the Self-Identity of Young British Muslims', in Clarke, Peter B., *New Trends and Developments in the World of Islam*, Luzac Oriental, 1998, pp.93-103.

Chapter 9

Endemically European or a European Epidemic? Islamophobia in a post 9/11 Europe

Christopher Allen

It can be without any doubt whatsoever, that the impact and significance of the events of 9/11 will have a deeply profound effect on the psyche of the American people;[1] not only those who experienced the traumatic events either directly or indirectly, but also those future generations who will need to try to understand and comprehend both the magnitude and relevance of the event in its rightful context. The same will no doubt be true for the wider world, watching the events dramatically unfold in the safety of their own homes and offices through the global lens of the world's media. It is still unclear some two years on, exactly how dramatically the events of 9/11 have affected the world today and what the legacy for tomorrow will be. To what extent 9/11 overshadows for example the ongoing 'war on terror', the worsening situation between Israel and Palestine, and the war in Iraq can only be guessed at as we are all unsure how such global tensions and relations would have otherwise unfolded. Before 9/11, such international flash-points were at best misty: since then however, the heavy metaphorical fog still rising from the twin towers makes everything increasingly difficult to see. The need for clarity is vital.

As Jorgen Nielsen recently described the predicament, 9/11 heralded a period of 'urgent history',[2] where considered analysis and reflective assessment has been quite impossible despite a pressing need to achieve otherwise. At the same time, the sheer hyperbolic overstatement that seems to have become such a vital component of any analysis of 9/11, has seen commentators describe this day and its aftermath as signifying everything from either the beginning of 'the end of history' through to the much dismissed until recent times, first throes of the 'clash of civilisations'.[3] However accurate these suggestions might be, what might be reasonably assumed is that the legacy of 9/11 will become deeply embedded within the collective memory of many future generations, not only in the United States (US) but also here in Europe and elsewhere. Whether future generations on both sides of the Atlantic will reflect upon and evaluate the events with the same clarity and understanding remains to be seen. What may well occur in the European psyche at least, is that the legacy of 9/11 will reinforce and feed into another enduring trait of the European mindset that has been there for a much longer period of time: the historical encounter and the ensuing dislike, mistrust and hatred of Islam and Muslims.

Writing in an article following 9/11 entitled, 'The politics of Islamophobia', Professor Yaqub Zaki suggested that the 'hatred of Islam and Muslims is endemic in the European psyche; endemic even if at times it becomes an epidemic. We are living through such an epidemic now'.[4] In his opinion, the events of 9/11 brought about an epidemic of Islamophobia by re-affirming an endemic prejudice and hatred that he suggests is as old as the religion of Islam itself. But whilst this may itself be seen to be sitting within the realms of 'hyperbolic overstatement', there is evidence to suggest that one of the most dangerous and worrying consequences of 9/11 has been a significant backlash against Muslims in Europe. This essay therefore sets out to reflect upon this evidence to re-evaluate the claims made by Zaki and to consider to what extent it might be termed an epidemic, before finally attempting to place this in the context of an endemic European legacy.

In beginning to consider this, it is worth considering some of those voices that would counter such a suggestion. For example, the British broadsheet *The Daily Telegraph* less than a month after 9/11, published a leader article under the heading 'Islamophilia'.[5] Denouncing the 'wave of Islamophobia' that many both inside and outside Muslim communities had become increasingly concerned with, *The Telegraph* preferred to describe the backlash against Muslims as 'the lie to this imaginary Islamophobia ... the backlash against [the British population's] Muslim neighbours is a myth ... this country in general cannot be fairly described as being even mildly Islamophobic'.[6] Whilst it is unfounded and unwise to suggest that Britain as a whole can be described as Islamophobic, it is probably just as unwise to suggest that Britain as a whole was entirely 'Islamophilic' either. What the Runnymede Trust noted some five years earlier would suggest something to the contrary: that Britain does quite clearly have traits of Islamophobia both in its attitudes towards Muslims, and in the social institutional infrastructures that exist.[7] Obviously Britain as a nation and as a society is immensely diverse and far from being uni-dimensional in any aspect of its collective identity, yet such a widespread and blanket dismissal of any suggestion of an ensuing backlash against Muslims in Britain would have appeared at such an early injunction to have been both premature and inaccurate. Within certain sectors of British society, both before and after the events of 9/11, Islamophobia could very easily tap into popular and quite widespread prejudices and beliefs. One needs to look no further than the explicitly anti-Muslim political campaigns, and the unprecedented electoral success gained from them, by the quasi-legitimate British National Party (BNP). Running campaigns entitled, 'Islam out for Britain' and 'No to fundamentalists', trying to suggest that anti-Muslim and anti-Islamic ideas could not strike a chord within some the predominantly white, socially deprived and culturally divided communities in the north of England would be quite ridiculous.[8] Such campaigns were clearly much more than just 'mildly Islamophobic'.

The fact that Islamophobia cannot be so readily dismissed is further reinforced by some of the statistics that were collated by concerned organisations throughout 9/11's immediate aftermath. Despite there being a lack of any governmental, UK wide effort to monitor reprisal attacks, the Islamic Human Rights Commission (IHRC)[9] was one of a number of organisations that attempted to do this at a much more localised level.[10] From its ensuing report, the IHRC's monitoring suggested that 674 attacks on Muslims or other Islamic targets were recorded as being directly motivated by the events of 9/11[11]. Ranging from instances of psychological pressure and harassment through verbal and written abuse, to the most serious cases of physical violence and damage against individuals and property, the report appears to counter the 'myth of Islamophobia' that *The Telegraph* preferred to suggest. When one also considers that 'the IHRC is aware that the vast majority of incidents including serious physical assaults go unreported',[12] and that its monitoring accessed only a very small cross-section of Britain's Muslim population, it is quite clear that if the same picture had been replicated nationwide, a backlash of some magnitude would have been in evidence.

Yet despite this, others preferred to dismiss both the data collated and the entire debate about Islamophobia as being irrelevant. Jennie Bristow, writing for the periodical *Spiked*, despite selectively quoting from the IHRC report, concluded that, 'a popular anti-Muslim racism did not happen'.[13] Dissecting, and at the same time dismissing, both the IHRC data and the fact that the Forum Against Islamophobia and Racism (FAIR) reported a staggering 600% increase in the number of callers to a helpline set up to record instances of anti-Muslim motivated attack,[14] Bristow like so many others remained unconvinced by the evidence. However, what Bristow's observations repeatedly overlooked was that whilst these figures in themselves were both substantial and worrying, both the IHRC and FAIR are London-based organisations that have relatively little permeation outside the greater London area. In this context alone, the abrupt dismissal by Bristow of Islamophobia as being a case of 'over-sensitivity' by Muslims would appear to be somewhat harsh at the very least. What her article and subsequently the periodical *Spiked* appeared to reinforce with their dismissive attitude was that, as the Runnymede Trust noted in *Islamophobia: a challenge for us all,*[15] anti-Muslim discourse was seen to be so natural and unproblematic that 'even organisations known for their liberalism and anti-racism express prejudice against Islam and Muslims'.[16] As *Spiked* prides itself on its liberal tendencies, it is clear that this aspect of the Runnymede report is still in evidence some half a decade after its publication. As the report continues, liberalism's prejudices are merely one element of a multi-faceted and multi-layered phenomenon that cannot be dismissed without any wider context.

Whilst only two examples against there being an upsurge, even less so an epidemic of Islamophobia, have been considered, they are both symptomatic and indicative of numerous other articles and features that appeared elsewhere across the various British media. Many print, visual and audio equivalents included ideas and expressions that maintained similar reservations about the legitimacy of the very concept of Islamophobia, openly questioning the reality of any backlash against Muslims in Britain and elsewhere.[17]And whilst the findings of both the IHRC and FAIR might be inconclusive through their respective limitations, similar findings have emerged from a number of other sources that undertook independent research through academic and other institutions. For example, the findings of Dr Lorraine Sheridan at the University of Leicester showed that following the attacks on the US, Muslims experienced the highest increase in incidents of racism and discrimination, becoming more prone to being a victim because of their religiosity and religious identity than because of their racial, ethnic or cultural identity.[18] Others, such as the Open Society Institute's investigation into the situation of Muslims in the UK, equally confirmed that racism was being honed into having a specifically anti-Muslim ethos, especially where 'following the events of 11 September Muslims and those perceived to be Muslim have faced unprecedented levels of attacks and violence'.[19] Enough evidence would therefore appear to exist to at least suggest that a backlash against Muslims was in fact somewhat a reality, albeit one that had been confirmed at a localised or regional level. In addition, the transition from racism being motivated by colour, ethnicity or nationality would appear to have begun to shift in this period as well, where the identifier for this new strand of racism became much more defined by religion and one's perceived rather than actual religious identity.

However, Zaki's statement referred directly to the situation across Europe and as such, the shift from the perspective of a locality or region to a pan-continental one is required if his observations are to be understood. To comprehend whether an epidemic of Islamophobia had swept Europe, a much more systematic approach to considering the issue would be required. Probably the most comprehensive and interesting resource that emerged out of the aftermath of 9/11 from the perspective of Europe, was the report published by the European Monitoring Centre on Racism and Xenophobia (EUMC) entitled, *Summary report on Islamophobia in the EU after 11 September 2001*.[20] In being quick to acknowledge the impact that international events have at the local, national and continental levels, on 12 September 2001 the EUMC implemented a monitoring mechanism to closely follow the situation across all fifteen of the European Union (EU) member states.[21] At this stage, it was decided as a matter of urgency that national short-term reports would be produced by the EUMC's RAXEN network of National Focal Points (NFPs), with each covering the following topics:

1. Acts of violence or aggression and changes in the attitude of the EU population towards ethnic, cultural, religious minorities, especially Islamic/Muslim communities but also other potentially vulnerable groups or new types of victims that may become targets as a result of the events of 9/11;
2. Good practices for reducing prejudice, violence and aggression;
3. Reactions by politicians and other opinion leaders including initiatives to reduce polarisation and counteract negative national trends.

In total, from the period commencing 12 September 2002 to the end of the calendar year, the NFPs were asked to produce five consecutive reports each. The first two sets of reports were published on the EUMC's website,[22] although a decision was made not to do so with the final three, the last of which became a summary and analysis of events for the whole period.

The ensuing summary report, published in May 2002, was a synthesis of all of the material, providing a comparative analysis of the reactions and changes in attitudes towards Muslims and Islam across the entire EU. As the EUMC quite categorically stated at the time of its publication, 'Muslims became indiscriminate victims of an upsurge of both verbal and physical attacks following the events of 11 September'.[23] The findings of this report alone, being the most comprehensive and wide-reaching monitoring project of Islamophobia anywhere in the world, would suggest that the spread of Islamophobia and anti-Muslim feeling became so virulent in the post-9/11 era that it permeated many levels of understanding: from the most basic of discourse at street level, to the rhetoric and politicising in the hierarchies of national and pan-European governance. From this basic premise, to preliminarily suggest that this permeation was an epidemic may not therefore be to underestimate the phenomenon. A new ferocity and dynamism emanating directly from the attacks on the US saw manifestations of anti-Muslim and anti-Islamic expression become much more extreme, much more explicit and much more widely accepted.

Irrespective of the variable levels of violence and aggression identified within each member nation, one of the report's most significant findings was the recurrence of attacks at street level upon the recognisable and visible traits of Islam and Muslims that exist across European society. Incidents included verbal abuse indiscriminately blaming all Muslims for the attacks, women having their *hijab* torn from their heads, adult men and women being spat upon, and children being called 'Osama' as a term of insult and derision,[24] all of which contributed to, and culminated in, a situation where a significant number of Muslims became random victims. Some of the most extreme of these saw the victims being left paralysed or hospitalised for many days.[25] Motivating the attacks appeared to be the assumption that the victims were legitimate merely because of their very Muslimness, usually being identified through the visual appearance of the victims, irrespective of whether they were Muslim or not. This was termed in the report as the 'visual identifiers': the visible and readily identifiable features of Muslims.[26] The visual identifiers therefore appeared to become a shorthand stimulant for those who felt that retaliatory attacks and violence were indiscriminately necessary and justified against all Muslims; whilst not enough evidence is available to suggest that this was the sole causal factor, it did appear to have some form of catalytic influence in those instances documented.

For Muslim women, arguably some of the most visibly recognisable religious adherents in contemporary European society, the situation across the EU was particularly dire where they became the primary target for anti-Muslim retaliation. In Denmark, for example, a woman wearing the *hijab* was thrown from a moving taxi after being accused of her role in the World Trade Center attack, whilst in Italy a woman wearing the *chador* was repeatedly shut in the door of a bus. In cities and towns across Austria, Germany, Ireland, Spain and elsewhere, women were spat upon and verbally abused. The most violent would appear to have occurred in Slough, England where a Muslim woman was beaten in broad daylight by men wielding baseball bats, apparently only because she was identified as being Muslim.[27] Only in Luxembourg, where Muslim women are largely visibly unidentifiable due to the absence of traditional Islamic attire and very few visual Islamic elements, were there no reports of any Islamophobically charged attacks on women. In fact the importance of considering the role and relevance of the visual identifiers, especially those attributed to women, may provide an additional insight into the motivations and causal tendencies of Islamophobia itself. It is clear that Muslim women are routinely and stereotypically represented and perceived through the distorting lens of anti-Muslim prejudice; whereas the Runnymede Trust observed, women are seen to be largely victims of faith, both as second class citizens and subservient to their husbands.[28] It is ironic that such a common perception of oppressed victimhood that had evolved in this period towards Muslim women, should result in those who were previously perceived to be victims of oppression to become the same victims of the so-called liberal societies that had defined them as 'oppressed' in the first place. Whilst this observation needs further investigation and thought, it would preliminarily appear that following 9/11 throughout Europe at least, Muslim women made the transition from perceived victim to actual victim, one where the empathiser became the perpetrator.

With regards to Muslim men, quite surprisingly the turban became the most prominent visual identifier, and by consequence, another target for pinpointing Muslims for further attacks and abuse. Surprisingly, only in France and Germany were Muslim men identified by their beards, despite this probably being a much more common characteristic of a Muslim man's appearance than that of wearing a turban. The focus upon the turban, however, must be attributed to the images that were widely disseminated through various media, where the visual image of Osama bin Laden and members of the Taleban all wearing turbans, became an essential and significant factor in the semiotics of the period. It was even reported in one British tabloid newspaper that Yusuf Islam – formerly the singer Cat Stevens – had become a target for abuse in this period for wearing a turban and had been repeatedly mistaken for looking like Osama bin Laden.[29] Whilst turbans are more appropriately associated with the attire of those adhering to the Sikh tradition, this particular focus for attack may indicate an apparent lack of knowledge about religious diversity across the EU and the inter-changeability between religions that in some parts of Europe commonly derive from the Indian subcontinent. Indeed this could have been the reason why in France and Germany the beard was more of a focus. As large percentages of their respective Muslim communities originate not from the Indian subcontinent but from North Africa and Turkey, so the beard may have been much more popularly seen to be an identifier of Muslims. Whereas in Britain, Muslims remain somewhat indiscriminately defined as Asian, and along with Hindus, Muslims and Sikhs are relatively undifferentiated. It was therefore unsurprising that the report subsequently acknowledged the number of times that Sikh men became victims of attacks because of this very fact. Whilst hostility towards Sikhs therefore was a feature of the aftermath of 9/11, it was a phenomenon that was largely incidental and one that was not deliberately motivated by religious hatred either of Sikhs or their religion.

In addition to the attacks on Muslim men and women, the relevance of visual identifiers could also be seen to be an essential factor in determining where attacks and damage were perpetrated against material constructs of Islam as well. Mosques, cultural centres, Islamic schools, and Muslim-owned businesses and property also became indiscriminate targets for retaliation. As a development of this premise, numerous examples were also cited where planning permission for proposed places of worship and other Islamic developments were also boycotted and restricted across the EU. In Italy, for example, one town mayor enlisted the support of local residents to petition against, and eventually stop, the development of any further mosques within a particular municipal region in the north of the country.[30] Similar, if somewhat less impacting, ventures were also identified elsewhere and it should be noted that still it remains illegal in countries such as Greece to build a mosque or other building for worship by Muslims.[31]

The EUMC report also noted that in the immediate aftermath of 9/11, the media increasingly cast its spotlight on Muslims, where speculation and sensationalism became asymmetrically balanced by an upsurge in genuine interest in each of the fifteen member states. At the same time, however, as Brian Whitaker notes, the newsworthiness of Muslims became so great in this period that in British newspapers the coverage given over to reporting with an Islamic or Muslim specific subject matter increased by just under 300% in the broadsheets, to an overwhelming 658% increase in the tabloids.[32] It is clear that the representation of Muslims in the media has always been an issue that many commentators have felt has perpetuated and reinforced Islamophobia through the repetitive and indiscriminate use of negativity attributed to Muslims, and common misunderstandings about the religion of Islam itself.[33] In the post-9/11 period, there is little evidence to suggest that this representation was any different. And whilst some medias attempted to differentiate between those that were believed to have perpetrated the attacks in the US from those Muslims that were both ordinarily resident and citizens of Europe, this was not the case everywhere. Inherent negativity, stereotypical images, fantastical representations, and grossly exaggerated and dangerously chimerical caricatures were all identifiable across the entire spectrum of European media. Balance, fairness and accuracy, whilst being present and identifiable in differing levels, were however in the minority.[34] As usual, the media preferred to rely heavily upon various historical archetypes and contemporary stereotypes that were immediately understood from the Euro-centric perspective. Neither should the effect of imported American satellite news channels nor the increasing disseminative audiences available to them, be underestimated in considering the overall impact and influence of the media. As Morley and Robins state, the ongoing removal of geographical spatial access that allows media to eradicate space, distance and time is a significant factor in the emergence of a homogenous television geography.[35]

Remaining within the European context, however, in Italy, the largest daily newspaper, the *Corriere della Sera* was described as being 'violent and insulting …' where '… the contents [were] explicitly anti-Muslim, anti-Arab and anti-migrant'.[36] In Ireland, concerns were raised about the effect that sensationalist journalism in imported British tabloids might have upon the newly established ethnic minority communities in Dublin and the subsequent relationship and interaction between them and the indigenous population. Without any doubt whatsoever, the Irish NFP felt that this type of reporting was ideal for initiating an atmosphere from which Islamophobia might easily evolve. But it was not just sensationalist journalism that caused concern with its ability to agitate and encourage anti-Muslim feeling. In Sweden for example, it was noted that even the most accurate and factual journalism was at the very best, 'quite shaky.[37] In acknowledging the seriousness of such assertions, the role of the media should not therefore be underrated or readily dismissed. As media societies emerge, and the dependency of such upon them for obtaining knowledge and information as well as formulating and establishing popular perceptions, the communication and perpetuation of such stereotypical images and ideas about Muslims and Islam may well have a significant impact both on the contemporary climate and many future ones as well.

Whilst the media were increasingly focusing on a myriad of issues relating to Muslims in Europe throughout this period, one of the most significant peaks of attention followed the realisation that some of the alleged perpetrators of the 9/11 attacks had previously resided in Europe. In addition to some Europeans being arrested in connection with the attacks, others were also arrested for their alleged links with al-Qa'eda, and in the British context, a number of British Muslims were detained in Afghanistan before being imprisoned in Guantanamo Bay by the US military. One significant consequence of this was the emergence, or re-emergence if one considers the historical encounter between Islam and Europe, of an increased sense of Muslims being presented as the 'enemy within'. This of course has always been an inherent stereotype of anti-Muslim expression, but throughout the immediate aftermath of 9/11, the media increasingly used these incidents as inconclusive yet accusatory evidence to condemn a seemingly uni-dimensional and transcendent anti-Western Muslim community. Possibly evolving out of the Islamic concept of the *ummah*, this post-9/11 media-driven interpretation was one that was, and remains, highly inappropriate, inaccurate and dangerously insidious. What with the hugely disproportionate coverage that was extended to small and largely unrepresentative fringe groups that vociferously supported the attacks in the US and Osama bin Laden,[38] trying to explain the role that the media played is extremely difficult. As the EUMC report stated, 'whilst no evidence exists to suggest that medias are influentially causal, they also cannot be dismissed either'.[39] Substantiating the influence and causality of the media therefore is something that is to some degree almost impossible, and one that would be better considered and attempted on a wider scale elsewhere.

In addition to the media, similar questions pertaining to issues relating to the ability to influence populations were also raised in the report concerning the role of some European leaders, politicians and other institutional figures with authority. At the level of 'mainstream politics' across the EU there appeared to be quite a significant awareness of the possibility of a very real negative backlash against Muslims.[40] In an attempt to pre-empt any potential backlash or unrest, whilst some political leaders made immediate verbal statements stressing the need to differentiate between 'Muslims' and 'terrorists', others such as the Irish Prime Minister, Bertie Ahern opted for a similar but much more visualised message by visiting the Islamic Cultural Centre in Dublin.[41] In countries such as Portugal where political leaders chose to remain silent on the issue, some voices emanating from Portuguese Muslims condemned the political inaction as an apparent absence of opinion or concern. Despite such suggestions, there was no evidence to suggest that any lack of comment actually shaped public views or reaction either positively or negatively.

This, however, was not the situation in those countries where political leaders were much more vocal with their anti-Muslim rhetoric and discourse. This was seen particularly in those countries governed by those on the right-wing of the political spectrum. Whilst a substantial amount of media reporting that incorporated inflammatory rhetoric against Muslims by political figures remained constrained by the national borders of the individual member states, a few incidents, most prominently those of Silvio Berlusconi the Italian Prime Minister, did resonate Europe-wide. When European and global medias reported Berlusconi's pronouncement that Western culture was superior to its Islamic counterpart, the same message was also being said, albeit less prominently, in other parts of the EU as well. Denmark for example, a country where Jan Hjarnø had earlier noted that 'there is now a tendency among many politicians and media to make Islam the explanation for all problems',[42] was one such country. It was also the first EU member to have national elections after 9/11 where, quite unsurprisingly, the main political thrust of the election was one based on an anti-Muslim/anti-immigration campaign culminating with those right-wing parties that had been highly Islamophobic seeing a significant percentage of the national vote shift towards them. Since Denmark's election, legislation specifically targeting 'foreigners' has been given top priority, although most worrying for Denmark's Muslim communities is the recognition that in Denmark, the word 'foreigner' usually means 'Muslim'.[43]

More recently, a similar pattern emerged following the assassination of the anti-Muslim, pro-liberalism politician, Pim Fortuyn in the Netherlands. Assassinated just nine days before the Dutch general elections, the Pim Fortuyn List (LPF), his political party, secured nearly 30% of the vote and became a part of the country's coalition government. How much the LPF's success was an outpouring of grief or a populist response to Fortuyn's assassination is unclear, but there is no doubt that his strong anti-Muslim and anti-Islamic views, at one point describing Islam as 'backward',[44] his anti-immigration standpoint, and his emphasis upon protecting the values of Dutch liberalism from the influence of immigrants was one that clearly tapped into the fears, beliefs and attitudes of a post-9/11 Dutch society. Even before his death, Fortuyn was being touted for government and would probably have won a substantial number of votes, albeit not as many as the LPF consequently did. Irrespective of the events surrounding his death, the success of the LPF was clearly one that did so via the dynamic of demonising and victimising Muslims through a campaign of Islamophobic rhetoric. It was this that initiated the primary shift in attitudes and subsequently votes.

Whilst the term 'mainstream' has already been used, a resurgence of far-right and neo-Nazi groups participating in 'street politics' across the EU was also noticeable.[45] An upsurge in activity saw, as mentioned beforehand, those such as the British National Party (BNP) not only finding a voice for their Islamophobic views but also a quasi-legitimacy. Other much more fluidly determined groups such as 'skins' in Spain and elsewhere gained a similar momentum from the events whilst remaining primarily street orientated. In Britain, the impetus given to these groups by this wave of anti-Muslim sentiment has seen the BNP win a number of successes in local council elections in Blackburn, Burnley and Halifax, to the extent where they are now planning to contest many more seats in the next European parliamentary elections. Despite this, there is no evidence to suggest that there was any collaborative or pan-European co-operation between far-right groups, even though a recurrent feature in their activity was the ideology to re-establish a European Christian identity – which by default must be white and non-Muslim – due to the threat that Islam was seen to be presenting. Those such as the extreme right-wing White Nationalist Party in the UK have tried to capitalise upon their white, Christian identity.

Whilst it remains unclear as to how far into the mainstream of European politics such groups will continue to go, it is important to note that their recent and varying levels of success have been founded entirely upon expressions and campaigns based upon the most explicit forms of Islamophobia. One measure of significance in this observation might be to compare the recent endeavours of the far-right, employing an agenda that is based on explicit anti-Muslim and anti-Islamic expression and hatred, to those founded upon prejudices and hatreds that assumed either racist or Anti-Semitic premises. Quite categorically, within the past 50 years in Europe, no political group - either mainstream or street - has made such an impact employing any such form of expression. The shockwaves and impact of Islamophobia in the EU therefore, and the growing acceptance by many Europeans of it, should be seen as the possible first signs of a more naturalised acceptance of the phenomenon across European societies. What is most worrying however is the observation by the EUMC that there would also appear to be some evidence to suggest that the gap between the bi-polar extremes of acceptability between the political mainstream and the street has begun to close, where derogatory and damaging language and ideas about Muslims and Islam has begun to infiltrate the wider spectrum, forming a bridge across this previously untenable and somewhat politically essential divide.

As a result, the EUMC report concluded that, 'a greater receptivity towards anti-Muslim and other xenophobic ideas and sentiments has, and may well continue, to become more tolerated'.[46] Indeed, this statement alone would seem to fit with Zaki's observation, especially when it is reconsidered in its fuller context. As he writes, '[Islamophobia's] intensity varies according to time and place, but hatred of Islam and Muslims is endemic in the European psyche; endemic even if at times it becomes epidemic'. As European receptivity has intensified in this period, it would appear that Zaki was correct in suggesting that anti-Muslim hatred must have pre-existed, as an endemic trait, the events of 9/11. In order for Islamophobia to increase or intensify, the phenomenon must have been there beforehand. In this respect, as the EUMC report states, there was a *greater* receptivity rather than a *newfound* receptivity. A brief retrospective of the European encounter with Islam and Muslims would also appear to reinforce the idea that such hatred has been and indeed remains, endemic in the development of the contemporary European experience. The report traces the history of encounter from the emergence of Islam in the seventh century to the Crusades, through the medieval, reformation, enlightenment and orientalist periods, to the onset of colonialism and the developments of the twentieth century including the dormancy of Islam throughout the Cold War. With the looming and exaggerated 'spectre of fundamentalism'[47] and the contemporary re-emergence of a dynamic and re-assertive Islam, the encounter that the West has, and indeed continues to have, remains one of mistrust and fear, built upon relations of superiority and subjugatory control. One that as Asaf Hussain puts it, has been where Muslims are 'either to be feared ... or to be controlled'.[48]

It would appear therefore that the fear factor involved in the European encounter with Islam has been an endemic feature of the historical and indeed contemporary psyche, leaving a legacy that can be seen operating not only in modern day Europe but also in other earlier paradigmatic periods as well. Following the events of 9/11 therefore and the hysteria about the threat posed to the security and safety of Europeans at all levels, as the recognition that 'prejudice may be triggered by threats' would suggest,[49] it is no surprise that one of the most noticeable emergent strands of response has been the dependence upon the historical archetypal Muslim enemies that continue to lurk in the European psyche's depths. From the blurring of contemporary concerns in Greece for example, where attitudes towards Muslims remain intermixed with pre-existent xenophobias towards ethnic Albanians and ethnic Turks, through to Spain where the widespread survival of the looming menace of 'el Moro'[50] continues to shape the racial stereotypes within the national consciousness, the archetypal influence is present across the whole of Europe. Sardar's view appears to substantiate both the claims made by Zaki's conclusions, and also the evidence that the EUMC report gathered, when he suggests that anti-Muslim expression is always a 're-emergence' rather than a new phenomenon. As he writes, 'Islamophobia and prejudice against Muslims, has a long memory and still thrives ...' where it '... resides so deeply in the historical consciousness [of Europe]'.[51] The endemic presence of fear, mistrust and hatred of both Muslims and Islam within the psyche of European society cannot, I would suggest, be contested. Endemically, therefore, Zaki's observations would appear to be justified.

As to whether the post-9/11 emergence of a new manifestation of Islamophobia has been an epidemic is something that will no doubt be much more subjective. With regards to the prevalence of Islamophobia, from the most brutal and vicious attacks through to the most implicit of media reporting, questions and doubts will always loom with reference to the processes of identifying and understanding the motives, causes and longevity of any shift in attitude or action. The result is that a lack of certainty will always be present in considering and subsequently analysing any evidence and data. As stated at the outset, some commentators had been quick to dismiss any suggestion that a 'wave of Islamophobia' had actually been apparent across Europe or indeed elsewhere. In providing evidence to suggest otherwise, the observation about a lack of absolute certainty that subsequently exists, is exactly what is exploited in order to dismiss actual realities by attempting to isolate and compartmentalise them within very strict, somewhat microscopic foci. In attempting to overcome this, and in attempting to shift the foci back onto a macroscopic perspective of a wider and broader Europe, the EUMC synthesis report and its systematic, if somewhat still incomprehensive and incomplete monitoring, must therefore be the primary authoritative resource against which such conclusions are drawn. Yet whilst it remains the largest project of monitoring Islamophobia ever undertaken, it still offers no more than a mere snapshot of a rapidly moving and protean time-frame. As Allievi metaphorically puts it, capturing the essence of Muslims in Europe is 'like photographs taken in motion, [they] will not be completely clear, because the situation is not stationary – it is moving, and quite fast'.[52] In the context of Nielsen's 'urgent history',[53] therefore, no other project has attempted similar in this respect and only the urgency of history can be captured in an urgency of monitoring, however flawed the systems and processes might have been.

From the perspective of the EUMC report, it must therefore be concluded that a marked and identifiable upsurge of Islamophobia did occur following 9/11, and has since continued to spread across Europe, and more accurately the EU. In defining epidemic as 'an outbreak or product of sudden rapid spread...prevalent to an excessive degree',[54] it is without question that the EUMC report has documented an epidemical phenomenon, one that may indeed spread further in future years as a result of the continuing spread of the EU. Islamophobia, in its myriad manifestations and multi-faceted expressions, existing on a multitude of levels within European society, has been prevalent throughout the EU since 9/11 and it would seem that not only has it shaped the common understanding and shared experiences of the well documented historic European character and soul, but also the contemporary manifestation as well. By doing so, a post-9/11 Islamophobia has seeped into the psyche of Europe and provided a catalyst to the re-awakening of that same endemic prejudice and hatred that has been disturbed in recent years following numerous other global, continental, national and local exchanges and encounters.[55]

Whilst it might be argued that the receptivity to anti-Muslim ideas and expressions was already increasing in pre-9/11 Europe, the epidemic that has swept across Europe will continue to shape, influence and determine events and policies for the foreseeable future. Consequently, 9/11 will irredeemably assert and overshadow the following debates that are contemporarily so prominent and important within present day European societal discourse: issues relating to the multicultural interchangeability within many of the EU member nations; the significance and development of debates relating to citizenship and identity; the social integration and cultural absorbency of those Muslim communities within Europe's boundaries or those seeking to enter as political or economic migrants; national and European identity, re-establishing the need for the perpetually asked question *European Muslims* or *Muslims in Europe*; the political demographic of the EU at local, national and continental levels; and the allegiance and loyalty of citizens within national and regional boundaries. Whatever debates and encounters emerge, it would seem highly likely that the endemic fears and prejudices of the European psyche remain imbued with the perception of a negative, dangerous and Islamophobically determined Muslim presence. The resonance of 9/11 and the greater receptivity of an ensuing Islamophobia will no doubt therefore outlast the contemporary period of urgent history.

So whilst the attacks themselves were geographically remote to Europe, both the events and aftershock of 9/11 has, and indeed would appear to continue to have a profound effect on both Europe and its inhabitants. What has emerged as a reality, some might prefer to use Baudrillard's definition of a 'hyper-reality' instead,[56] has been a phenomenon to epidemic standards that has seen attitudes and actions towards Muslims both in Europe and elsewhere deteriorate at alarming rates. The historical encounter that continues to sit so firmly within the European psyche is the very same psyche that has historically constructed the Eurocentric 'Other': the 'Other' that Muslims have so regularly been seen to be. Whilst the idea or embeddedness of the 'Other' is neither new or unique to European understanding, what has been previously termed the almost eternalised xenophobic dualism,[57] in the current climate, 9/11 has served as a dramatic catalytic reminder of both who and what Europe's historical foes are perceived to be, and more so, what they are perceived to be capable of achieving. The expression of anti-Muslim and anti-Islamic expression and feeling, along with the associated fear and hatred that has emanated directly from the tragedy of 9/11, has made Islamophobia increasingly more acceptable and legitimised. What 9/11 and its aftermath has instigated is a situation where such prejudices and hatreds are now much more than just an endemic feature of Euro-culture: contemporarily, a much more unnoticed, acceptable and increasingly necessary facet of understanding.

As the European psyche has been unable to rid itself of the endemic streak of Islamophobia over the past 14 centuries, so it would also seem highly unlikely that Islamophobia's evolutionary metamorphism through history, both retrospectively and progressively, will be halted within the current climate of urgent history. Whilst the intensity of the current epidemic may lessen, it is improbable that it will ever be completely eradicated, and as the legacy and impact of 9/11 lives on in the collective memory, so it would seem that the ensuing collective acceptance of Islamophobia within the contemporary understanding might signal that another defining moment in the (urgent) historical encounter between Europe and Islam has been formed. It can only be hoped therefore that a less urgent history that reflects upon and attempts to contextualise 9/11, will be able to disassociate itself from the endemically Islamophobic response that the current urgent historical understanding has intensified to epidemic proportions.

Notes

[1] The term 'psyche' is used here not entirely in the context of a purely Jungian interpretation. Whilst Jung defined the psyche as the 'collective unconscious' where a psychic inheritance is common to all humankind that subsequently transforms and determines how we interpret the world and our relationship within it, my use of the term reflects a much less rigid, psychological understanding, where it can be understood as being, say, the spirit or ethos that underlies the principles affecting a group's attitudes or beliefs.

For an overview of the term psyche and Jung's theories relating to it, see Jung, C.G. (1969) *On the nature of the psyche*. London: Routledge.
[2] As part of an as yet unpublished research paper entitled, 'Racist backlash and Islamophobia after 11 September – the UK record'.
[3] This refers to the many references made primarily in the media and political environs of both Europe and the United States (US) to the 'end of history' theory of Francis Fukuyama and the 'clash of civilisations' theory of Samuel P. Huntington.
[4] Zaki, Y. (2002) 'The politics of Islamophobia'. *Re-present*, Winter/Spring 2002, pp.8-18.
[5] Anon, (2001), 'Islamophilia', *The Daily Telegraph*, 1 October 2001.
[6] Ibid.
[7] Ruunymede Trust, The (1997) *Islamophobia: a challenge for us all*. London: Runnymede Trust. From hereon, this report will be referred to as the Runnymede report.
[8] Details of these campaigns can be found at the BNP's website, http://www.bnp.org.uk
[9] For more information about the work of the IHRC, see http://www.ihrc.org
[10] In addition to the IHRC, the Muslim Council of Britain and the Forum Against Islamophobia & Racism also did similar. Both of these organisations' data was included within the report published by the IHRC.
[11] Islamic Human Rights Commission (2002) *The hidden victims of September 11: the backlash against Muslims in the UK*. Wembley: Islamic Human Rights Commission.
[12] p.8, ibid.
[13] Bristow, J. (2002) 'Who's afraid of Islamophobia?', *Spiked*, http://www.spiked-online.com/Articles/00000006D95B.htm (last updated 2 July 2002, accessed 12 November 2002).
[14] Statistics taken from internal sources at FAIR. For more information about the work of FAIR, see http://www.fairuk.org.
[15] *The Runnymede report*.
[16] Ibid., p.11.
[17] The most prominent of these were Polly Toynbee and Julie Burchill in *The Guardian*, Nick Griffin on BBC2's 'Newsnight' and Norman Lamont in *The Daily Telegraph*. In addition, tabloids such as *The Daily Mail* and *The Daily Express* included so many negative and stereotypically charged articles against Muslims and Islam that they are too numerous to be listed here.
[18] Sheridan, L., (2002) *Effects of the events of September 11th 2001 on discrimination and implicit racism in five religious and seven ethnic groups: a brief overview*. Leicester: University of Leicester.
[19] Choudhury, T. (2002) *Minority protection in the EU: the situation of Muslims in the UK*. Budapest: Open Society institute, p.73.
[20] Allen, C. and Nielsen, J. (2002) 'Summary report on Islamophobia in the EU after 11 September 2001'. Vienna: European Union Monitoring Centre on Racism and Xenophobia. From hereon, this will be referred to as the EUMC report. For more information about this report and the work undertaken by the EUMC, see its website at http://www.eumc.eu.int.
[21] The fifteen member nations of the EU at the time of the report's publication were Austria, Belgium, Denmark, Finland, France, Germany, Greece, Ireland, Italy, Luxembourg, Netherlands, Portugal, Spain, Sweden and the United Kingdom.
[22] http://www.wumc.eu.int/publications/terror-report/index.htm.
[23] Press release from the EUMC at the launch of the report's publication.
[24] As reported in one of the unpublished Belgian national focal point reports.
[25] This refers to the incident of a taxi driver in London being left paralysed following a particularly vicious assault. The story was reported extensively in the British press, although this source refers to one of the unpublished reports compiled by the UK NFP.
[26] *EUMC report*, p.34.

[27] Ibid.
[28] *The Runnymede report.*
[29] *The Sun*, 24 September 2001.
[30] Sourced from unpublished material supplied by the Italian NFP.
[31] Sourced from unpublished material supplied by the Greek NFP.
[32] Whitaker, B. (2002) 'Islam and the British press' in Anon (ed.) *The quest for sanity: reflections on September 11 and its aftermath.* London: Muslim Council of Britain, pp.53-57.
[33] See for example, Said, E. (1997) *Covering Islam: how the media and the experts determine how we see the rest of the world.* London: Vintage; or Poole, E. (2002) *Reporting Islam.* London: IB Tauris.
[34] *EUMC report*, p.47.
[35] Morley, D. and Robins, K. (1995) *Spaces of identity: global media, electronic landscapes and cultural boundaries.* London: Routledge.
[36] Sourced from unpublished material supplied by the Italian NFP.
[37] Sourced from unpublished material supplied by the Swedish NFP.
[38] In Britain this was seen primarily with groups such as Al Muhajiroun, and Muslim clerics such as Shaykhs Abu Hamza al-Masri and Abu Qatada.
[39] *EUMC report*, p.48.
[40] By this, 'mainstream politics' is used to mean the legitimised parliamentary political structures and organisations that exist within Europe, whether at the level of the European Parliament or those national, democratically elected governments within each member state.
[41] *EUMC report*, p.43.
[42] Hjarno, J. (1996) 'Muslims in Denmark', in Nonneman, G. et al. (eds.) *Muslim communities in the new Europe.* Reading: Ithaca, p.300.
[43] *EUMC report*, p.45.
[44] As reported by BBC Online http://news.bbc.co.uk/1/hi/world/europe/1988306.stm (accessed 30 November 2002, last updated 15 May 2002).
[45] Following on from the term 'mainstream', 'street politics' is used to describe those political groups that exist outside of the parliamentary process. Typically extreme in their ideologies, 'street' politics is primarily the politics of those groups that operate at that level. See p.42 of the EUMC report for its definition.
[46] EUMC report, p.43.
[47] This was a term given to describe the rise of the fear of 'fundamentalist Muslims' since the Iranian Revolution in 1979. For a further explanation see, Allen, C. (2001) 'Islamophobia: Western perceptions of Islam in the contemporary world'. University of Wolverhampton dissertation, June 2001.
[48] Hussain, A. (1990) *Western conflict with Islam: survey of the anti-Islamic tradition.* Leicester: Volcano books.
[49] Beit-Hallahmi, B. and Argyle, M. (1997) *The psychology of religious behaviour, belief and experience.* London: Routledge.
[50] Del Olmo VIicen, N. (1996) 'The Muslim community in Spain' in Nonneman, G. et al. (eds.) *Muslim communities in the new Europe.* Reading: Ithaca, p.307.
[51] Sardar, Z. (1995) 'Racism, identity and Muslims in the West' in Abedin, S. Z. and Sardar, Z. (eds.) *Muslim minorities in the West.* London: Grey Seal, pp.7 and 15.
[52] Allievi, S. (1997) 'Muslim minorities in Italy and their image in Italian media' in Vertovec, S. and Peach, C. (eds.) *Islam in Europe: the politics of religion and community.* Basingstoke: Macmillan, p.211.
[53] As before, it forms part of a yet unpublished research paper entitled, 'Racist backlash and Islamophobia after 11 September – the UK record'.
[54] Definition from the 2002 edition of the *New Penguin English Dictionary.*

[55] For an in-depth analysis of some of these pre-9/11 encounters and their significant consequences, see Kepel, G. (1997) *Allah in the West: Islamic movements in America and Europe.* Cambridge: Polity Press.
[56] Baudrillard describes hyper-reality as a construct, or many constructs, where the real and imaginary collapse into each other. Baudrillard has used various places and events to substantiate his theory, the most notable being Disneyland and the Gulf War.
[57] *EUMC report*, p.37.

Chapter 10

Sharí'ah Sanctions and State Enforcement: A Nigerian Islamic Debate and an Intellectual Critique

Lamin Sanneh

The Background: Containment or Dialogue

The terrorist attacks in the USA on 9/11, sparked a wide-ranging debate on inter-cultural relations between East and West. Nearly everyone seems agreed about the fact that we have entered a new phase in the relation between the Muslim world and the West and the need, therefore, to recognize retreat and resignation as impractical. But beyond that attitudes vary greatly. Some people favour dialogue and inter-cultural solidarity in the belief that concessions will mollify, others that it will isolate the misguided minority. Some assume confrontation to be inevitable in a world of irreconcilable difference and hostility, with war and armed vigilance the terms of engagement. There are still others who believe the global imbalance of economic resources is to blame, with the solution lying in programs of debt relief and poverty alleviation. Material security, it is argued, would make potential terrorists more amenable to reason and moderation and, by implication, that much easier to wean from religious fanaticism. You can get at the mind of the terrorist by appealing directly to their self-interest, it is believed.

The present crisis has prompted many analysts to look to past experience as a guide, and so they find an analogy in what went before rather than seeing the crisis as something new. The closest analogy they find is the Cold War and its totalitarian ideology. The comparison now is between truth, *jihad*, and martyrdom in the Muslim world and liberal democratic values in the West. The anachronism of Islamic utopianism is opposed to the progressivism of Western liberalism. As Paul Berman expressed it, what is happening today is a 'war of ideas' every bit as fierce as the anti-totalitarian struggles of the twentieth century[1]. The old weapons of vigilance and containment are needed to deal with the new Islamic threat.

Analogies, however, can distract as much as they can inform, for they are never exact and should, therefore, be adopted cautiously. The Cold War habits of global menace, for example, spawned the doctrine of mutually assured destruction (MAD) as a deterrent, with the nuclear arms race a corollary. As Caspar Weinberger once expressed it, your being credible depended on a calculus of the balance of terror, one that equipped you for the struggle of moral pre-eminence as much as it diminished the other side. Ultimately, the margin of security you enjoyed reflected the economic resources you controlled. The arms race, accordingly, had a dislocating effect on the Soviet Union's command economy, whereas for the West's liberal capitalist system it had a rejuvenating effect. By 1989, the strain had become too great on the Soviet empire and it collapsed like a pack of cards. As a frustrated Gorbachev put it, the Soviet Union's ability to put a man in space counted for nothing when simple utensils like a can opener in the home did not work.

It is difficult in light of the now well-known outcome of the Cold War to believe that Islamic radicalism has any similarity with the ill-fated Soviet Union. The fundamentalists are not a state or an empire, though they hanker after a similitude of one such. Too, their blueprint is not a messianic classless society or a workers' commune, but, instead, the truth of God divinely mandated and historically constituted, a truth that transcends the dialectics of exploiter and exploited, of labour produced and labour consumed, with masters and servants locked in an accelerating process of internal contradiction. The new radical ideology is immune to considerations of strength and weakness, or of wealth and poverty. Blowing yourself up in the cause is as meritorious as blowing up the enemy, and so the method of terror is morally fail-proof. How do you confront or contain a foe like that? The Cold War analogy, for that reason, is unilluminating, and merely throws us off the scent.

The Cold War, it should be stressed, promoted the goal of national and international security as part of a culture of competitive advantage from the open exchange of goods and ideas, and, thus, with restraining and subduing the forces of monopoly and regulation. Such a goal, however, is woefully short of coming to grips with the deeper moral issues of the present crisis. The enemy being in our case a radical ideology, rather than a nation state that has mutually binding obligations and countervailing interests vis-à-vis other states, it behoves us to ask different questions. Homeland security, for example, begs the massive question about civil commitment and common values: how do you corral a fractious, distracted nation? Terrorists thrive by secrecy, violence, and intimidation, and seem emboldened by a response employing more of the same methods, or indeed, by evidence of domestic contentiousness that terrorists naively construe as weakness. Suppleness of mind is a virtue they know not. The balance of terror as mutually assured destruction appears to them more like a concession than deterrence. In part, that is because their radical ideology is a vortex of extremist ideas and values that spins appealingly on moderate, conventional versions of the faith that sustains rank and file Muslims, and in part because for the West to be credible against an unscrupulous foe can be self-damaging, like grasping the blade that cuts you. A US installed government in Baghdad, for that reason, has only aggravated the widening hostility that the mere presence by invitation of US troops on the sacred soil of Saudi Arabia first provoked. A credible exit strategy for the US in Iraq has now become more urgent, and no less fraught with menace, than taking down Saddam Hussein.

Even if conflict is not inevitable, or inevitably calamitous to the West, that does not mean that there is no enduring struggle of ideas and values. Thus the twin towers of the World Trade Center in their mass and thrust represented faith and confidence in the West's global pre-eminence. Yet in the eyes of the terrorists the twin towers were phallic symbols of the supine humiliation and powerlessness of their societies, and, provoked, they attacked it twice, showing their fixation with it. The West remains none the wiser, stubbornly adhering to the line that economic aid will win friends and overcome enemies. For their part, the terrorists feel their humiliation and powerlessness are a moral outrage. They remember that their societies are the inheritors of the mantle of the divine authorization to subdue and rule the world according to God's commands, and, with their lives, they will contest with the West that global role.

Since America has now assumed a global franchise for its hemispheric idea of Manifest Destiny but acknowledges no divine mandate for it, that suggests a covert hostility towards God, the true source of all power, and towards those on God's side. Power not only corrupts but also incriminates when it repudiates God, in which case it demands to be resisted absolutely in God's name. The West has, accordingly, been called the Great Satan and the *Jahiliyah* ('ignorance') because its undeniable greatness has been severed from divine obedience, while its unredeemed ignorance is removed from the divine light. The radicals who have lived and studied in the West can thus speak with field authority about the West's moral deficiency by virtue of the West's disobedience and its blindness, with the despairing masses at home left to concur from the evidence arrayed before their own eyes on television, in pornographic magazines, and from Hollywood. A god-deficient West is condemned by the global sins it taints others with.

This litany of the West's failings shows the flammable dimensions of the 'sacred borders' of fundamentalist ideology as well as the charmed circle of its self-propelling logic that western hegemony represents at long range moral peril for the Muslim world. Even an unsuccessful defiance of a corrupt West is to be preferred to profitable partnership with it, a pointed censure of the West's Muslim allies and its licensed diaspora communities. In the view of the radicals, believers cannot be friends with infidels, and this is a judgment about truth, not about temporal gain. To appreciate this properly, it is crucial to scrutinize these ideas and values scrubbed of their conspiratorial undertones. Only within the healthier 'open borders' of moderate Muslim values can we come within safe range of the otherwise strange and convulsive world of terrorist rage or begin to grasp the murky logic of the terrorist mind.

The repellent side of radical terror has thus an approachable side that is a lot more complex and much longer enduring than merely a visceral rejection of the West.[2] That complicates matters for us, for it sidesteps the US administration's spread-eagle rhetoric about taking sides without a convincing definition of what the sides are. The simplistic view that the terrorists are motivated by hatred and intolerance of everything Western overlooks, or else stigmatizes, the complexity of the values that have shaped and in turn been shaped by the broader culture of mainstream religious life and practice.

Shari'ah and colonial advocacy

It is a fact that the Muslim encounter with the West has not necessarily led to conflict or to radicalism. At its most provocative, such as in its far-flung colonial enterprise, the modern West encountered Muslim populations on a more or less amicable basis, with periods of repression and dogged resistance alternating with periods of glad cohabitation. Thus did Súfí brotherhoods, for example, take turns in opposing and collaborating with local administrators. Large sections of the Islamic world came under direct colonial rule without that fomenting the radical extremism we are familiar with today. There was, needless to say, much uncertainty about how exactly Muslim leaders should comport themselves before their new masters, but a lot of that was due to untested assumptions and mutual ignorance. Once that initial barrier was overcome, a genuine partnership developed in which Muslims participated actively in the colonial venture, resulting in irreversible gains for Islam. For example, the tax engine of the colonial state enabled the Muslim *'ulamá* to organize more effectively *waqf,* charitable endowment, acquiring enhanced political clout as a result. And so the imperial *cordon sanitaire* expanded Islam's *halál* outreach into remote districts. Almost everywhere in the colonial empire Islam remained as firmly entrenched at the end as it had been at the beginning, and often in a strengthened form. The Muslim encounter with western overlordship was seldom at the expense of the religion, a fact that may have shielded minority Muslim communities from open hostility from their subdued neighbours. The Makurdi riots in Nigeria in 1949, for example, suggest the potential for such hostility. Partition as a response to the end of British rule is another example of Muslims' lack of confidence in a Hindu-ruled India once the colonial cover was withdrawn. Equally pertinent is the case of Peninsular Malaya under colonial rule. A post-independent Malaysia, reconstituted in 1963, now comprised of East Malaysia, (northern Borneo, Sarawak and Sabah) and West Malaysia, and has adopted a policy of state-sponsored islamization to consolidate gains achieved under British rule: a modern bureaucratic state, endowed with great wealth, can now serve the cause of what Sultan Sharafuddin Idris Shah of Selangor called maintaining a 'sharp focus of the Islamic image' through public patronage to mosques as symbols of Islam's greatness and the religion's beauty. Islam lost little of its momentum from the effects of colonial rule; rather, it was the large non-Muslim ethnic minorities who lost out and who had to scramble for survival.

It is true that colonial infidels had their faults; but they never sold out on Islam's natural assets. Not a stone, not a pillar, for example, was dislodged from the Islamic holy shrines of Mecca and Medina, a lot more than can be said for the Christian holy places of Bethlehem and Jerusalem. Rome as a consolation is a compromise already with the classical pagan residue. Consequently, nobody has been able to persuade Muslims, or, for that matter, many Catholics, that Rome is comparable to Mecca and Medina. Who prays, for instance, in the direction of Rome? And so Roman Catholic East Timoris qua Roman Catholic made little moral impression on their tormentors. Accordingly, for the Muslims concerned there still lingered in the air a whiff of *'ajamí* 'auslander' stigma concerning the eternal city, and this before any of the radical vitriol that breeds terror.

On the level of irreconcilable differences *Sharí'ah* law has played a crucial part in the radical fundamentalist rhetoric as well as in western perceptions of Islam. But *Sharí'ah* as civil law in general was a crucial administrative element in the colonial bureaucratic system, showing how present day rhetoric and perceptions are far removed from reality. It is, in fact, the sudden withdrawal of colonial rule and the pressure of nationalist demands that made the appeal of religious radicalism so attractive. This radical distrust of pluralism in a post-colonial state has been a pattern repeated in numerous parts of the Muslim world, with Nigeria an outstanding example. There the debate also shows the exigencies of the process that Sir Muhammad Iqbal once characterized as the 'reconstruction of religious thought'[3]. The challenge calls to mind a critical strain in Muslim thought about truth and dissent, about community and difference, and has implications for intercultural understanding.

In the language of political expedience, *Sharí'ah* is being promoted as the constitutional right of Nigerian Muslims, including the right of establishing an Islamic state and abrogating the secular constitution regarded as incompatible with the *Sharí'ah*. Fundamentalists oppose secularization, or so they claim, and the western powers that spread it. In turn, they back *Sharí'ah*, understood here as the divine law and its accompanying tradition of jurisprudence and legal scholarship, known as *fiqh*. Anti-secular fundamentalism tries to ground itself in the tradition of *fiqh*, tracking the adopted course of political change with the help of rules of guidance and precedent available to Muslims. While it is true that such opposition feeds the anti-western radical sentiment, it is, however, not always the case that it leads to violence, though sometimes it does, admittedly.

Sharí'ah civil law in the main is a conventional code, involved routinely in guidance, encouragement, reconciliation, and assurance, and widely observed as such in the Muslim world. Colonial rule, for instance, made the decision to engage Islam's intellectual tradition by concluding that nowhere is that intellectual tradition better represented than in Islamic legal science. One such colonial assessment described it as 'a vast science [representing] the genius of the same people which gave arithmetic, algebra, trigonometry, astronomy, optics, chemistry and medicine to the Western world, and generally stood at the cradle of modern science'. It is in legal scholarship that the genius of Islam 'has exhibited itself in all its power and exactitude'.[4]

Sharí'ah was administered in Islamic *Qádí* courts directed by Muslim magistrates. In 1956, a Muslim Court of Appeal was set up in Kaduna, the then northern capital, later upgraded to have jurisdiction in *Sharí'ah* appellate cases. Law manuals were identified and translated from Arabic and placed in the hands of justices; schools and institutes were founded by government to train Muslim officials; students were recruited to enrol in these places of higher learning; tribunals were set up to handle Muslim issues; Islamic appellate procedures were instituted; and budgets created to underwrite the costs of implementing the *Sharí'ah* code. What emerged from the synthesis of classical Islamic law and the customs and exigencies of Muslim African societies under western colonial rule represents an important venture in comparative law. With a possible few exceptions, there is little earlier evidence of such hybrid legal work being carried out anywhere in the modern Muslim world.[5]

The motivation behind such legal work was the colonial government's utilitarian interest in investing in the local legitimacy and stability of alien suzerainty over Muslim populations. In the process, Muslims were trained and equipped to run a modern state, the sort of political apprenticeship administrators were unwilling to extend to Christian subjects except as trustees of the secular state.[6] As I shall make clear presently, this policy disparity would come to have an important bearing on the divergent attitudes of Muslims and Christians towards secularism.

The colonial authorities were, notwithstanding, opposed to *Sharí'ah* as penal law because of their desire to preserve the distinction between criminal and civil law, with the state as the sole repository of criminal justice.[7] Officials desired to maintain uniformity in the administration of justice throughout the colonial territories, and, accordingly, restricted *Sharí'ah* to the status of customary law, leaving the state free to design and enforce the criminal code. The state legislated and levied taxes; customary law, including *Sharí'ah* personal law, filled the permitted gaps. A principle of great importance was involved in this arrangement, namely, that the British were prepared to divide state authority between them and their Muslim subjects. *Sharí'ah* law intervened, in effect, to prevent state monopoly of power, while at the same time accommodating itself to an adjustment of the normative boundaries of Islamic jurisprudence. Colonial directives and African customary law combined with *Sharí'ah* stipulations to broaden the scope of Muslim civil society.

This *modus vivendi* created an identity of interest between administrators and Muslim officials, and allowed the Muslim objection to western infidel power to be modified in favour of accommodation. In appreciation, colonial officials embraced their Muslim protégés as partners and future heirs, turning a Nelson's eye to peculiar domestic practices like slavery and polygamy.

The roots of controversy: The politics of Sharí'ah enforcement

It was inevitable that once colonial rule ended, the issue of the north's political participation based on *Shari'ah* prescriptions for the integration of religion and politics would reassert itself. Nationalist politics had no stomach for pragmatic conciliation lest that detract from the logic of proud sovereignty. (This writer remembers an interview in the 1970s with the Wazirin Junaidu, a scion of the ruling house of Sokoto, in which the Wazirin spoke of the duty not to surrender the north's Islamic legacy to secular influences emanating from Lagos in the south. Islam, he felt, should not be gambled in the cause of national sovereignty.) Military rule under the repressive regime of Sani Abacha (1993–1998) kept the lid on *Sharí'ah* sentiments. The 1979 Constitution had recognized *Sharí'ah* courts by giving them jurisdiction over civil matters, a reversion to the colonial status quo. The provision was confirmed in the 1999 amendment to the Constitution which now contained an ambiguous reference to 'other jurisdiction as may be conferred upon [*Sharí'ah* courts] by the law of the State.'

Abacha's predecessor, General Babangida (ruled 1985-1993),[8] gave an international twist to the controversy when it changed Nigeria's observer status by enrolling it as a member of the Organization of Islamic Countries (OIC) (Ar. *Munazzamah al-Mu'tamar al-Islámí*). It sparked local unrest, prompting a decision to form the Christian Association of Nigeria (CAN) in 1986 as an ecumenical grouping of Protestants, Catholics and African Independent Churches. CAN issued a statement protesting the federal government's backing for *Sharí'ah* courts in north Nigeria and asking for an identical public status for Christianity.

The Council of *'Ulamá* in a press statement in May, 1990, pounced on CAN's charge that Nigeria as a member of the OIC had become an Islamic country by pointing out that Nigeria's secular constitution prescribes a secular state, the OIC notwithstanding. The *'Ulamá* persisted:

> Strictly speaking, the government [of Nigeria] has more to do with Christianity than [with] Islam[,] since secularism as practised by the government is an extension of the church concept of government. In Islam, politics and religion are inseparable. For a government to be Islamic, Allah has to be the legislator through the Qur'án and the *Sunna* of the Prophet.[9]

The idea of secularism as church doctrine leaves the field to the *'ulamá,* or else to the radicals, to make the religious case.

The *Sharí'ah* debate: Round two: National integration and religious autonomy

A second and particularly acrimonious round of controversy erupted, coinciding with the election in May, 1999, of Retired General Olusegun Obsanjo, a southerner, and a Christian to boot. The *Sharí'ah* issue assumed explosive force with the announcement on October 22, 1999, of the inauguration of *Sharí'ah* rule in Zamfara State by its youthful governor, Alhaj Ahmed Sani Yerima, to the alarm of Nigerian federal authorities and civil rights groups. Yerima had shelved his clean 'corporate' image[10] and instead sprouted a shaggy beard that highlighted his handsome face as that of a medieval religious crusader. He declared that the *Sharí'ah* announcement was the culmination of the hopes, ideals and aspirations of Nigerian Muslims, the long-delayed awakening of the dormant *ummah* from its silence and inactivity. National independence in 1960, Yerima charged, had given the north's Muslim majority only a partial victory, leaving the way open for the full implementation of the *Sharí'ah* code some day. That day had now arrived with his announcement, he declared. As a corollary, a controversial *dhimmí* status was implied for non-Muslim fellow Nigerians.

Basking in the glow of his success, Governor Yerima was greeted with cheers when he went on tour in Egypt, Pakistan, Qatar, Sudan, and Saudi Arabia.[11] The governor has dismissed complaints against *Sharí'ah* law, saying popular support for *Sharí'ah* seals it against outside objections. *Sharí'ah* law is now a consumer confidence index, "a dividend of democracy," in the words of Hamza Y. Kurfi, the Solicitor General of Katsina State.[12]

Against the criticism of civil rights groups, Yerima is adamant that *Sharí'ah* law does not breach the boundary between the islamization of the state, which he opposes, and the islamization of society, which he favours. This crucial distinction has roots in a broader Islamic tradition, such as in Turkey, but its specific source in this context comes from other Nigerian Muslim leaders. One such was Alhaji Abubakar Gumi (d. 1992), Grand Kadi of Northern Nigeria and leader of the influential Wahhabi-inspired *Izala* reformist movement,[13] and another is the Iranian-inspired cleric, Shaykh Ibrahim Yaqoub El [Az-] Zakzaky, the Shí'ite head of the Islamic Brotherhood (sometimes Muslim Brothers) Movement based in Zaria, with a branch in Kafanchan, according to some reports.[14] According to El Zakzaky, who visited Teheran in 1990, the state superstructure must be islamized first on the pattern of the 1979 Iranian revolution before *Sharí'ah* could be introduced. In that argument the constitution creating the state, presumed to be infidel, must be replaced with an Islamic one based on *majlis* and *shúra* (religious counsel and consultation). Only then can the state be considered *halál* (licit) and acceptable. What exists now, instead, is a schedule of constitutionally mandated popular elections that has no foundation in Islamic law. El Zakzaky, an economics graduate of the University of Zaria, has acquired national prominence as an opponent of the constitution which he regards as an instrument of secularization. He declared:

> Islamic law is meant to be applied by an Islamic government in an Islamic environment. If you introduce Islamic laws under [sic] an un-Islamic environment, under a system of government which is not Islamic, then it is bound to be an instrument of oppression.[15]

On its own terms, however, the distinction between the islamization of society and the islamization of the state offers a potentially productive way of re-framing the debate on the proper relationship between religion and statehood in Muslim thought in general and among Nigeria Muslim leaders in particular. Its great intellectual merit is to shift the focus from the role of the state exclusively to the role of civil society in dealing with issues of tolerance, diversity, and pluralism. The distinction does not deny the challenge of secularism, but instead mitigates it by restructuring it as a matter of the civil order. Modernist Arab thought as a general matter, for instance, has tended to oppose a public role for religion as something outside the purview of public reason, and instead to embrace secularization as the proper domain of democracy.[16] The reasoning is that religion is incompatible with freedom while secularization is conducive to freedom.[17]

The idea of secularization rather than religion fomenting democracy is supported by the dissenting statement of the Council of *'Ulamá* in Nigeria about secularism being a part of the 'church concept of government', implying that Muslims should oppose secularism, and, therefore, democracy, as incompatible with Islam.[18] In the particular case of its advocates, however, the islamization of society in Nigeria would not politicize religion, or oppose democracy, as the islamization of the State is likely to. Furthermore, the islamization of society, involving a code of strict personal standards of religious observance, such as prayer, pilgrimage, *zakát*, and devotion, could proceed with the dual affirmation of a laic State, on the one hand, and, on the other, of the role of Muslims in promoting Islam without denying a similar role for members of other religions. In other words, the effects of civil agency could neutralize combative secularism.

Thus could Alhaji Aliyu, the Magaji Gari, a senior political councillor of the Sokoto Sultanate, dismiss the idea of political Islam as mere academic diversion, as 'the view of radical academics' who ingratiate themselves with the government.[19] Aliyu's argument allows for the islamization of society by preventing the *Sharí'ah* from being turned into a bullyrag and instead enhancing the civil scope of society by promoting human community, and enjoining moral standards for conduct and behaviour without state authorization. In that way Muslims may embrace a mild form of secularization by supporting the separation of 'church and state' and taking their rightful place in national affairs alongside others. The proponents of the islamization of the State, on the other hand, favour a different course of action. Shaykh Gumi spoke for such proponents when he said that politics was more important than prayer or pilgrimage for reasons of scale.[20] A delinquent Muslim at his or her prayer and devotion brings harm only to themselves, whereas a politically remiss Muslim implicates the larger Muslim community, both present and future. On this philosophical issue, El Zakzaky was proposing to assume the mantle of Gumi, a Sunni, unlike himself, and who, as such, has greater legitimacy in the north's political culture. Yet El Zakzaky's pro-Iranian rhetoric has echoes in unrest elsewhere in the north.

Gumi, in that light, advocated islamization of the State even though he had no known Iranian Shí'ite sympathies or links. The resemblance, then, between the approach of Gumi and that of El Zakzaky's Iranian-inspired campaign may be nothing more than circumstantial, even if the cause of advancing northern Muslim rights is a common goal between them. That common goal may explain why Gumi, for instance, could make the pronouncement, without risk of repudiation or sanction, that politics (*siyásah*) is more important than prayer (*salát*) even though prayer, unlike politics, is one of the five pillars of faith. For all his reputation as a religious maverick, El Zakzaky has stirred a fiercer controversy without going that far.

The debate about secularism, then, has deep roots in Muslim circles, and is not just the pet theme of Nigerian academic radicals.[21] It is in that context that El Zakzaky's objections, in spite of their marginal Shí'ite significance, have deepened existing fault lines in a common attempt by all interested parties to shift power from the south to the north. To all intents and purposes, and declarations to the contrary notwithstanding, Yerima, with foreign aid and succour, has in fact turned Zamfara into an Islamic State. He admitted as much in giving evidence to the members of the human rights commission. He said he had been upfront on the matter when he campaigned in the elections. To quote him, 'when I was campaigning for this office [of governor], wherever I go, I always start with *Alláhu Akbar* (Allah is the greatest) to show my commitment to the Islamic faith. Therefore, as part of my programme for the state, I promised the introduction of *Sharí'ah*.'[22] The reference, however, to the *takbír* in the context of constitutional national elections that never administered or invoked the *shahádah* scarcely constitutes a safe religious foundation for government and public order in Islam: it might attest to nothing more than a self-help personal mandate. Other states pondered Zamfara's example, with Kano, Kaduna, and Niger States, for example, declaring their intention to adopt *Sharí'ah* law.[23]

As if to make penance for his southern connections, Obasanjo proceeded to crack down on the unrest in the south, mobilizing police and military units to rein in vigilante groups, such as the Oodua Peoples Congress (OPC) in Lagos State, whom the federal government accused of acts of 'ethnic cleansing'. The crisis was threatening to assume an ethnic guise in the south.

Wole Soyinka, the Nigerian Nobel Laureate, gave voice to this ethnic sentiment in a statement in which he was quoted as saying that, being neither a Christian nor a Muslim,[24] he wished to assert the virtues of what he called 'traditional Orisa' as something authentically African and as such equally entitled to the primary loyalty of Nigerians like himself. He imputed political motives and moral duplicity to those advocating *Sharí'ah* penal law. In the final analysis, claims Soyinka, these advocates are wolves in sheep's clothing, hiding their political ambitions behind a smokescreen of pious pretence. As an argument, the statement is conspicuous more by what it opposes than by what it advocates. In any case, by the same logic traditional Orisa may be accused of being a cover for the south's own political ambition. Which all amounts to saying the statement is tantamount to an evasion of the real challenge the country faces. Defending 'traditional Orisa' in the name of indigenous rights soon runs out of steam against the heavy artillery of cumulative Islamic legal scholarship ranged against it, and may explain why Muslim Yoruba leaders have not rushed to intercede with Orisa, or to Soyinka for solidarity. At any rate, here is Soyinka's statement:

> I am neither a Christian nor a Moslem. Definitely, if I have any religion at all it is our traditional [Yoruba] Orisa. As far as I am concerned, both Islam and Christianity are interlopers in Africa spiritually. That is my position. Even though I say I am neither a Christian nor a Moslem, let me make it clear that I studied comparative religions and so I know quite a bit of the Qur'an. We are not totally ignorant even though we are 'infidels' and 'Kafirs'. We are not totally ignorant about the provisions of the Qur'an. And we are saying that some of these people [*Sharí'ah* advocates] are lying, misusing and abusing the Qur'an. And we also know that we have studied the religious sociology of many countries even in contemporary times and we know very well that their own interpretation of the *Shari'ah* is at least different from the one which is being imposed on this country...So let them stop claiming some kind of very special knowledgibility

> [sic]. They are abusing knowledge. They are abusing faith. They are abusing piety and they are showing themselves to be nothing but real impious secularists who are merely manipulating religion for political ends.[25]

In the north, ethnicity, however, has been superseded by religion as the driving force of the debate. Press and media reports emanating from the south, exhibiting all the classic symptoms of religious privatization, have tended to downplay religion and to look instead for a similar ethnic interpretation of the unrest in the north. And so reports spoke of Obasanjo's slowness in taking similar action in areas of Muslim unrest in the north, though they also noted his failure to take on the *Sharí'ah* issue as a root cause. The Catholic Bishops Conference of Nigeria (CBCN), responding to the religious nature of the crisis, nevertheless looked for a solution short of the long-term challenge of *Sharí'ah* legislation. It issued a statement regretting the slowness of the federal government to respond to the troubles in Kaduna and elsewhere. Archbishop John Onaiyekan, the vice president of the Catholic Bishops Conference, said in a public statement that the government should have acted much sooner than the Kaduna riots and taken decisive military action in October, 1999, when Yerima was in full tilt mobilizing his followers in Zamfara.[26] Like others in the debate, Onaiyekan was looking to government to overcome the handicaps of government.

The State: Friend or foe? The critique of Muslim jurisprudence

The northern strategy to advance its political aims by deploying theological arguments, namely, that religion is too important to abandon it in private hands as personal choice, evades the other half of the argument, namely, that religion is too important to entrust to the State, whether civilian or military. Gumi's defence of the northern strategy perpetuates the problem, however much it may resonate with pious sentiment that sound religion requires public state enforcement, for in his view without public enforcement the ideals of religion are empty and pander to wrongdoers and the wicked. In this reasoning, the law of God demands the law of the State for proof and safeguard. Gumi, accordingly, concedes that Muslims and non-Muslims, including Christians, cannot be equal under one government. On principle, Muslims would not accept the authority of a non-Muslim ruler except under special circumstances, such as military rule.[27] Gumi saw partition, perhaps on the Indian model, as the radical answer for Nigeria, though it is not clear whether he means by that secession by the Muslim north or a loose confederal system allowing for local autonomy. El Zakzaky, for his part, comes at the same issue from a purist angle. The secular State, according to El Zakzaky, is the illegitimate child of the secular constitution, and to overthrow the State it is necessary to overthrow the constitution that gave it birth. Only so can Muslims save themselves from what El Zakzaky calls the idolatrous worship of the secular State.[28] A sovereign secular constitution and a sovereign national State represent a double assault on revealed law and the chosen *ummah*. They are an unholy combination, and must be opposed by Islam's unitary mandate.

One would have to say, however, that these religious arguments are laden with the flaws they wish to remedy. The argument against compromise with the secular State, for example, spirals into the requirement of a *shahádah*-based State of *Sharí'ah* prescription. Yet religious or secular anointing of the State does not solve the problem of the State; they merely exacerbate it. A religious State would allow government to redeem revealed truth with the instrument of political self-interest. In that case, by co-opting religious dogma, the secular State transforms itself into an organic public truth. It is thus revealing that both Shaykh Gumi and Shaykh El Zakzaky offer little religious critique of the history of military rule in Nigeria in spite of the doctrinaire secular State military rule fostered and in spite of the conspicuous absence of a religious warrant either for military rule or for an ideological State, both vanguards of secularism.

The Muslim opponents of *Sharí'ah* law, for their part, insist that State sponsorship threatens the moral foundations of religion (*la ikráha fí-d-dín* Q. ii: 256), and that, far from solving the secular challenge within, *Sharí'ah* rule leaves Muslims helpless before it. For these opponents, if religion is too important for the State to ignore, it is equally too important for the State to co-opt. *Sharí'ah* belongs with the end and purpose of our temporal and eternal felicity, with what al-Ghazálí called our higher moral happiness, *sa'ádah*, not with the strategem and means of State control in the Aristotelian sense. Responding to the criticism, Governor Yerima argues popular support entitles him to the mantle of upholder of revealed truth.

Many contest Yerima's claim, including Dr Suleman Kumo, a Muslim lawyer in private practice in Kano and himself a prominent *Sharí'ah* activist since 1978. He belongs to the loose circle of critics of the politicization of *Sharí'ah*. Although known for his pro-Iranian leanings, Dr Kumo, nevertheless, states his objections to *Sharí'ah* law, saying incompetent and corrupt judges, many of whom would fail a simple character test, are meting out justice. Abuse is prevalent in these courts. 'They are the worst courts. Ninety percent of the area judges, if you were to apply the *Shari'ah* rules that witnesses must be upstanding citizens, would not even be competent to testify.'[29] Called to serve on a State government appointed committee called the Kano Forum, Dr Kumo opened a dialogue with members of the militant Ja'amutu (Jamá'atu) Tajidmul Islami, a breakaway group from El Zakzaky's Muslim Brothers. Kumo noted that the members were well-educated: engineers, medical students, and university-age young men. These people wanted to be self-reliant, to be independent of the government, but felt nevertheless that Islam should have a public role, though what that role is, they did not say.

In any case, Tajidmul is an example of the roots of secularization spreading among the fundamentalists, their assertions to the contrary notwithstanding. In the meantime, fundamentalists face formidable obstacles. Thus Maitama Sule, a Kano power broker and friend of the emir, wants to scotch any signs of militant Islam lest a political stampede ensue and religion becomes mere fodder. He was taunting of El Zakzaky's Muslim Brothers, calling them 'a group of disgruntled elements who are out to vent their anger and who are joined by undesirable waste products of humanity.'[30]

Another example of opposition to the political misuse of *Sharí'ah* is Mohammed Sani, a tailor and reportedly a devout Muslim. In August, 2000, Sani preached at an open air meeting to a crowd of fellow Muslims about the banners, bumper stickers, and posters featuring governor Yerima's photograph. He pointed out that such partisan displays were a mockery of the claim that all this was about *Sharí'ah*. 'This is a political campaign, not *shari'ah*', he protested. *Sharí'ah*, he assured his audience, is from God, not from a governor. For his pains Sani was thrown in jail for four months, his enemies charging him with disloyalty to the government. Said Abdul Kadir Jelani, a leading Muslim scholar and an advisor to the government, 'Islam does not permit someone to criticize the government.'[31] The sentiment echoes the statement of the Council of *'Ulamá*, to the effect that, 'for a government to be Islamic, Allah has to be the legislator through the Qur'án and the *Sunna* of the Prophet.' Public dissent is anathematized in such a government. Few should miss the irony that it was a secular constitution that sanctioned public dissent and allowed *Sharí'ah* advocates to mobilize in the first place.

This loose coalition of dissidents has in a city like Zaria a liberal environment, a hinge community of the disaffected that is most hospitable to their reform ideas. Zaria has been a stronghold of anti-establishment sentiments that challenge the government and those who set themselves up as champions of Islam, as if being champions of justice for the common person is less worthy or desirable. Exemplary of this attitude is Sabo Bako of the Ahmadu Bello University. He castigates those in power as feudalistic and corrupt. 'The only way you can remain in power', he charges, 'is by keeping people down. You must not allow people to know what you are doing and how much money you have. So don't give them education, don't give them fertilizer, don't establish industries for them.'[32]

Immunity or double jeopardy?

The West looms so large in the debate about *Sharí'ah* penal law that it seems reasonable to conclude that it is the cause of the problem. But, as I argued at the outset, the colonial concordat shows Islam and the West cohabiting quite successfully. At any rate, the heart of the issue would seem to be the role assigned to the state by each side in the debate. One side feels that the islamization of the State, with religion and government united in a single source, will make government a source of grace and assure immunity for God's truth, while the other side feels that such a step will result in double jeopardy for political stability and religious integrity.

This intellectual cleavage has driven much of the momentum of the debate in Nigeria and elsewhere. The demand by Nigerian secularists, mostly from the south, for a constitutional separation of religion and government provokes in the Muslim north criticism on two fronts: first, that separation is a ruse to hand government a carte blanche to embark on innovation, and, second, that religion would be reduced to a personal and private option, having no standing in the public square. It is the major reason why the Council of *'Ulamá* allege that secularism is a Christian Trojan horse deployed to assail Islam from within. The allegation, however, befuddles Christian Nigerians and others who have not the least rudimentary notion of 'Christendom' as a political system. Typically, Christian Africans, such as Archbishop John Onaiyekan of Kaduna, defend political secularism on pragmatic grounds of equality under the law, national stability, and participation in public life, not for theological reasons. The prominence, in contrast, of religious reasons in the Muslim case creates a grave imbalance in the national debate, and polarizes attitudes. That secular pragmatism has been the Christian failure, though Muslims misunderstand it by attributing it to theological self-interest. Pragmatism as a relative ethic is its own reward.

Secularism remains deeply suspect among Muslims because it promotes political innovation as the prerogative of an emancipated people. In Islamic terminology, 'innovation' is a code for heretical adding, subtracting, or alteration. Muslims recall that the Prophet Muhammad discharged his mission by claiming only that it was a confirmation and continuation of earlier messages rather than a break with them. His successors felt they had, and should have, no different mandate with respect to his legacy.

In the secular scheme, by contrast, political innovation is the right of the sovereign national State, with the elected legislature the inviolable shrine of the people's will. The argument by the secularists for constitutional separation belongs with that of popular sovereignty, and, as such, provokes among the Islamists a counterproposal of State-sponsored piety. Given the reality of weakened and ineffective government institutions and structures at both the federal and state levels in Nigeria or elsewhere, and of the accompanying widespread public disenchantment with failed reforms, it is easy to see why *Sharí'ah* law has popular appeal among the rank and file. Yet amidst all the contentions and diverse agendas of *Sharí'ah* advocates, it is striking that not a word has been uttered about Third World debt relief or about programs of poverty alleviation. The question remains, then, as to whether even a *Sharí'ah*-mandated State can do better by offering a solution to the existing failures of mismanagement, public incompetence, judicial corruption, social injustice, the absence of safety and security, falling standards of living, and widespread loss of morale, or whether, instead, *Sharí'ah* would add just another twist to the discontent, and become thereby compromised. In the end, whatever the moral merit of a cargo, it cannot save the ship of state that is out of trim.

By common consent government is necessary, even if considered a necessary evil, for otherwise anarchy and mutual hostility would menace life and property. In the pragmatic view, say, in that of Oliver Wendell Holmes, Jr. (1841-1935) or of Roscoe Pound (1870-1964), government is normative to the degree that it is publicly effective, or perceived to be effective, and not the other way round lest, as Holmes put it, puritan prudes muscle in to prevent pigs from putting their feet in the trough. (Holmes, it should be remembered, advocated a program of public sterilization of the mentally retarded and other economic disposables as a perfectly logical corollary to the sacrifice of the strong and able-bodied in war: both are for the public good.) Yet effectiveness, or the public good, does not insure against tyranny, and so theocratic power, as a reaction against secular monopoly of power, risks making effectiveness a sacrament of obedience, with prayer and politics commodities of public manipulation. For sound religious as well as secular reasons, we need to separate obedience to God from submission to the instruments the state employs to enforce such obedience,[33] so that claims about God do not get reduced to matters of public enforcement, of imposition of belief, and so that doctrine and political expedience do not become currency for constituency leverage. A likely outcome of that gallery view of truth claims is the demagogic state, pointing to a religion of utility. Those obfuscate the issue who fault religion for the despotic and intolerable consequences of its interchangeability with politics, and of politics with religion. The current bitter anti-secular campaign is unlikely to spare the religion that inspires it.

The legal and normative tradition that has helped shape and define Islam's historical identity has depended crucially on the open borders the religious community has shared with its neighbours whose experiences and insights were reformulated and adopted into the code. Customs and ideas that were once regarded as alien and remote, or worthless and irrelevant, became by virtue of their proximity and familiarity no longer heretical and strange, and no longer feared and ignored, and so the canon could expand from cumulative interaction, experience, and observance. *Sharí'ah* evolved in the crucible of life and experience.[34]

Worldly affairs and the spiritual caliphate

Government is a trust from God, in the Muslim view, and from the people, in the view of the West. In both cases, however, the exercise of government is constrained by the requirement of stewardship as a spiritual caliphate (*khiláfah*),[35] under God or His *ummah* in the Muslim case, or under the people and those in whom they vest authority in the Western case.

For moderate Muslims, the danger of an Islamic State is religion becoming political fodder, to the detriment of the poor and weak, as the women and poor victims of *Sharí'ah* penal law illustrate. As Muslim moderates see it, an Islamic State would necessarily implicate Islam in political and historical compromise, an outcome that, oddly enough, fundamentalists, too, oppose. Moderates would agree on Islam as divine truth rather than as a historical construction, though they would be chary of saying it is the cure for all finite ills, including disobedience. In the end, however, both fundamentalists and moderates would concur that rulership (*hukm*), however necessary, is not a sufficient safeguard for Islam's absolute truth claims. As the Qur'an testifies, force and great might will not by themselves accomplish the purpose of God. 'Kings, when they enter a city, disorder it and make the mighty ones of its inhabitants abased (Qur'an 27: 34). It is a view that has a familiar ring in the evangelical stream in early modern Christianity, the pronouncements of Roger Williams and William Penn being a case in point, not an insignificant advantage in the dialogue with the Muslim world.

The *Sharí'ah* debate in Nigeria should shed light on the larger issue of the worldwide agitation of Muslim radicals against what they view as secular fundamentalism, and against the West that harbours and fosters it. Religious fundamentalists often come across as foes of secular governments and of democratic freedom. They sound medieval in their values and backward in their outlook, scandalized by the thought of people as free and enjoying themselves, and particularly of men and women mixing freely in social company. Furthermore, fundamentalists cherish the machinery of instant justice, including chopping off limbs and heads and reducing people to grovelling fear and abject submission. What they fail to recognize, however, is that legal coercion is a flawed instrument for securing moral persuasion. As the Caliph al-Ma'mún (ruled 813-833) trenchantly observed, it is impossible under the threat that overhangs society from *Sharí'ah* political sanctions to distinguish between political expedience and moral duty, between opportunism and sincerity. Threats corrupt, and absolute threats make absolute hypocrites. There is a class of Muslims, al-Ma'mún noted, 'who embrace Islam, not from any love for this our religion, but thinking thereby to gain access to my Court, and share in the honour, wealth, and power of the Realm; they have no inward persuasion of that which they outwardly profess.'[36] The lesson here is, if the state must procure the allegiance of believers, then religion cannot pretend that its truth claims have intrinsic persuasive merit, and so religion must disingenuously yield right of way to behavioral norms dispensed by the State. In that case, the caliph's disquiet has sounder religious roots than the scheming '*ulama* with their supple conscience.

Religion and the cultural project: Postscript

Religious groups in the West have come at the issue of secularism from the antinomian tendencies of the privatization of faith. Some of these groups have withdrawn into communes and farmsteads where in isolation they nurse a sectarian view of the world. Others make a bid for power to turn back the tide of vice. All such groups seem of the mind that the modern status quo is complicit in the emergence of a fundamentalist secular culture bereft of a sense of the holy and transcendent. Secularism has declared open war on religion, prompting religious groups into invoking *jihád* to condemn secularism and the liberal democracy promoting it.

The secular status quo from the left and the right has remained controversial. To resolve the issue, we should take seriously the moral insight of personal salvation grounded in freedom as a response to God's grace as important not only for sound religion but also for social tolerance and democratic renewal. That means we must resist the view that religion is detrimental to individual freedom and that only a begrudged private piety must be allowed room in a secular democracy. Neither the legislative authority of an elected parliament nor the will of a dictator can ever muzzle the voice of conscience without risk of social instability and political disaffection. As Durkheim contended, religion is not unconnected to the social order. The costs of postponing rational discussion of how religion may impinge on politics to tame doctrinaire secularism and its religious nemesis are high. That is the unacknowledged hidden corollary of the impact of 9/11. It is not just the military and economic interest of the West that is under threat. The modern cultural project at large is itself at stake.

Notes

[1] Paul Berman, *Terror and Liberalism*, NY: W.W. Norton, 2003.

[2] In an uncannily prescient statement, A.J. Arberry, an eminent life-long student of things Muslim and Islamic, reflected more than fifty years ago on the challenge of Islam to the West, saying it is an old one. 'Present-day Oriental contempt for Europe, to my way of thinking the most terrible and menacing aspect of contemporary politics, is not to be dismissed simply as a triumphant reaction against a defeated or a penitent imperialism. Doubtless there is much of that in it; but the roots go deeper. Underneath all of it lies the challenge flung down more than thirteen centuries ago, and taken up again and again by' leading Muslim thinkers. 'Islam claims specifically to be the final revelation of God to mankind, and an overthrow of all other religions ... The tables have been turned. Christian Europe, adventuring into the East upon its self-appointed civilizing mission, is now informed that it is itself in need of civilizing anew from the East ... If the threatening and so unnecessary conflict is to be avoided, it is imperative that we should make a renewed and unremitting effort to understand each other's viewpoint, and to study what possibilities exist for, first, a diminishing of tension, next, a rational compromise, and, ultimately, an agreement to work together towards common ideals.' Arberry's Preface to his edition and translation of Muhammad Iqbal, *The Mysteries of Selflessness: A Philosophical Poem*, London: John Murray Publishers, 1953, xivff.

[3] That was the title of Iqbal's influential book published in 1934. It became a national charter for the posthumous state of Pakistan, created in 1948. In the book, Iqbal wrote that the Muslim community, now scattered perforce in a multiplicity of free independent units must strive to have their 'racial rivalries adjusted and harmonized by the unifying bond of a common spiritual aspiration. It seems to me that God is slowly bringing home to us the truth that Islam is neither Nationalism nor Imperialism but a League of Nations which recognizes artificial boundaries and racial distinctions for facility of reference only, and not for restricting the social horizon of its members.' His was a voice for open borders of intellectual exchange.

[4] Alexander David Russell and Abdullah al-Ma'mún Suhrawardy, *First Steps in Muslim Jurisprudence*, 1906, reprinted London: Luzac & Co. Ltd., 1963, viii.

[5] At about the same time similar efforts were going on in Egypt. Sir Norman Anderson's book, *Law Reform in the Muslim World* (1976) offers a comprehensive overview and summary of developments in the field. See also his *Islamic Law in Africa*, London: HM. Stationery Office, 1954; reprinted London: Frank Cass Publishers, 1970. Anderson, it should be pointed out, was not, however, concerned with issues of normative or prescriptive coherence in the administration of law.

[6] Some Muslim spokesmen have contended that secularism divested the Muslims of their right to *Shari'ah* law while imposing no similar disability on Christians, a contention that does not accurately reflect the fate that, according to R.H. Tawney, had befallen Christianity when it was subjected to privatization in early modern Europe, with the church removed from having any public role in society. Tawney, *Religion and the Rise of Capitalism: A*

Historical Study, Penguin Books: Harmondsworth, UK, 272. Under much of colonial rule, accordingly, the churches were severely restricted by being privatized, Nigeria not excepted.

[7] *Hadd* (pl. *hudúd*) is the sphere of *Sharí'ah* criminal law, and comprises i) *sariqa* (cutting off the hand for theft), ii) *zinà* (caning or execution for fornication and adultery), iii) *qadhf* (slander or false accusation for fornication and adultery punishable by caning), iv) *haraba* (highway robbery or rebellion, for which the punishment is amputation of the right hand and left foot, exile, imprisonment, or sometimes execution by crucifixion, v) *shurb al-khamr* (alcohol consumption, punishable by caning), and, sometimes vi) *al-ridda* (apostasy, which is punishable by death).

[8] For a study of contemporary Nigerian politics, including the regime of Babangida see Eghosa E. Osaghae, *Crippled Giant: Nigeria Since Independence*, Bloomington: Indiana University Press, 1998.

[9] Birai, 'Islamic Tajdid', 1993, 190. The implication here is that there is no ground for dialogue with Christians. They are responsible for secularism.

[10] Yerima was appointed as an official participant at the August, 2000 Democratic National Convention in Los Angeles, California, a measure of his range and appeal.

[11] *Christian Science Monitor*, 22 February, 2001.

[12] 'As Stoning Case Proceeds, Nigeria Stands Trial', *New York Times*, 26 January, 2003, A3.

[13] The name, *Izala* is Arabic for 'eradication' and occurs in the name of the movement, the Society for the Eradication of Heresy and the Establishment of the Prophet's *Sunnah*, founded in 1978.

[14] For a report on El Zakzaky and the 1996 religious riots in Kafanchan and Kaduna he inspired, see 'Bloody Riots in the North', *Tell* magazine, September 30, 1996. According to the magazine's report, the government crackdown commenced on September 12, 1996 in Zaria, when El Zakzaky gave himself up to the authorities. The following day after the Friday *Jum'ah* prayer, his followers mounted public demonstrations in various parts of the country, including Katsina and Kaduna, and Zaria, demanding his release. There was bloodshed from these demonstrations. On the background to El Zakzaky, see also Ousmane Kane, 'Mouvements religieux et champ politique au Nigeria septentrionale: le cas de réformisme musulman au Kano', *Islam et Sociétés au Sud du Sahara*, 4, 7-24.

[15] Muyiwa Akintunde, 'This Isn't the Sharia We Know', *Africa Today*, December, 1999.

[16] Some Egyptian modernists follow Leo Strauss and Karl Popper in making this distinction. Among them was Faraj Fúda, assassinated in 1992. He accused *Sharí'ah* advocates of offering a false panacea for present ills. Like Mamadou Dia, one time Prime Minister of Senegal, Fúda called for a dynamic understanding of *Sharí'ah* and Islamic history. See Ibrahim M. Abu-Rabi', *Intellectual Origins of Islamic Resurgence in the Modern Arab World*, Albany: State University of New York Press, 1996, 255ff. In this respect, a report on Iran says that the clerical leaders of the revolution there have climbed down from their high theocratic positions and opted for 'a minimalist' approach in order to reduce the risk of popular backlash and to connect with the youth. But this is not surrender to secularists who also admit that Islam has a role in society. Thomas L. Friedman, 'Iran and The War of Ideas', Op-Ed article, *New York Times*, 19 June, 2002. This sentiment is in line with the distinction being made in Nigeria in the contrasting roles of State and society which promises a more fruitful avenue of thinking, if only because it accepts the coexistence of islamization and secularization. The issue of democracy and *Sharí'ah* rule was taken up also by the influential Pakistani scholar, Maududi, but with unsatisfactory results. S. Abul A'la Maududi, *Political Theory of Islam*, Lahore: Islamic Publications Ltd., 1980, 21-25, 34-42. See, too, James Piscatori, *Islam, Islamists, and the Electoral Principle in the Middle East*, Leiden: International Institute for the Study of Islam in the Modern World, 2000.

[17] In an irate editorial, 'Faith in the Public Sphere', the *New York Times* invoked this argument when it chided Rod Paige, the African American Secretary of Education, for advocating Christian values in schools. Dr Paige's statements confirm 'the suspicions that the [Bush] administration is in sympathy with the religious right's drive to undermine the public school system in favour of a voucher-financed nationwide network of religious schools.' According to the *Times*, Dr Paige's religious views are destructive of the public interest. *The New York Times*, April 11, 2003. Precisely what justifies the Times' alarmist view is not made clear. Is it Paige's advocacy of Christian values in schools or the boost it might give to the religious right? What are the Christian values in question, and why are they a matter only for the religious right? What about Roman Catholic schools in the inner cities of America? Does religious involvement in that case undermine the public school system? Scarcely.

[18] Maududi's influential opinions include guarded support for 'theo-democracy', i.e., democracy qualified by Islamic restrictions. See Piscatori, 2000, 20-21.

[19] Interview, *This Week*, 6 April, 1987. This condemnation of those 'ulamá who are under the thumb of temporal rulers is a well rehearsed one in the literature. As far back as Jalál al-Dín al-Suyútí (d. 1505) we hear of attacks on religious scholars who ingratiate themselves with rulers.

[20] Report in *Quality*, Lagos, October, 1987, and cited in S. Ilesanmi, *Religious Pluralism and the Nigerian State*, Athens, Ohio: Center for International Studies, 1997, 186.

[21] The example of Dr Mohammed Tawfiq Landan, senior lecturer in law and Head of the Department of Public Law at Ahmadu Bello University, Zaria, is a case in point. In a major dissenting article, he attacked the method of *Sharí'ah* implementation as flawed and 'violative of the rights of life and security' of the poor. *The Guardian*, 8 January, 2002.

[22] Report of the commission: 'Sharia and the Future of Nigeria: Report of the Trip by the Civil Liberties Organization, CLO, Hurilaws and other NGOs to Zamfara State', p.9.

[23] BBC reports of 23 December, 2000, spoke of continuing public campaigns demanding *Sharí'ah* law in other parts of the north.

[24] Mr Soyinka's own justifiable protestations notwithstanding, the northern Muslim leaders prefer to consider him a Christian for the purposes of legal classification. Thus, when he received the 1986 Nobel Prize for Literature, Shaykh Gumi was awarded by Saudi Arabia an Islamic equivalent created for the occasion.

[25] 'This is Prelude to War', Soyinka interview, *The News*, Lagos, March 6, 2000. 'One must allow for some editorial shoddiness in this copy. Only academic essentialism can make us persist with equating *sharí'ah* with Orisa: the two have Nigeria fortuitously in common; otherwise in historical range, scale, and claim, they move in very different spheres altogether.'

[26] *The Guardian*, Tuesday, February 29, 2000.

[27] Umar M. Birai, 'Islamic *Tajdid* and the Political Process in Nigeria', in Martin E. Marty & R. Scott Appleby, editors, *Fundamentalism and the State: Remaking Polities, Economies, and Militance*, Chicago: Chicago University Press, 1993, 184-203, 196.

[28] Birai, "Islamic *Tajdid* and the Political Process in Nigeria," 197.

[29] Maier, 2000, 178.

[30] Maier, 2000, 170-171, 172. The leader of Tajidmul, Shaykh Abubakar Mujahid, is a self-declared uncompromising admirer of the Iranian Revolution and of the Talibans. He expressed disquiet about Iran's reformist president, Mohammad Khatami, saying Khatami was slipping from the old moorings, was 'getting loose', as he put it. He wishes to use Western education, including its technology, to inculcate Islamic values. Tajidmul ran a small school in Kano, a pharmacy, and a wholesale food store for its members, showing secular inroads in fundamentalist theology.

[31] *Christian Science Monitor*, 22 February, 2001.

[32] Maier, 2000, 172-173.

[33] For a discussion of some of these issues, see Wael Hallaq, 'From Fatwas to Furú': Growth and Change in Islamic Substantive Law', *Islamic Law and Society*, vol. i, no. i, 1994, 29-65; and the same author's *Authority, Continuity and Change in Islamic Law*, Cambridge: Cambridge University Press, 2001.

[34] Ibn Khaldún (1405/06), pioneering historian and sociologist of Islam, affirms the importance of contingency and difference in Muslim jurisprudence as follows: 'It should be known that the jurisprudence described, which is based upon religious evidence, involves many differences of opinion among scholars of independent judgment. Differences of opinion result from the different sources they use and their different outlooks [methodologies], and are unavoidable ... [These differences] occupied a very large space in Islam.' Ibn Khaldún, *The Muqaddimah: An Introduction to History*, ed. & tr. Franz Rosenthal, Princeton: Princeton University Press, 1958, 3 volumes, vol. iii, 30-31. In an important study of the subject, Muhammad Khalid Masud appended a notice by Abu Ishaq al-Shatibi (d. 1388) to set the tone of his book: 'God made this blessed righteous *Sharí'ah* accommodating and convenient and thus won the hearts of men and invoked in them love and respect for law. Had they had to act against convenience they could not have honestly fulfilled their obligations'. Muhammad Khalid Masud, *Islamic Legal Philosophy: A Study of Abu Ishaq al-Shatibi's Life and Thought*, Delhi: International Islamic Publishers, 1989, frontispiece. For a summary see Muhammad Khalid Masud, *Muslim Jurists' Quest for the Normative Basis of Sharí'a*, inaugural lecture, University of Leiden, 2001.

[35] For a study of this theme in the Qur'án, see Kenneth Cragg, *The Privilege of Man*, London, 1968.

[36] 'Abd al-Masíh ibn Isháq al-Kindí, *The Apology*, ed. & tr. Sir William Muir, London: SPCK, 1887, pp. 29-30.

Chapter 11

Perspectives on Radical Islamic Education in Contemporary Indonesia: Major Themes and Characteristics of Abu Bakar Ba'asyir's Teachings

Muhammad Sirozi

Background notes

The term *radical* comes from the Latin *radix*, meaning 'root', used in the sense of 'from the roots up' or 'through'.[1] In politics, *radical* has been used to describe those 'who advocate fundamental or extreme measures to challenge an established order'.[2] The meaning of *radical* has been shifting, imprecise, and inflammatory.[3] In the late eighteenth century, after the French Revolution, the term *radical reformer* was used to describe respectable leaders and right wing agendas.[4] Since the end of the Cold War and the resurgence of international terrorism, 'radicals' has been used to describe the terrorists. Since many terrorist suspects are Muslims, the term *radical* tends to be associated with Islam, such as 'radical Muslims', 'Islamic extremism', 'Islamic fundamentalism', or 'radical mosques'.[5] After 9/11, Robyn Blummer observes, 'the "radical Islamist" has become the bogeyman of academe'.[6] Radical is often synonymous with fanatic, a term that refers to 'the irrationality of religious or political feeling'.[7] 'For most Americans', said Herbst, 'Muslim radicalism bristles with images of cruel violence'.[8]

Irrespective of its shifting, imprecise, and inflammatory use, radicalism has been an important part of Islamic history. Radical Islamism has grown rapidly as the ideology of Islamic intellectual, social, and political movements at local, national, and international levels. Contemporary radical Islamism can be traced back to the works of Abul al-Ala Mawdudi (d. 1979),[9] Sayyid Qutb (d. 1966),[10] and Imam Khomeini (d. 1989).[11] These radical Islamists claim that 'Islam is for all aspects of social as well as personal life ... that Islam is flexible and that un-Islamic "superstitions" must be eliminated'.[12] They accept 'the need for absolute *ijtihad*,[13] but they are likely to grant it less scope and they emphasize that it must be done in an authentically Islamic way and not as a covert means of copying the West'.[14] Radical Islamists 'tend to accept more of the past *ijtihad* of the scholars and to emphasize somewhat less the failings of the community in pre-modern times and somewhat more the distortions caused by Western colonialism'.[15] They strongly emphasize 'the distinctiveness of Islam' and distinguish Islam from 'democracy', 'communism', or 'dictatorship'. They tend to reject modified terms, such as 'Islamic socialism'.[16] For them, 'Islam as a whole is a distinct and integrated system [way of life], so that even if individual elements do not seem distinctive, their place in the Islamic system makes them different'.[17]

In order to assure the authenticity and distinctiveness of Islam, radical Islamists avoid being apologetics and emphasize the importance of adopting and implementing the *Sharí'ah* at individual, community, and state level.[18] For them, *Sharí'ah* 'is not only an ideal to be known and revered, but a law to be put into effect and obeyed'.[19] For these purposes, some of them adopt a 'gradualist approach' by emphasizing negotiation, cooperation, and persuasion towards Islamic law. Some others, however, prefer to adopt a 'revolutionary' approach to Islamic law. They legitimize violence, terrorism, and repression for the sake of implementing *Sharí'ah*.[20]

Although anti-West and anti-modernity in character, radical Islamists accept and apply some western and modern ideas. As in the name of the Islamic Republic of Iran, Khomeini rejects the word 'democratic' because of its close connection with modernity, but accepts the word 'republic' which is equally close to modernity. Mawdudi describes *jihad* as a 'revolutionary struggle', and Sayyid Qutb describes Islam as 'a universal proclamation of the liberation of man'.[21] Although emphasizing the importance of following the Islamic way of life adopted by Prophet Muhammad and his companions in seventh century Arabia, radical Islamists accept the idea of 'progress' and insist that Islam is the way to get 'progress'.[22] Khomeini describes Islam as a 'progressive' religion and Mawdudi believes that adopting the moral values of Islam will allow Muslims to accelerate the onward march to progress.[23] Although strongly emphasizing the importance of preparing for life in the hereafter (*akhirah*), radical Islamists do not ignore the worldly orientation (*dunya*) of Muslim life. Their thoughts and activities are characterized by what Weber described as 'inner worldly asceticism'.[24] 'They [radical Islamists] are not unconcerned for otherworldly things, and to some extent their emphasis on this-worldly things is a function of the fact that it is mainly in this-worldly sphere that secularism has called Islam into question'.[25]

Indonesia has always been a fertile ground for the development of radical Islamism despite the secularization policies adopted by the government and a majority moderate Muslim population. Radical Islamists have played a role in the dynamics of social, religious, and political changes in the country. The rise of reform and democratization movement after the fall of Suharto government in 1998 paved the way for the resurgence of radical Islamism. The reform movement allows radical Islamists to organize their activities, develop their networks, and consolidate their power. One leading figure in the resurgence of radical Islamism in contemporary Indonesia is Abu Bakar Ba'asyir, better known as Ustadz Abu.[26]

Ba'asyir has been described in national and international media as a radical Muslim leader and a terrorist suspect linked to al-Qaeda. His involvement in the radical Islamic movement began in early 1980s when he opposed the Suharto government's policy requiring all mass organisations to adopt *Pancasila*,[27] the national ideology, as the sole base (*asas tunggal*). After the fall of Suharto, Ba'asyir was one of the founders and first Chairman of an Islamist non-government organization called Indonesia Mujahidin Council (*Majelis Mujahidin Indonesia*, MMI) established in 2000.[28] At the second national MMI conference on August, 5-7, 2002 in Yogyakarta,[29] he was re-elected as Chairman.[30] Since the 9/11 tragedy and Bali bombings on October 2002, Ba'asyir has been accused of being involved in international terrorist networks, particularly in the Southeast Asia region. The accusation is based on a CIA document which refers to a statement made by Omar al-Faruq, a mysterious suspected member of *Jamaah Islamiyah* (JI),[31] according to *Time Magazine* (September 23, 2002). The report said that Ba'asyir is al-Qaeda's highest representative in Southeast Asia and that he was involved in serial bombings in Jakarta. It also said that Ba'asyir planned to blow up a US military base in the Southeast Asia region and kill President Megawati. Al-Faruq claimed that he is familiar with Ba'asyir and indicated that Ba'asyir received money from bin Laden for buying ammunition. In December 2001, the governments of Singapore,[32] Malaysia, the Philippines, and the USA put Ba'asyir on the list of leading figures involved in international terrorist networks. They accused him of being the 'spiritual leader' of *Jamaah Islamiyah* (JI) and described him as the 'Osama bin Laden of Southeast Asia',[33] and 'number 2 enemy of America' (Osama bin Laden is number 1).[34] Malaysian security officials described him as the 'godfather' of JI.[35] On October 2002, under pressures from the US government, Indonesian police formally declared Ba'asyir a terrorist suspect and arrested him on the next day. Referring to a source at the American Embassy in Jakarta, *Tempo Interaktif*, September edition, 2003, confirmed that Ba'asyir remains on the top of current list of CIA terrorist suspects.[36]

One thing that tends to be less noted in discussions and publications about Ba'asyir is the fact that he is an experienced and influential Islamic teacher. He is an *ustadz* (teacher) and a *musrif* (adviser) at *Pondon Pesantren*[37] *Al-Mukmin*, Ngruki, more popularly known as Pondok Ngruki, a traditional Islamic boarding school that he co-founded in March 1972.[38] He was a key figure in the establishment of *Madrasah Diniyah* which later become Sekolah Menengah Atas Islam (Islamic Senior High School) in Pasar Klewer (Klewer Market), Solo, a few years before the establishment of Pondok Ngruki. While managing *Madrasah Diniyah*, he was also teaching daily at *Kuliah Zhuhur* (Noon prayer study group) in Surakarta Agung Mosque. While in exile in Malaysia from 1985 to 1998,[39] Ba'asyir, under the name of Abdus Samad, was a *pendakwah lepas* (freelance preacher) in many *pengajian* (religious study groups) that he describes as 'Qur'an recitation groups' aimed at 'purifying Islamic teaching following the *Ahl as Sunnah wal Jamaah* school of thought'.[40]

This article explores radical Islamic education in contemporary Indonesia with particular reference to Ba'asyir's teachings. It focuses on the major themes and characteristics of the teaching, the way Ba'asyir configures religiosity and identity in Muslim society, and the educational implications of his teachings. It is supplementing previous studies, such as *Meeting Ustadz Abu, Preaching Fundamentalism: The public teachings of Abu Bakar Ba'asyir*, and *Reading Past the Myth: Public Teachings of Abu Bakar Ba'asyir* by Tim Behrend; *Kontroversi*

Ba'asyir: Jihad Melawan Opini 'Fitnah' Global by Idi Subandy Ibrahim and Asep Syamsul M. Romli; *Dakwah & Jihad Abu Bakar Ba'asyir* edited by Irfan Suryahadi Awwas; *Ngruki & Jaringan Terrorisme: Melacak Jejak Abu Bakar & Jaringan dari Ngruki sampai Bom Bali* by E.S. Soepriyadi; and *Abu Bakar Ba'asyir Melawan Amerika* edited by Arie Ruhyanto.

Identifying the themes and characteristics of Ba'asyir's teachings, the way he configures religiosity and the educational implications of his teachings allows us to assess the type of Muslim community that the radicals expect to develop and the possible impact of radicalism on the future development of Islam in Indonesia. In particular, it allows us to identify the strengths and weaknesses of the radical Islamic movement in contemporary Indonesia and to assess the extent to which Islamic education needs to be redirected for designing strategies and setting up agendas for the reform of Islamic education in the country.

Ba'asyir's teaching

There are eight major related themes in Ba'asyir's public teachings: *Tauhid* (Islamic monotheism), *Sharí'ah* (Islamic law), *Ibadah* (worship), *Daulah Islamiyah* (Islamic State), *Jihad, Dawah* (Islamic missionary), *Wahn* (worldly life) and *Mutraf* (luxury), and the authenticity of Islam.

Tauhid, the core element of *Din al-Islam*

Tauhid is the Islamic monotheistic doctrine of the oneness and unity of God.[41] The Qur'an suggests that *Tauhid* is the original creed of mankind that has been introduced by all prophets of Islam. *Tauhid* forbids any form of partnership to God and suggests that God is the only Creator, Lord, and Maintainer of every thing in heaven and on earth. Adopting *Tauhid* requires one to believe in God (Allah) and behave according to the demands of His doctrines.[42] *Tauhid* is 'a powerful symbol of divine, spiritual, and sociopolitical unity'.[43] Islamic reformers and activists, such as Muhammad ibn Abd al-Wahab (d. 1792),[44] Muhammad Abduh (d. 1905),[45] Ismail al-Faruqi (d. 1986),[46] Ali Sharíati (d. 1977),[47] and Ayatollah Ruhollah Khomeini (d. 1989)[48] used the concept of *Tauhid* as the basic principle for developing their ideas regarding the development of Muslim society.

Ba'asyir shares the position of these reformers and activists. The first and most important theme of his teachings is *Tauhid*. He believes that every single human being is born with the spirit of *Tauhid*[49] and *Tauhid* is the core of *Din al-Islam* (the religion of Islam). He also believes that *Tauhid* is a factor that determines whether a human's *amal* (deeds) are accepted or rejected by Allah *Subhanahu wa Ta'ala* (SWT).[50] 'Failure to accept *Tauhid* or committing *shirk* (polytheism)', he stresses, 'is an unforgivable sin'.[51]

There are three elements of *Tauhid* introduced by scholars of Islam. First, *Tauhid Rububiyah*, believing that *Allah Subhanahu wa Ta'ala* is the conqueror and controller of the universe, who determines human life, death, and fate. Second, *Tauhid Asma' wa Sifat*, believing that Allah is omniscient and has exclusive characteristics as indicated in *al-Asmaul Husna*.[52] Third, *Tauhid Uluhiyah*, obeying what is permitted and forbidden by Allah as regulated by *Sharí'ah* or *hukmullah* (the law of Allah).[53] In order to free him/herself from any worldly power, Ba'asyir says, a person needs to adopt the above three *Tauhid* altogether. He stresses that *Tauhid Uluhiyah* is essential. 'Without *Tauhid Uluhiyah*, someone's *Tauhid* is defective'. Those who simply adopt *Tauhid Rububiyah* and *Tauhid Asma' wa Sifat* and reject *Tauhid Uluhiyah* because of arrogance and logical reasoning are among *Iblis laknatullah* (devils condemned by Allah). In this regard, Ba'asyir refers to verse 34 of Chapter 2 (*Al Baqarah*) of the Qur'an[54] which explains that Iblis rejected Allah's command to bow to Adam because he thought he was superior to Adam. *Iman* (Islamic belief), said Ba'asyir, is 'believing and implementing the truth'.[55] The essence of *Tauhid*, he further states, is 'believing in Allah's existence, in *Rububiyah* (that Allah creates, enlivens, terminates life, arranges universe etc.), in Allah's perfection'.

Realizing *Tauhid* through *Sharí'ah*

Sharí'ah comes from *shar*; 'the path leading to the water hole'.[56] It is a 'God-given prescription for the right life in this world and for salvation in the world to come'.[57] It is 'God's eternal and immutable will for humanity, as expressed in the *Qur'an* and Muhammad's example (*Sunnah*), considered binding for all believers'.[58] In brief, it is an ideal Islamic law.

Ba'asyir is committed to the implementation of *Sharí'ah* at an individual and collective level. He teaches that *Sharí'ah* is 'a system of life designed by Allah for His worshippers and brought by His messenger (*Rasulullah Shallallahu 'alaihi wa Sallam*)'. It includes *hukum far'i* (laws on empirical deeds) or *hukum fiqih* (fiqh law) and the principal law on the aspects of belief as discussed in *ilmu kalam* (Islamic theology).[59] Ba'asyir believes that implementing *Sharí'ah* is a condition for true *Tauhid*. 'Obeying and implementing *Sharí'ah* comprehensively', he said, 'is the realization of *Tauhid*'.[60] Referring to the Qur'an, Chapter 16 (*An-Nahl*) verse 36, Chapter 7 (*Al A'raf*) verse 85 and 65, Chapter 23 (*Al-Mukminun*) verse 23, and Chapter 51 (*Adz-Dzaariat*) verse 56, he concludes that Islamic *Tauhid* will be defective if a Muslim commits *shirk* (idolatry) and disobeys the *Sharí'ah* or replaces it with man-made laws. True *Tauhid*, he suggests, is implementing *Sharí'ah* comprehensively.[61] Ba'asyir particularly stresses that *Tauhid Uluhiyah* is required for the implementation of *Sharí'ah* and those who reject the implementation of *Sharí'ah* because of arrogance and logical reasoning are among *Iblis laknatullah* (condemned by Allah).[62] Referring to the *Qur'an*, verse 85 of Chapter 2 (*Al-Baqarah*), he stresses that implementing *Sharí'ah* comprehensively will bring happiness in this world and in the hereafter as well as many positive results in the life of Muslims, such as preserving the purity of *din al-Islam* and strengthening its existence, making public security real, purifying the implementation of *Tauhid*,[63] purifying wealth,[64] securing wealth,[65] maintaining a healthy mind,[66] preserving offspring,[67] avoiding forceful means in religion,[68] protecting the rights of the *kufr* (disbelievers),[69] avoiding *pemurtadan* (apostate) from *din al-Islam*,[70] securing life,[71] and inviting *barakah* (blessings) from heaven and earth.[72]

'In this life', Ba'asyir teaches, 'there is nothing more valuable than struggling to implement Allah's *Sharí'ah*'.[73] *Sharí'ah* must be implemented consistently and comprehensively. 'No bargaining in this process [of implementing *Sharí'ah*]. Accept every thing or reject every thing'.[74] Ba'asyir believes that failure to implement the *Sharí'ah* will cause difficulties in worldly life and lead to punishment in the hereafter.[75] In this world, he explains, failure to implement *Sharí'ah* will cause various types of *musibah* (disaster) in the life of all Muslims, such as moral decadence, sickness, chaos, and depression, particularly psychological depression, so that Muslims will be frustrated and commit suicide. Ba'asyir further explains that failure to implement *Sharí'ah* will cause continuous conflicts and arguments among Muslim leaders.[76] He believes that without *Sharí'ah* Muslims will always be the losers. To be the winners, he teaches, Muslims do not need sophisticated science and technology. What they need is the blessings of Allah that can only be gained through the implementation of *Sharí'ah*. In his words: 'Muslims can be the winners only if they are committed to *Sharí'ah*, Allah's *Sharí'ah*. If we [Muslims] cannot implement *Sharí'ah*, we better give up [from this worldly life]'.[77]

Worshipping (*Ibadah*) according to *Sharí'ah*

Ibadah (worship) literally means 'servanthood, slavehood'.[78] The technical meaning of *ibadah* is 'an act of worship performed in obedience to God [Allah], in accordance with His command, and in order to seek His pleasure'.[79] In term of ritual, *ibadah* includes *salat* (prayer), *zakat* (religious tax), *saum* (fasting), and *hajj* (pilgrimage). In general, *ibadah* also includes 'any act done in recognition of one's proper relationship with God, the relationship, that is, of a servant or slave to his master'.[80] *Ibadah* covers the whole of human life.[81] *Ibadah* is 'acts of devotion' or 'the religious duties of worship incumbent on all Muslims when they come of age and are of sound body and mind'.[82]

Ba'asyir stresses that the main objective of human being along with the *jinn*[83] is to worship Allah.[84] The right way to worship Allah is to speak and act according to His will, that is to follow *Sharí'ah* or Allah's law sincerely, *lillahi ta'ala* (only for the sake of Allah), in search of His *ridha* (blessings).[85] Ba'asyir teaches that "*ibadah* (worshipping Allah) means implementing Allah's *Sharí'ah* in a comprehensive way (*kaffah*) for the sake of gaining His *ridha* (blessings)".[86] He further suggests, the main duty of human beings in this world is 'to implement all Allah's *Sharí'ah* (law) only for the sake of gaining His *ridha* (blessings)'.[87] According to Ba'asyir, 'other worldly activities, such as earning for life and seeking knowledge are only supplementary ways of perfecting *ibadah*'. He warns that in the process of *ibadah*, human beings will face challenges and difficulties from the *shaitan* (devil)[88] because Allah has decreed it.[89] He teache]s that Muslims can continuously improve the quality of their *ibadah* (worship) by two ways: (1) Pray to Allah so that we gain the strength to perform the *ibadah* well and (2) Fight bravely, strongly, patiently, and with perseverance against all challenges from the

Shaithan.[90] The fight must be meant to support *Din al-Allah* (Allah's religion) through implementing *Sharí'ah* consistently, without tolerating any form of *kebathilan* (wrong deed).

Daulah Islamiyah for implementing *Sharí'ah*

Establishing *Daulah Islamiyah* (Islamic State) has been a goal of Islamic movements since pre-modern times. This goal is based on the belief that religion and government are closely related and cannot be separated. It is also based on the fact that Prophet Muhammad was both a religious and state leader. In the seventh century, the *Khawarij* (seceders)[91] was the first movement to claim/proclaim the doctrine of divine governance (*hakimiyyah*) and rule (*hukm*) and the ultimate authority of the Qur'an as the only reference for Muslims. They rejected the legitimacy of human arbitration unless it was supported by the text. Ibn Taymiyyah and his followers, especially the Wahhabis, called for the purification of Islam by returning to the Qur'an and the *Sunnah* (way) of the Prophet. Similar arguments were adopted by other Islamic movements, such as *al-Sanusiyah* in Libya, *al-Mahdiyyah* in Sudan, *ikhwan al-Muslimun* in Egypt, *Jamaat Islami* in Pakistan and the Islamic revolution in Iran.[92]

Like the Wahhabis and other proponents of Islamic purification, Ba'asyir rejects the secular state and strives for a *Sharí'ah* oriented one. For example, he rejected *Pancasila*[93] and promoted the adoption of *Sharí'ah* in Indonesia. He believes that the major cause of backwardness and moral bankruptcy in many Muslim countries, including Indonesia, is the failure of their leaders to implement *Sharí'ah*[94] and the one and only way for solving these problems and enlightening Muslim life is by strictly implementing *Sharí'ah* principles. Without an Islamic State, he believes, Muslims will not be able to implement the *Sharí'ah* and sooner or later the *Sharí'ah* will simply be a name. For him, establishing an Islamic State is a leadership strategy that needs to be considered in an effort to implement *Sharí'ah* effectively. He believes that *Sharí'ah* can be implemented purely and comprehensively (*secara kaffah*) if Muslims are united under one leadership of *Daulah Islamiyah*. He also believes that the current environment in Indonesia is far too permissive and fatally flawed. The reason, he suggests, is because the country is established not based on *Sharí'ah*, but on the principles of *kufr* (disbelief), including popular democracy, a usurious banking system, social equality of the sexes, and licensing of immoral (and culturally unacceptable) behaviour for economic gains.[95]

Performing *Jihad*

Jihad is an Arabic word meaning 'to strive', 'to exert', 'to fight' or 'to struggle' with something distressful or hostile or against some wrong.[96] Muslim scholars and jurists generally agree that *jihad* is 'the use of the powers, talents, and other resources of believers to live in this world in accordance with God's plan as known through the Islamic Scriptures'.[97] *Jihad* includes 'any endeavour that is made to further the cause of God, whether in promoting good or eradicating evil'.[98] It can be in the form of social action or private effort, financial assistance, physical struggle, or against the enemy.[99] There are two categories of *jihad*. First, *Jihad Akbar* (the greater *jihad*) which means 'the inner struggle for one's own soul against the flesh and for righteousness against the forbidden', and including striving for justice and compassion, for example, parents' concern for children.[100] Second, *Jihad Asghar* (the lesser *jihad*), which means 'literal warfare against the infidels – holy war by way of the sword'.[101]

Some western critics of Islam, such as Daniel Pipes, interpret *jihad* as a 'holy war', 'to extend sovereign Muslim power'. [102] In the western media *jihad* is used to refer to 'terrorist attacks organized by so-called militant fundamentalist Muslims'.[103] However, for Muslims *jihad* is waged in defence of Muslims. Thus, for Hamas, *jihad* is a struggle to liberate Palestine, to end the Israeli occupation of the land of Muslims.[104] Raphael Israeli refers to the following definition of *jihad* provided by Hamas:

> When our enemies usurp our Islamic lands, *Jihad* becomes a duty binding on all Muslims. In order to face the usurpation of Palestine by the Jews, we have no escape from raising the banner of *Jihad*. This would require the propagation of Islamic consciousness among the masses on all local, Arab and Islamic levels. We must spread the spirit of *Jihad* among the Islamic *ummah*, clash with the enemies and join the ranks of *Jihad* fighters.[105]

Jihadist groups, such as *The International Islamic Front for the Jihad Against Jews and Crusaders* led by Osama bin Laden, *Laskar Jihad* led by Ja'far Umar Thalib in Indonesia, *Harakat ul-Jihad-i-Islami* in Kashmir, *Palestinian Islamic Jihad*, *Egyptian Islamic Jihad*, and *Yemeni Islamic Jihad* wage war in defence of Muslims.

However, for most Muslims *jihad* 'simply refers to a spiritual striving to attain nearness to Allah'.[106] Thus, the Qur'anic scholar Muhammed Abdul Malek writes, '*Jihad* is a duty of Muslims to commit themselves to struggle on all fronts – moral, spiritual and political – to create a just and decent society. It is not a 'holy war' against the non-believers as is commonly understood'. He maintains that 'the doctrine of *jihad* never encourages war or violence'. Malek argues that 'the phrase "holy war" was coined by the West in its struggle against the Muslims during the time of the Crusades (a war instigated by the Church for religious gain).'[107] Similarly, for Ibrahim Abu-Rabi from Hartford Seminary, *jihad* is an 'effort against evil in the self and every manifestation of evil in society'.[108] Farid Eseck also emphasizes that *jihad* is a struggle for justice: 'resisting apartheid or working for women's rights'.[109] Western scholars of Islam also support this interpretation of *jihad*. Bruce Lawrence writes, *jihad* is 'being a better student, a better colleague, a better business partner. Above all, to control one's anger'.[110] Historian, Karen Armstrong describes *jihad* as 'the effort or struggle to achieve [a just] world where you learn to lay aside your own selfishness and recognize the needs of the poor, elderly and sick … Islam condemns violence except in self-defence'.[111]

Ba'asyir teaches that *jihad* is a fundamental article of Islamic faith that must be performed by all Muslims. In performing *jihad* a Muslim must be: (1)

sincere (*ikhlas*) and expect no worldly rewards, (2) patient (*sabar*), never discouraged by calamity (*musibah*), never lazy in the path of Allah, and never giving up to the enemy, and (3) modest (*zuhud*). Ba'asyir teaches that *jihad* requires 'proportionate self-defence'. This understanding of *jihad* led him to support the involvement of *Laskar Jihad* (Muslim Fighters)[112] in the conflicts between Christians and Muslims in Maluku and Poso as well as the terrorist attack on the World Trade Center by Osama bin Laden and Al-Qa'eda on 9/11. Ba'asyir argues that these were appropriate self-defensive actions in response to the violence of the USA against the entire Islamic world.[113] Behrend describes this understanding of *jihad* in 'inter-confessional and political terms' as 'active defence of Islam wherever and whenever it is threatened'.

> When a threat to Islam, or a Muslim community, takes the form of propaganda, *jihad* requires a proportionate response in kind - education and dissemination through comparable media of the Truth undermined by anti-Islamic lies. When the threat is violent and results in the destruction of life and property, a proportionate and equitable *jihadi* response can justifiably take the same form.[114]

Performing *Dawah*

Dawah means 'to call', 'to invite', or 'to ask' from the root of *da'aa – yad'uu – du'aa-an* or *da'watan.*[115] *Dkwah* can be described as a call or invitation to an individual, family, and others to take Islam as a way of life, to live in accordance with Allah's will, with wisdom and consciousness, nourished by His blessings. Islamic scholars teach that *da wah* is 'God's way of bringing believers to faith and the means by which prophets call individuals and communities back to God'.[116] For militant Islamic movements, *dawah* means 'calling Muslims back to the purer form of religion practiced by Muhammad and the early Muslim community'.[117] Radical Islamists, such as Abu al-Hasan al-Nadawi, Hasan al-Banna, Sayyid Qutb, and 'Abd al-Jawad Yasin taught that *dawah* at the individual, family, and society levels will provide Muslims with the power they need to take over leadership of the world from the West.[118]

In Malaysia, *dawah* is the name for a political Islamist movement that emerged in the 1970s through the activities of youth organizations. It seeks greater application of Islamic laws and values in national life and articulates a holistic Islamic perspective of social, economic, and spiritual development.[119] Muhammad Natsir, the leader of a political *dawah* movement in Indonesia,[120] teaches that *dawah* aims to refine the relationship between human beings and their Creator (*hamblun minallah* or *hamblun ma'a al Khaliq*); the relationship among human beings (*hablun minannas* or *mu'amalah ma'a al-khalqi*); and to develop balance (*tawazun*) and harmony between the two relationships. For Natsir, *dawah* and politics are two sides of a coin: *dawah* can be performed through politics and politics can be performed through *dawah.*[121]

For Ba'asyir, 'm*endawahkan* (propagating) and *menegakkan* (lifting up) *din al-Islam* is compulsory to all Muslims'. He teaches that *dawah* will make Islam spread so that it becomes a way of life. He describes those who strive to lift up

Islamic values as winning the 'two righteousnesses (*al-hasanain*): winning or dying as a martyr'. Those who promote other values, he warns, 'will receive punishment directly from Allah or through the hands of Muslims'.[122] According to Ba'asyir, *dawah* is 'giving information regarding *Sharí'ah* to Muslims and non-Muslims'.[123] Ba'asyir follows Natsir in his commitment to various forms of *dakwah*.[124] He teaches that *dawah* can be performed through education, mass media, and social activities.[125] In 1969, he helped to establish Surakarta Radio for Islamic *Dawah* (*Radio Dawah Islamiyah Surakarta* or RADIS) to broadcast the call to Islam. Ba'asyir and his colleagues also used the radio to oppose Suharto's secularization policies and to invite Muslims to perform *jihad* to stop the regime.

Avoiding *Wahn* and *Mutraf*

For Ba'asyir, *wahn,* an Arabic word meaning 'love of worldly life and 'fear of death' is a disease that must be avoided by a Muslim. 'If someone is infected by *wahn*', he teaches, he will gradually begin to commit bad deeds ... to fulfil the worldly needs that he thinks will satisfy him'. Those who are infected by *wahn* will be trapped in a luxurious lifestyle (*mutraf*), which is the lifestyle of *kufr* (disbelief). Ba'asyir contrasts this lifestyle with the life of Prophet Muhammad and his companions, who lived modestly (*zuhud*). He teaches that 'luxury will only make the heart fragile and doubtful in matters related to *Sharí'ah.*'.[126] Ba'asyir teaches that Muslims must adopt Islamic principles in their lives. The principles include *tasdiq*, accepting and obeying every thing that comes from Allah and His messenger without questioning (*sami'na wa atho'na*) and *taslim*, accepting *taqdir* (Allah's will).[127]

Islam is the only true religion

The central theme in Ba'asyir's public teaching is that Islam is the only true and authentic religion: '*Din al-Islam* is the only *din al-haq* (true religion)'.[128] Islam is the true order and law of Allah for all His creatures given to them through His last Messenger, Muhammad. Ba'asyir teaches that 'Islamic order and law is superior to all other social forms, wherever and whenever'.[129] He reminds his listeners that the enemies of Islam, internal and external, have tried many times to destroy it, but Islam survives and attracts millions of peoples in all parts of the world.[130] Ba'asyir describes Islam as a light from Allah that no one can dim. Because of their inner potential for faith (*fitrah*) 'human beings will always search for the authentic truth of Islam'. 'The truth that comes from Allah', he further describes, 'is not fabricated by human beings, nor is it simply history or philosophical analysis'. 'Those who reject the truth', said Ba'asyir, 'are controlled by their passions, apply too much logic, or lack of knowledge'.[131]

Assessing the teachings of Ba'asyir

In Ba'asyir's teachings, Islam is not a spiritual path as understood in western culture and in the mystical tradition of the Sufis. It is a complete 'way of life' based on Islamic faith and law (*aqidah wa Sharí'ah*). Islam is not simply a moral guide, it is more like an ideology, a complete package of rules and guidance for all aspects of life. The teachings invite Muslims to view Islam as a total, comprehensive, and all-encompassing way of life. They reflect a desire to unite Muslims in a worldwide Islamic community (*ummah*) through the formation of national and international Islamic organizations, which can pressure policy makers to implement Islamic law as derived from the teaching of Prophet Muhammad and his companions.

In the following section of the paper I discuss seven major characteristics of Ba'asyir's public teachings: 1) Islam as a normative-ideal; 2) Islam as an absolutist-exclusionary ideology; 3) the denial of different traditions within Islam; 4) the literal interpretation of scripture; 5) the lens of conspiracy, 6) inconsistencies, and 7) anti-modernism and anti-intellectualism.

Islam as a normative ideal

Ba'asyir's public teachings are about Islamic ideals rather than the realities of Islam and Muslims. They idealize sixth and seventh century Islam as exemplified by Prophet Muhammad and his companions as the best society for Muslims for all times. The teaching is based on interpretations of the texts of the Qur'an and *Hadiths* that refer to concepts developed centuries ago under different circumstances. The Islamic ideals of the Qur'an and *Hadiths* are not translated into concrete terms, practical guidelines, or logistical strategies.[132] Ba'asyir teaches about *Islam*, not about *being Muslim*. His teachings do not address Muslims' real needs and daily life concerns, such as how to solve individual problems and participate in community development. The teachings focus on the obligatory aspects of Islamic values without showing the practical benefits of the values. Ba'asyir seems to believe that Muslims will follow Islamic moral teachings if they are simply reminded that these are required of them. In fact, as Tauhidi argues, Muslims will follow Islamic teachings if their hearts and minds can see how Islamic values will lead to a better life.[133] Instead of giving Muslims the prospect of a better life, Ba'asyir frightens Muslims with punishments and teaches them that they and their religion are under attack from the West.

Islam as an absolutist-exclusionary ideology

Behrend describes Ba'asyir as an 'absolutist' and 'exclusionist' teacher.[134] Ba'asyir stresses that *din al-Islam* is a complete religion and the only true religion on earth that is accepted by Allah.[135] 'In consequence', he argues, 'whoever follows [a religion] other than Islam or regards all religions as the same, his/her deeds will be rejected [by Allah]'. 'All deeds guided by other than Islam,' Ba'asyir teaches, 'bring imbalance, chaos, and destruction to the individual, family, society, and state'.[136] In contrast, 'all deeds guided by *din al-Islam* will certainly bring goodness for individual, family, society, and the state'.[137]

Ba'asyir emphasizes that Islam is the one and only true faith and only those who follow Islam will gain Allah's blessings: '*Din al Islam* is sent by Allah to human beings . . . If you want to be safe, take the Islamic way. . . if you choose other ways, sooner or later you will face a disaster . . . do not mix Islam with other ways of life'.[138] For Ba'asyir, Muslims must either struggle to implement *Sharí'ah* or reject *din al-Islam.*[139] He calls leaders in Muslim countries who fail to implement *Sharí'ah* apostates (*murtad*), unbelievers (*kufr*), despots (*dhalim*) and godless (*fasik*).[140] Islam is a comprehensive (*syumul*) way of life (*manhajul hayah*). Implementing the *Sharí'ah* is an obligation for every Muslim, no matter who they are, what they are, and where they are.[141] In their efforts to implement *Sharí'ah*, Muslims have two extreme choices: 'living with dignity or dying as a martyr' (*hidup mulia atau mati syahid*).[142] 'Dying as a martyr is being killed by the enemy of Islam while striving in the path of Allah (*jihad fi sabilillah*) or being killed by a despot (*dhalim*) because of expressing the truth'.[143] Ba'asyir teaches that worshipping Allah is not limited to ritual practices, such as prayer (*salat*), fasting (*saum*), pilgrimage (*hajj*), and remembrance of Allah (*dhikr*). The implementation of *Sharí'ah* comprehensively (*secara kaffah*) with sole intention: to please Allah and obey His commands forbids gambling, corruption, and prostitution.[144] Rejection of one part of *Sharí'ah* places a Muslim among those who commit idolatry (*mushrikin*).[145]

Denial of different traditions within Islam

The Qur'an serves as both record and guide for the Muslim community, transcending time and space. It is true that some verses of the Qur'an and texts of *Hadith* are precise in meaning (*qat'iyah*), but many of them have to be interpreted (*dzanni*). They can be interpreted in the light of their linguistic, juristic, and theological contexts. Traditionalist, modernist, revivalist, and liberal Islamic scholars may apply different methods of interpretation and produce different legal principles from the Qur'an and *Hadith.* Since different methods and contexts of interpretation may produce different understandings and applications, it is necessary to define which method and context of interpretation is to be adopted. However, Ba'asyir teaches that *Sharí'ah* is the law of Allah (*hukmullah*) based on the Qur'an and *Hadith* and is in opposition to man-made laws.[146] He does not acknowledge that the Qur'an and *Hadith* need to be interpreted to produce legal principles.

Because there are no clear guidelines on *Sharí'ah,* many Muslim groups in Indonesia, particularly *Nahdatul Ulama* (NU) and *Muhammadiyah*, are reluctant to adopt *Sharí'ah* as State law although they do not deny the importance of Muslims implementing *Sharí'ah* in daily life. They reject the formalization of *Sharí'ah* as State law because the negative impacts (*mudharat*) exceed the benefits (*manfaat*).[147] Instead, they promote informal practice of *Sharí'ah* values in State affairs and daily life. The Chairman of Masyumi Islamic political party, Muhammad Natsir, once raised the following question: 'Which one is better, pig oil in a camel can or camel oil in a pig can?' The Chairman of National Mandate

Party and House Speaker, Amien Rais, distinguishes between 'salt politics' (*politik garam*) and 'flag and lipstick politics' (*politik bendera dan gincu*). 'If flag and lipstick politics is adopted', said Rais, 'it will wave and shine. But it will invite reactions from other [religious] groups'. 'On the contrary, if salt politics is adopted, it will not wave or shine, but the society will taste it'. Rais believes that 'salt politics will produce an inclusive social attitude . . . If we see with a clear perspective, many Islamic values are not much different from those of Christianity'.[148] However, Ba'asyir seems to prefer lipstick politics, demanding the adoption of *Sharí'ah*, but he does not explain what type of *Sharí'ah* is to be applied and how to apply it. Nor does he say whether he advocates adopting a 'persuasive' approach or a 'revolutionary' one.

The Literal interpretation of scripture

Intellectual, contextual, and systematic interpretation of the verses of the Qur'an is essential for producing their relevant meanings. The Islamic scholar Fazlur Rahman writes:

> If the Muslims' loud and persistent talk about the viability of Islam as a system of doctrine and practice in the world of today is genuine ..., then it seems clear that they must once again start at the intellectual level. They must candidly and without inhibitions discuss what Islam wants them to do today. The entire body of the *Sharí'ah* must be subjected to fresh examination in the light of the *Qur'anic* evidence. A systematic bold interpretation of the *Qur'an* must be undertaken.[149]

Rahman suggests that there are three steps in interpreting the Qur'an. The first is to adopt a historical approach. The Qur'an should be studied in a chronological order in order to understand the relation between the struggle of Prophet Muhammad and the Qur'an, so that one can avoid exaggerated and artificial interpretations and bring out the overall meaning of the Qur'anic message in a systematic and coherent manner. The second is to distinguish between Qur'anic law and the objectives these laws were expected to serve in order to identify the reasons provided by the Qur'an for its specific legal pronouncements. The third is to identify the sociological setting of the Qur'an, the environment in which the Prophet lived and worked. Rahman believes that such steps will limit the interpreter's bias and lead to a clearer understanding of the Qur'an and is 'the only real hope for a successful interpretation of it [Qur'an] today'.[150] With the three steps, he argues, Muslims can move from literal interpretation of the Qur'an to metaphorical or intellectual and systematic ones. This method of interpretation of the Qur'an, he suggests, is 'honest', 'true', and 'practical', thus 'the most satisfactory and perhaps the only possible one'.[151] The traditionalists, Rahman notes, often criticize this approach as being too total and abrupt, as sacrificing too much of tradition, and suspect it of being Western oriented. He admits that such an interpretation of the Qur'an requires living intellectualism and cannot grow if stifled by conservatism.[152]

Ba'asyir's public teachings are based on a literal interpretation of selected verses of the Qur'an and *Hadith*, without considering their linguistic, historical, and cultural contexts. Ba'asyir does not pay attention to chronological order and fails to distinguish between Qur'anic legal dicta and the reasoning behind the dicta, ignoring the sociological setting of the law. He does not provide the basis for his interpretation of the Qur'an.

The lens of conspiracy

For the most part, Ba'asyir's public teachings are reactionary in character. They are reactions to liberal Muslim scholars who promote moderate Islamic teachings and whom he perceives as agents of an international conspiracy of Zionists, Christian missionaries, and the government of the USA. Ba'asyir accuses liberal Muslim scholars of introducing an 'evil version of *Tauhid*' (*Tauhid versi iblis*) based on pride in human rationality. Ba'asyir believes that today, secularism and liberalism dominate the thinking of Muslim scholars, thus an 'Iblis version of *Tauhid* is gaining momentum'. He accuses liberal Islamic scholars of promoting a misleading understanding of Islamic teachings and leading Muslims from the straight path to the wrong one by suggesting that all religions are the same and the followers of a religion cannot claim that their religion is the only true one.[153] For Ba'asyir, liberal Islamic scholars are allies of an international Zionist and Christian conspiracy to separate Muslims from Islam. They also separate Muslims from one another by creating divisions, such as radical Islam (*Islam Radikal*) or fundamentalist Islam as distinguished from moderate Islam (*Islam Moderat*).

Ba'asyir accuses secular and liberal scholars of rejecting the Qur'an and making Muslims superior over the Qur'an. He points out that verse 221, Chapter 2 (*Al-Baqarah*) of the Qur'an forbids inter-religious marriage,[154] and the liberals argue that this verse is unacceptable because it discriminates on the basis of religion. Here Ba'asyir indirectly criticizes Nurcholis Madjid, who allowed his daughter to marry a Jewish man and thereby promoted universal marriage (*perkawinan universal*). Ba'asyir also criticizes secular and liberal scholars for rejecting the pattern of inheritance distribution set forth in the Qur'an,[155] by arguing that such a pattern of distribution reflects gender bias.[156] He further accuses liberal scholars of rejecting the Qur'anic verses that require Muslims to perform *jihad* and of accepting the western view that such verses are violent in character and encourage terrorism.[157]

Ba'asyir believes that liberal Islamic scholars persuade Muslims to follow a new belief that has no textual basis (*nash*).[158] He accuses the scholars of arrogance because they accept some of the laws set forth by Allah and reject others based on their own ideas. They dare to correct Allah's regulations and reject the words of His Prophet, but accept the words of infidels (*kafir*). And Ba'asyir accuses all those who criticize him of attacking Islam. Accusations against Ba'asyir are 'part of efforts of the infidel to dim the light of Islam by using terrorism as a camouflage. . . What they [US and its allies] mean by terror is everybody who defends *Sharí'ah*, including myself'. Ba'asyir describes those who accuse him as 'Allah's enemies' (*musuh-musuh Allah*) and claims that accusations connecting him to *Jamaah Islamiyah* and *Al-Qa'eda* are part of a scenario to corner Muslims.[159]

Ba'asyir believes there is an international Zionist and Christian conspiracy with the US government to destroy Muslim countries and eliminate Islam from earth. Behrend notes, 'His public statements with respect to political issues inevitably refer to supposed manipulation and conspiracy by the US, and to its never-ending war against Islam'.[160] He urges his followers to ban all American products and to pressure the Indonesian government to break off diplomatic relations with the US government.[161] Ba'asyir expresses his admiration for Osama bin Laden whom he considers a 'true Islamic warrior[162] or 'a true Muslim fighter.'[163] He says that bin Laden 'has dared to represent the Islamic world in combat against the arrogance of the United States and its allies'. 'The real terrorist', said Ba'asyir, 'is not bin Laden, but the US which is waging war on Islam, not terrorism'.[164]

Ba'asyir's anti-Americanism does not differentiate between American values and the American political system and President Bush's foreign policy toward the Muslim world. His views are reactive to what he interprets as attacks on Islam, and he believes that attacks on him are simply attacks on Islam.

Inconsistencies

Fazlur Rahman has described as 'janus-faced' the view of some Islamists.[165] This criticism can be applied to Ba'asyir's teachings on an Islamic State (*Daulah Islamiyah*) and *jihad*. Ba'asyir teaches that Muslims need an Islamic state that will enforce *Sharí'ah* comprehensively and consistently. He calls Muslim leaders who fail to implement *Sharí'ah* apostates (*murtat*), infidels (*kaffir*), despots (*dhalim*), and godless (*fasiq*). He teaches that Muslim nations must be united under a single and righteous leadership of one caliphate. However, he denies that he wants to develop an Islamic state in Southeast Asia, including parts of the Philippines, Malaysia, Singapore, Brunei, and Indonesia in Nusantara Islamic State (*Negara Islam Nusantara* or *Daulah Islam Nusantara*).[166] He has called such a plan 'really irrational', asking: 'How could it be possible to unite countries that have different ideologies and ethnic groups into one *Daulah Islamiyah*?' [167] He argues that the idea of a Southeast Asian Islamic state is only an effort (made by Arroyo and George Bush) to create horizontal conflict in Indonesia and Southeast Asia. Behrend has tried to explain this inconsistency by saying that what Ba'asyir means by a caliphate is a concept of moral leadership and shared vision without necessarily establishing an over-arching super state.[168] Ba'asyir's lawyer, Adnan Buyung Nasution, defends him by arguing that '[Ba'asyir] is simply fighting for the implementation of *Sharí'ah* as Indonesian law, not to bring down the Republic of Indonesia'. However, given Ba'asyir's teaching it remains difficult to understand how *Sharí'ah* could be implemented if *Daulah Islamiyah* simply means 'moral unity' and 'vision'.

Ba'asyir claims: 'I never teach violence'.[169] His follower at Pondo Ngruki, Farid Ma'ruf, describes him as a person with a soft (*lembut*) personality who does not justify violence and who 'never criticizes other groups of Muslims, except those who have committed wrong deeds (*lalim*)'.[170] When on trial in Jakarta in September 2003, Ba'asyir told his students (*santri*) and supporters not to use violence in their protests. He said that those who used violence were provocateurs (*provokator*). Wahyudin, Deputy Director for Pondok Ngruki, said that Ba'asyir's followers would 'not take anarchistic actions in protesting [Ba'asyir's four year prison sentence]. We will do every thing according to the rule of law, namely by bringing the case to higher court'. [171] However, a political manifesto entitled 'The Latest Indonesian Crisis: Causes & Solutions' composed in late May 1998, as Ba'asyir and Abdullah Sungkar were preparing to return to Indonesia after the fall of Suharto, presented Indonesian Muslims with a simple and stark alternative: 'We have two choices before us: 1. Life in a nation based upon the *Qur'an* and the *Sunnah*; or 2. Death while striving to implement, in their entirety, laws based upon the *Qur'an* and the *Sunnah*'. [172] Indeed, Ba'asyir does not object being described by the media as the 'Osama bin Laden of Southeast Asia'.[173] Ba'asyir asks Allah to help bin Laden and destroy his enemies:

> O Allah, please help every one who help your religion [Islam], save Osama bin Laden, and also save the *mujahidin* all around the world. Oh Allah, destroy every one who wants to destroy your religion, as you have destroyed those who disobeyed you. Destroy George Bush, Sharon, Howard, Lee Kuan Yew, demolish Tony Blair, Goh Tjok Tong. And demolish all your enemies. Please answer [my prayer] oh Allah.[174]

Anti-modernism, anti-intellectualism

Modernity, a product of the Renaissance, the Reformation, and the discovery of the New World, promotes rationality and individualism.[175] According to Habermas, 'modernity cannot and will no longer borrow the criteria by which it takes its orientation from the models supplied by another epoch; it has to create its normativity out of itself'.[176] Modernity challenges and revises tradition by adopting scientific mode of thinking and introducing other social and cultural values.

Bernard Lewis argues that the Muslim world has responded to modernity in three different ways. The first he calls 'supermarket style'. Muslims learn, select, and finally adopt certain modern values and practices that they consider beneficial without necessarily becoming western in terms of religion and culture. They remain hostile to the West, and they see western civilization as immoral and dangerously corrupting. This is the response of Ayatollah Khomeini and his followers. In the second way Muslims combine what they consider as the best elements of Islamic and modern civilizations, but often result in 'a promiscuous cohabitation of the worst'. The third response to modernization is that of Kemal Ataturk and the Young Turk movement, which accepted modernization as the peak of the development of human civilization and believed that Muslims must follow it in order to be part of the civilized world. [177]

The dismissive analysis of the Muslim response to modernity of Bernard Lewis contrasts with the analysis of the modernist Islamic scholar Fazlur Rahman. He suggests that although very careful and selective, Muslims tend to respond to modernity positively, intellectually, and spiritually. For example, the most important characteristics of the classical Muslim modernists of the nineteenth century was an 'intellectual *élan* and the specifically intellectual and spiritual issues with which it dealt'.[178]

Ba'asyir's public teachings reject modernity for its emphasis on rational and liberal thinking. Modern values that are in line with Islamic teachings, such as progress, justice, and egalitarianism are ignored. Ba'asyir criticizes, ridicules, and rejects modern values and adopts an uncompromised, uncritical, and unreflective approach to the Qur'an and the *Sunnah*. Ba'asyir's teachings maintain that Muslims will be able to revive the quality of their life only by going back to models provided by Prophet Muhammad and his companions in the sixth and seventh centuries. The teachings focus only on the negative effects of modernization, such as egotism, materialism, social inequities, and moral degradation, but fail to appreciate the achievements of modern civilization. In particular, Ba'asyir teaches that embracing modernity and westernization has caused moral degradation in Muslim society. He denies the significance of systematic, creative, and intellectual effort for solving Muslims' problems.

Concluding remarks: Some educational implications

Radical Islamic teachings as introduced by Ba'asyir are on the line with the teachings of *Wahabiyyah*, eighteenth-century reformist/revivalist movement for socio-moral reconstruction of society led by Muhammad ibn Abd al-Wahab. The teachings are 'intolerant', 'fanatic', and 'extreme', emphasizing a particular interpretation of the fundamental role of *Tauhid* (uniqueness and unity of God). They promote *Tauhid* as a primary doctrine and propose a return to an ideal Islamic monotheism based on Qur'an and *Hadith*. They invite Muslims to internal reforms and to unite against the West, especially the USA and its allies, and totally oppose any form of modernization and secularization, promising to dismantle western civilization as well as replacing it with an Islamic one. The teachings place Islam and modernity in a binary opposition, as if the two of them are totally hostile to one another – exaggerating their differences and ignoring their sharing points. Ba'asyir's teachings may be able to raise a feeling of 'religiosity' or 'Muslimness' and a feeling of 'Islamicity'[179] among Muslim youths, but may not be able to provide them with the quality and type of knowledge, skills, and mode of thinking that they need to solve their daily life problems and come to term with the future challenges of modern civilization.

Ba'asyir's teachings confront Muslim real life situation in contemporary Indonesia where modernization has dominated many aspects of public life and discourses. Such teachings may not be popular among Indonesian Muslims who are getting along with modern lifestyle. However, their emphasis and claim on the authenticity of Islam, their ability to call for commitment, their attention on the inner characteristics of Islam for bringing dignity and respect to Muslims, and Ba'asyir's sincerity and dedication in promoting them can make his teachings attractive, particularly to the beginner, modernists who are still doubtful about modern values and those who are disappointed with modernity, such as many young people and recent urban immigrants who are threatened by the alienation of life in cities. For oppressed groups, Ba'asyir's teachings may be attractive as a vehicle for protesting against unjust authorities. Opportunistic and pragmatic Muslim politicians who look for a shortcut to gain support may use Ba'asyir's teachings as part of the rhetoric of their political campaigns. With regard to their anti-West characteristics, Ba'asyir's teachings can create an opinion in the West as well as in the Muslim world that Islam is not compatible with the West. In the light of their rejection to modernity and democracy, Ba'asyir's teachings can hinder democratization and modernization in Indonesia.

If Muslim leaders in Indonesia still believe in the importance of partnership with the Western world and the need to pursue modernization and democratization for a better future of Indonesia, they need to counter the spread of Islamic radicalism by all means. They need to develop and disseminate moderate Islamic teachings at all levels of education by designing Islamic teachings that do not only raise a feeling of 'religiosity', 'Muslimness', and 'Islamicity', but also raise a very real openness to change and constructive attitude toward modernity. They need to elicit a moral commitment not only to be critical toward modernity, but also being able to reconstruct it based on Islamic values. Indonesian Muslim leaders need to utilize Islam as spiritual salvation and inspiration within modernity in order to develop an Islamic path to modernity. This approach will allow them to design social, economic, cultural, political, and religious modes of modernity that suit Islamic values and principles. In turn, this will allow Muslim youth to adapt to a modernity that is relatively different from secular western forms. It will enable them to be modern, competitive, and play an important role in the global world without losing their cultural, national, and religious identity.

Today, many Islamic educational ideas in Indonesia come from anti-modernist and anti-West scholars. They control many Islamic education institutions, such as *Pesantren* and *Madrasa* as well as many Islamic study groups all around the country. These scholars tend to believe that Muslim youth will be ready to face future challenges if they memorize a number of Qur'anic verses and *Hadith* as well as be familiar with the basic teachings of *Fiqh* (jurisprudence), *Sharí'ah* (Islamic law), *Tauhid* (Islamic theology), *Dawah*, and *Jihad*. These scholars also tend to believe that all problems in Muslim society can be solved by going back to the sixth century model of Muslim life adopted by Prophet Muhammad and his Companions. They tend to suggest that being losers in this worldly life is not a problem for Muslims as long as they champion the hereafter. They also tend to suggest that various modern scientific disciplines are the treasure of the West that has nothing to do with Muslims. I share Khan's opinion that such as narrow understanding of knowledge has caused lack of creativity, dynamism, vitality and power in the Muslim world.[180]

Muslim scholars in Indonesia need to address the future challenges of Muslims in the country realistically and rationally. They need to develop a proper sacred vision of Islamic life based on a workable synthesis between Muslim traditional values and the modern ones. They need to base Islamic teachings on a *dynamic,* rather than static and legalistic view of Islam and on a belief that the mission of Islam is to positively affect and transform the world. Muslim teachers, including Ba'asyir, need to redefine what they mean by knowledge, what contents need to be prioritized in their teachings, what approach is appropriate, what standard is used to measure effective teachings, and what quality is required for Muslims to be able to compete in modern and global world. They need to develop an open-minded intellectual environment and forward looking attitude in order to develop a new vision of Islamic teaching that can bring Muslims to the level of understanding, commitment, and social responsibility to serve Islam and humanity effectively. They need to introduce and explain Islam as both *normative* and *empirical* ideal and link fundamental Islamic teachings, such as *Tafsir*, *Hadith*, *Fiqh*, *Tauhid*, *Dawah*, and *Jihad* to the natural concerns of Muslims and their relation with the whole world.[181] Islamic teachings need to equip Muslim youth with traditional and modern disciplines as well as a proper understanding of the contemporary world in term of social, political, and religious diversity.

Ba'asyir and other radical Islamists in Indonesia need to reconsider their understanding of the relationship between modern and Islamic civilization and the role that Muslims need to play in the dynamic of the relationship. At the educational level, they need to develop new materials and approaches to produce an open-minded and skilful generation of Muslims who are capable of synthesizing Islamic and modern concepts of successful living. Such a generation of Muslims will replace West-phobia, modernity-phobia, and America-phobia with a creative attitude and constructive mode of thinking. They will be knowledgeable about Islam and capable of being good Muslims, playing their role as the viceregent of God on earth (*khalifatullah fil Ardhi*). In the words of Dawud Tauhidi, Muslim teachers need to move from teaching *facts about Islam* to teaching *about being Muslims*.[182] 'The goal of Islamic education', he explains, 'is not to fill our children's minds with information about Islam, but rather to teach them about *being* Muslim'.[183] Indeed, Islamic mission is *rahmatan lil alamin*, being part of the world and sharing the responsibility to make it a better place to live.

If Indonesia, the largest Muslim country in the world, is to be able to compete in an era of globalisation and play a role in the future development of world civilisation, more realistic, rational, and contextual Islamic teachings need to be developed. More visionary Islamic teachers need to be trained, and a more faithful, creative, open-minded, thoughtful, and skilful generation of Muslims needs to be produced. Above all, more affordable and accessible modern Islamic education institutions need to be developed. It is in this regard that radical Islamic teachings as presented by Ba'asyir need to be carefully and critically treated. It is also in this regard that agendas and strategies for Islamic education reform in the country need to be developed.

Notes

[1] Philip Herbst 2003. *Talking Terrorism a Dictionary of the Loaded Language of Political Violence*. Westport, Connecticut, London: Greenwood Press, p. 144.
[2] *Ibid.*, pp.144-145.
[3] *Ibid.*
[4] *Ibid.*, p. 144.

[5] *Ibid.*, p. 145.
[6] See *This Week*, February 8, 2002, p. 4.
[7] *Ibid.*
[8] Philip Herbst 2003, p. 145.
[9] Sayyid Abu al-Ala Mawdudi is an Indo-Pakistani Muslim revivalist thinker, prolific writer, politician, and founder of Jamaat Islami in 1941. He is the author of more than 150 books. Mawdudi believed that 'the salvation of Muslim culture lay in the restitution and purification of Islamic institutions and practices'. See John L. Esposito 2003. *The Oxford Dictionary of Islam.* New York: Oxford University Press, pp. 196-197.
[10] Sayid Qutb is an Egyptian literary critic, novelist, and poet who became an important Islamic thinker and activist. For Qutb, Islam is 'a call to social commitment and activism'. He believes that 'Islam is timeless body of ideas and practices forming a comprehensive way of life, rendering non-adherence to Islamic law inexcusable'. See *ibid.*, p. 257.
[11] Ruhollah al-Musavi Khomeini is the Iranian Shii cleric, leader of the Islamic revolution, and ideologue of the Islamic Republic of Iran. See *ibid.*, p.173 and William E. Shepard 1987. Islam and Ideology: Towards a Typology, in *International Journal of Middle East Studies*, Vol. 19, No. 3, p. 314.
[12] See William E. Shepard 1987, *ibid.*, p. 314.
[13] Along with the Qur'an, *Sunnah*, and *Ijma'* (consensus), *Ijtihad* (independent reasoning) is a source of law in Sunni tradition. It is used when the Qur'an and *Sunnah* do not provide sufficient legal explanation. Sunni scholars suggest that *ijtihad* is fallible since more than one interpretation of a legal issue is possible. To do *ijtihad* or to be a *Mujtahid*, one must have thorough knowledge of theology, revealed texts, legal theory (*usul al fiqh*), a sophisticated capacity for legal reasoning, and thorough knowledge of Arabic. See John L. Esposito 2003, p. 134.
[14] William E. Shepard 1987, p. 314.
[15] *Ibid.*
[16] *Ibid.*
[17] *Ibid.*
[18] *Ibid.*, pp. 314-315.
[19] *Ibid.*, p. 315.
[20] John L. Esposito 2003, p. 259.
[21] William E. Shepard 1987, p. 315.
[22] Quoted in *ibid.*, p. 316.
[23] Quoted in *ibid.*, p. 315.
[24] Quoted in *ibid.*, p. 316.
[25] *Ibid.*
[26] Other radical leaders in Indonesia are Habib Rizieq Shihab of Islamic Defenders Front or *Front Pembela Islam* (FPI), Agus Dwi Karna of The Warrior of God's Militia or *Laskar Jundullah*, and Ja'far Umar Thalib of Jihad Fighters or *Laskar Jihad*. See Martin van Bruinessen 2002. 'The violent fringes of Indonesia's radical Islam', in *ISIM Newsletter*, 11 December.
[27] *Pancasila* is a Sanskrit word meaning 'Five Principles'. It is the national ideology of the Republic of Indonesia consisting of belief in God, Indonesian nationalism, humanitarianism, democracy, and social justice.
[28] Ba'asyir's organizational activities began from his *Santri* time in Gontor. In 1961, he was Chairman of *Gerakan Pemuda Islam Indonesia* (GPII) or Muslim Youth Movement of Indonesia for Gontrol branch. In Solo, he was Secretary of *Pemuda Al-Irsyad* (Al-Irsyad Youth) and was Head of *Lembaga Dawah Mahasiswa Islam* (LDMI), a division of *Himpunan Mahasiswa Islam* (HMI) for Solo branch. See Idy Subandi Ibrahim and Asep Syamsul M. Romli 2003. *Kontroversi Ba'asyir: Jihad Melawan Opini 'Fitnah' Global.*

Bandung: Penerbit Nuansa, p. 34. With its strong emphasis on the importance of adopting and implementing *Sharí'ah*, many observers began to see MMI as an umbrella group for people wanting to push for the adoption of strict Islamic *Sharí'ah* law in Indonesia and turn the country into an Islamic state. According to Ba'asyir, MMI mission is simply to say right is right and wrong is wrong according to *Sharí'ah*. Although it deliberately advocates the implementation of *Sharí'ah*, MMI never formally states its intention to establish an Islamic state, because it has not been able to formulate the approach to be employed to do so. See *Asia Times Online*, February 6, 2002. 'Southeast Asia, The Osama bin Laden and al-Qa'eda of Southeast Asia'. Available on http://www.atimes.com/se-asia/DB06Ae01.html See also Ibrahim and Romli 2003, p. 39.

[29] The conference was attended by 'hard line' Muslim leaders who were very critical at Suharto's secularization policies. They were Abu Bakar Ba'asyir, Deliar Noor, and some ex political prisoners from various provinces during Suharto, such as Sahirul Alim and Irfan Suryahadi Awwas (Yogya), Nur Hidayat (Lampung), and Mursalim Dahlan (Bandung). See Ibrahim and Romli 2003, *ibid.*, p. 40.

[30] Being MMI national Chairman often put Ba'asyir in the spot light of Islamic politics in Indonesia. The new position also changed the way people looked at him. His public image began to change from a modest preacher to a powerful radical leader. Ba'asyir repeatedly explains that there is nothing special about MMI. It simply promotes *dawah* and *jihad* as exemplified by *Rasulullah* (the Messenger of Allah). He emphasizes that MMI never involve in anarchy. Islam, said Ba'asyir, prefers peace among Muslims and between Muslims and other believers. He also said: *Mencaci maki* (abusing) other groups is forbidden and forcing others to follow Islam is forbidden. See *ibid.*, pp. 39, 47.

[31] JI is a mysterious organization suspected as the umbrella organization of many radical Islamic organizations in the Southeast Asia region and of being responsible for a series of bombings in Southeast Asia, including the Bali bombing in October 2002 which killed more than 200 people. JI has been described as an al-Qa'eda type terrorist organization that aims to redraw national boundaries in Southeast Asia in order to set up a pan-Islamic state or 'Islamic super state'[31] or *Daulah Islamiyah*, covering Indonesia, Malaysia, Singapore and the southern Philippines island of Mindanao. ABC News, September 2, 2003. Profile: Abu Bakar Ba'asyir. Available on http://news.bbc.co.uk/2/hi/asia-pacific/2339693.stm. See also *Asia Times Online*, February 6, 2002. 'Southeast Asia, The Osama bin Laden and al-Qaeda of Southeast Asia'. Available on http://www.atimes.com/se-asia/DB06Ae01.html.

[32] See Sydney Jones 2003. 'Indonesia Backgrounder: How the *Jemaah Islamiyah* terrorist network operates', International Crisis Group. Jakarta and Brussels, 11 December, p. 5. See also discussion in Tim Behrend 2003. *Reading Past the Myth: Public Teachings of Abu Bakar Ba'asyir.* Available on http://www.arts.auckland.ac.nz/asia/tbehrend/radical-islam.htm.

[33] Tim Behrend 2003. *Ibid.*

[34] Quoted in Idi Subandy Ibrahim and Asep Syamsul M. Romli 2003, p. 31.

[35] Quoted in *Asia Times Online*, February 6, 2002. 'Southeast Asia, The Osama bin Laden and al-Qa'eda of Southeast Asia'. Available on http://www.atimes.com/se-asia/DB06Ae01.html.

[36] *Tempo Interaktif*, September 21, 2003. Wawancara: 'Abu Bakar Ba'asyir: "Saya Tak Kenal Umar Al-Faruq"'. Available on http://www.tempo.co.id/harian/wawancara/waw-Baasyir01.html.

[37] Ministry of Religious Affairs (MORA) notes that by the year 2002-2003 they were more than 14,000 *Pesantrens* throughout Indonesia. See Departemen Agama RI 2003. *Statistik Pondok Pesantren Seluruh Indonesia*, brochure issued by the Educational Data and Information Division of the Directorate of Muslim Educational Institutions. For a discussion of the possible role of Pondok Ngruki in international terrorist network, see ES. Soepriyadi 2003. *Ngruki & Jaringan Terorisme: Melacak Jejak Abu Bakar Ba'asyir dan Jaringannya dari Ngruki sampai Bom Bali.* Jakarta: Al-Mawardi Prima.

[38] Among the founders of Pondok Ngruki are Ba'asyir, Abdullah Sungkar, Yoyo Rosywadi, Abdul Qohar Haji Daeng Matase, Hasan Basri and Abdullah Baraja. For further information on Ba'asyir's *dakwah* activities, see *Asia Times Online*, February 6, 2002. 'Southeast Asia, The Osama bin Laden and al-Qa'eda of Southeast Asia'. Available on http://www.atimes.com/se-asia/DB06Ae01.html; Ibrahim and Romli 2003, p. 35; and *Tempo Interaktif*, September 21, 2003. *Ibid.*
[39] In 1985, after being arrested by Suharto's security agents, Abu Bakar Ba'asyir and Abdullah Sungkar decided to leave for Malaysia. They took the chance to leave while they were given home detention and waiting for higher court decision. They crossed to Malaysia through Medan, the Northern part of Sumatera, in order to escape another prison term. They stayed in Malaysia for 13 years and back to Indonesia after the 1998 downfall of Suharto. See *Tempo Interaktif*, September 21, 2003. *Ibid.*
[40] See Ibrahim and Romli 2003, p. 36.
[41] This understanding of *Tauhid* refers to Chapter 112 (*Al Ikhlas*) of the *Qur'an* which says: 'Say: He is Allah, the one; Allah, the eternal, the absolute; he begetteth not, nor is He begotten; and there is none like unto Him'. See Ludwig W. Adamec 2001. *Historical Dictionary of Islam*. Lanham, Maryland, and London: The Scarecrow Press, Inc., p. 255.
[42] Mustansir Mir 1987. *Dictionary of Qur'anic Terms and Concepts*. New York & London: Garland Publishing, Inc., pp. 137-138.
[43] John L. Esposito (editor in chief) 2003, p. 318.
[44] According to this eighteenth-century Arabian reformer, *Tauhid* is 'a remedy for spiritual stagnation and excesses'. For him, Muslims must not compromise Islamic unity with sectarianism, praying to saints, angels, and prophets. He also stresses that Muslims must not claim knowledge based sources other than the Qur'an, *Sunnah*, and results of logical processes. See *ibid.*, p. 317.
[45] This nineteenth-century Egyptian reformer synthesized *Tauhid*, human free will, and obedience to God's revealed word. For him, rational approach can be applied in inquiring into the Qur'an, because there is no conflict between reason and revelation. He stressed that 'the Qur'an validates and encourages humans' exercise of reason'. See *ibid.*
[46] This Palestinian scholar argued that 'all life must be ordered according to divine will, so Islamic law must both legislate every aspect of life and be the dominant legal system throughout the world'. *Ibid.*, p. 317-318.
[47] For this ideologue of Iranian revolution, 'the purpose of human existence is agreement or trust between God and creation'. '*Tauhid*', he stresses, 'is, therefore, designed to transform a religion that justifies and accepts the status quo into a religion of awareness, activism, and revolution'. See *ibid.*, p. 318.
[48] For Khomeini, *Tauhid* is the centre of Islamic spiritual and material life and the source of Muslim social and political unity and harmony. See *ibid.*
[49] He supports this view with the Qur'an, Chapter 7 (*Al A'raf*) verse 172, one *Hadith* narrated by Ahmad and Muslim, and one *Hadith* narrated by Bukhari and Muslim. See discussion in Irfan Suryahadi Awwas 2003. p. 45.
[50] Ba'asyir bases this view on the following verses of the Qur'an: Chapter 39 (*Az-Zumar*) verses 46-67; Chapter 25 (*Al Furqan*) verses 22-23; and Chapter 24 (*An-Nur*) verse 39. See *ibid.*, p. 46.
[51] Ba'asyir bases this view on two verses of the Qur'an: (1) Chapter 4 (*An-Nisa*) verse 116 and (2) Chapter 9 (*At-Taubah*) verse 113 and one *Hadith* narrated by Bukhari and Muslim. See *ibid.*, pp. 46-47.
[52] This literally means great names. It refers to 99 names of Allah as mentioned in the Qur'an and *Hadiths* and introduced by the *ulama* (scholars).
[53] See Irfan Suryahadi Awwas 2003. *Dakwah & Jihad Abu Bakar Ba'asyir*. Yogyakarta: Widah Press, pp. 41-42.

[54] See *ibid.*, p. 42.
[55] *Ibid.*, p. 45.
[56] See Ludwig W. Adamec 2001. *Historical Dictionary of Islam*. Lanham, Maryland, and London: The Scarecrow Press, Inc., p. 141.
[57] See *ibid.*, p. 141.
[58] See John L. Esposito (editor in chief) 2003, pp. 287-288.
[59] Quoted in Irfan Suryahadi Awwas 2003, p. 42.
[60] *Ibid.*, pp. 49-50.
[61] *Ibid.*, p. 50.
[62] *Ibid.*, p. 42.
[63] The first three points are referring to the Qur'an Chapter 24 (*An-Nur*) verse 55 and Chapter 5 (*Al-Maidah*) verse 33.
[64] Referring to the Qur'an Chapter 9 (*At-Taubah*) verse 103, Chapter 3 (*Ali Imran*) verse 130, Chapter 2 (*Al Baqarah*) verse 188, 275-279.
[65] Referring to the Qur'an Chapter 5 (*Al-Maidah*) verse 38.
[66] Referring to the Qur'an Chapter 2 (*Al-Baqarah* verse 219 and Chapter 5 (*Al-Maidah*) verse 90-91.
[67] Referrring to the Qur'an Chapter 24 (*An-Nur*) verse 2 and a *Hadith* narrated by Al Bukhari and Muslim.
[68] Referring to the Qur'an Chapter 2 (*Al-Baqarah*) verse 256.
[69] Referring to the Qu''an Chapter 60 (*Al Mumtahanah*) verse 8. In the Qur'an, *Kufr* is to disbelieve in or reject God, a prophet, a scripture, the hereafter, the truth, etc. The root meaning of *kufr* is 'to hide, conceal'. To disbelieve means to hide the truth or deny recognition to it. See Mustansir Mir 1987, p. 52. The word *kufr* or one of its derivatives appears 482 times in the Qur'an. It also means 'ingratitude', the wilful refusal to appreciate the benefits that God has bestowed. For modern reformists and revivalists, 'current Muslims beliefs and practices have been so corrupted from true Islam that they constitute *shirk* (idolatry) or *jahiliyyah* (ignorance)'. For premodern reformers, *kufr* occurs in popular Islam, including *sufi* practices. See John L. Esposito (editor in chief) 2003, pp. 176-177.
[70] Referring to a *Hadith* narrated by At Tirmidzi. *Murtadd* (apostate) is 'one who has renounced her or his religion'. According to classical Islamic law, a *murtadd* is subject to the death penalty or banishment. See John L. Esposito (editor in chief) 2003, p. 216.
[71] Referring to the Qur'an Chapter 2 (*Al-Baqarah*) verse 178-179.
[72] Referring to the Qur'an Chapter 7 (*Al A'raf*) verse 96. For complete version of the verses, see Irfan 2003, pp. 55-60.
[73] See 'Taushiah Ustadz Abu untuk Muslim Indonesia', in *Majalah Islam Sabili*, No. 12 TH. X 2 Januari 2003/29 Syawal 1423, p. 35.
[74] See *ibid.*
[75] Irfan Suryahadi Awwas 2003, p. 51.
[76] Ba'asyir explains this view by referring to the Qur'an Chapter 8 (*Al-Anfaal*) verse 25, Chapter 20 (*Thaha*) verse 124, and a *Hadith* narrated by Ibnu Majah. See Irfan Suryahadi Awwas 2003, p. 54.
[77] See 'Taushiah Ustadz Abu untuk Muslim Indonesia', p. 35.
[78] Mustansir Mir 1987, pp. 217.
[79] *Ibid.*
[80] *Ibid.*, pp. 217-218.
[81] See *ibid.*
[82] See John L. Esposito (editor in chief) 2003, p. 123.
[83] *Jinn* can be described as 'creatures known in popular belief in pre-Islamic Arabia and mentioned numerous times in the Qur'an, parallel to human beings but made out of fire rather than clay. Believed to be both less virtuous and less physical than humans, but like

humans, endowed with the ability to choose between good and evil'. See John L. Esposito (editor in chief) 2003, p. 160.

[84] He refers to the following verses: Chapter 51 (*Adz-Dzariyat*) verse 56; Chapter 16 (*An-Nahl*) verse 36; and Chapter 98 (*Al Bayyinah*) verse 5.

[85] Abu Bakar Ba'asyir, 'Renungan dari Penjara'. Foreword for Irfan Suryahadi Ahwaz 2003, pp. xi-xiv.

[86] *Ibid.*

[87] *Ibid.*

[88] Shaitan literally means 'reckless, headstrong, defiant, violent'. This Arabic term used in the Qur'an in both the singular (*Shaitan*) and the plural (*Shaiyatiin*), often interchangeably with *Iblis* (considered to be a particular *shaitan*). There is no satanic species as such. Shaitan are among men and jinn who defy God. Scholars agree 'only that the term represents at least a principle (if not personification of evil)'. See John L. Esposito (editor in chief) 2003, p. 279-280 and Mustansir Mir 1987, p. 189.

[89] Abu Bakar Ba'asyir 2003, pp. xi-xiv.

[90] *Ibid.*

[91] *Khawarij* is 'early sectarian group in Islam, neither *Sunni* nor *Shii*, although they originally supported Ali's leadership on the basis of his wisdom and piety. They turned against Ali when he agreed to submit his quarrel with Muawiyah to arbitration; a group of his followers accused him of rejecting the Qur'an. Ali was forced to fight them in 658; in revenge, Ali was murdered at the Mosque in Kufa in 661. The group survives today, known as the *ibadis*, with fewer than one million adherents'. See John L. Esposito 2003, p. 171.

[92] See further discussion in Ahmad S. Moussalli 1999. *Historical Dictionary of Islamic Fundamentalist Movements in the Arab World, Iran, and Turkey*. Lanham, Maryland, and London: The Scarecrow Press, Inc. pp. 131-132.

[93] Ba'asyir began to become a 'problematic' religious leader in the late 1980s when he began to publicly express his strong and uncompromised opposition to Suharto's secularization policies. He rejected the forceful implementation of *Pancasila* as *asas tunggal* (sole base) for all mass organizations. He also refused to fly and pay respect to the national flag in State ceremonies as well as display presidential icons at Pondok Ngruki. He criticized such policies from an Islamic theological perspective and argued that such policies are the practice of *syirik* (idolatry). For him, '*Asas tunggal Pancasila* is indeed a trick of the Christians/Catholics to destroy all Islamic institutions in this country [Indonesia]'. See Tim Behrend, 2003.. 'Preaching fundamentalism: The public teachings of Abu Bakar Ba'asyir'. *Inside Indonesia*, April. Available on http://www.insideindonesia.org/edit74/behrend.html. See also 'Perjalanan menuju Allah', in *Majalah Islam Sabili*, No. 12 Th.X 2 Januari 2003/29 Syawal 1423, p. 25.

[94] Tim Behrend, 2003, *ibid.*

[95] *Ibid.*

[96] See Mustansir Mir 1987, p. 112.

[97] *Ibid.*

[98] *Ibid.*

[99] *Ibid.*

[100] Philip Herbst 2003, p. 99.

[101] *Ibid.*

[102] Daniel Pipes 2002. What is Jihad, in *New York Post*, December 31.

[103] Philip Herbst 2003, p. 100.

[104] See discussion in Beverly Milton-Edwards 1992. The Concept of *Jihad* and the Palestinian Islamic Movement: A Comparison of Ideas and Techniques. In *British Journal of Middle Eastern Studies*, Vol. 19, No. 1, pp. 48-52.

[105] Raphael Israeli 2001. The Islamic Doctrine of *Jihad* Advocates Violence. In Jenifer A. Hurley (ed.), *Islam: Opposing Viewpoints*. San Diego, California: Greenhaven Press, pp. 118-119.

[106] Mohammed Abdul Malek 2001. The Islamic Doctrine of Jihad Does not Advocates Violence. In Jenifer A. Hurley (ed.), *Islam Opposing Viewpoints*. San Diego, California: Greenhaven Press, p. 121. For Maled, the exact meaning of *jihad* can only be found from the *Qur'an, and one must pay attention to the context in which jihad appears* (pp. 121-124).

[107] Malek quotes Haji Ibrahim Golightly, who writes, '*Jihad* means to strive or make an effort, usually in an Islamic context, so that anything which requires an effort to be made is *Jihad* and the person doing it is a *mujahid* ... Making time in a busy schedule to study the Qur'an; going to a *halal* butcher rather than the closest or most convenient one; discussing Islam with both Muslims and non-Muslims and helping them to understand it better; studying *ayat* (signs), both of Qur'an and in nature and science, in order to increase *ilm*, or knowledge; setting other Muslims a good example and showing non-Muslims the true way of Muslims; are all examples of *Jihad* in daily life. *Jihad* is the effort made, not just against internal and external evils, but also to live at peace with oneself and one's community (Muslim and non-Muslims). *Ibid.*

[108] Quoted in Daniel Pipes 2002, *ibid.*

[109] *Ibid.*

[110] *Ibid.*

[111] Karen Amstrong 2001. 'The Roots of Islamic Fundamentalism'. In *These Times*, 24 December, p. 12.

[112] *Laskar Jihad* was a radical Islamic organization founded by Ja'far Umar Thalib in January 2000 and disbanded in October 2002. According to Ja'far, there are three major reasons for the disbandment of *Laskar Jihad*. First, due to advice (*fatwa*) from some *ulamas* in Mecca and Madinah, such as Syekh Rabi bin Hadi Al Madkhali. Second, because *Laskar Jihad* has been followed by political interests, that some political elites have approached the organization for their own political interests. Third, because some members of *Laskar Jihad* have violated *akhlak* and the principles of *ahlussunnah wal jamaah*. See *Suara Merdeka*, October 20, 2001, p. 1.

[113] See Tim Behrend 2002, p. 8.

[114] *Ibid.*

[115] See 'Da'wah dan Berbagai Persoalannya', in *Al Muslimun*, no. 394 Tahun XXXIII (46) Syawal/Dzulqa'idah 1423 H – Januari 2003, pp.19-23. The word *dakwah* can be found in many verses of the Qur'an, such as verse 33 of Chapter 41 (*Fushshilat*), verse 125 of Chapter 16 (*an Nahl*), and verse 24 of Chapter 8 (*al Anfal*), and verse 108, Chapter 12 (*Yusuf*).

[116] John L. Esposito 2003, p. 64.

[117] *Ibid.*

[118] Ahmad S. Moussalli 1999, p. 45.

[119] John L. Esposito 2003, p. 64.

[120] Muhammad Natsir (1908-1993) is one of the few Indonesian Muslim leaders who has national and international experience. From 18 August 1945 until 3 January 1946, he was a member of BP KNIP (*Badan Pekerja Komite Nasional Indonesia Pusat*), a nationalist committee for the formation of the new republic of Indonesia. From 1946-1948, Natsir was the Minister of Information and a member of the DPRS (*Dewan Perwakilan Rakyat Sementara)* or the Temporary People's House of Representatives. From 1950-1951, he was the Chairman of the modernist Muslim party of Masyumi and, most importantly, the Prime Minister of the Republic of Indonesia. His political career began to face difficulties in the early 1960s when he strongly and openly opposed President Sukarno's concept of *Demokrasi Terpimpin* (Guided Democracy). He also rejected the involvement of PKI or the

Communist Party in parliament, and was involved in a local separatist movement known as PRRI (*Pemerintah Revolusioner Republik Indonesia*) in West Sumatera. In 1960 Sukarno had Natsir and other Masyumi leaders detained. Natsir was held in jail for seven years until the New Order government released him in 1967. At the international level, Natsir is known as one of the most consistent supporters of independence movements in Muslim countries in Asia and Africa. He worked to strengthen cooperation among the newly independent Muslim countries. Natsir was a consultant for many international Islamic movements, including the PLO, the Mujahidin of Afghanistan, Moro in the Philippines, and movements in Bosnia, Japan, and Thailand. From 1967 until his death in 1993, he was the Vice President of the World Islamic Congress based in Karachi, Pakistan and one of the founding members of *Rabithah al-'Alam al Islami* based in Saudi Arabia. See Muhammad Sirozi 1998. Politics of Educational Policy Production in Indonesia: A Case Study of the Roles of Muslim Leaders in the Establishment of the Number 2 Act of 1989. Thesis submitted to Education Faculty, Monash University, Australia, pp. 124-125.

[121] Quoted in *Khutbah Jum'at*, 'Laporan Utama', No. 253 Rajab 1422H/Juli 2002, p. 84-85; 87.

[122] See Irfan Suryahadi Awwas 2003, p. 61. Ba'asyir supports this view with the Qur'an, Chapter 74 (*Al Mudatsir*) verse 1-2: 'O thou wrapped up (in the mantle)! Arise and deliver thy warning!' (translation by Abdullah Yusuf Ali).

[123] Quoted in Ibrahim and Romli 2003, p. 39.

[124] Further information on Ba'asyir's *dakwah* activities. See *Asia Times Online*, February 6, 2002. 'Southeast Asia, The Osama bin Laden and al-Qaeda of Southeast Asia'. Available on http://www.atimes.com/se-asia/DB06Ae01.html; Ibrahim and Romli 2003, p. 35; *Tempo Interaktif*, September 21, 2003. *Ibid*; and *Asia Times Online*, February 6, 2002.

[125] See Irfan Suryahadi Awwas 2003, p. 61.

[126] See 'Taushiah Ustadz Abu untuk Muslim Indonesia', in *Majalah Islam Sabili*, No. 12 Th. X 2 Januari 2003/29 Syawal 1423, p. 36. Ba'asyir suggests that it is alright for Muslims to adopt *mutraf* lifestyle in the hereafter, citing verse 77, Chapter 28 (*al Qasash*) of the Qur'an: '*But seek, with the (wealth) which Allah has bestowed on thee, the Home of the Hereafter, nor forget thy portion in this world: but do thou good, as Allah has been good to thee, and seek not (occasions for) mischief in the land: for Allah loves not those who do mischief*' (translation by Abdullah Yusuf Ali).

[127] See 'Taushiah Ustadz Abu untuk Muslim Indonesia', pp. 36-37.

[128] Tim Behrend 2003, p. 8.

[129] Irfan Suryahadi Awwas 2003, p. 65.

[130] *Time Asia* notes that Islam is the fastest growing religion in the world (25%) with 1.3 billion adherents: 670 million in Asia, 320 million in Africa, 132 million in the Middle East, 40 million in Europe, 6 million in North America, 1.5 million in Latin America, and 0.5 million in Oceania. See http://www.time.com/time/asia/covers/501030310/wahhabism.html.

[131] Ba'asyir cites verse 8, Chapter 61 (*Ash-Shaaf*), verse 32, Chapter 9 (*At Taubah*), and Chapter 2 (*Al-Baqarah*) verse 147 of the Qur'an. Irfan Suryahadi Awwas 2003, p. 64, 65.

[132] Tim Behrend 2003. Reading Past the Myth, p. 6.

[133] *Ibid.*

[134] Tim Behrend 2003, p. 7.

[135] Ba'asyir cites verse 3, Chapter 5 (*Al-Maidah*) of the Qur'an, '*Forbidden to you (for food) are: dead meat, blood, the flesh of swine, and that on which hath been invoked the name of other than Allah; that which hath been killed by strangling, or by a violent blow, or by a headlong fall, or by being gored to death; that which hath been (partly) eaten by a wild animal; unless ye are able to slaughter it (in due form); that which is sacrificed on stone (altars); (forbidden) also is the division (of meat) by raffling with arrows: that is impiety. This day have those who reject faith given up all hope of your religion: yet fear them not but*

fear Me. This day have I perfected your religion for you, completed My favour upon you, and have chosen for you Islam as your religion. But if any is forced by hunger, with no inclination to transgression, Allah is indeed Oft-forgiving, Most Merciful' (translation by Abdullah Yusuf Ali). Irfan Suryahadi Awwas 2003, p. 66.

[136] *Ibid.*

[137] Ba'asyir cites verse 19 and 89, Chapter 3 (*Ali Imran*) of the Qur'an, *Ibid.*

[138] This explanation of Ba'asyir refers to verse 29, Chapter 18 (*Al-Kahfi*) and verse 256, Chapter 2 (*Al-Baqarah*) of the Qur'an.

[139] See full description in Irfan Suryahadi Awwas 2003, p. 68.

[140] Ba'asyir cites the Qur'an, Chapter 5 (*Al-Maidah*) verses 44, 45, and 47, *Ibid.*, pp. 53-54.

[141] In this regard, Ba'asyir refers to the following verses of the Qur'an: Chapter 4 (*An-Nisaa* verse 65 and 105; Chapter 33 (*Al-Ahzab*, verse 36; and Chapter 24 (*An-Nur*) verse 51.

[142] The Arabic version of this is '*Isykariman au Musytahidan*'.

[143] Abu Bakar Ba'asyir, 'Renungan dari Penjara', in Irfan Suryahadi Awwas 2003, pp. xi-xiv.

[144] Ba'asyir cites Chapter 2 (*Al-Baqarah*) verse 208 of the Qur'an (Irfan Suryahadi Awwas 2003, p. 35, 51).

[145] Ba'asyir refers to the following verses of the Qur'an when he explains this view: Chapter 4 (*An-Nisa*) verse 65; Chapter 24 (*An-Nur*) verse 51; Chapter 33 (*Al-Ahzab*) verse 36; and Chapter 6 (*Al-An'am*) verse 121. See Irfan Suryahadi Awwas 2003, pp. 51-52.

[146] *Ibid.*

[147] *Tempo Interaktif*, November 11, 2001. 'Siapa Mau Syariat Islam'. Available on http://www.tempo co id/harian/opini/opi-07112001 html.

[148] *Ibid.*

[149] Fazlur Rahman 1970. Islamic Modernism: Its Scope, Method and Alternatives. In *International Journal of Middle East Studies*, Vol. 1, No. 4, October, p. 329.

[150] *Ibid.*, pp. 329-331.

[151] *Ibid.*, p. 331.

[152] *Ibid.*

[153] *Ibid.*

[154] Translation by Abdullah Yusuf Ali:

> *Do not marry unbelieving women (idolaters), until they believe: A slave woman who believes is better than an unbelieving woman, even though she allures you. Nor marry (your girls) to unbelievers until they believe: A man slave who believes is better than an unbeliever, even though he allures you. Unbelievers do (but) beckon you to the Fire. But Allah beckons by His Grace to the Garden (of bliss) and forgiveness, and makes His Signs clear to mankind: That they may celebrate His praise ...*

[155] Key figure in this regard is Munawir Sjadzali. Based on his idea of the 'Reactualization of Islamic Teachings', Sjadzali suggests that the distribution of *harta waris* must not be based on gender, but rather on merit. See See Munawir Sjadzali 1997. *Ijtihad kemanusiaan / Munawir Sjadzali*; pengantar, Busthanul Arifin, Nurcholish Madjid. Jakarta : Paramadina. See also Munawir Sjadzali 1994. *Bunga rampai wawasan Islam dewasa ini /* oleh H. Munawir Sjadzali. Jakarta : Penerbit Universitas Indonesia.

[156] Verse 11, Chapter 4, *An Nisa* (Irfan Suryahadi Awwas 2003, p. 44).

[157] *Ibid.*

[158] *Ibid.*

[159] Ibrahim and Romli 2003, pp. 45-47.

[160] Tim Behrend 2002, p. 5-6.

[161] See 'Taushiah Ustadz Abu untuk Muslim Indonesia', p. 37.

[162] BBC News World Edition, October 15, 2002. 'Spotlight turns on radical cleric'.

[163] *Asia Times Online*, February 6, 2002. 'Southeast Asia, The Osama bin Laden and al-Qaeda of Southeast Asia'. Available on http://www.atimes.com/se-asia/DB06Ae01.html
[164] *Ibid.*
[165] Fazlur Rahman 1970, p. 324.
[166] According to CNN's Maria Ressa, Ba'asyir wants to develop an Islamic super state, including Indonesia, Malaysia, Singapore, parts of the Philippines, Thailand, and Myanmar. If Philippines national security adviser Roilo Golez's claim is correct, Ba'asyir also intends to include northern Australia as part of his theocratic state, Daulah Islam Nusantara. See discussion in Tim Behrend 2003. *Reading Past the Myth: Public Teachings of Abu Bakar Ba'asyir*, p. 5.
[167] Irfan Suryahadi Awwas 2003, p. 34.
[168] Tim Behrend 2003. *Reading Past the Myth*, p. 8.
[169] Quoted in Ibrahim and Romli 2003, p. 39.
[170] Another student (*Santri*) at Pondok Ngruki, said: 'As far as I am concerned, Pak Abu (Ba'asyir) is far from violence. He is even too soft, that I used to think that he is a coward.' (*Kompas Cyber Media*, November 3, 2002. Nasional, Ustad Menanam Dakwah, Ustad Menuai Teror. Available on http://www.kompas.com.
[171] See *Republika Online*, September 3, 2003. Berita Utama, 'Melawan Dengan Ketenangan'. Available on http://www.republika.co.id.
[172] This Manifesto was later published in a bulletin called *Nida'ul Islam*, July-August 1998. See Irfan Suryahadi Awwas 2003, p. 51. It has been one of the important documents used by government authorities in Malaysia, Singapore and Philippine to interrogate terrorist suspects. *Asia Times Online*, February 6, 2002, *ibid.*
[173] ABC News, September 2, 2003, *ibid.*
[174] See 'Hari Fitri Bersama Ust. Abu', in *Majalah Islam Sabili*, No. 12 Th. X 2 Januari 2003/29 Syawal 1423, p. 21.
[175] Quoted in Daniel Miller 1994. *Modernity: An Ethnographic Approach*. New York: Berg Publishers , p. 61.
[176] See Jurgen Habermas 1987. *The Philosophical Discourse of Modernity*. Cambridge: MIT Press, p. 7.
[177] Bernard Lewis 1997, 'The West and the Middle East', in *Foreign Affairs* 76 (1), p. 127.
[178] Fazlur Rahman 1970, p. 318.
[179] These terms are adopted from Hussin Mutalib 1990. Islamic Revivalism in ASEAN States: Political Implications. In *Asian Survey*, Vol. 30, No. 9, September, p. 883.
[180] Muqtedar Khan, 2003. [Globalist Paper Global Education] Islam's Future and the Importance of Social Sciences. Available on:
http://www.theglobalist.com/DBWeb/StoryId.aspx?StoryId=3255. Downloaded on Sept 19, 2003.
[181] Dawud Tauhidi. A Vision of Effective Islamic Education, edited by Anas Coburn. http://islamic-world.net/parenting/parenting_page/a_vision_of_effective_islamic_ed.htm. Dowloaded on September 19, 2003.
[182] Dawud Tauhidi 2003. *Ibid.*
[183] *Ibid.*

Chapter 12

Israel as a Focus for the Anger of Muslims Against the West

Colin Chapman

No single cause fuelled Muslim rage as much as the establishment of Israel[1]

I am in a dream. I never believed that one day the US would come to pay a price for its support to Israel.[2]

It is time to accept that the Arab-Israeli conflict is the main source of tension between the Muslim world and the West and act to resolve it.[3]

Journalists and diplomats alike, returning from the Middle East, attest that our almost blind support of Israel is a major cause of the anti-Americanism that is sweeping the Islamic world.[4]

Is it surprising to find an Indian Muslim journalist, a young Palestinian in Jerusalem, a *Guardian* editorial in the UK and a right-wing American conservative Christian all agreeing in recent months that the State of Israel is a major reason for the anger that many Muslims feel against the West? We may want to argue about whether it is 'the main source of tension', one major source of tension or one source of tension among many. We may also want to distinguish between the mere existence of Israel, its actions since 1948 and Western support for Israel. But we can hardly escape the fact that, in the eyes of most Muslims all over the world, Israel today is closely associated with the West and totally identified with the US, and that we are dealing here with one of the most important and the most bitter of all the complaints that Muslims direct towards the West.

Any attempt to analyse and understand the anger of Muslims against the West needs to begin with history and attempt to explain the Muslim perception of the great reversal, in which a successful civilization which dominated the Middle East and North Africa for centuries gradually weakened to the point of finding itself subject to Western domination. Between the eighteenth and twentieth centuries the whole of the Muslim world (except for Arabia, Turkey and Afghanistan) for shorter or longer periods was under Western imperial rule. And in the last fifty years this has been replaced by a new imperialism – political, economic and cultural – which is perceived to be just as powerful and perhaps even more sinister and destructive than the old kind of imperialism. In its present position of superiority the West (and especially the US) arrogantly claims to be bringing civilization, freedom and democracy to the rest of the world. At the same time, however, it manipulates world markets to maintain its own dominance, applies double standards to resolve local conflicts to further its own interests and coopts the governments of most Islamic countries as 'stooges'.[5]

In this context the creation of Israel is seen by Muslims as one of the last examples of a Western colonial movement. With the help of the West (first Britain and then the US), the number of Jews in Palestine increased through steady immigration from just under 5% in 1880 to 30% by 1948. The Jewish state, established in 1948 at the heart of the Arab world and the Islamic world, has been seen by Muslims worldwide as a dangerous transplant or a cancerous growth, sustained as if on a life support machine by the moral, political and economic support of the US. Its aggressive policies towards the Palestinians and its skilful manipulation of successive American administrations since 1967, with the support of Jewish and Christian lobbies in the US, have enabled it to exploit every weakness among the Palestinians, to defy resolutions of the UN Security Council, and to make it harder, if not impossible, for any meaningful Palestinian entity to be created. Israel, in short, is seen as an anachronism in the post-colonial world, a misfit in a place where it does not belong, and 'a surrogate of America'. [6] Its very existence represents 'the absolute trough of the decline of Islamic civilization'.[7]

Is there any justificiation for this perception of Israel in the minds of Muslims all round the world? The moment we ask this question we are faced with the almost impossible task of separating politics from religion. How much of the reaction of Muslims is determined by an Islamic worldview, and how much of it is a natural reaction to a perceived injustice? How do we separate the issues relating to human rights from those related to religion? Would Palestinians and Arabs have been just as angry if they had been Hindus or Buddhists?

Some answers to this question say that the fundamental conflict here is between Islam and Zionism. 'These Arab Islamic countries', wrote A Carlebach, a Jewish writer, in 1955, 'do not suffer from poverty, or disease, or illiteracy, or exploitation; they only suffer from the worst of all plagues: Islam. Wherever Islamic psychology rules, there is the inevitable rule of despotism and criminal aggression. The danger lies in Islamic psychology ... You can talk "business" with everyone, and even with the devil. But not with Allah ... The heart of the conflict is not the question of the borders; it is the question of Muslim psychology ...'.[8] Similarly Bat Ye'or interprets the present conflict largely in the light of traditional Islamic ways of relating to the Jews: 'In international forums, the world can today observe the age-old hatred towards the rebellious *dhimmis* projected onto Israel'.[9]

Answers at the other end of the spectrum tend to say that the religious factors related to Islam are very secondary, and that Palestinian, Arab and Muslim reactions to Israel are no different in principle from the reactions of any people who have been oppressed by another people. A political scientist like Fred Halliday, for example, argues for 'the modernist, anti-essentialist, anti-perennialist approach', which insists on addressing the specific factors in any given situation before appealing to abstract principles or any overarching ideology. In trying to understand the Arab-Israeli conflict he suggests that, instead of appealing to 'an immutable, recurrent, historical archetype' or 'any essence of Western or Christian or non-Muslim society', we should be looking at 'a set of contemporaneous national conjunctures, in which politicians and their associate ideologues draw on themes present in history or in the discourses of other states for their own current and specific purposes ...'.[10]

This essay focuses on the *Islamic* dimension of the Palestinian-Israeli conflict not because it is felt to be the only or the most important factor, but because the Islamic dimension doesn't seem to be sufficiently understood in the West. 'They have Mecca and Medina as their holy cities – so why do they want Jerusalem as well?' Remarks of this kind reveal not only a total lack of sympathy and respect for the religious feelings of Muslims but also (dare we say) complete ignorance about how Muslims see the world. We therefore attempt, firstly, to understand the place of Palestine, Jerusalem and the Jews in the world-view of Islam in order to understand why Muslims tend to be very critical of the state of Israel. The second stage is to reflect on some Western responses to the Islamic case concerning Israel, and we conclude by asking whether the different sides in the dialogue are listening to each other and whether there is any possibility of defusing the anger felt by most Muslims.

Islamic assumptions contributing to the anger of Muslims

1. *The land and Jerusalem in the Qur'an*

There are two clear references to the land in the Qur'an. The first is in a passage which speaks about Moses encouraging the Children of Israel to enter the land: 'O my people! Go into the holy land (*al ard al-muqaddasa*) which Allah hath ordained for you ...' (Qur'an 5:21, Pickthall). This conveys the idea that this land has been set apart by God for the Children of Israel, who are related to the Arabs through their ancestor, Ishmael. The second is a verse which speaks about Abraham and Lot in the land, where God says, 'We delivered him (Abraham) and Lot, and brought them to the land which We had blessed for all mankind' (*allati barakna fiha lil'alamin.* Qur'an 21:71, Dawood). The single reference to Jerusalem comes in a verse referring to Muhammad's Night Journey from Mecca to Jerusalem: 'Glory be to him who made His servant go by night from the Sacred Temple [of Mecca] to the Father Temple [of Jerusalem] whose surroundings We have blessed (*alladhi barakna hawlahu*), that We might show him some of our signs' (Qur'an 17:1. Dawood). These three verses make Muslims feel that the whole land, and Jerusalem in particular, are sacred and that a special divine blessing rests upon it.

2. *Muhammad and Jerusalem*

According to Islamic tradition, earlier in his life and before his call to be a prophet, Muhammad visited Gaza and Palestine, perhaps including Jerusalem. When he first received his revelations, he and the Muslim community in Mecca said their prayers facing in the direction of Jerusalem. The first significant link between Muhammad and Mecca, therefore, was that this was their first *qiblah* until about eighteen months after the *Hijrah*, when the Prophet received a further revelation instructing them to change the *qiblah* to face Mecca. The second important link was the Night Journey (*isra'*) and the Ascent to Heaven (*mi'raj*), which was either a miraculous event (as some Muslims believe) or a vision of some kind, in which Muhammad was transported during the night from the Ka'aba in Mecca to Jerusalem, and from there taken up into heaven, where he met with Adam, Abraham, Moses, Jesus and other Prophets. The magic steed which transported Muhammad from Mecca to Medina, known as Buraq, was tied up at the Wailing Wail, which is therefore known to Muslims as the Buraq Wall.

It is hard to exaggerate the importance of the *isra'* and the *mi'raj* in the thinking of Muslims, because it links Muhammad with Jerusalem and is seen as a commissioning of Muhammad for his ministry as Prophet. It also indicates a significant change in the role of the Jews in relation to the Arabs in the purposes of God, symbolizing a kind of spiritual conquest of Jerusalem by Muhammad.[11] Since the Jews forfeited their right to the land and to Jerusalem by breaking God's covenant, the promises now have to be fulfilled through the descendants of Ishmael. 'Prophethood', says Zachariah Bashier, 'switched from the Israelites to the Arabs ... This change is symbolized in the act in which the Prophet, ushered by Gabriel, led the prayer, in the Aqsa Mosque, with all the Prophets including Adam and Abraham lined up with him ... According to the Qur'an, the Bani Israe'il are no longer the 'chosen people'. The Muslims are the best people if they fulfil the conditions of being true to the mission of Islam: You are the best nation (*ummah*) brought forth to mankind ... (*Al 'Imran* 3:110).'[12] According to Mohammed Abdul Hameed Al-Khateeb, 'Al-Quds has sanctity for Muslims because of the events that took place there within Muslim sacred history which extends to the beginning of time ... The assertion of the sanctity of Jerusalem for Muslims is fundamentally an assertion of the continuity of Islam with a tradition going back to Ibrahim [Abraham] and beyond'.[13]

3. *Muhammad's relations with the Jews of Medina*

The change in the status of the Jews symbolized by the *mi'raj* was worked out more painfully in the deteriorating relationship between Muhammad and the three Jewish tribes in Medina, who opposed him partly because they could not accept the new faith of Islam, and partly because they found it difficult to recognize his growing power in the community. During the series of battles that took place between the Muslims and the Meccans, the Muslims felt that although the Jews in Medina were bound by a covenant to support the new Islamic community, they were in fact working against them and conspiring with the Meccans. As a result, one Jewish tribe, the Banu Nadir, were expelled from Medina and sought refuge in a Jewish community at Khaybar to the north. Between 600 and 900 men from another tribe, the Banu Qurayza, were beheaded and thrown into a ditch and their wives and children sold into slavery, while a third tribe, Qaynuqa, were expelled from Medina and went eventually to Syria.

These developments provide the context for understanding several verses in the Qur'an which are critical of the Jews. The sin of the Jews, we are told, is that they 'broke their covenant, denied the revelations of God and killed the prophets unjustly ...' (4:155). The vast majority of them do not have faith (4:46). The enmity and hatred which God has stirred up 'will endure till the Day of Resurrection' (5:64). One of the strongest criticisms is found in a verse which makes a clear distinction between Jews and Christians: 'You will find that the most implacable of men in their hostility to the faithful are the Jews and the pagans and the nearest in affection to them are those who say: "We are Christians ..."' (5:82–83, Dawood). These words are generally interpreted by Muslims not only as a reflection of the difficult relationship between Muhammad and the Jews of Medina but also as the basis for a particular attitude towards Jews in general. Commenting on the way this verse is understood today in the writings of Hizbullah, Amal Saad-Gharayeb writes: 'On the most explicit level, this verse reveals God's immense dislike of the Jews. As the people who display the strongest enmity towards the Muslim believers, the Jews are clearly the Muslims' greatest enemy ... But the generalisation does not only relate to the Jews of Muhammad's time, but to all Jews throughout history ... the Jews of yesterday, today, and the generations to come, are necessarily included in those who are cursed, damned and generally demonised in the Qur'an ...'.[14]

4. *The status of Jews as dhimmis*

During the centuries following the initial Islamic conquests Jewish communities survived throughout the Middle East and North Africa as a tiny minority of around 1-2 %, presenting no threat to the Muslim authorities.[15] Muslim interpretations of these relationships are generally very positive, pointing out that the Jews who were expelled by Christian Spain in the fifteenth century were welcomed in different parts of the Muslim world. They argue that persecution was the exception rather than the general rule, and that Islam worked out its own kind of tolerance and pluralism long before the West developed its own pluralist societies. This is why Zaki Badawi is able to say 'We have always had a good relationship in history with the Jews but it is this which has been put at risk by the fifty years of conflict with Israel'.[16]

Jewish writers, however, are not usually able to put such a positive gloss on the relationships during these centuries. The legal basis for Islamic thinking about Jews within the empire is explained by Bat Ye'or as follows:

> Muslim jurists fixed the rights of conquest on the basis of Muhammad's treatment of the Jews of Arabia. This treatment became a model serving as a universal norm to be applied to all Jews, Christians, Zoroastrians, and others vanquished by *jihad*. In the same manner as Muhammad had spared the Jews of Khaybar, who had recognized his sovereignty, so the Arab conquerors concluded 'toleration' treaties with all the other peoples who, faced with *jihad*, submitted to their domination. The *dhimmi* condition, which is a direct consequence of *jihad*, is connected with this same contract. It suspends the conqueror's initial rights over the adherents of the revealed religions on payment of a tribute such as the Jews had agreed to give to the Prophet of Khaybar.[17]

While there is no basis, therefore, for speaking about an 'eternal enmity' between Muslims and Jews, there is no denying that for many centuries the proper place in Islamic thinking for Jews was as a tolerated minority living under Islam. The growing conflict with the Zionist Jews in Palestine from the end of the nineteenth century no doubt revived in the minds of many Muslims painful memories of the difficult relationship that Muhammad had had with the Jews of Medina. It must have looked as if Jews in the modern period were simply repeating in modern history the behaviour of fellow Jews many years before towards the Prophet of Islam

5. *Jerusalem in Islamic tradition and history*

A significant number of the reported sayings of Muhammad in *hadith* literature illustrate the special sanctity that Jerusalem came to have for Muslims: 'Journeys should not be made except to three mosques: this my mosque (in Medina), the sacred mosque (in Mecca), and Al-Aqsa.' 'Whoever dies in the Jerusalem sanctuary is as if he has died in heaven'.[18] When the caliph Umar reached Jerusalem with his army in 638, Sophronius, the Christian patriarch, came out of the city wearing his robes to surrender to Umar who was wearing his battle clothes. Umar gave orders that a place of worship should be built on the site of Muhammad's 'ascension' into heaven. It was here that the Umayyad caliph Abd al-Malik built the Dome of the Rock *(qubbat al-sakhra)* in 691 as a pilgrim ambulatory, providing Muslims with a place of pilgrimage similar to the Christian Church of the Holy Sepulchre. The *al-Aqsa* mosque was built a few hundred yards to the south of the Dome of the Rock in around 810, to replace the original mosque that had been built there by Umar. Many other important names in Islamic history were associated with Jerusalem, including Bilal, the first *muezzin*, the Umayyad caliph Mu'awiya, Rabi'a the mystic, the legal scholar al-Shafi'i, and the theologian al-Ghazali. For many centuries pilgrims, travellers, scholars and students made their way to the city. Muslims point out repeatedly, therefore, that the land was in their hands for around 1,300 years (i.e. from the first Islamic conquest in 638 until the end of the Ottoman Empire in 1918, with the exception of the years of Crusader rule), and under Arab rule for around 900 of those years.

6. *Jerusalem and the Crusades*

'The Crusades', according to H.S. Karmi, 'gave Jerusalem a new significance in the eyes of the Muslims ... The position of Palestine as a holy country for Muslims derives very strongly from the Crusades... It is little wonder that Arabs and Muslims regard Palestine as holy, as a reaction to such aggressive designs'[19]. Similarly Zaki Badawi says, 'It was the Crusaders who transformed Jerusalem into a potent symbol of Islam once again'.[20] One particular incident during the Crusades gives a special insight into the thinking of Muslims concerning Jerusalem. At the time when the Crusaders had lost Jerusalem to Saladin in 1191 and were trying to reestablish their control over the whole country, Richard the Lion Heart wrote to Saladin making the bold suggestion that Richard's sister, Joanna, should marry Saladin's brother, Malik al-Adil; they should reign together as king and queen of Jerusalem, and all Palestine should come under Christian rule. Saladin in his reply explained how unthinkable it was for him as a Muslim to surrender Jerusalem to Christian rule:

> Jerusalem is ours as much as yours. Indeed it is even more sacred to us than it is to you, for it is the place from which our Prophet accomplished his nocturnal journey and the place where our community will gather on the Day of Judgement. Do not imagine that we can renounce it or vacillate on this point. The land was originally ours, whereas you have only just arrived and have taken it over only because of the weakness of the Muslims living there at the time. God will not allow you to rebuild a single stone as long as the war lasts ... [21]

7. *Jerusalem and the land in eschatology*

Saladin in his letter was referring to the whole series of events centred on Jerusalem which, according to Muslims, will take place at the end of the world. In stories about the Day of Judgement that developed over the centuries, one widely accepted idea was that when Jesus comes again to the earth in Damascus, he will kill the Anti-Christ and return to Jerusalem, where he will pray in the mosque, kill all the pigs, break all the crosses, and destroy the synagogues and churches, thus vindicating Islam as the one true religion. He will reign in Jerusalem for fifty years, then die and be buried in Medina beside the Prophet Muhammad.[22] Some Shi'ite Muslims today make a clear link between the appearance of the Mahdi and the liberation of Jerusalem.[23] Two frequently quoted sayings contain predictions made by the prophet Muhammad concerning the conflict that would take place in Jerusalem and between Muslims and Jews: 'O Mu'adh, Allah will conquer the land of Syria after me for you, from al-'Arish [Egypt] to the Euphrates [Iraq]... Whoever of you chooses to remain along the coastal region of Syria or in Bait al-Maqdis [Jerusalem] will be engaged in constant jihad until the Day of Judgement'.[24] 'The Last Hour will not come until the Muslims fight against the Jews, and the Muslims kill them until the Jews hide themselves behind a stone or a tree and the stone or tree will say: "O Muslim, or slave of Allah, there is a Jew behind me; come and kill him" ; but the *gharqad* tree will not say that, for it is the tree of the Jews.' [25]

8. *Some recent statements of Islamic assumptions*

The following are examples from two different Islamic sources illustrating how some of these traditional assumptions have been expressed in relation to the Palestinian-Israeli conflict. While they do not in any way represent the whole range of views among Muslims, they indicate the general approaches that Muslims are likely to adopt if they are faithful to their history and consistent in working out traditional Islamic ideas in the present context.

Ismail R. Al-Faruqi, a Palestinian scholar who spent much of his life teaching in the USA, strove to present a 'holistic, activist Islamic worldview'.[26] In his *Islam and the Problem of Israel*, written in 1980, he began by saying that Islam is not opposed to Judaism, but only to Zionism, and then went on to outline what he saw as 'the Islamic solution of the problem of Israel', which involves the dissolution of the Zionist state and the return to a single Islamic *umma*, with Jews once again living as *dhimmis*.

> For its crimes against the individual Palestinian men and women, against the corporate existence of the Palestinians, against the individual Arabs of the surrounding countries as well as the *ummah*, Islam condemns Zionism. Islam demands that every atom's weight of injustice perpetrated against the innocent be undone. Hence, it imposes upon all Muslims the world over to rise like one man to put an end to injustice and to reinstate its sufferers in their lands, homes and properties. The illegitimate use of every movable or immovable property by the Zionists since the British occupation of the land will have to be paid for and compensated. Therefore, the Islamic position leaves no chance for the Zionist state but to be dismantled and destroyed, and its wealth confiscated to pay off its liabilities ...
>
> Islam offers a perfect solution to the Jewish problem which has beset the Jews and the West for two millennia. This solution is for the Jews of the world to be given the right to dwell wherever they wish, as free citizens of the state of their choice ... *Ex hypothesi*, there must be an Islamic state comprehending these territories; an Islamic state whose constitution is the Quran, whose law is the *shariah*, and whose constituency is only partly non-Muslim. Such an Islamic state, extending from the Atlantic to the Malay Basic, is certainly obliged to open its gates to any Jewish immigrant who travels thither. ... the Arab states of the Near East must undergo a transformation from being caricatures of the Western national states to becoming a single, united Islamic state ... They must all be dismantled and their population reorganized into the Islamic state ... Only if this is achieved may the Arab Muslims of the Near East stand ready to implement the Islamic solution of the problem of Israel...[27]

The Covenant of *Hamas*, the Islamic Resistance Movement, first published in 1988, contains 36 items which sumarize the ideology of the movement. Some of these articles, as summarized by Peter Riddell, show how the movement attempts to relate traditional Islamic assumptions to the conflict with Israel:

> (1) Hamas is based on Islam; (3) Hamas is for Muslims who favour Jihad; (5) Allah is the target, the Prophet is the example, and the Qur'an is its constitution; (6) Hamas aims for every inch of Palestine; (7) Hamas is a universal movement, for Muslims throughout the world; (8) Jihad is the path and death for the sake of Allah is the loftiest of its wishes; (11) Palestine is Islamic 'waqf' till Judgement Day. No part of it should be given up; (14) Palestine is sacred land; (34) as Crusaders were defeated, so will Zionists be ...[28]

While drawing on models and assumptions drawn from the past, Hamas is also open to modern ideas and even incorporates many of them into its thinking. 'The ideology of *Hamas*', says Andrea Nusse, 'is far from being static or simply reverting to an ancient Islamic model. It can rather be characterized as based on traditional Islamic teaching, enriched with modern concepts and ideas of mainly Western origin ...'. Her summary of the goals of the movement illustrates how traditional and modern ideas are combined:

> The goal of the Islamists is to liberate Palestine from occupation by the 'Zionist' enemy and re-establish an Islamic state. With the Islamic conquest, Palestine ... had become Islamic patrimonium of *waqf* which does not belong to any person, party or state ... In Palestine, Muslims are fighting to reconcile history to Islamic beliefs and convictions. Thus the outcome of the struggle over Palestine is decisive for the whole *Umma*. A victory in this struggle would prove that Muslims are again on the right path and will continue to succeed in the world. This also means that the fight for Palestine can only be won under the banner of Allah ... The establishment of an Islamic state in Palestine is seen to be the only possible political solution: a state which will be part of a wider Islamic domain that will finally embrace the whole world.[29]

In attempting to describe the main assumptions which have influenced the attitudes of Muslims concerning the conflict over Israel, we have to reckon with the fact that many Muslims know little of their tradition and history. Some may be aware of Islamic assumptions but be much more pragmatic in their approach, deeply influenced by secular and non-Muslim ways of thinking. Recent developments within the Palestinian movement, for example, have underlined the widening gap between the more secular approach of the PLO and the explicitly Islamic approaches of groups like Hamas and Islamic Jihad. One further problem is that many moderate Muslims want to distance themselves as far as possible from the outlook of Islamists, alarmed that through 'guilt by association' they are inevitbaly identified with the views and actions of extremists.

Having taken all this into account, however, we can hardly escape the conclusion that if we are talking about the *Islamic* dimension of the conflict (as opposed to the political dimension or Jewish, Christian or secular dimensions), all these ideas seem to add up to a consistent world-view which provides Muslims with strong additional reasons for reinforcing their claims to the land and to Jerusalem that are otherwise based simply on continuous occupation over many centuries. As we shall now see, non-Muslims in the West have reacted strongly to the anger of many Muslims over Israel and to the explicitly Islamic elements in their case for establishing sovereignty over the land and its capital city.

Some Western responses to the Islamic case against Israel

In what follows we are attempting to listen both to the ways in which many non-Muslims respond to the Islamic arguments over the Israeli-Palestinian conflict and to how Palestinians and Muslims tend to respond to this critique. If at times we find ourselves straying into history and politics, it is because it is often hard in this particular conflict to separate the political and the religious.

1. *'The typically Islamic rhetoric concerning Palestine is relatively recent. Most Palestinians have seen the problem as a national struggle without all the religious overtones. Hamas was only created in 1987'.*

Organised Muslim opposition to Zionist plans in Palestine, including a number of calls for *jihad* by religious leaders, began in the 1920s, and during the same period Muslims and Christians came together to form Muslim-Christian Associations to resist Zionism. The Mufti of Jerusalem, al-Hajj Amin al-Hussayni, was one of the leaders of the Arab Revolt in 1936, and the first occasion when any Arab government invoked the doctrine of *jihad* was in 1969 when, following the arson attack on the Al-Aqsa Mosque, King Faisal of Saudi Arabia called for *jihad* in order to liberate Jerusalem. Summit conferences of Muslim states since that year have issued similar calls.[30] The Islamic basis for these concerns has been articulated very clearly in recent years by organisations like Hamas and Hizbullah. It is true, therefore, that the Zionist challenge has forced Muslims to articulate these ideas. The basic Islamic assumptions, however, about Jerusalem and the land are evident in the Qur'an, the *hadith* and at many other stages in history, and did not need to be articulated as clearly as they have been in recent years.

2. *'Palestinian nationalism is a by-product of Jewish nationalism'*

Four centuries under oppressive or negligent Ottoman rule hardly created a natural context for the growth of any national movement in Palestine. Palestinians like Edward Said, however, are in no doubt that even in the nineteenth century the Palestinians felt that they were different from other Arabs: 'For any Palestinian there was no doubt that his country had its own character and identity ...'[31] They would probably not disagree, however, with Benny Morris's judgement that 'Paradoxically it was in large part the thrust and threat of Zionism that generated this consciousness of collective self, that is, a distinct Palestinian Arab identity and nationalism'.[32] If Israeli Jews feel that their identity is bound up with land, culture and religion, they have no reason to despise Palestinian Arabs for understanding their own identity in very similar terms. They can hardly deny to their Palestinian neighbours a right that they have claimed for themselves, and have no right to pour scorn on Palestinian nationalism for being largely generated and stimulated by Jewish nationalism.

3. *'The Islamic theology of the land is simply a carbon copy of the Jewish theology of the Land'*

'The idea of the sanctity of the Palestinian territories', says Andrea Nusse, 'seems clearly to have been taken over from the enemy's doctrine'.[33] It could easily be argued, however, that there are bound to be strong similarities beeen the two theologies since the history of the Children of Israel in the Promised Land is seen by Muslims as part of Islamic history. Several of the Old Testament prophets are included in the line of prophets that ended with Muhammad, and the whole of Biblical history (from Adam to Jesus) is therefore, as it were, co-opted and incorporated into Islamic history. This is all part of what Nusse calls 'an Islamisation of all history before Muhammad'.[34] It is also inevitable that response to challenges from outside at different stages of history was bound to be inspired by Islamic ideas. Saladin's reply to Richard the Lion Heart's proposal is fully understandable in Islamic terms without any reference to the Hebrew Bible. And the growth of Islamic fundamentalism among the Palestininians on the West Bank and Gaza can be seen to a large extent as a response to the refusal of every Israeli government to withdraw from the territories occupied in 1967 and Jewish settlement in these areas. If Israel had withdrawn as it was required to do by UN resolutions, would Hamas and Islamic Jihad ever have come into existence? If Israel had not invaded Lebanon in 1982 and stayed on occupying the south until 2001 would there be a Hizbullah in Lebanon?

4. *'The Zionist movement has been under attack from Arabs from the very beginning. They have suffered from the inveterate hostility of the Arabs'*

'It's all the fault of the Arabs', we are told, for being so hostile to the Jews. 'Look at poor little Israel surrounded by all those warlike Arabs.' It is significant, however, that some Israeli Jews like Benny Morris are prepared to challenge this perception. The conclusion of his *Righteous Victims: A History of the Zionist-Arab Conflict (1881-1999)* begins with these words: 'In 1938, against the backdrop of the Arab rebellion against the Mandate, David Ben-Gurion told the Political Committee of Mapai:

> When we say that the Arabs are the aggressors and we defend ourselves – that is only half the truth. As regards our security and life we defend ourselves ... But the fighting is only one aspect of the conflict, which is in its essence a political one. And politically we are the aggressors and they defend themselves.

Ben-Gurion, of course, was right. Zionism was a colonizing and expansionist ideology and movement.[35]

5. *'Blaming others is simply a way of avoiding the need to accept one's own responsibility'*

Bernard Lewis speaks of 'the blame game' in which Muslims have blamed one party after another for all their problems - the Turks, the Mongols, the imperialists, the Jews, the Americans:

> For the governments, at once oppressive and ineffectual, that rule much of the Middle East, this game serves a useful, indeed an essential, purpose – to explain the poverty that they have failed to alleviate and to justify the tyranny that they have intensified. In this way they seek to deflect the mounting anger of their unhappy subjects against other, outer targets.[36]

In his recent book *What Went Wrong? The Clash between Islam and Modernity in the Middle East* the one brief mention of Israel refers to 'the intolerable humiliation' felt by Muslim Arabs, the dissemination of European anti-Semitism in the Arab world and the attitudes that 'blame all evil in the Middle East and indeed in the world on secret Jewish plots'.[37] Apart from these references there is no recognition of the role of Zionism in the clash between Islam and the West in the Middle East. It is surely significant, however, that some of the new generation of Israeli historians are prepared to speak, for example, about the ethnic cleansing of the Palestinians at the time of the creation of the State of Israel and even describe this process as part of 'the original sin' of Israel. If Muslims could hear Israel's supporters in the West speaking with similar honesty about the price paid by the Palestinians in the creation of the state, they might be be more willing to accept their own share of responsibility and not constantly be blaming others for all that has happened.

6. *'Most Muslims all over the world are concerned about immediate issues in their own context; it's only religious and political leaders and demagogues who stir their people up to be concerned about Israel. The Palestinian cause is just a diversion.'*

No doubt a large proportion of Muslims all over the world are more concerned about surviving in their own situation than about political problems in the Middle East. But all Muslims who have more than a superficial knowlege of their faith and history are bound to have some feeling for fellow-Muslims elsewhere and to recognise the significance of Jerusalem within the world-view of Islam. It must be hard for Israeli Jews to feel that they have to deal not only with the Palestinians themselves, but behind them with the whole Arab world and beyond them with the whole Muslim world. 'Why', they must ask 'can't the rest of the Arab world and the Muslim world just get off our backs and leave us Israeli Jews and Palestinians to sort out these problems betweeen ourselves?' If the Zionist homeland had been set up in Uganda or Argentina, any subsequent problems might have been confined to the immediate area. But when Herzl and others insisted on Palestine as the location of 'the Jews' state', were they unaware that they were inviting themselves to make their homeland/state in the heartlands of Islam? Did they know anything about the world-view of their new Muslim neighbours and did they have any idea of the world they were stepping into?

7. *'Islamic anti-Semitism today is just as pernicious as European (Christian) anti-Semitism has been in the past'*

This may be one area where Palestinians, Arabs and Muslims need to be pressed very hard. Can they demonstrate that there is a *qualitative* difference between what many of them have said about 'the Jews' in the last thirty years and the things that Christian leaders at different times of history and Nazis have said against 'the Jews'? Was Hannadh Arendt right in observing that totalitarian movements tend to be intrinsically anti-Semitic?[38] Is Daniel Pipes justified in claiming that 'the historically Christian phenomenon of anti-Semitism is now primarily a Muslim phenomenon; Christians have passed the hate-filled baton to Muslims. The main locus of anti-Semitism has moved from the Christian countries to the Muslim world. Muslims, not Christians, now pose the greater danger to Jews'.[39] Or should we believe Amal Saad-Gharayeb, who, while admitting that 'the anti-Judaism of Hizbu'llah is as vituperative against Jews, if not more than, conventional anti-Semitism' still argues that 'Islamic anti-Semitism is fundamentally different from its Western Christian predecessors' and that 'it would be a gross fallacy to claim that contemporary Islam is anti-Semitic'.[40] Are Muslims willing to recognise how their rhetoric concerning 'the Jews' is often perceived by the rest of the world?

Conclusion: a defusing of anger or a dialogue of the deaf?

At this particular time in history we face a situation in which the escalation of the conflict is raising the stakes and intensifying the human suffering on both sides day by day. The combination of politics and religion increases the sensitivity and the complexity of the issues all round. It is hard enough to deal with the clash of two nationalisms in which two peoples claim the same piece of land for different reasons. But now these two nationalisms have given birth to two fundamentalisms in which Jewish settlers, using the Hebrew Bible and dreams of 'the Greater Israel' to support their claims to the West Bank, confront Palestinian Muslims, who think of their struggle to establish a state and regain Jerusalem more and more in terms of *jihad.* Both sides provoke each other to greater fury.

The contention of this paper is that a serious attempt on the part of the West (and especially the USA) to understand the anger of Palestinians, Arabs and Muslims and to deal with this conflict in a more even-handed way would go a long way – perhaps even a very long way – towards defusing the anger that many Muslims feel towards the West. This will not happen, however, if western governments continue to defend themselves and respond by venting their own anger, disappointment and frustration on the Muslim world. Many Americans have felt that what happened on September 11 was so serious and so traumatic that they are justified in putting all their energies into 'the war against terrorism' – including the 'terrorism' of those who resist Israel's illegal occupation of the West Bank. Refusal to understand their anger or to admit any guilt on the part of the West, however, closes the door to any meaningful communication and leaves both parties totally isolated from each other. Responding to anger by overwhelming force is likely to increase the anger rather than make it go away.

An alternative response is for people in the West to stand back and ask themselves, 'why are these people so angry?' If they can separate the religious and the political issues, and if on reflection they can admit – at first to themselves and then perhaps gradually to others – that at least *some* of the anger may be justified, then it is possible for dialogue to begin. When individuals and governments in the West admit even a small amount of responsibility for what has happened, they may still want to defend themselves against other criticisms that they feel are not justified. But if they recognise that serious injustices have been done (in the creation of Israel and all that has flowed from it), and are still being done (in resisting the aspirations of the Palestinians), they will no doubt want to affirm the words of the *Guardian* editorial already quoted: 'It is time to accept that the Arab-Israeli conflict is the main source of tension between the Muslim world and the West and act to resolve it.'

If in this dialogue Muslims are listening to non-Muslims, they will have understood the different reasons why many in the West support the state of Israel. They will also no doubt have understood that many others in the West have considerable sympathy for the Palestinian cause, but are beginning to have genuine concerns about the Islamic ideology with which it now so often associated. They are alarmed at the resurgence of Islamism in groups like Hamas, Islamic Jihad and Hizbullah and the resultant conflict and division within the Palestinian movement, and appalled at the suicide bombings and the terrorism directed against Israeli civilians that are sanctioned, if not actually encouraged, by particular kinds of Islamic teaching. They understand that these actions often spring from a profound despair, but fear that ultimately they are likely to be counter-productive, because they play into the hands of hard-line Israeli governments. When they hear the expectation of some, if not many, that any future Palestinian state would have to be an Islamic state, they begin to be concerned about the status of Christians and other non-Muslims in such a state.[41]

For these reasons many sympathisers in the West fear that the more the Palestinian cause is argued and fought *in Islamic terms*, the more it is likely to lose support from the rest of the world. The stronger the emphasis on Islam, the less sympathy they can expect from non-Muslims. In challenging Palestinians in this way they are not asking Muslims to give up their Islam. They are simply saying that the Palestinian cause is strong enough to stand on its own as a cause based on internationally accepted understandings of human rights. It does not need the underpinning of Islamic ideas in order to be supported in the West, and is likely to be weakened by too close an association with Islam.

A recent book responding to 9/11 by Ziauddin Sardar and Merryl Wyn Davies has the provocative title *Why Do People Hate America?* It ends with the hope that hatred would be overcome: 'The key to a viable and sane future for us all lies in transcending hatred. Since America is both the object and the source of global hatred, it must carry the responsibility of moving us all beyond it. America needs to unwrap itself from the flag, and envelop itself in the prayer of St Francis of Assisi:

> O Master, grant that I may never seek
> So much to be consoled as to console,
> To be understood and to understand,
> To be loved, as to love, with all my soul.[42]

This prayer came from the lips of St Francis who at one time in his life (1219) left the Crusader army encamped at Damietta on the Nile in Egypt to spend two days in dialogue with the Fatimid Sultan Malik el-Kamil of Egypt, the nephew of Saladin. Could it express the post-9/11 hopes and longings of Jews, Christians, and Muslims, of people of all faiths and of none – in the West and the East – for justice and peace in Israel/Palestine and in Jerusalem?

Notes

[1] A.G.Noorani (2002), *Islam and Jihad: Prejudice versus Reality*, London: Zed p.126.
[2] Mustafa, a young Palestinian boy, quoted in *The Sunday Times*, September 23, 2001.
[3] Comment and Analysis, *Guardian Weekly*, October 24-30, 2002, p.12.
[4] Pat Buchanan, *American Conservative Magazine,* January 13, 2003.
[5] M.J. Akbar (2002), *The Shade of the Swords: Jihad and the conflict between Islam and Christianity*, London: Routledge, p.192.
[6] *Ibid.*
[7] Andrew Rippin (1993), *Muslims: Their religious beliefs and practices. Volume 2: the contemporary period*, London: Routledge, p.16.
[8] Quoted by Edward Said (1979) 'Zionism from the Standpoint of its Victims' in *The Question of Palestine*, Time Books; also in (2000) *The Edward Said Reader*, edited by Moustafa Bayoumi and Andrew Rubin, Vintage, p. 145.
[9] Bat Ye'or (1985), *The Dhimmi: Jews and Christians under Islam*, Associated University Presses, p.125.
[10] Fred Halliday (2002), *Two Hours That Shook the World: September 11, 2001: Causes and Consequences*, Saqi Books, pp.211 and 120.
[11] Sami Aoun (1990), 'The Muslim Perspective' in *Jerusalem, a shared trust*, MECC Perspectives, Issue No. 8, July, p.14.
[12] Zakaria Bashier (1991), *The Makkan Crucible*, The Islamic Foundation, p.216.
[13] Mohammed Abdul Hameed Al-Khatib (1998), *Al-Quds: The Place of Jerusalem in Classical Judaic and Islamic Traditions*, Ta-Ha Publishers, pp.181–182.
[14] Amal Saad-Ghorayeb (2002), *Hizbu'llah: Politics and Religion*, Pluto, pp.175, 179, 180.
[15] Youssef Courbage and Philippe Fargues (1998), translated by Judy Mabro, *Christians and Jews under Islam*, I.B.Tauris, p.41.
[16] Zaki Badawi (1997), 'Jerusalem and Islam' in Ghada Karmi (ed.), *Jerusalem Today: What Future for the Peace Process?*, Ithaca, p.142.

[17] Bat Ye'or, op.cit, p.46.
[18] Quoted by H.S. Karmi (unpublished) in 'How Holy is Palestine to Muslims?', p.5.
[19] *Ibid*, p.25.
[20] Zaki Badawi in Ghada Karmi (op.cit.), p.141.
[21] Quoted in James Reston, Jr., *Warriors of God: Richard the Lionheart and Saladin in the Third Crusade*, Anchor, p.257.
[22] See under 'Isa' in the *Encyclopedia of Islam* (1978), E.J. Brill, vol. IV.
[23] Quoted by Fadeel Abul-Nasr (2003) in *Hizbullah: haqa'iq wa-ab'ad (Hizbullah: Facts and Dimensions)*, Beirut: World Book Publishing, Beirut, p.169.
[24] Quoted by Al-Khateeb (op.cit.), p.101.
[25] *Ibid*, pp.161-162.
[26] John L. Esposito (1995) in *The Oxford Encyclopedia of the Modern Islamic World*, Oxford University Press, under Faruqi, Isma'il Raja Al-.
[27] Ismail R. al Faruqi (1983), 'Islam and Zionism' in John L. Esposito, ed., *Voices of Resurgent Islam*, Oxford University Press, pp.261–267.
[28] Peter Riddell (2002), 'From Qur'an to Contemporary Politics: Hamas and the Role of Sacred Scripture' in C. Partridge (ed.), *Fundamentalisms*, Paternoster, pp.52-74.
[29] Andrea Nüsse (2002), *Muslim Palestine: The Ideology of Hamas*, Routledge Curzon, pp. 47-52.
[30] Shukri B. Abed (1995), *The Oxford Encyclopedia of the Modern Muslim World*, under Arab-Israeli Conflict.
[31] Edward Said (1980), *The Question of Palestine*, Vintage Books, pp.117-118.
[32] Benny Morris (1999), *Righteous Victims: A History of the Zionist-Arab Conflict, 1881-1999*, John Murray, p.653.
[33] Andrea Nüsse (op.cit.), p.176.
[34] *Ibid.*
[35] Benny Morris (op.cit), p.652.
[36] Bernard Lewis (2002), *What Went Wrong? The Clash Between Islam and Modernity in the Middle East*, Weidenfeld & Nicolson, p159.
[37] *Ibid.*
[38] See Daniel Pipes (2002), *Militant Islam Reaches America*, Norton, 2002, pp.41 and 203.
[39] *Ibid.*, p.212.
[40] Amal Saad-Ghorayeb (op.cit.), pp.172-173.
[41] Andrea Nüsse (op.cit.), pp.101-103, 177.
[42] Ziauddin Sardar and Merryl Wyn Davies (2002), *Why Do People Hate America?*, Icon Books, p.211.

Chapter 13

Conclusion

Jane Idleman Smith

The authors of this volume are unanimous in their opinion that since 9/11, and probably as a direct result of it, there have been observable and sometimes dramatic changes in the world, in the West in general and in the USA and Britain in particular. They also agree that the fateful September day must be seen in the context of a history of centuries of interaction between Islam and the West, and of many decades in which the emigration of Muslims to Europe and the Americas has changed western countries both demographically and ideologically. The impact of the series of events of 9/11 for relations between what are often distinguished as the Islamic world and the West, for American and European understanding of who Muslims are and what Islam stands for, and for any hope of progress in the crucial arena of improved interfaith relations is still in the process of being determined.

For more than 14 centuries citizens of the West, until recently mainly self-identified as Christians, have faced the reality of living and interacting with an entity known as Islam (though they have called it by many other, generally derogative, names). A long and diverse history of fear and conquest, misconceptions and misrepresentations has preceded the current encounter of Islam and the West, but it has also been a history with notable periods of cooperation and even the acknowledgement of cultural and religious commonalities. From the early centuries when Muslim armies, merchants and explorers knocked at the gates of Europe, the Christian West has shuddered at the reality of what it recognized as a serious military, cultural and theological challenge. At the same time, the Muslim memory of Christian armies marching under the cross to kill Muslim infidels, of the Reconquista of the fifteenth century and of the arrival of missionaries and colonial powers during the nineteenth and first half of the twentieth centuries has left many Muslims enraged at what they perceive as a new age of imperialism aimed at dis-empowering, dispossessing and even eradicating Islam. Meanwhile, as Christendom and Islamdom have struggled and warred with each other, and religious spokespersons have challenged the nature of the other faith and even its right to exist, cultural, commercial and personal relationships between Muslims and Christians as fellow citizens have always been developed and maintained.

Why did the specific events of 9/11 occur? What is it that the USA could have done to justify such unprecedented violence on American soil? The complex of historical, political and economic realities that may offer some answers to these questions seems to remain quite incomprehensible to many in the West, certainly in the USA As Christopher Allen puts it in his chapter for this volume, '...the heavy metaphorical fog still rising from the twin towers makes everything increasingly difficult to see.' Arguing for what he calls a need for more trenchant self-criticism among Christians, Muslims and Jews, John Shepherd says we need to recognize that the roots of religious extremism really do lie in religion. Ron Geaves believes that a primary reason for the violent attacks is economic, involving a growing disparity in wealth and economic resources, and a continuing imbalance of international power. Geaves insists that the voices of militant Muslims, while often speaking in 'religious' [Islamic] language, are using that mode to express their outrage at what they perceive to be political and social injustices and are the natural outcome of deep and growing international economic imbalance. And the West remains none the wiser, laments Lamin Sanneh, 'stubbornly adhering to the line that economic aid will win friends and overcome enemies.'

Life for Muslims, both in the West and in other parts of the world, and for the citizens of western countries in which Muslims are now a sizeable minority, has unquestionably changed since the fateful September day. The chapters presented here have attempted to suggest some of the ways in which these changes have manifested themselves. Many make reference to attempts by the West to categorize Muslims so as to distinguish between terrorists at one extreme and those who are acceptable in the western context at the other. President George Bush has recently been cited in the press for having confessed to Senator Joe Biden that 'I don't do nuance.' This seems to be borne out in his defining 'with us or against us' post-9/11 rhetoric that has helped push Americans into what many observers see as dangerously bifurcating ways of thinking. As Theodore Gabriel notes, the perception that Islam is somehow 'against' and even hostile to the western world has been around for awhile, and has gained ground since 9/11. Such a perspective clearly helps reinforce the we/they thinking that the US government seems bent on fostering. The efforts of both the US and Britain to differentiate between moderate and extremist – acceptable and unacceptable – Islam serve to set up what can only be a false dichotomy within Islam itself, an analysis that Geaves calls 'overwhelmingly simplistic.'

Despite the call of many westerners to eschew dichotomous language, and to avoid thinking in either/or dimensions, we have been encouraged by governments and scholars alike, and to some extent perhaps even by some western Muslims themselves, to employ exactly such distinctions. Those who are labelled by both Muslims and non-Muslims as 'moderate,' a designation carefully examined in this volume, may also be referred to as secularist (the equation of moderate with secularist is problematic for some Muslims, who prefer to say that a better term is 'democratic'), progressive, and sometime even pluralist. The US and British governments have invested a great deal of time and resource since 9/11 cultivating the image of 'moderate Muslims' as the kind we can deal with, the kind who makes good citizens in our reasonable western democracies. Moderate Muslims are encouraged to speak in the media and in public events on behalf of moderate Islam.

At the other end of the spectrum are those Muslims who, in reality as well as in western imagination, are not moderate, democratic, or progressive. It is those whom the West finds most alarming Hovering in the background of this dichotomous conversation, of course, is the reality of the vast body of Muslims living in most areas of the world, very many as refugees of one sort or another, who are simply quietly struggling to survive. Their Islam is not moderate or modern, to say nothing of progressive, but neither is it radical, political or extremist. Islam provides a cultural identity, a way of life and of relation, and a means of hope for a future existence whose rewards will ensure a release from endlessly difficult circumstances.

The spectre of another kind of Islam, however, one made shockingly real by 9/11, does of course correspond to a reality or multiple realities that have manifested themselves in various parts of the world. By what terms can Muslims whose vision of justice includes violence, sometimes by the most extreme means, be designated? Extremist, radical, revolutionary, reactionary, militant, fundamentalist all come to mind. Whatever we call them, or they call themselves, they represent a basic challenge to western secularism and democracy, as well as to Christians as such (Sanneh reminds us that from the perspective of radical Islam, and based on the Qur'an itself, believers cannot be friends with infidels), and certainly to the kind of moderate Islam that our governments and many of our Muslim citizens are trying to cultivate.

The development of militant Islamism, with its frequent calls for the imposition of Islamic law on an international scale, its apparent sanction of the use of violence (or, in some cases, the appropriation of violence on the part of some of its adherents), and its increasingly wholesale condemnation of the various modalities of western imperialism, must not be underestimated, argue the contributors to this volume. Colin Chapman identifies this imperialism as political, economic and cultural. In Chapman's view Muslims find it obvious that the West, especially the US, manipulates world markets for its own gain, applies double standards in the resolution of local conflicts so as to pursue its own interests, manipulates many governments of Islamic countries by means of financial aid incentives, and in general portrays itself as arrogant and imperialist. Often seen by the West as a reactionary movement, which in some sense it may be, Islamic extremism (always keeping in mind that it is not a monolith) for some time has been recognized as a particularly modern set of responses, developed in reaction to events of the last century and in particular the last half century, and making use of some of the most advanced forms of technology. Gabriel notes that although many conservative Muslims oppose technology because it may lead to westernisation, there is no question that it is being used to propagate revivalist Islam and that the kind of networking that is now possible has allowed Muslims from a variety of contexts to communicate with and influence each other.

Many of the chapters herein address the issue of globalisation; readers may consider it one of the signal contributions of the collection. Has economic globalisation turned America into a colonial power, asks Gabriel? Has President Bush's 'go it alone' policy, at least until he realised that it led him into a quagmire in Iraq, seriously undermined basic principles of international cooperation? 'The inter-penetration and inter-dependence of human societies are manifest on every count of sanity and compassion and, indeed, brutal fact,' observes Kenneth Cragg. The still smouldering Iraq war, which many Muslims look at as US invasion of an

Islamic country, was waiting in the wings at the writing of some of these chapters, and its consequences continue to unfold. Among them are the frequent accusations on the part of Muslims and others of US and British war profiteering. The war has also brought another kind of 'dichotomy' in the world of Islam onto the international screen in recent months, and one that most likely will serve to further complicate the attempts (such as they are) of western populations to understand Islam. This dichotomy is between Shi'ite and Sunni Islam, evident especially as events play out in the attempt to govern the new Iraq, illustrating what the media refer to as 'competing urgencies.' Shi'ite/Sunni tensions, which were so formative in the early political development of the world of Islam, began to bubble up again in the Iran-Iraq war of the 1980s. Now they may become even more significant, fomented in the current power struggle in the state of Iraq that some observers feel may eventuate in civil war and a destabilisation of the region. The massacres at Kerbala and Baghdad at the end of Ashura in March 2004, apparently intended to foment sectarian strife, will only further confuse a bewildered and shocked western audience, particularly as they are interpreted in ways that lay more blame at the door of the occupying coalition forces. The recent victory of hard-line core Islamic leadership in Iran, to the detriment and even exclusion of moderates and with far fewer women in the new parliament, will surely raise more questions in the minds of the western public about the nature of Islam.

It is also the conviction of virtually all of the contributors to this volume that if accusations of imperialism in all of its many forms against the West, and in recent decades especially against the US, are justifiable, nowhere are they more evident than in its ongoing, unflinching and apparently irrevocable support of the state of Israel. It would appear that invasion of Iraq and other parts of the Arab world notwithstanding, no factor is as powerful in encouraging the animosity with which much of the Islamic world regards the West as the reality of its intransigent attitude which favours not only the survival of Israel but its steady advance into Palestinian territories. Yvonne Haddad notes that since 9/11 American politicians have had to be cautious in their affirmation of even a moderate form of Islam for fear of the Jewish backlash. The Christian right, with powerful allies in the US government, has stepped up its demonisation of Muslims and Islam. This is often in the context of support for Israel, which is conflated with hopes of millenarian Christians for the intensification of conflict in the land of Israel so as to bring the final redemption of Jews and the end of time. Preachers such as Jerry Falwell and others, as Shepherd observes, have tried to reinforce the strong alliance between evangelical Christians in America and messianic Jews in Israel. If the proposed scenario of a revival of Israel as a precursor to the conversion of Jews to Christianity (or else their destruction) at the millennium is not in the long run advantageous to either secular or religious Jews in Israel, it surely serves the interim purpose of providing a context for the demonisation of Islam. (One need only think, for example, of the Holy Land Experience theme park in Orlando, Florida, which promotes a rabidly anti-Arab and anti-Islamic rhetoric in the context of an 'entertainment' park.) Shepherd also observes that anti-Semitism is alive and well, and that it is not hard to find examples of it in most countries of the West. Such anti-Semitism is growing visibly more apparent, suspected to be fostered at least in part by Arabs and Muslims whose anger at western support of Israel is growing stronger; major international conferences are now being held in Europe to address this growing phenomenon. Shepherd's concern is to avoid the charge of anti-Semitism while recognizing that it is crucial to identify what are obvious racist tactics of the current Israeli government. (A mid-1990s European Union poll found that a majority of Europeans believed Israel to be the greatest threat to world peace.)

Colin Chapman has written most comprehensively in this volume about the crucial importance of the reality of Israel and the Palestinians in understanding the rise of extremist Islam. Whether it is seen as the main source of tension between Islam and the West, he says, or one among many reasons, its importance cannot be underplayed; Israel, he insists, is a prime example of western arrogance and imperialism. He discusses the complex relationship of religion and politics in the area, and especially in relation to Jerusalem, and the exceedingly important role of Zionism in the growing tensions between Islam and the West in the context of the Middle East. The importance of Jerusalem to Muslims, generally unknown or ignored in the West, the perceived unfair policies of (especially) the US in its unwavering support of Israel, and the injustices that such support allow the Israeli government to perpetrate on the Palestinians, are simply huge in the eyes of international Islam. For many in the West, sympathy with the Palestinian plight is quickly ameliorated by the resurgence of violence from groups such as Hamas, Islamic Jihad and Hizbullah, and most obviously and especially, the suicide bombers.

Today changing political, economic and social realities result in growing numbers of Muslims living in the West. The distinction generally posited between Islam and West is thus another dichotomy that must be avoided, despite its convenience, precisely because it supports the persisting sense that such entities are somehow still separate and incompatible. Paradoxically, the rising number of Muslims in the West both belies such a distinction and promotes it insofar as non-Muslims in western countries worry about and even fear their presence, especially given the rise of tensions since 9/11. Until recently Europe and America have absorbed their new residents with relatively little sense of disruption of the continuity of their basically Christian heritage. Now Islam is the second major religion in terms of numbers of adherents in all the countries of western Europe, and is probably that also in the USA today. As Muslims struggle with issues of personal, cultural and religious identity in western countries, they are haunted both by the various forms in which their presence is not fully welcomed in the western context, and by the legacy of western colonialism in their own histories which continues as a powerful force affecting the relationship between Muslims and citizens of Europe and America.

The events of 9/11 have placed Muslims in the West in a particularly tight spot. How can they publicly condemn the acts of those who misguidedly claim to have performed their deeds in the name of Islam, in ways that are heard and believed by sceptical western audiences? Muslims in the West are often asked why they do not Muslims speak out against acts of atrocity and terrorism? The fact is that they have struggled to address such concerns, both in public statements and in conversations among themselves. But it is difficult for them to be heard because the media often find such attempts at reflection and explanation less interesting than reports of continued violence – conflicts in which Muslims are involved – in various parts of the world. Since the 9/11 attacks, Muslims in the West, particularly in the USA, have vied for the role of spokesperson for 'real' (though not essentialised) Islam. While there has also been a proliferation of new Islamic and political organisations to promote the advocacy of Islam, it is interesting that many of its new spokespersons are not speaking on behalf of any given group or organisation.

Western understanding of Islam is not aided by the brash and insulting commentary of some of the most prominent Christian evangelical leaders, notoriously saying that Islam is an evil and wicked religion, that Muhammad was a fanatic, a pedophile and a killer. The American public does not always recognize that such references are part of a larger picture that includes the rise in global efforts at evangelisation of Muslims, and has clear and obvious implications for US foreign policy abroad. Muslims, meanwhile, have to live with the humiliation of such criticism of their faith and its founder, whom they see as a model for belief and behavior, and with US intervention in and control of the Middle East with which they vehemently disagree. Muslims in the West who have found the courage to condemn not only Islamic extremism but what they see as the terrorism supported or perpetuated by the US government itself in its invasion of Islamic lands, in its treatment of 'suspected Muslim terrorists,' and in its support of Israel, face severe reprisals on the part of the general public for being (as long suspected) basically anti-American. How, Muslims wonder, is it possible to voice their disagreement with US policies in the Middle East or elsewhere without being branded as terrorists or asked by fellow citizens why they don't 'go home' if they don't like it here.

The efforts of the US government to foster, nurture and empower moderate Islam, as Haddad observes, are not without a price for the Muslim community, namely the forfeit of their right to define their own identity. Haddad charts the recent history of the disappointment of Muslims who had voted for Bush, and his belated efforts to bolster the moderate image by inviting a specially selected cadre to White House functions. Efforts by the US State Department to foster good will, and especially to reassure Muslim allies abroad that America is welcoming of its Muslims, have resulted in many visits by overseas Muslims to see what life is like for their co-religionists in America. The government has also produced a number of 'Apple-Pie' videos for export abroad in which American Muslims talk about how good it is to be Muslim in the US (Such efforts seem not always to have served their purpose, however, and many Muslim around the world worry about what they see as a worsening situation for American Muslims.) Marcia Hermansen is direct in her article in showing how this effort to foster a certain brand of Islam has led to a kind of checklist of 'good Muslims' and 'bad Muslims,' depending on the degree to which they conform to the moderate ideal, and cites a British scholar's suggestion that the search is on for a liberal Muslim who can be 'manipulated and domesticated.'

Geaves suggests that one reasonable way to 'categorize' Muslims, looking at their historical development, is into what he calls reform and renewal, Sufis, modernists, and those who are nominal or non-practicing. American and British governments generally prefer the modernist or the nominal Muslims, he says, but the problem comes when they try to decide who among those groups are 'moderates.' Geaves argues that British affinity for moderate Islam suggests a kind of religious pluralism that has as its basis a common worldview. It is possible, he says, that such a pluralistic worldview itself might actually be another kind of absolutism. It does seem clear that the effort of the American and British governments in particular to define moderate Islam is both fuelling moderate Muslim efforts to make their own definitions, which may in fact rather push the 'accepted' definition of moderation, and encouraging some elements of the international Muslim contingent to espouse interpretations of Islam that are clearly more radical. Especially since 9/11, Muslim communities in the West have acknowledged and assumed the responsibility for speaking publicly about 'moderate Islam' at the same time that they are turning individually and in groups to their scripture, texts and traditions to understand as accurately as possible what these sources say about moderation as well as about violence, as John Shepherd describes. Implicit in this effort is the recognition that extremism can and did lead to the kind of horror perpetuated on 9/11, and must therefore be renounced.

So where have the events of 9/11 and the subsequent 'war on terror' and its ramifications left the western public in its understanding and appreciation of Islam? Certainly many attempts have been made on local levels to engage in conversation with Muslims, to identify the Muslims who might be one's neighbours in Europe or America as different from the extremists and the terrorists, and in effect to endorse the Bush and Blair administrations' processes of identification and support of moderate (good) Muslims. Nonetheless, few can argue with the reality that Muslims in the West in many ways are worse off since those cataclysmic September attacks. In America Muslims worry deeply that such realities as the US Patriot Act, 'Operation Green Quest' (involving the invasion of Muslim homes and businesses), profiling in airports and other public places, and monitoring the activities and freezing the assets of Muslim charities are resulting in a loss of Muslim civil liberties. Haddad notes that some have likened the situation of post 9/11 Muslims in America to that of German-Americans during World War I and interned Japanese during World War II. Are the measures taken by the Bush government ostensibly to counter terrorism really anti-terrorist, she says many Muslims are asking, or are they in fact anti-Islam? As of this writing US Muslim charities continue to claim that actions taken against them constitute a 'witch hunt' that intimidates donors and severely hampers their work. Stricter US regulations mean heftier costs to those charities that are allowed to function, resulting in smaller percentages of donated *zakat* monies actually reaching the needy for who they are intended.

Before 9/11 many Muslims in the US and Europe identified anti-Islamic prejudice as the major concern they face trying to live as Muslims in the West. Without question the stakes have been raised higher in the last several years, and anti-Islamic feelings are on the rise. Despite efforts by Muslims and others to define and defend themselves, polls show that fewer Americans and Europeans understand or appreciate Islam today than immediately after 9/11. Although Muslims and others in Europe and the US repeatedly voice strenuous objection to media distortions, religiously sponsored negative stereotypes and other modes of publicly demeaning Islam, increasing numbers of people worry that somehow in its 'essential' form Islam is suspect if not downright evil as a religion. A number of contributors to this volume discuss the rising tide of anti-Islamic sentiment, including Dilwar Hussein whose detailed study examines the history of public opinion in Britain since the 1997 Runnymede Trust coined the term 'Islamophobia' in its report of the same name. Contributing to the increase in anti-Islamic feelings since 9/11 is the fact that such a defining historical event has resulted in a strengthened Islamic identity on the part of many immigrant Muslims, with ethnic affiliation playing a secondary role. Hussein notes, however, that significant rise in physical and verbal attacks on Muslims, and an increase in what he calls a heightened climate of discrimination, have been countered by the opening of new opportunities for dialogue as well as the impetus for members of the Muslim community (or communities, as Hussein argues is more appropriate) themselves to become more public in their efforts to speak out against extremism.

The same point about changing from ethnic to religious identity is raised by Christopher Allen in his chapter on Islamophobia in post-9/11 Europe. Allen describes a shift from racism defined by colour, ethnicity or nationalism to what he calls a new strand of racism, one that is defined specifically by religion. He sees a direct relationship between anti-Muslim feelings and incidents and the wearing of such visible Islamic symbols as the *hijab* (veil). All of Europe, and in some ways the rest of the world, awaits the ramifications of the recent French decision to ban the wearing of such obvious religious symbolism on the part of its citizens in public institutions, most particularly in schools. Public outcry has been raised on the part of Muslims, Sikhs and others who consider doffing their headdress not to be a religious option, and we wait to see how members of these communities will respond when the law actually takes effect in the fall of 2004. (Some Muslims have advised women to make their *hijabs* as stylish as possible so that they will appear more a fashion statement rather a religious affirmation.) Allen says that his research shows that anti-Islamic feelings are not new, though probably rekindled, since 9/11 but are the re-emergence of long-standing endemic responses that Europeans have harbored virtually since the emergence of Islam. In terms of European Muslims, or Muslims in Europe, according to Allen 'it would seem highly likely that the endemic fears and prejudices of the European psyche remain imbued with the perception of a negative, dangerous and Islamophobically determined Muslim presence.'

On the surface one might claim that there is a real difference between Europe and the US in terms of its acceptance of Muslims. While the latter has never been the melting pot it is often claimed to be, it has also not until recently had the kind of direct experience of armed conflict with Islamic lands that has characterized the long history of Europe. Haddad, however, argues that the experience of Arabs and Muslims in America from the beginning has been one of prejudice, showing how anti-Arabism has transmuted in more recent days into anti-

Islamism. Such external responses to Muslims in the US would seem to mirror the identity transformation within the immigrant Muslim community itself observed by Hussein and Allen in Europe. Certainly Islamophobia is a term that has slid across the Atlantic into American parlance and is much used by agencies such as the Council on American Islam Relations to describe what it perceives as anti-Islamic behavior in public arenas of the US Religious leaders, politicians, employers, public school officials, citizens accused of prejudicial behavior against Muslims are increasingly identified by CAIR and other Islamic organisations as Islamophobic, and are being called to public account for their discriminatory behaviour.

The theme of rising Islamic self-identity as over against racial-ethnic identification has clear ramifications for the American Muslim community, which is unique in its blend of African Americans who are Muslim through a range of affiliations and those who are themselves immigrant or whose parents immigrated at an earlier period. On the one hand such a movement toward emphasis on identity as Muslim would seem to encourage the kind of inclusive community that African Americans believe is characteristic of true Islam and that other Muslims in the American context have affirmed if not always practiced (at least in the perception of the African Americans). On the other hand, it may also serve to mask the real issues that African American Muslims are now publicly raising, challenging what they sometimes see to be their effective exclusion from the American public forum either as spokespersons or as interpreters of Islam. Marcia Hermansen's section on race and identity in her essay in this volume highlights the work of black intellectual Sherman Jackson in raising issues of race and Islamic authority and revealing some of the ideological differences among American Muslims. African Americans, Hermansen argues, have felt generally underrepresented, and particularly in the media, during recent efforts to present a realistic and honest picture of Islam in the public realm.

One of the very noticeable effects of 9/11 has been the heightened encouragement of active Muslim participation in national political life. The term political Islam, which for some time has been used to designate a kind of religion that brings concern to the hearts of many non-Muslims, is now being appropriated by Muslims living in the West as an affirmation of their legitimate role as citizens of western countries and therefore their responsibility to participate seriously in the political process. As Cragg notes, perhaps as many as a quarter of all Muslims live outside Muslim states and are trying to adjust to Islam being 'just a religion' in contexts where religion and politics are separated. Political Islam thus means for them not a means of pressuring for the implementation of Islamic law, but of participating in western secular political processes.

American Muslims are said to have decided to vote as a bloc in 2000 for candidate George W. Bush. Mention has already been made of the disillusionment of most Muslims at their treatment after Bush gained the presidency. The post-election time also revealed something else, namely feelings of exclusion from the political process on the part of African-American Muslims. Not only were they not involved in the decision to support Bush, they argued, but they were asked to back a political party that traditionally has not done much for African-Americans. The 2004 American elections, therefore, are marked by two important themes: the urgency on the part of American Muslims as a whole to involve as many Muslims as possible in the voting process, and the increasing insistence of some members of the African-American community that their voices be heard among those who are distinguishing themselves as spokespersons for a viable American Islam.

Implicit in the presentations of several of the chapters of this volume is the importance of women in post-9/11 developments. One way in which women are highlighted has to do with the obvious fact of increased veiling in Europe and America as a result of heightened Islamic rhetoric, and western response to obvious forms of Islamic dress. Allen, for example, notes the direct relationship of anti-Muslim incidents, some violent, to women's wearing of the *chador* or *hijab*. Another indication of the importance of women goes back to western rhetoric about good Muslims and bad Muslims. The US government and press took as one of the signal proofs of the rightness of its mission in bombing Afghanistan and (apparently) routing the Taliban the fact that women can now allow their faces to be shown in public. Here again the definition of appropriate Islam seems to Muslims to be imposed by the West. Although the press makes much of the fact that the current draft constitution in Iraq insists on more representation of women, little mention has been made, correspondingly, of the fact that the 'war of liberation' in Iraq has resulted in women increasingly putting on the veil out of concern for possible violence against them done in the name of conservative Islam. A third way in which women are playing an important role in the post-9/11 world that is referred to in this volume, particularly in the essay by Hermansen, is their role in assuming responsibility for new definitions and interpretations of Islam. To the extent to which they find support in this effort, it comes not only from other women but from the men who identify themselves as part of progressive, or reformist, Islam. First on the list of six characteristics that Hermansen notes for those who want to promote this kind of progressive Islamic understanding is gender justice. Obviously not all Muslims are in agreement with the fundamental assumptions of 'progressive Islam,' but it is clear that the recognition that it is being given is a clear result of the many efforts to understand, or re-understand, what Islam means in the contemporary world.

As new realities impose new definitions of the relationship between Islam and the West, and of Muslims themselves both in the West and in other parts of the world, serious issues demand some resolution. What, for Muslims living in the West, is the price of their decision to become citizens and are they willing to pay it? Will western governments and societies succeed in their efforts to identify and foster moderate Islam? If not, how will citizens of the West who are not Muslim find ways in which to accommodate to an Islam that they may consider alien and frightening, particularly if more radical forms continue to assert themselves in the Middle East and elsewhere? How long can the West continue to press its will on the Middle East before experiencing reprisals in its own lands perhaps as devastating as the events of 9/11? These questions may turn out to be more insistent and compelling than any in the long history of relations between Islam and the West. One can only hope that they are increasingly addressed by thoughtful and well-informed citizens, Muslim and non-Muslim, and not left to be determined by those whose words and actions are guided by frustration, anger and intolerance.

Index

A
9/11 *see* September 11 (2001)
Abacha, Sani 151
Abraham 19, 42
Abu Bakr 38
Abu Hamza 70
Afghanistan
  Soviet Union, invasion 4, 5
  Taliban
    defeat 7
    victory 5
Afrikaners, as chosen people 35
al-Azhar University, Cairo 40
al-Banna, Hasan 3
al-Faruqi, Ismail R., *Islam and the Problem of Israel* 201
al-Haqq, Zia, General 57
al-Qa'eda 5, 6, 7, 9, 137, 174
Algeria 4, 5
Allen, Christopher 130-45, 210-11, 217, 218, 219
American Muslims
  acceptable stereotypes 77
  in American society 97
  'bad' Muslims 88
  and the Bush Administration 101-11
  civil rights, restrictions 100, 104-7, 216
  converts 89
  as 'enemy within' 88-9
  'good' Muslims 83-7
  identity 88-90
  ideological differences 90, 91-2
  immigrants 98
  response to 9/11 77-96, 215
Amir, Yigal 31
anti-Semitism 28, 29, 41
  Biblical sources 37
  Islam 206
apartheid 35
Appleby Project 1
Arab
  immigration, US 98-9
  organizations, US 98
Arendt, Hannah 206
Armstrong, Karen 31, 79
  Islam: A Short History 81
Ashcroft, John 97, 105

B
Ba'asyir, Abu Bakr 10
  publications on 168-9
  teachings 169-84
Badr, Battle 63
Balfour, Lord 21
Balkans 4
beard, as Muslim identifier 135
Ben-Gurion, David 204-5
Berlusconi, Silvio 138
Berman, Paul 146
Bhagavad Gita 10
bida 24
Bosnia 5
Bristow, Jennie 132
Britain
  Islamic Cultural Centre 117
  Islamophobia 131-3, 217
  loyalty, Asian religious groups 127
  Mosque Trust 117
  Muslim communities 116-17
  Muslim immigration 116
  religion 116
    affiliation 117
    regional distribution 118-19
  and Zionism 21
British Muslims
  civil rights, restrictions 125
  Guantanamo Bay 137
  impact of 9/11 115-29, 216
  loyalty to Britain 127
  political life 119-20
  regional distribution 118-19
  statistics 117-20
British National Party, Islamophobia 126, 131, 138-9
Bunting, Madeleine 69-70
Burgat, François 126
Burke, Jason 72

Burma *see* Myanmar
Bush Administration, and American Muslims 101-11
Bush, George W. (President) 211, 218

C
Cairo, al-Azhar University 40
Caliphate 3, 56-7, 83, 160
Carroll, Robert 37
chador 134, 219
Chapman, Colin 8, 194-209, 212, 214
Chechnya 4, 5, 6, 22
China 8
Christian Association of Nigeria 152
Christianity
and Islam 210
and the Qur'an 14
Christians
as chosen people 35
and Messianic Jews 34-5
Chung, Connie 100
civil society, and Islam 58
civilisation, clash of 69, 70, 115, 130
Clinton Administration, Islamo-friendly acts 99-100
Clinton, Bill (President) 99
Cold War 3, 146-7
colonialism, and Islam 2, 71, 149-51, 194
community
and Islam 123-5
and the Qur'an 123
Cox, Peter 70, 71, 72
Cragg, Kenneth 10, 20, 51-61, 212
Crusades 14
and Jerusalem 200

D
dar al-'Ahd 123
dar al-'Amn 123
dar al-Harb 17, 38, 55, 64, 72, 123
dar al-Islam 17, 38, 55, 59, 64, 72, 123
dar al-Kufr 123
dar al-Sulh 17, 123
Darby, John 34
Daulah Islamiyah, and *Shari'ah* 172, 180
Davies, Merryl Wyn (co-author), *Why Do People Hate America?* 208
dawah 174-5
dawlah 57, 58
D'Costa, Gavin 69
Denmark, Islamophobia 138
Derby University, *Project on Religious Discrimination* 126
dhimmis 39, 55-6
Jews as 198-9, 201
Nigeria 152
din 57, 58
din moser 30
din rodef 30

E
Eck, Diane 72-3
Eickleman, Dale 83
Eid ul-Adha 101
El Fadl, Khaled Abu 84-5, 90
Emerson, Steven 99, 100
Ernst, Carl 67
eschatology, Jerusalem 200-1
Esposito, John 77
Europe
expansion 2
Islamophobia 133-42, 217
European Monitoring Centre on Racism and Xenophobia, *Summary Report...Islamophobia* 133-4

F
Falwell, Jerry 34, 87, 101
fatwa 15, 40
Finsbury Park mosque 70
fiqh 150
Fortuyn, Pim 138
Forum Against Islamophobia and Racism 132
Foucault, Michel, on identity 121
Foxe, John, *The Book of Martyrs* 36
Francis of Assisi, St., prayer 208
freedom
and religion 153
and secularism 153-4

G
Gabriel, Theodore 8, 13-26, 211
Geaves, Ron 9, 62-74, 211, 216
Gellner, Ernest 123
Gentiles, and Jews 31-3
Giddens, Anthony 121
Gilliat-Ray, Sophie 128
globalisation 1
and Islam 16, 66, 212-13
Goldstein, Baruch 29, 31, 32, 40

Graham, Franklin 87
Greater Israel movement 31
Guantanamo Bay 125
British Muslims 137
Gulf War (1991) 13, 98, 99

H
Habermas, Jürgen 181
Haddad, Yvonne 8, 97-114, 213, 215, 217
hadith 10, 15, 23, 177
hajj 171
halacha 31
Hamas, Covenant of 202
Hanson, Hamza Yusuf 79, 86-7
Haqqani, Husain 111
Hebron massacre (1994) 29, 40
Henzell-Thomas, Jeremy 72
Hermansen, Marcia 8, 77-96, 215, 218, 219
Herzl, Theodore 20-1
Hewitt, Patricia 120
hijab 134, 135, 217, 219
hijrah 18, 51, 56, 57, 59, 197
Hizb al-Tahrir 83
Hizbollah 40
Holmes, Oliver Wendell 159-60
Huntington, Samuel 8
Hussain, Asaf 140
Hussein, Dilwar 9, 115-29, 217, 218
Hussein, Saddam 4, 6, 7-8, 99

I
ibadah, and *Shari'ah* 171-2
Ibn Hait, Ahmad 14
Ibn Khaldun 124
identity
formation 120-1
Michel Foucault on 121
Muslim 122-5, 218
ideology, Wahhabism 24, 64, 86
iftar 100, 101
ijma 23
ijtihad 15, 166
Wahhabism 23
ikraha 56
India
Muslims, and Christians 15
Soviet Union, relations 4
and Western values 17
Indonesia
Padre Wars 14
radical Islam 167-84
Indonesia Mujahidin Council 168
Internet, and Islam 16
intifada 4
Iran, and Islam 16
Iraq
War (2003) 213-14
WMD 8
Ireland, Islamophobia 136-7
islah 65
Islam
as absolutist-exclusionary ideology 176-7
anti-Semitism 206
as Christian heresy 14
and Christianity 210
and civil society 58
and colonialism 2, 71, 149-51, 194
and community 123-5
conspiracy against 4
expansion 2, 37-8
and globalisation 16, 66, 212-13
'hypocrites' 63-4
and the Internet 16
and Iran 16
and Israeli-Palestinian conflict 207
and Jerusalem 199
Jesus in 14
and Judaism 19
meaning 13
militant 71-2, 212, 214
'moderate' 65-7, 97, 108-10, 211
and modernity 181-2
and morality 16
as normative ideal 176
as other 104
'progressive' 81-3, 167
in public life 123
purification 172
radical, Indonesia 167-84
revival 71
Salman Rushdie on 80
Shi'ite/Sunni tensions 213
and the state 157-8
traditions within 177-8
as the true religion 175
varieties 65-8
war ethos 38-9
as way of life 176
and Zionism 195-6

see also Shari'ah
Islam, Yusuf (Cat Stevens) 135
Islamic Cultural Centre
Britain 117
Dublin 137
Islamic Human Rights Commission 70, 132
Islamic Jihad 202
Islamic organizations, US 85, 88
Islamic Society of Britain 126
Islamic Society of North America 103
Islamic State 3, 160
Islamophilia 131
Islamophobia 28
Britain 131-3, 217
British National Party 126, 131, 138-9
Denmark 138
Europe 133-42, 217
Ireland 136-7
Italy 136, 138
Netherlands 138
reports 126
and September 11 (2001) 130-42
Sweden 137
US 217-18
Israel
establishment 195
Jewish settlers 29-31, 41
lobby, US 99, 101, 108
ultra-religious influence 31
US support 4, 21-2
Israeli-Palestinian conflict 18, 81, 201-3
and Islam 207
Western responses 203-6
Italy, Islamophobia 136, 138

J
Jackson, Sherman 88, 90-1
jahiliyya 15, 17, 64, 148
Jenkins, Roy 117
Jerusalem
al-Aqsa Mosque 33
and the Crusades 200
Dome of the Rock 33, 34
eschatology 200-1
in Islamic tradition 199
and Muhammad 197
in the Qur'an 196
Temple Mount 33, 34
Jesus, in Islam 14
Jews
as *dhimmis* 198-9, 210
and Gentiles 31-3
and Muhammad 39, 197-8
jihad 4, 5, 17, 62, 203, 206
meaning 18, 24-5, 40, 167, 172-4
in the Qur'an 39
and September 11 (2001) 58, 79-80
Jinnah, M.A. 57
John of Damascus 14
Judaism
and the chosen people 31
and Islam 19
and the Promised Land 20, 21, 29, 31, 34
and racial purity 32-3
Juergensmeyer, Mark 43

K
Kabbani, Shaykh Hisham 85, 86
Kashmir 4, 5, 22
significance 18-19
khalifat 3
see also Caliphate
Khan, Muqtader 83-4, 89, 91
American Muslims... 84
Khomeini, Ayatollah 16, 167, 181
Kittel, Gerhard 33
Kumo, Suleman 157

L
language, September 11 (2001) 79-80
law, and natural justice 16
Lemche, Niels P. 31-2
Leonard, Karen 83, 92
Levine, Mark 16
Lewis, Bernard 99, 181
What Went Wrong? 80-1, 205
Lieberman, Joseph (Senator) 99
Lindbeck, George 68-9
Lindh, John Walker 89
London Central Mosque 117
loyalty, Muslims 124-5

M
McVeigh, Timothy 100
madrasas 5, 24, 42
Mahdi rebellion, Sudan 14
Maimonides 32, 42
Makkah *see* Mecca
Manifest Success doctrine 1-2, 62-4, 66, 72

Mappila Rebellion (1920) 14
Mattson, Ingrid 89
Mawdudi, Maulana 3
Mawlawi, Shaikh Faisal 124
Mecca (Makkah) 4, 18, 51, 63
Medina 4, 14, 18, 19, 51, 63
modernity
  and Islam 181-2
  and religion 70-3
Mongol invasions 2, 63
morality
  and Islam 16
  and the West 15-16
Morris, Benny, *Righteous Victims...* 204
Mosque Trust, Britain 117
Muhammad 14, 19, 63
  and Jerusalem 197
  and the Jews 39, 197-8
mujaddid 89
mujahiddin 4, 5, 7
muriji'un 58
Muslim Association of Britain 120
Muslim Brotherhood 90
Muslim chaplains, US armed forces 99-100
Muslim communities, Britain 116-17
Muslim Council of Britain 125
  The Quest for Sanity... 127
Muslims
  Bosnia 4
  and Christians
    common ground 14-15
    hostility 14, 19
    India 15
  civil liberties
    UK 8
    USA 8
  identity 122-5, 218
  loyalty 124-5
  in non-Muslim countries 3
  see also American Muslims; British Muslims
mutraf 175
Myanmar 8

N
Nasr, Syed Hossein 16
natural justice, and law 16
Nazim, Shaykh 85
Netenyahu, Bibi 99
Netherlands, Islamophobia 138
Nielsen, Jorgen 130
nifaq 56
Nigeria
  dhimmis 152
  secularism 158-60
  Shari'ah
    application 151-8
    colonial era 150-1, 158
  ulama 152, 154
North Korea 8
North-West Provinces (Pakistan) 5, 6
Northern Ireland, religious strife 35-6
Nusse, Andrea 13, 18, 20, 202, 204

O
Oklahoma City bombing (1995) 100
Oliveti, Vincenzo 24
Ong, Aihwa 107
Organization of Islamic Countries 152
orientalism, and the West 66
Origen 27-8, 37
Osama bin Laden 5, 6, 7, 70, 135, 174
Oslo Agreement (1993) 30
other, Islam as 104

P
Padre Wars, Indonesia 14
Pakistan 57
  creation 55
  US, relations 4, 99
Palestine 5
  nationalism, and Zionism 203-4
  see also Israeli-Palestinian conflict
Pancasila 167, 172
Parekh Report, *The Future of Multi-Ethnic Britain* 126
Patriot Act, US 104-5
Pentagon, attack (2001) 7
Pipes, Daniel 99, 108-9, 206
PLO (Palestine Liberation Organisation) 202
pluralism, religion 69
Pound, Roscoe 159
Powell, Colin 101
Powell, Enoch 116
power
  and the Qur'an 51-2
  and religion 53-4
Protocols of Zion 4, 20
public life, Islam in 123

Q
qawm 123, 124
qiblah 56, 197
qiyas 15, 23
Qur'an 10
  and Christianity 14
  and community 123
  contemporary significance 53
  idolatry 53
  inclusiveness 52-3
  interpretation 178-9
  Jerusalem in 196
  jihad in 39
  and power 51-2
  and war 40
Quraysh 19
Qutb, Sayyid 3

R
Rabin, Yitzhak 30-1
radical, meaning 166
Rahman, Fazlur 178, 181-2
Ramadan, Tariq 83, 123
Reconquista, Spain 14
religion
  Britain 116, 117
  and freedom 153
  and modernity 70-3
  pluralism 69
  and power 53-4
  and secularism 161-2
  and the state 156
Revelation, Book of 33-4
Riddell, Peter 202
Runnymede Trust, *Islamophobia...* 126, 132
Rushdie, Salman
  on Islam 80
  The Satanic Verses 71

S
Saeed, Agha 102
Safi, Omid, *Progressive Muslims...* 82, 107
Safieh, Afif 21
Said, Edward 66, 81, 203
Saladin 200, 204, 208
salat 171
Sanneh, Lamin 2, 10, 146-65, 211
Sardar, Ziauddin (co-author), *Why Do People Hate America?* 208
Satyagraha 9
Saudi Arabia
  US troops 4
  Wahhabism 9, 64
  Western links 18
saum 171
secularism
  and freedom 153-4
  Nigeria 158-60
  and religion 161-2
  and the *Shari'ah* 161
September 11 (2001) 5, 6, 7, 10, 25, 174
  context 210-11
  and Islamophobia 130-42
  and *jihad* 58
  language 79-80
  Muslims
    American 77-96, 215
    in the West 214-15, 216
Serbia 4
Sharí'ah 7
  and *Daulah Islamiyah* 172, 180
  and *ibadah* 171-2
  meaning 170
  Nigeria
    application 151-8
    colonial era 150-1, 158
  and radical Islam 167
  scope 15
  and secularism 161
  and *tauhid* 170-1
Shariati, Ali 15
Sharon, Ariel 6, 30
Shepherd, John 10, 15, 27-50, 211
Sheridan, Lorraine 133
shirk 15
Siddiqui, Muzzammil 103
sirah 51
Sirozi, Muhammad 10, 166-93
Six-Day War (1967) 34, 98
Smith, Jane Idleman 210-19
Soroosh, Abdol Karim 83
South Asia 4
Soviet Union
  Afghanistan, invasion 4, 5
  collapse 4, 104, 147
  India, relations 4
Soyinka, Wole 155-6
state
  and Islam 157-8
  and religion 156

statistics, British Muslims 117-20
Sudan, Mahdi rebellion 14
Sufism 65, 67-8
suicide, Islam 25
suicide bombing 4, 9, 40-1
Sunnah 2, 16, 40, 123, 170, 182
Sunni Muslims 63
Sweden, Islamophobia 137

T
tafsir 23
tajdid 65
Taliban, Afghanistan
  defeat 7
  victory 5
Talmud 30
tariqas 67
tauhid 15, 169-71, 179
  and *Shari'ah* 170-1
  and Wahhabism 182
terror
  war on 28, 128, 130
  see also September 11 (2001)
terrorists, motivation 148
Thomas, David 14
Torah 30, 31
turban, as Muslim identifier 135

U
UAE, Western links 18
Uhud, Battle 63
ulama 9, 15
  Nigeria 152, 154
ummah 3, 9, 13, 15, 17, 18, 22, 25, 54, 58, 124, 137, 201
US
  Arab immigration 98, 98-9
  Arab organizations 98
  armed forces, Muslim chaplains 99-100
  Islamic organizations 85, 88
  Islamophobia 217-18
  Israel
    lobby 99, 101, 108
    support for 4, 21-2
  Middle East, perceived role 22
  Pakistan, relations 4, 99
  Patriot Act 104-5
  Wahhabism 85, 88
USS Cole, attack on 7

W
Wahaj, Siraj 91
Wahhabism
  ideology 24, 64, 86
  ijtihad 23
  Saudi Arabia 9, 64
  spread 23-4
  and *tauhid* 182
  US 85, 88
wahn 175
wala' 124
war, and the Qur'an 40
Weapons of Mass Destruction *see* WMD
Weinberger, Caspar 146-7
West, the
  meaning 1
  morality 15-16
  orientalism 66
Whitaker, Brian 136
WMD (Weapons of Mass Destruction), Iraq 8
Wolfe, Michael 88-9
  Taking Back Islam... 79, 87
Wolfowitz, Paul 107
women, Muslim, attacks on 134-5, 219
World Trade Center
  attack (1993) 5
  attack (2003) 7

Y
Yerima, Alhaj Ahmed Sani 152-3, 154-5, 156, 157

Z
zakat 39, 106, 154, 171
Zaki, Yaqub 131, 139
Zionism
  and Britain 21
  ideology 20
  and Islam 195-6
  and Palestinian nationalism 203-4